MW01193871

GATHERING TOGETHER

THE LAMAR SERIES IN WESTERN HISTORY

The Lamar Series in Western History includes scholarly books of general public interest that enhance the understanding of human affairs in the American West and contribute to a wider understanding of the West's significance in the political, social, and cultural life of America. Comprising works of the highest quality, the series aims to increase the range and vitality of Western American history, focusing on frontier places and people, Indian and ethnic communities, the urban West and the environment, and the art and illustrated history of the American West.

Editorial Board

Howard R. Lamar, Sterling Professor of History Emeritus, Past President of
    Yale University
William J. Cronon, University of Wisconsin–Madison
Philip J. Deloria, University of Michigan
John Mack Faragher, Yale University
Jay Gitlin, Yale University
George A. Miles, Beinecke Library, Yale University
Martha A. Sandweiss, Princeton University
Virginia J. Scharff, University of New Mexico
Robert M. Utley, Former Chief Historian, National Park Service

Recent Titles

*Gathering Together: The Shawnee People through Diaspora and Nationhood,
    1600–1870,* by Sami Lakomäki
*Nature's Noblemen: Transatlantic Masculinities and the Nineteenth-Century
    American West,* by Monica Rico
Rush to Gold: The French and the California Gold Rush, 1848–1854, by
    Malcolm J. Rohrbough
Sun Chief: The Autobiography of a Hopi Indian, by Don C. Talayesva, edited
    by Leo Simmons, Second Edition
Before L.A.: Race, Space, and Municipal Power in Los Angeles, 1781–1894, by
    David Samuel Torres-Rouff
Geronimo, by Robert M. Utley

Forthcoming Titles

George I. Sánchez: The Long Fight for Mexican American Integration, by
    Carlos Kevin Blanton
*The Yaquis and the Empire: Violence, Spanish Imperial Power, and Native
    Resilience in Colonial Mexico,* by Raphael Brewster Folsom
American Genocide: The California Indian Catastrophe, 1846–1873, by
    Benjamin Madley
The Cherokee Diaspora, by Gregory Smithers
Ned Kelly and Billy the Kid, by Robert Utley

GATHERING
TOGETHER

The Shawnee People through Diaspora
and Nationhood, 1600–1870

Sami Lakomäki

*Published in cooperation with the William P. Clements Center
for Southwest Studies, Southern Methodist University*

Yale
UNIVERSITY PRESS
New Haven & London

Copyright © 2014 by Yale University.
All rights reserved.
This book may not be reproduced, in whole or in part,
including illustrations, in any form (beyond that copying permitted
by Sections 107 and 108 of the U.S. Copyright Law and except by
reviewers for the public press), without written permission from the
publishers.

Yale University Press books may be purchased in quantity for
educational, business, or promotional use. For information, please
e-mail sales.press@yale.edu (U.S. office) or sales@yaleup.co.uk (U.K.
office).

Set in Electra type by IDS Infotech Ltd., Chandigarh, India.
Printed in the United States of America.

Library of Congress Cataloging-in-Publication Data
Lakomäki, Sami.
Gathering together: the Shawnee people through diaspora and
nationhood, 1600–1870 / Sami Lakomaki.
pages   cm. — (The Lamar series in Western history)
Includes bibliographical references and index.
ISBN 978-0-300-18061-9 (hardback)
1. Shawnee Indians — History. 2. Shawnee Indians — Social life
and customs. I. Title.
E99.S35.L34 2014
974.004'97317 — dc23
2014000586

A catalogue record for this book is available from the British
Library.

This paper meets the requirements of ANSI/NISO Z39.48–1992
(Permanence of Paper).

10 9 8 7 6 5 4 3 2 1

CONTENTS

ACKNOWLEDGMENTS

Researching and writing this book has taken some fifteen years, although for a long time I had no idea that what I was then doing would eventually become a book. During all this time I have been fortunate in having great mentors, colleagues, and friends without whose guidance, generosity, and company I would never have been able to finish—or even start—this book. First and foremost, I wish to thank Professor R. David Edmunds. In 2009 he agreed to become what in Finland is called the "opponent" in my doctoral defense. In that capacity, he offered a careful and encouraging assessment of my dissertation (and kindly made the public examination a relatively painless experience for me); later, he continued to advise me patiently on how to turn a rather unreadable thesis into a book. When I moved to Dallas to research and write, he helped me to feel at home in the unfamiliar landscape—for example, by guiding me to the best places to eat. Throughout, Dave's own scholarship has been a constant source of inspiration for me, as well as a model that I have sought to emulate in my work.

Several other individuals, too, read and commented on the manuscript or parts of it at various stages, helping me tremendously to sharpen my arguments and improve my writing. I thank especially Stephen Aron, Daniel Richter, Colin Calloway, John Wunder, Gunlög Fur, Ben Johnson, Sherry Smith, Stephen Warren, Edward Countryman, Andrés Reséndez, Michael Coleman, Matt Liebmann, Jason Mellard, Dan Arreola, Rani Andersson, Hannu Heikkinen, Markku Henriksson, Jukka Pennanen, Riitta Leinonen, and the anonymous reader for Yale University Press for their thoughtful feedback, suggestions, and critiques. I am likewise grateful to all who participated in my manuscript workshop at the Clements Center for Southwest Studies for their comments and the stimulating discussion. Numerous conversations with Rob Harper, David Preston, Laura Keenan Spero, and James Buss proved invaluable for my work, as did the panel on Shawnee history that Laura invited me to organize with her at the 2011 SHEAR meeting in Philadelphia. Tom Arne Midtrød, Penelope Drooker, and A. Gwynn Henderson generously shared their research with me. Various parts of this book first came into being as conference papers, and I benefited greatly from the comments received at those occasions from many of the people already named and several others. Special thanks here to Christina Snyder.

I am greatly indebted to Andrew Warrior, Henryetta Ellis, Leroy Ellis, Karen Kaniatobe, and other Shawnees who not only patiently discussed my research with me but also made me more aware of contemporary Shawnee life and the politics of research.

Much of the research and most of the writing for this book took place at the Clements Center for Southwest Studies at Southern Methodist University in Dallas. I cannot think of a more inspiring, productive, and hospitable place to work; the people at the center and the Department of History made my time at SMU a great professional and personal experience. I thank especially Ben Johnson, Andrew Graybill, Andrea Boardman, and Ruth Ann Elmore for their friendship and guidance of various kinds (which often extended to rather mundane issues such as finding furniture and making sense of such American oddities as checks). At the last stages of writing, the support and friendship of my colleagues in the Program of Cultural Anthropology at the University of Oulu were likewise immensely important to me (not least because they helped me to survive the oddities of Finnish academia that far surpass anything mere checks have to offer).

Various institutions have supported my research financially. I would not have been able to write this book without grants and fellowships from the Clements Center for Southwest Studies, the Academy of Finland, the Fulbright Center, and the Finnish Cultural Foundation. I am also grateful to Jessie Dolch and the people at Yale University Press for their expertise and professionalism in producing this book. Many thanks likewise to Terhi Tanska, who drew all the maps.

Finally, none of this would matter without family and friends. My deepest thanks for everything in general, as well as for all the specifics, to my family, Heli Maijanen, Paul Kaczmarczyk, Hannu Heikkinen, Timo Ylimaunu (despite his unreasonable taste in soccer teams), Riitta Leinonen, David Rex, Belinda Viesca, Norwood Andrews, Carla Mendiola, Dan Blackie, Hanna Laako, Kirsi Laurén, Pekka Kilpeläinen, Aki "Stephen Bloomer" Rossi, Luis Garcia, Diego Casillas (who will be happy to know that I have finally written the acknowledgments), Ryan Booth, and Adrian Burke. And last, but certainly not least, there is Isis, without whom life would indeed be a tale told by an idiot: *gracias por traerme tu cariño y salero a mi vida.*

To all of you: *kiitos.*

GATHERING TOGETHER

INTRODUCTION

"Our Straggling Nation"

In March 1790 two Shawnee headmen called a council at Kekionga, a populous cluster of Shawnee, Miami, and Lenape (Delaware) towns located at the forks of the Maumee River, where Fort Wayne, Ohio, now stands. Both local Indians and resident British and French traders collected to listen to the renowned war leader Peteusha (Snake) and a younger hereditary civil chief named Biaseka (Wolf). Later that evening one of the merchants, Henry Hay, wrote down the substance of the Shawnees' talk in his journal. According to Hay, Peteusha and Biaseka had declared that they planned to build a new town for the Shawnees farther down the Maumee, for they were "now going to gather all our straggling nation together." Such an announcement may have surprised some of the headmen's audience. Colonists had long known Shawnees as "the greatest Travellers in America," "dispersed all over the Face of the Earth" from the Mississippi Valley to the Atlantic Coast and from the Deep South to the Great Lakes. From the seventeenth through the nineteenth century the Shawnees were so scattered, fragmented, and mobile that modern scholars speak of a "Shawnee diaspora." And yet Biaseka and Peteusha understood their "straggling," diasporic people as something Hay translated as a "nation." Their words challenge us to rethink the reconfigurations of Native peoplehoods, spaces, and politics in postcontact America; to ask what it meant to be a "straggling nation" in a world of colonialism, displacement, and Euroamerican state-building; and to investigate how Indian social formations shaped that world.[1]

This book is about Shawnee diaspora and nationhood and the transformation of North America from Native homelands to Euroamerican nation-states. It traces how the military, economic, and epidemiologic ripple effects of the European invasion dispersed the Shawnees from their Ohio Valley homes across eastern North America in the seventeenth century, how hundreds of Shawnees coalesced again on the Ohio in the mid-eighteenth century to face off the expansionist British empire, and how Shawnees espoused both consolidation and fragmentation to create autonomous spaces for themselves within the expanding United States in the nineteenth century. Shawnees were not the only people who underwent repeated diasporas and consolidations during these centuries. Many of their Native neighbors, including Lenapes, Kickapoos, Cherokees, Haudenosaunees (Iroquois), Tuscaroras, and Alabamas, shared similar experiences as they struggled to cope with the Old World epidemics, colonial warfare, land loss, and globalizing trade that remade America after 1500. Nor were such experiences limited to the Indian peoples. In Europe, overseas colonial expansion went hand in hand with the rise of modern, centralized states. Wealth from the colonies funded the state-building projects of the nascent central governments in Europe; yet violent political and religious strife over the future of the new states, as well as new economic opportunities offered by the colonies, also dispersed the English, Irish, French, Spaniards, Germans, Dutch, and other Europeans across the globe and led to the development of new peoples and polities in America and elsewhere. In West Africa, local communities raided their neighbors and rivals for captives and sold them to European slavers who shipped their human cargo to the colonies overseas. The slave trade supported the consolidation of some African societies into powerful states, while their neighbors were scattered across the Atlantic world in a cruel diaspora. Nation-building and diaspora, fueled by violent conflicts over power and resources, were both inseparable elements in the rise of the "modern world-system," a world of colonial expansion and globalizing economic networks. The history of the Shawnees provides a prism through which we can trace these immense global transformations from one local perspective and discern how Indigenous peoples, often forgotten in sweeping world-system theories, drew from their culture, creativity, and power to shape the new geopolitical order that was emerging around them.[2]

American history has long been framed as a narrative of nation-building and diaspora. The casting for this epic has traditionally followed ethnic lines. In most histories, it is the European newcomers who build new nations and states in their New World. The role of the Indian peoples, in contrast, has generally been to "resist, retreat, and struggle to survive." Faced with the colonial onslaught, they scatter, sometimes disappear, and rarely create anything new. The strong state-centric tradition of historical scholarship has strengthened this dichotomy between nation-building colonists and dispersing Indians. In particular, popular histories and textbooks often concentrate so intensively on the development of the three modern North American nation-states that almost every historical event is seen either as leading to their birth or following from it.

Such a focus leaves little room for alternative projects of nation-building in the American past. Many historians have sought to remedy this problem. In the past two decades the "borderlands" school in particular has drawn attention to the contingency of nations in North America by examining the contested evolution of borders across the continent. Borderlands historians have detailed the histories of transnational peoples, spaces, and networks, demonstrating that the modern national boundaries in America are products of centuries of struggles and negotiations among empires, states, Indians, and Euroamerican settlers. But even borderlands scholars have tended to focus on Euroamerican nationhoods and boundaries. Indians, in turn, are typically portrayed as "peoples in between," living on "porous" borderlands between rival colonial empires and states—not as nations living on their own "bordered lands." While borderlands studies have greatly advanced our understanding of the geopolitical strategies of the Native peoples through the era of European colonialism, they sometimes risk neglecting the complex ways in which the Indians conceptualized themselves as nations at the center of their world.[3]

Until very recently, Native American perceptions of nationhood and boundaries have received scant attention even from specialists in Indian history. Ethnohistory and "new Indian history," two research traditions that emerged in the 1950s and 1970s, respectively, have produced a canon of outstanding Nativecentric scholarship. Researchers in these fields have foregrounded Indian agency in history and contextualized Indian actions within the framework of Indian cultures. Both ethnohistory and new Indian history have, however, concentrated more on the diverse interactions between Natives and newcomers—trade, diplomacy, warfare, missionizing—on multiethnic "middle grounds" than on the politics and political ideologies within Indian societies located on "Native grounds." In general, these studies have identified Indian-Euroamerican encounters as the principal engine of historical dynamics in postcontact America. While certainly valid, such a focus downplays the importance and complexity of Native American politics and underestimates how political dynamics within Indian societies have molded the continent. Only recently a growing number of ethnohistorians have begun to interrogate Indian political action, power relations, and ideologies in ways that "embed" Native politics "in the broader context of [Native] culture." Such "ethnopolitical history" retains the old interest in the cultural, military, and economic interactions between Indians and Euroamericans, but it is equally interested in Indigenous ideas of peoplehood, power, and society and Native debates over these ideas. Most crucially, this approach maintains that Native projects of imagining, debating, and constructing communities, confederacies, and nations constituted a powerful creative force in postcontact North America that shaped the world of both Indian and Euroamerican societies.[4]

Profound theoretical assumptions have hindered scholars from tackling Indian ideas and debates about peoplehood and power. In both scholarly and everyday language Native Americans are commonly referred to as "tribes." Anthropologists define a tribe as a decentralized and egalitarian coalition of communities that are loosely bound together by kinship networks and shared rituals but not by any overarching political leadership or institutions for collective decision-making. There are two anthropological models for explaining the formation of tribal societies, both with problematic ramifications for writing American Indian history. The more traditional of these conceptualizes tribes as one stage in the universal political evolution of human societies, located between "simple" (that is, egalitarian and decentralized) societies called bands and "complex" (that is, centralized and hierarchical) societies labeled chiefdoms and states. Like many typological constructions, the evolutionary concept of tribe lacks internal dynamism. It is a static ideal type that leaves little room for real people competing for power and arguing about politics. Consequently, anthropologists have usually attributed the band-tribe-chiefdom transformations to external influences such as environmental pressure. A revisionist approach in turn claims that tribes are products of European colonial expansion. According to this position, colonial warfare, land loss, population decline, and capitalist economies broke older and more complex Indigenous polities across the globe into loose and shifting tribal societies. Both views rob tribal peoples of their political creativity and predispose scholars to portray American Indian societies as either static or disintegrating. Moreover, such theoretical underpinnings shift attention from Native political ideas and debates to external engines of social change such as colonialism or ecology.[5]

Narrative models of Native disintegration and declension have powerfully shaped depictions of Shawnee history. An Algonquian people, the Shawnees figured prominently in the pan-Indian military and spiritual resistance movements against Anglo-American expansion in the interior of eastern North America from the mid-eighteenth to the early nineteenth century. Shawnee war leaders, most famously Tecumseh (ca. 1768–1813), captured the imagination of U.S. historians early on. In the 1840s and 1850s Benjamin Drake and Francis Parkman immortalized the Shawnees as savage yet noble defenders of Native freedom who would rather die than submit to "White" oppression. Ever since the days of these pioneer historians, Euroamerican scholars have been fascinated by the bewildering peregrinations of the militant Shawnees. In the late seventeenth century Iroquois warfare, the colonial slave trade, and changing patterns of trade scattered the Shawnees from their Ohio Valley homelands across the East. For the next two centuries dozens of Shawnee groups crisscrossed the continent from the Atlantic seaboard to northern Mexico and from the Gulf Coast to the Great Lakes, constantly fragmenting and amalgamating in complex and seemingly confusing ways. Baffled by such mobility and social fluidity, some historians have vilified the Shawnees. For Parkman, they were "a tribe of bold, roving, and adventurous spirit," whose "eccentric wanderings . . . perplex the antiquary, and defy research." Others have instead romanticized the "roving" Shawnees, celebrating how "the Shawnee held best to certain ideal Indian patterns of behavior; fearlessness; contempt for property and comfort; arrogance toward Whites; disregard for authority; reserve; unbridled, forthright expression of aggression, and other emotions."[6]

More recent historians have moved away from such moralizing statements that treated Shawnee mobility as an expression of Shawnee personality. Instead, scholars now seek to understand Shawnee migrations and dispersals by contextualizing them within the transforming landscapes of colonialism, violence, and Atlantic trade created by the Columbian encounter. In a groundbreaking study, historian Laura Keenan Spero has analyzed Shawnee history as a diaspora. This concept helps to identify and trace "a people who migrate through shifting and ephemeral political borders in search of a new space and yet retain some kind of connection (emotional or otherwise) to their past homelands." For Spero, diaspora is not merely a metaphor for describing Shawnee dispersal. Rather, she sees diaspora as a Shawnee strategy for adapting to a rapidly changing and often dangerous world. When Shawnees scattered across eastern North America, they created an extensive social network that allowed individuals, families, and communities to move over great distances and ally with widespread Native and Euroamerican peoples flexibly in order to address local needs. Diaspora, then, empowered rather than weakened the Shawnees.[7]

Diasporic identities remain difficult to grasp. Often described as fluid, shifting, and multiple, such identities appear endlessly malleable and ever-changing. Shawnee identities, too, have perplexed scholars. Because of the dispersal and apparent disunity of the Shawnees, even careful historians routinely dismiss their collective identity as "weak" or claim that they "lacked an abiding sense of tribal identity" altogether. Such statements entirely miss an important alternative strand in Shawnee history. Colonial documents from the eighteenth and nineteenth centuries are littered with speeches of Shawnee leaders declaring, like Biaseka and Peteusha, that they planned to "Gether two Gather" their scattered people to be "again re-united as one nation." Nor was this mere talk. Beginning in the 1720s, hundreds of Shawnees did indeed gather together in the Ohio Valley where they shared land and built institutions of collective decision-making. When the British victory over France in the Seven Years' War remade the geopolitics of all of North America in the early 1760s, the Shawnees intensified their cooperation. They began meeting at "a Council of their whole Nation" to discuss the common problem of how to cope with an aggressive imperial neighbor. Likewise, the various Shawnee groups created rituals to share their spiritual power in order to strengthen the nation. When the expansive United States threatened to swallow autonomous Indian communities across eastern North America in the early years of the nineteenth century, the Ohio Shawnees drew increasingly strict geographic boundaries and sought recognition for their territorial integrity from both the federal government and their Native neighbors. Finally, when the U.S. government forcibly relocated diverse Shawnee communities from the East, Midwest, and South to a single reservation in Kansas after 1825, some Shawnee leaders advocated national cooperation in order to defend Native sovereignty and property rights. In 1852 they established the National Council, a republican institution that claimed the right to represent all Shawnees in international politics and to control such national assets as land and treaty monies. Gathering together, then, formed a recurrent theme in Shawnee history. From the 1600s to the late 1800s the Shawnees created diverse ways to gather together, ranging from sharing land to collective decision-making and from communal ritual to centralized leadership.[8]

Yet gathering together never went uncontested among the Shawnees. While some leaders and communities collected in the Ohio Valley and later in Kansas, others kept their distance and settled instead among their relatives and allies among the Creeks, Lenapes, Haudenosaunees, and Cherokees. Every time one group of Shawnees called for political consolidation to protect their lands and independence from Euroamerican encroachments, others preferred to rely on mobility, flexible community fissions, and multiethnic alliances. If some leaders evoked spiritual power to advocate Shawnee unity, others referred to that same power to argue for local and kin group autonomy. Many Shawnees, especially after the mid-eighteenth century, envisioned a collective, bounded Shawnee country; others shared land with various Native allies. Clearly, from the seventeenth to the nineteenth century diaspora and consolidation represented two alternative Shawnee strategies for surviving and asserting power in the colonial world. Moreover, diaspora and consolidation were not simply alternative reactions to oppressive exigencies. Instead, both strategies were based on complex and constantly evolving understandings of peoplehood, power, and land. In other words, Shawnee diaspora and nationhood were sophisticated, creative, and historically changing Indigenous political ideologies that profoundly shaped Shawnee actions and, through them, the history of North America.

The complexity and creativity of Shawnee politics challenge us to rethink our models for analyzing Native histories. Such a reappraisal has been in full swing for well over a decade, as a growing number of scholars have focused on Indian peoples and communities in the making. Anthropologists and historians working in the American South have shown how the European invasion transformed the region in the sixteenth and seventeenth centuries into a violent "shatter zone," where slave-raiding and epidemics killed thousands of Indians, displaced many more, and initiated the collapse of centralized societies known as Mississippian chiefdoms. But they have also demonstrated that this chaos did not spell an end to the Native peoples of the South. Across the region survivors joined together for security and assistance and formed new, often multiethnic and even multilingual "coalescent societies." Forging new kinship networks, creating new collective symbols and rituals, and building new institutions for shared decision-making, these new peoples had by the eighteenth century acquired nascent collective identities as the Chickasaws, Choctaws, Cherokees, Creeks, Alabamas, and others. Similar processes shaped Indian societies to the north as well. In the mid-Atlantic river valleys diverse but related Algonquian-speakers sought to offset population decline and land loss due to colonial encroachments by intensifying their cooperation, forging alliances based on kinship, and sharing land with neighbors and relatives. By the first half of the eighteenth century they increasingly identified themselves collectively as Lenapes, while the British recognized their growing unity by calling them Delawares.[9]

Recent scholarship has traced how these emergent Indian nations across the East continued to transform and adjust to the rapidly changing colonial world after the mid-1700s. In the face of relentless Anglo-American expansion Creeks, Lenapes, and Cherokees, for instance, began drawing territorial boundaries and meticulously sought international recognition for them. In the process they subtly changed themselves from kin-based alliance networks to territorial nations. During the early nineteenth century many Southern nations, in partic-ular, also formed centralized and hierarchical governmental structures in hopes that a consolidated political order would help them defend their sovereignty and lands against the United States. But coalescence and centralization were not the only paths for eastern Indians. From the sixteenth through the nine-teenth century many communities relied on migration and fragmentation to battle colonialism. Rather than signaling Native decline and weakness, such actions often constituted highly successful political and economic strategies. Constructing mobile and fluid communities that could disperse and reamal-gamate flexibly, many Shawnees, Haudenosaunees, Alabamas, and others found security, trading advantages, and autonomy through violent and unpredictable times.[10]

Shawnees and other Indian peoples, then, constructed diverse and complex societies to survive and assert power in postcontact America. As the old image of static tribes has been replaced by interpretations emphasizing the dynamism and hybridity of Native societies, scholars have rethought the very terms they use to describe Indian history. Some have even banished the word "tribe" from their vocabulary, claiming that the concept indicates too much political and ethnic unity and stability to capture the far messier social reality of diasporic peoples and polyglot coalescent societies with multiple origins and often rampant internal factionalism. Instead, many recent historians have focused on local communities as the nexus of Native politics and identities. Innovative community-centric Indian histories have thrown into sharper relief how local networks, viewpoints, and interests shaped Native lives and molded the fates of even colonial empires and states in eastern North America. Emphasizing localism should not lead scholars to neglect how Indian peoples conceptualized larger political and ethnic entities, however. Despite diasporas and powerful local identities, from the seventeenth through the nineteenth century most eastern Indians portrayed themselves as larger political and national units in the arenas of international diplomacy. When colonial-era Southern Natives drew maps of their world, they used circles and squares to designate bounded, named, and distinct groups of people—what Europeans at the time called nations. Even the scattered Shawnees consistently referred to themselves as *šaawanwaki*, the Shawnee people, thus linking their local community to dozens of others spread throughout eastern North America. Moreover, the Shawnee word *lenaweeki*, the plural of *lenawe*, or "person," could be attached to a place name or an ethnonym to underline the collectivity of a group of people. When speaking of the Seminoles, for example, Shawnees might say *šimanooleewilenaweeki*, the "Seminole people." Other Indian languages had similar ways to express peoplehood and collective identity.[11]

Drawing from such evidence, historian Nancy Shoemaker has argued that Indians in the postcontact East took "the existence of national categories" for granted and "used labels such as 'Cherokee' and 'French' as though these terms could capture tangible phenomena, discretely bounded and unambiguous political entities." In other words, despite diasporas and localism, Native peoples portrayed and experienced themselves as members of larger entities that can be best described as nations. In the Western academic tradition, the emergence of "nations" is often equated with the post-Enlightenment development of nation-alism and nation-states in Europe. This view restricts nations to the modern era and equates them with politically centralized state societies. Dissatisfied with such a narrow and Eurocentric understanding of nationhood, ethnohistorians, Indigenous scholars, and medieval historians have espoused a broader defini-tion. They argue that a nation should be defined as any collectivity of people who lack direct face-to-face contact but still "imagine"—that is, envision and experience—themselves as a community because they share (or believe they share) both a common origin and a common future. As Creek-Cherokee scholar Craig Womack writes, "a key component of nationhood is a people's idea of themselves, their imaginings of who they are."[12]

Imagining a nation does not imply inauthenticity. Rather, it calls attention to the historicity and contingency of nations. All nations are imagined dynamically, because the vicissitudes of war, internal conflicts, contrasting interests, and economic shifts constantly force individuals and groups to reconsider who they are, where their interests and loyalties lie, and how they are connected to other people. A nation, then, is never a static or unified "thing," although its members may like to think so. Instead, it is a historical "process of forcing conformity and resisting it."[13] Any nation evolves constantly, as various local, kin, or class-based groups negotiate and argue about the proper order, membership, and future of their society. In addition, exactly what "nations" were—how coherently they would or should act; how national identities intertwined with local, kin-based, and regional ones; and what it meant, socially and politically, to be Shawnee or Choctaw—was often ambiguous and contested among the Indians in postcontact eastern North America. As Shawnee history demonstrates, groups that identified themselves as šaawanwaki could still disagree bitterly over the merits of centralized leadership versus local autonomy, or over the relations of power among the various kin groups and towns constituting their nation. Political order and the meanings of peoplehood were actively debated in Indian societies, as they are in any society.

Emphasizing the importance and creative power of such debates, historian Joshua Piker has advocated an "intranational approach" to Native American history. According to Piker, historians should "consider the ways in which national affiliation and community identity were intertwined and the ways in which they diverged" in Indian societies.[14] Taking a cue from Piker, this book focuses on the relationships among the diverse and often dispersed Shawnee communities, the meanings given to those relationships by Shawnees and others, and the negotiations in which such relationships and meanings were constructed, debated, and refashioned or broken. Seen from such a perspective, the Shawnee people appear not as a static or disintegrating tribe with a "weak" collective identity, but as a complex and dynamic historical process, emerging from the actions and cultural ideas of diverse individuals and groups living and making decisions in a world shaped by the powerful global forces of colonialism, capitalism, and state-building.

Historicizing Native American nations and ideas of peoplehood forms a crucial task for historians, anthropologists, and Indigenous scholars. For one thing, it will help us write more complex, nuanced, and culturally informed histories of America. Scholars have long recognized that the late-eighteenth and early-nineteenth-century consolidation of Indian nations involved a complex interplay between Natives and Europeans. By and large, historians have stressed the colonial side of this interaction. They have analyzed how British, French, Spanish, and American agents sought to control Indians by appointing puppet chiefs for loosely allied Native communities and forcing diverse local groups to gather on "tribal" reservations. Such colonial projects, it is often argued, transformed multiethnic Native towns into consolidated but subdued nations. This is an important but lopsided interpretation. To be sure, Euroamericans interfered aggressively in Indian politics and tried to mold Indian societies, often with harsh measures. But Shawnee history makes clear that Shawnee diasporas and coalescences, even though powerfully shaped by colonialism, were also based on Indigenous agendas and ideas. These, in turn, were never mere reactions to the Columbian encounter but stemmed from far older roots. To understand Shawnee communities in the postcontact world, one must therefore begin with their precontact ancestors and investigate the ways in which the political, economic, and ecological dynamics among these ancestors molded subsequent Shawnee ideologies and actions. One likewise needs to situate Shawnee actions within the context of Shawnee cultural and spiritual traditions but envision these traditions as dynamic and debated. Traditions guided Shawnees in their transforming world, but their traditions were never frozen in time. Like all traditions, they involved "the creation of novel cultural forms which are tied to the rich and dynamic context of the past."[15]

Historicizing Native American nationhoods and identities will also encourage scholars to further historicize Euroamerican nationhoods and identities. As borderlands historians have shown, Euroamerican nations and borders, too, were the outcome of complex interactions between Natives and newcomers. Shawnees played a central role in their construction. From the 1770s to the 1790s the determined resistance of the Shawnees and their Native neighbors against Anglo-American expansion to Kentucky and the Ohio Valley forced the notoriously independent American settler communities in these regions to seek the protection of the nascent national government of the United States. Likewise, the destructive Native military campaigns compelled the government in the East to assert its power in the Trans-Appalachian West for fear that otherwise the western citizens might look for solace from another Euroamerican empire. During and after the War of 1812 the mobility of anti-American Shawnees and their allies between the territories claimed by the British empire and the United States led to tightening state control of the U.S.-Canada border.[16] From the 1810s through the 1840s mobile and autonomous Shawnee communities on the Texas borderlands forced Spain, Mexico, Texas, and the United States to consolidate national borders and assert national authority in this socially fluid and contested region. Far from a marginal sidestory in the grand epic of the westward expansion of the United States, Shawnee history thus becomes a crucial element in the far broader history of North America.[17]

Finally, how we conceptualize and historicize Indian politics and societies of the past is not a mere academic exercise. At worst, in the United States claims that "tribes" are simply figments of colonial imagination or products of Euroamerican policies have been used in court against Native peoples pursuing their land and other rights. Federal law defines Indian tribes as sovereign governments. Since the foundational Supreme Court rulings that recognized Native Americans as "domestic dependent nations" in the 1830s, federal authorities have, however, interpreted both Indian sovereignty and Indian nationhood in wildly different ways, usually restricting rather than respecting Indigenous autonomy. Based largely on Euroamerican political and legal traditions, the debates surrounding Native nationhood and sovereignty in the United States would benefit greatly from perspectives grounded in Indian cultures and histories.[18]

As these issues demonstrate, the study of Native American histories is inevitably wrought with complex questions of power, responsibility, and ethics. Indian history has been written predominantly by Euroamericans, for Euroamericans, based on Euroamerican documentary sources, methodologies, and theories. No wonder many Indians have felt that their past has been colonized by academics. As a Finnish anthropologist, I too am an outsider to the Shawnee society, both past and present. Likewise, I have traced Shawnee history largely on the basis of Euroamerican documents. To offset these obvious problems, I have sought Shawnee voices in the documents written by American, British, French, German, and Spanish colonists. In fact, colonial papers are filled with speeches, letters, and messages by Shawnees, and even though these were usually compiled by leading, elderly men rather than by, say, young women, they tell volumes of past Shawnee viewpoints and motivations. Until the mid-nineteenth century such Shawnee voices were written down by Euroamerican scribes in Euroamerican languages, however. This makes it crucial to investigate how much cultural information was lost in translation. What did Peteusha and Biaseka, for instance, actually say, when Henry Hay recorded that they intended to gather together their "straggling nation"? To interpret Shawnee voices in Euroamerican documents I have employed ethnographic and linguistic materials, a standard ethnohistorical practice. When available, I have also complemented and contrasted the documentary evidence with archaeological data and Shawnee oral histories recorded between the late eighteenth and early twentieth centuries. Archaeology and oral histories often illuminate areas of Native life consistently neglected in colonial papers, such as material culture and spirituality. Yet all these research strategies cannot change the fact that mine remains one interpretation of Shawnee history, made from a particular cultural and academic perspective. Other scholars, Native and non-Native, will, I hope, engage this interpretation, to complement, refine, or contradict it.[19]

As one effort to honor Indigenous voices and perspectives, throughout this book I use Native personal names when referring to individual Indians. This runs counter to the standard practice of using English translations of Native names or nicknames given to Indians by Euroamerican traders, diplomats, and missionaries. Thus the famous late-eighteenth-century Shawnee war leader usually known as Blue Jacket appears here first as Sepettekenathé (his name until the mid-1770s) and then as Waweyapiersenwaw (his name later in life). Neither of these names translates to anything like Blue Jacket (they are translated as Big Rabbit and Whirlpool, respectively). "Blue Jacket" was simply a nickname given to the Shawnee leader by Anglo-American traders for unknown reasons. Here, such names will be mentioned only in parentheses when the person first enters the narrative. I have adopted this practice because many of the English translations of Shawnee personal names are inaccurate, while the nicknames are often pejorative. I have made no effort to reconstruct a linguistically correct form of the Native names. I have simply used one rendering that is common in the original (Euroamerican) documents. By the second quarter of the nineteenth century some Shawnees, especially those interested in adopting selected features of Euroamerican economic, cultural, and spiritual traditions, began using English personal names, at least when dealing with Americans. Even though most of these individuals also had Shawnee names, their new English names seem to have formed a part of their self-representation, perhaps even identity. Therefore, I call these individuals by their English names. The grandsons of Waweyapiersenwaw thus appear here as Charles and George Bluejacket.[20]

When I began the research for what eventually became this book, I imagined that the end result would be a neat evolutionary narrative following the transformation of the Shawnees from a diasporic people to a consolidated and politically centralized nation. But Shawnee history defies such simple models. There was never a single moment when the Shawnee nation was "invented." Neither was there ever a single moment when all Shawnees agreed what "being šaawanwaki" entailed in terms of power, politics, and loyalties. From the seventeenth through the late nineteenth century the people called Shawnees underwent repeated diasporas and coalescences, constantly changing, but also constantly retaining connections to past ways of being. Throughout, Shawnee towns, kin groups, and individuals debated the meanings of peoplehood, power, and land. So, in fact, do all people.[21]

"The Greatest Travellers in America"

The Shawnee Diaspora, 1600–1725

"They are Stout, Bold, Cunning, and the greatest Travellers in America."[1]

Thus Edmond Atkin, a seasoned British Indian trader and the future superintendent of Indian affairs, described Shawnees in 1754. Like other colonists, Atkin was baffled by the Shawnees. Since the late seventeenth century, seemingly countless bands of these people had crisscrossed the eastern third of North America, turning up now on the lower Mississippi River, next in Charles Town, Carolina, then on the streets of Albany, New York. Equally baffled by such mobility and dispersal, generations of subsequent scholars condemned the "sudden appearances and disappearances" of the Shawnees as "very obscure." More recently, historians have come to understand that the Shawnees' fragmentation and mobility were emblematic of a whole world set in motion by the immense demographic, political, and economic changes that shook North America during the seventeenth century. Scholars now conceptualize the dispersal of the Shawnees as a diaspora, a forced scattering of a people from ancestral homelands. In the seventeenth century epidemic disease, slave raiding, and globalizing economic networks spread across eastern North America with European explorers, traders, and settlers. These upheavals transformed the region into a "shatter zone," a violent and unstable territory characterized by warfare, depopulation, displacement, and community fragmentation. The diaspora of the Shawnees was a strategy for survival in this chaos, for escaping violence and exploiting new trading opportunities. It was based on Shawnee ideas and networks of alliance, kinship, and community, but the diaspora also transformed those ideas and networks. By the 1720s some Shawnees had learned to regard a mobile life within multiethnic networks of kin and allies as the normal way of life. Others concluded that dispersal was dangerous and began seeking unity and permanent homelands.[2]

THE EMERGENCE

It all began, the Shawnee elders always knew, in the Upper World above the Sky.

According to Shawnee oral histories recorded in the late eighteenth and early nineteenth centuries, the Creator, Meteelemelakwe, made the ancestors of twelve Shawnee divisions in the Upper World, a place of great spiritual power and sacred harmony. Meteelemelakwe then lowered these first people down to the Earth in a basket and taught each division a set of sacred songs that gave the group unique spiritual power and a distinct identity. Once these Shawnee ancestors were on the Earth, the Creator instructed them "to go to Shawnee river, which was the centre of this Island." Thus began a series of epic migrations. Setting out in "a northern direction," the diverse Shawnee divisions crossed oceans and rivers and fought Underworld monsters and hostile peoples. Along the way they allied with one another and gradually formed a powerful confederacy that pushed human and nonhuman enemies out of its way. When they finally reached their promised land at the center of the island Earth, Meteelemelakwe visited them and declared that "they should thenceforth be called Shāūwonoa." A new people had been born.[3]

While Shawnees have always known their own origins, historians and archaeologists have remained more puzzled. In general, archaeological and documentary evidence, like oral histories, points to the importance of migrations and alliances in the emergence of the people called Shawnees. By the eighteenth century the Shawnee people consisted of five "divisions": the Chalaakaathas, Mekoches, Pekowis, Kishpokos, and Thawikilas. These groups spoke closely related dialects of the same language and shared largely similar culture, yet they were often scattered geographically and divided politically. Most scholars assume that the divisions were originally separate groups that had joined together into a confederacy and acquired a collective identity as Shawnees. But exactly when, where, and why this happened remains poorly understood. The difficulty in answering these questions is rooted in the nature of the archaeological and documentary materials at our disposal. Although scholars commonly speak of "archaeological cultures," the term refers merely to roughly contemporaneous archaeological sites that share a similar assemblage of material remains, consisting of, for example, potsherds, discarded tools, and abandoned dwelling structures. What such similarities in material culture may have meant in terms of ethnicity, politics, or language is often difficult to say. Connecting postcontact Native ethnicities to precontact archaeological cultures is therefore always challenging. The widespread diaspora of the Shawnees in the late seventeenth century compounds this problem. Because few Europeans met Shawnees before the 1670s, colonial texts and maps offer no detailed information on their exact locations before they were already scattering throughout the East from wherever their homes had been.[4]

On the basis of studies of ceramic styles, linguistic connections, oral histories, and seventeenth-century documents, most archaeologists nevertheless believe that the majority of the postcontact Shawnees descended from some of the numerous precontact communities in the central Ohio Valley known as Fort Ancient cultures. The connection between Shawnees and Fort Ancient peoples is complex. "Fort Ancient cultures" is a scholarly shorthand for dozens of diverse farming societies that flourished in the region stretching from southern Indiana to West Virginia between 1000 and 1700 CE. While the people living in this area shared some similarities in pottery styles, architecture, and clothing, many regional and temporal differences in their material cultures suggest that several different ethnic and linguistic groups lived in the Fort Ancient territory. Therefore, it is likely that the descendants of the Fort Ancient peoples included many historically known Native groups in addition to the Shawnees. These probably included some Central Algonquian speakers related to the Shawnees, as well as unrelated Siouans and Iroquoians. Furthermore, some Shawnees may have originated elsewhere. The dialects of the five postcontact Shawnee divisions were so closely related that these groups must have shared a common background of considerable time depth. Other cultural differences, for example in ritual cycles, nevertheless suggest that all divisions may not have shared the same origins. Seventeenth-century French documents often place some Shawnee communities on the lower Ohio and the Cumberland River, known as the Shawnee River well into the eighteenth century. Quite likely, the postcontact Shawnees represented a coalition of various precontact populations from the central and lower Ohio and the Cumberland.[5]

In order to understand how these diverse peoples coalesced together it is essential to explore the development of the Late Fort Ancient communities after 1400 CE. Although all Shawnees did not necessarily descend from Fort Ancient populations, it was the complex political and social processes in these communities that laid the groundwork for the formation of the Shawnee people, the politics in early Shawnee towns, and the strategies the Shawnees espoused when the Columbian encounter transformed eastern North America into a hotbed of violence, migration, and population decline. The Fort Ancient cultures first emerged around 1000 CE, when small hunter-gatherer-farmer communities throughout the central Ohio Valley added maize agriculture to their traditional livelihoods. Taking full advantage of a warm climatic period known as the Medieval Warm Period, they developed an efficient, if precarious, economic system that combined several subsistence pursuits. During summers the Fort Ancient peoples lived in small villages in river valleys where women farmed maize, squash, and beans; during winters the villagers dispersed in small family and kin groups to upland woods where men hunted deer and other game. For much of the year gathering and fishing supplemented the diet.[6]

The fifteenth century witnessed the beginnings of several social, political, and ecological transformations in the Fort Ancient territory that gradually led to the emergence of the Shawnee people over the following two centuries. Most importantly, population distribution and settlement patterns underwent a radical transformation. Before about 1400, dozens of small Fort Ancient communities had been scattered evenly over a wide area extending up to sixty miles from the Ohio on both sides of the river. During the fifteenth century, however, the population concentrated on a drastically circumscribed region that lay within a radius of a mere twelve miles from the Ohio. In the process the numerous small villages amalgamated into a handful of larger towns, with populations varying from one hundred to five hundred people. The causes behind these changes are not clear. The transformation may have been prompted by the onset of cooler and moister climatic conditions, known as the Little Ice Age, which forced people to concentrate on prime agricultural lands close to the Ohio River. The reconfiguration of the Fort Ancient settlements was also almost certainly connected to similar demographic and social changes across eastern North America. Throughout the East communities that previously had been distributed evenly across the landscape concentrated now into smaller, densely populated centers separated by large uninhabited areas. It is possible that deteriorating climatic conditions over the entire region sparked conflicts over land and resources, forcing small villages to band together for security. The palisades around some Late Fort Ancient towns and many contemporary settlements elsewhere in eastern North America point to this direction. However, archaeological records also offer abundant evidence of increasing peaceful exchange between the population centers across the East. Large communities established close to important trade routes, such as the Ohio River, were certainly better positioned to benefit from this exchange than scattered villages.[7] The consolidation of the Fort Ancient populations and communities was, then, intimately connected to major transformations in broader regional networks of warfare, diplomacy, and trade.

When previously separate peoples gather together to form new settlements, they face the daunting task of transforming a collection of strangers into a viable community. They must construct new social ties and symbols to bind them together, rethink their loyalties and relations of authority, and create shared identities. When the Fort Ancient villagers gathered into the new, big towns in the fifteenth century, they accomplished many of these tasks through the creative use of one important traditional social institution: the clan system. Anthropologists define a clan as a kin group whose members believe that they descend from a common ancestor, even though they may not know the exact genealogical relations between all clan members. Clan membership is inherited either through the father (patrilineally) or through the mother (matrilineally). Anthropological studies of clan societies across the globe demonstrate that clans constitute an efficient way of organizing large numbers of people and regulating their interaction.[8]

Linguistic and archaeological evidence suggests that some Fort Ancient villagers and even their ancestors had been organized into clans or similar kin groups long before the fifteenth century. When Fort Ancient villages amalgamated into larger towns, clans took a more prominent role in structuring social, political, and economic life in the new communities. This can be seen most powerfully in the changes in the Fort Ancient household architecture. After the fifteenth century small, single-family dwellings common in earlier Fort Ancient villages were replaced by much larger, rectangular longhouses. With floor spaces varying from approximately 680 to 2,100 square feet, these dwellings housed an estimated thirteen to thirty-three people. Such a group probably formed a clan segment or an extended family. Houses in a town were often grouped in distinct clusters, suggesting that related families, possibly belonging to the same clan, settled near one another. The strength of kinship and clan identities were also demonstrated through mortuary ritual. In some settlements the deceased were buried under or near the house where their relatives continued to live. Other towns had communal cemeteries that were divided into distinct, probably clan-based sections. Clans further solidified their importance by adopting a new food storage system, as people living in the same household began digging deep storage pits under their homes. Large amounts of corn could be preserved in these pits for long periods, which strengthened the self-sufficiency and independence of households and, by extension, clans.[9]

It is always risky to extend information on postcontact Native cultural patterns back into precontact times. Nevertheless, the picture of the Late Fort Ancient clans that emerges from archaeology bears a close resemblance to eighteenth- and nineteenth-century Shawnee and other Central Algonquian clans. In the eighteenth century the social life of Shawnees and other Central Algonquians revolved around clans. Known as *m'shoma*, or "name," in Shawnee, these were patrilineal and exogamous descent groups; that is, an individual always belonged to her or his father's clan and had to marry a person from a different clan. Each Shawnee m'shoma was believed to descend from a mythical ancestor who had given the group its name. From the ancestor a clan derived unique spiritual power, also called m'shoma, that gave the clan special potency in a specific field of life. The Turkey and Turtle clans, for example, were believed to possess power over the fertility of the earth. Individual members of a clan received a share of their group's m'shoma power through their personal names, which were connected to the clan eponym.[10]

Clan membership greatly shaped both social life and individual identity among the postcontact Shawnees. In 1753 one Shawnee explained: "We are distributed by different names, the Cow, the Bear, the Buffaloe. There are also Wolf Shavanahs and other Names given us." The postcontact clans were political as well as spiritual units. According to one early-nineteenth-century Native description, each m'shoma had its own leadership and various political officials. Every clan had a *hokima*, a male civil or peace chief, who represented his kin group to outsiders in communal and international affairs and fostered good relations between his m'shoma and other people. Most clans also had a *neenaw-tooma*, a male war leader, whose duty was to defend his kinspeople against threatening outsiders. Side by side with these male officials worked corresponding female ones, the Peace Woman and the War Woman. Known as *hokima wiikwes*, or "chief women," these influential women oversaw the agricultural work of their m'shoma, organized planting and harvest rituals, and participated in decision-making concerning war and peace. Well into the nineteenth century Shawnee leaders stressed that their authority was embedded in kinship relations and portrayed themselves as m'shoma leaders. Typically, a hokima or a neenawtooma, for example, signed a treaty with Europeans with the picture of his clan eponym. This suggests that leaders conceptualized themselves first and foremost as spokespeople of their clan members. We cannot know how far such eighteenth- and nineteenth-century information is applicable to the Fort Ancient clans. In all likelihood the postcontact Shawnee m'shomas had deep precontact roots, and the Fort Ancient clans were at least roughly similar spiritual and political units.[11]

As strong corporate groups with a distinct identity and unique sacred power, clans both divided and united the people collecting in the growing Late Fort Ancient towns. It is likely that clans related through descent or marriage often moved to the same settlements. Marriages also quickly bound previously unrelated clans together. So did rituals. In postcontact times Shawnee and other Central Algonquian clans performed various kinds of ritual tasks on behalf of one another. The deceased, for example, were prepared for burial by members of a clan other than their own, while leadership roles in communal planting and harvest rituals were assigned to specific m'shomas. It is possible that such ritual cooperation was created deliberately in Late Fort Ancient towns to tie the incoming clans into a cohesive community whose members would feel mutually dependent on one another. Ethnographic and historical studies demonstrate that such a strategy is common across the world in "coalescent societies" formed of previously disparate peoples and communities.[12]

The most important archaeological evidence of clan cooperation in the Late Fort Ancient towns is the appearance of large, centrally located rectangular buildings at some settlement sites. These structures resemble postcontact

Central Algonquian "council houses," known as *mšikamekwi* in Shawnee. Built of bark or logs and sometimes reaching a length of ninety feet, the postcontact Shawnee mšikamekwis housed the meetings of a town council, composed of "Chiefs & . . . old men," clan elders and matrons, war leaders, and warriors. The emergence of similar buildings in Late Fort Ancient towns suggests that as the settlements grew, the diverse clans moving in from different villages found it important to establish a shared arena for discussing common concerns. Similar councils emerged in other late precontact settlements throughout the East to facilitate harmonious social life in communities that were rapidly growing and incorporating groups with disparate backgrounds. Importantly, eighteenth-century Shawnee and other town councils recognized no majority decisions. Instead, they sought to construct a unanimous position through a long, often grueling, process of negotiation and compromise. Therefore, town councils both fostered clan cooperation and protected clan autonomy.[13] It is likely that this was the very goal of the Fort Ancient clans when they established councils. When political, economic, and ecological transformations forced disparate kin groups and communities to join together, clans sought to ensure social harmony by creating a political institution based on collective decision-making and sharing power. Unlike the highly centralized Mississippian chiefdoms to the south, the Fort Ancient peoples cultivated clan egalitarianism and decentralized leadership as strategies for adapting to a rapidly changing world.

It seems that the Late Fort Ancient communities also constructed an elaborate system of checks and balances to impede the rise of aggressive individuals and groups to political prominence during this era of growing settlement size and intensifying clan collaboration. Such a system certainly existed by 1824, when the Shawnee holy man Tenskwatawa described it to American ethnographers. He explained that although the position of a clan hokima in principle passed from father to son, in actual fact the "chiefs & principal men" of a town selected one of the sons of a deceased hokima to become his successor. Their decision was then declared to the community in "a great feast" where the new hokima was ceremonially installed. The community exerted similar control over the rise of new war leaders. In theory, any man could become a war leader if he managed to lead four victorious military expeditions against enemy communities. Yet even a man who accomplished this feat had only the right to "demand" war leadership. He became a neenawtooma only after the other leaders of his town had recognized him as such, again in a communal feast. These customs bound each new leader intimately to the other powerful people and m'shomas of their community. They made it next to impossible for any individual to rise to a position of authority without the support and acceptance of several clans and their leaders.[14]

In addition to new forms of political cooperation, the appearance of council houses suggests that new communal identities were emerging in the Late Fort Ancient towns. Postcontact Shawnee mšikamekwis housed not only council meetings, but also town rituals and nighttime social dances that drew the community together for prayer, entertainment, and celebration. An increasingly communal orientation in the Late Fort Ancient towns is further indicated by open plazas located at the center of some settlements. Some of these served as communal cemeteries, but the plazas also may have been used for collective rituals like similar spaces in many precontact and postcontact communities in the South. While clans clearly remained central to the Late Fort Ancient peoples, new town-based identities, rooted in cohabitation, collective decision-making, and shared rituals, were also becoming increasingly important. It seems likely that the towns formed the foundations for the historically known Shawnee divisions. Certainly by the first decades of the eighteenth century Shawnee towns often bore divisional names, suggesting an intimate link between the two.[15]

New supra-local social networks and identities emerged as well. From the late fifteenth century on, the Fort Ancient towns created new ties to one another. Archaeologically this can be seen best in the gradual unification of material culture, especially ceramics, throughout the Fort Ancient country. This development probably demonstrates increasing interaction, visiting, and intermarriage among the Fort Ancient communities. Because women manufactured most pots in postcontact Indian societies in the East, the growing similarity of ceramics suggests that women in particular were moving between the Late Fort Ancient towns, probably to marry men from other communities. Doing so, they weaved intimate social and emotional bonds among the various local groups and gave their children social networks that extended beyond the hometown. New kinds of political alliances took shape, too. In the late sixteenth and early seventeenth centuries several adult men were buried at four western Fort Ancient sites in Ohio and Kentucky with strikingly similar copper pendants, decorated with rattlesnake engravings, and large white or light gray pipes. Pipes and the color white played a central part in Native diplomatic rituals throughout the postcontact East. Snakes, in turn, symbolized spiritual power among Shawnees and many neighboring Natives. Following these ethnographic analogies, archaeologist Penelope Drooker has argued that the individuals buried with such prestigious objects served as leaders in a nascent multisettlement alliance network or confederacy. This may represent the earliest roots of a coalition of towns that would in time evolve into the Shawnee people.[16]

When explaining Shawnee origins, Native oral histories emphasize just such alliance building between previously distinct groups. Three oral histories describing tribal origins were recorded by British and U.S. officials in 1795,

1824, and 1825. The first was narrated by the Mekoche headmen Catahecassa (Black Hoof), Biaseka (Wolf), and the Red-Faced Fellow; the second by the Kishpoko prophet Tenskwatawa; and the third again by Catahecassa. In addition, in the 1920s a tribal official, teacher, and historian named Thomas Wildcat Alford wrote down tribal traditions that he had learned decades earlier from Pekowi, Thawikila, and Kishpoko elders. Since the three earliest histories were narrated in the context of heated political disputes, they reflect the politics and interests of their day; therefore, one must use them cautiously as records of Shawnee origins. But despite their obvious partisanship, all versions agree on several key points, suggesting that they contain valid historical information and should not be discarded as sources of the past.[17]

The oral histories describe how numerous migratory groups in search of land and security came together, formed alliances, and gradually embraced a collective identity as Shawnees. Most versions identify the five divisions known from eighteenth-century colonial documents as the original members of this alliance network. In addition, Catahecassa's narratives suggest that other groups also joined the emerging Shawnee confederacy but were later assimilated into the five divisions. Oral histories detail two strategies that the divisions employed to forge alliances with one another. Catahecassa in particular emphasized the creation of ceremonial kin ties. In his two versions the proto-Shawnee groups transform strangers into allies by recognizing one another reciprocally as brothers or as grandfathers and grandchildren. Creating ceremonial kinship was a common method for uniting unrelated communities throughout postcontact Native eastern North America. Conceivably, the Fort Ancient peoples would have seen it as a safe and efficient way to turn strangers into allies.[18]

Tenskwatawa and Alford, in turn, stressed the role of sacred power and reciprocal ritual duties in linking the proto-Shawnee communities together. In Tenskwatawa's history, the Shawnee divisions meet during their migrations toward the land the Creator has made for them. They negotiate alliances and assign each division a specific role that the division has to perform on behalf of all the confederated groups. The Pekowis, for example, are "appointed head of the warriors of the Shawanese nation," while the Mekoches are recognized as "the counsellor for the whole nation." Alford explained that these responsibilities were connected to a specific form of spiritual power possessed by the divisions. According to him, the Creator had given each division a sacred bundle, or *miišaami*, which Tenskwatawa described as a collection of spiritually powerful objects "rolled in a dressed deer skin, which is again wrapped in a dressed Buffaloe skin." Each bundle contained tremendous power, also known as miišaami, which could be mobilized by ritually opening the bundle and singing a set of sacred songs connected to it. Miišaami formed an essential part of the identity of a division. Alford called it "the potency of life" that gave a division "its very life and inspiration." The miišaami power of each Shawnee division was unique: the power of one division might be suited for healing, that of another for warfare. In Alford's history, the proto-Shawnee divisions meet, compare their respective miišaamis, and then conclude alliances in which each group is given specific responsibilities on the basis of the nature of its sacred power. These reciprocal duties bind the various groups together into a united Shawnee confederacy.[19]

While we do not know how such a system of reciprocal duties may have worked in practice, it is likely that the responsibilities described by Tenskwatawa and Alford were largely ritual. Throughout the late precontact and early postcontact East, many Indian communities coalescing into larger confederacies created complex reciprocal rituals to forge and solidify alliances. Such rituals were much more than simply functional strategies for building political cohesion, however. Like the Shawnee case suggests, the goal was to share spiritual power in order to make all the allies stronger than they would have been alone. As historian Daniel Richter writes about the Iroquois League, this confederacy of five Iroquoian tribes constituted "spiritual and temporal force marshaled by alliances among the people, kin groups, and villages of the League."[20]

One thing the proto-Shawnee communities did *not* create was centralized leadership. There is no evidence of intertown hierarchies or overarching decision-making institutions in the Fort Ancient archaeological record. If the men buried with the rattlesnake pendants and white pipes truly were proto-Shawnee leaders, their duty was more to foster peace and harmony among their respective communities through ritual and ceremonial gift exchanges than to make and enforce collective decisions.[21]

Late Fort Ancient communities had good reasons to cultivate intertown alliances and harmony. For one thing, the Little Ice Age was forcing people to crowd to the best farmlands close to the Ohio River. In such potentially explosive conditions both ceremonial kin ties and reciprocal rituals would have helped communities to share the land and its resources peacefully. The emergence of the Shawnee confederacy was probably also a response to wider geopolitical transformations. During the sixteenth and early seventeenth centuries the complex Mississippian chiefdoms that had dominated much of the Southeast for hundreds of years began falling apart, creating political instability and migrations and disrupting trade routes. At the same time long-distance exchange, slave raiding, and warfare intensified across eastern North America, and Old World diseases, introduced by the first European explorers, created havoc along the Atlantic and Gulf coasts. Many communities throughout the East sought to survive these tumultuous times by forming alliances with their neighbors. This led to the emergence of multiethnic coalitions and confederacies such as the Iroquois, Choctaws, Cherokees, and Upper and Lower Creeks.

In such a competitive and conflict-ridden environment, forging intertown alliances and networks of cooperation was a sensible political, economic, and spiritual strategy for the Fort Ancient communities.[22]

The early Shawnee confederacy probably emerged and grew gradually between the late fifteenth and mid-seventeenth centuries, as several local communities forged multiple and overlapping ritual and kin ties with one another. It was a dynamic alliance network in constant flux, for the allies had to find a balance between local interests and a collective identity. Oral histories, for example, describe how the Mekoches wanted to ally with the Chalaakaathas as "brothers," but the Chalaakaathas insisted that they were "to be called *grandfathers*," a strong symbol of authority in a society that venerated old age and the wisdom of grandparents. In other versions the Chalaakaathas and Mekoches argue bitterly about the potency of their miišaamis and thus their respective status, rights, and responsibilities. Many oral histories further suggest that through time some groups separated from the confederacy and new ones joined in.[23]

Despite the flux, a collective identity did gradually evolve among the communities increasingly connected by kinship, ritual, intermarriage, and political alliance. This is evidenced by the emergence of the most powerful symbol of a shared identity: a collective name. In the mid-seventeenth century French explorers, missionaries, and traders active in the St. Lawrence Valley, around the Great Lakes, and on the Mississippi River began collecting information on the Ohio Valley from their Native allies, converts, and trading partners living north or west of the Ohio. From the Indians the Frenchmen heard stories of several great rivers crosscutting the land between the Mississippi and the Atlantic and of many populous Native peoples living along these streams. Among these Indians were groups known to outsiders as the Moseopelas, Casas, Honniasaontkeronons, and Chaouanons. In many Algonquian languages words like "Shawunogi" mean simply "Southerners." Thus the "Chaouanons" of the early French journals and maps do not necessarily refer to a distinct political or ethnic group. Sometimes the name may denote anyone living to the south of whoever was providing the information to the French. But the French documents place the "Chaouanons" fairly consistently somewhere on or near the Ohio River, next to groups known by other names. This suggests, at the very least, that by the late seventeenth century many Indians in the surrounding regions saw some of the communities in the Ohio drainage constituting a collectivity known as the "Shawnees." It is impossible to say when these people adopted "Shawnee" as their self-designation—or whether they had invented the name in the first place. When Shawnees scattered from the Ohio in the late seventeenth century, they consistently introduced themselves to strangers as Shawnees (*šaawanwaki* or *šaawanooki* in Shawnee). This provides strong evidence that the name must have had considerable time depth among them. By the late 1600s it was part and parcel of the identity of the communities that had been forging alliances over the previous two hundred years.[24]

But the nascent Shawnee identity did not eradicate older town, divisional, and clan identities. The French records are replete with the names of the Shawnee divisions, such as Chaskepe (Kishpoko) and Meguatchaiki (Mekoche). This is evidence for the ongoing importance of the divisions. French documents also speak of geographical divisions among the "Chaouanons." In 1673 Indians living near the mouth of the Ohio explained that there were no fewer than thirty-eight Chaouanon "villages" in two "districts" higher up on the Ohio. Other early documents place some Shawnees on the Cumberland River in addition to the Ohio. While no reliable population figures exist, one oft-used but probably conservative estimate puts the number of the early postcontact Shawnees somewhere between two thousand and four thousand. Clearly, such a population living in dozens of towns that stretched from the Cumberland River to the central Ohio Valley cannot have been politically united or culturally homogenous.[25] Like other Indian peoples throughout the East, the early Shawnees of the sixteenth and seventeenth centuries thus constructed multiple overlapping networks of kinship, alliance, and exchange, within which clans and towns remained the foci of the most fundamental identities and loyalties.[26]

DIASPORA

In the sixteenth century the Fort Ancient peoples must have heard disturbing rumors of strange newcomers who had appeared at the margins of their world. Several Spanish entradas marched violently through the interior South during the 1500s. From the Florida coast to the Mississippi Valley military defeats and population decline shattered the economic and political foundations of the centralized Mississippian chiefdoms and triggered the disintegration of these hierarchical societies. The Spaniards and other European visitors also carried new germs to America. During the sixteenth century smallpox and other Old Word diseases ravaged Mississippian communities in the South. From 1616 to 1619 smallpox devastated Indians in what is now called New England, and fifteen years later it spread death in the eastern Great Lakes region. Such "virgin soil epidemics" killed untold numbers of Natives during the seventeenth century. Population loss led to further political turmoil when survivors fled from their homes and looked for safety in new regions.[27]

On the northeastern Atlantic Coast a more peaceful pattern of interaction developed between Natives and newcomers, when local Indians and visiting French, Basque, Portuguese, and English fishermen began trading in the 1530s.

Native peoples exchanged animal furs and skins for European metal tools and glass ornaments that soon spread far and wide through Indigenous exchange networks that crisscrossed the East. When Indians incorporated European materials and goods into their economy, art, and spirituality, they became enmeshed in emerging commercial networks that extended across the Atlantic. Soon, global currents of supply, demand, and warfare would increasingly frame their lives. By the seventeenth century growing European demand for beaver furs sparked intertribal conflicts over trade routes and hunting territories and intensified warfare throughout the Northeast. In the South, the founding of the English colonies of Virginia and Carolina created another kind of commerce, when wealthy colonial plantation owners began looking for Indian slaves to labor on their fields and to be sold to the Caribbean. Encouraged by high prices, many Southeastern Native communities transformed into "militaristic slaving societies" that raided other Indians for captives and then sold these to the English. Brutal warfare spread through the South, and perhaps as many as fifty thousand Natives were enslaved. The Mississippian chiefdoms fragmented, as the survivors fled and banded together, forming new refugee communities and coalescent societies. Within a century the European invasion had remade eastern North America into a shatter zone, where war, migration, and population decline broke older social formations into "a world made of fragments." It was a world on the move, full of transforming societies and diasporic peoples.[28]

Although no European set foot in the Ohio Valley before the late seventeenth century, shockwaves from the Atlantic and Gulf coasts quickly reached the region. The first indicators of trouble appear in the archaeological record in the early seventeenth century. Ever since the mid-1500s the Ohio peoples had acquired European copper kettles, glass beads, and scrap iron through Native down-the-line exchange networks from peoples living closer to the Atlantic. Many of these goods had become part and parcel of the everyday life, dress, and ritual of the locals. By about 1640, however, such items no longer reached the Ohio Valley. This suggests major reconfigurations in regional exchange networks and, much worse, disruptions in the webs of trade and alliance that had long connected the Fort Ancient communities to surrounding peoples to the north, east, and south.[29]

When trade and diplomacy withered, violence followed. In the 1640s the Haudenosaunees, or the Iroquois Confederacy of Mohawks, Oneidas, Onondagas, Cayugas, and Senecas, also known as the Five Nations, launched a series of devastating attacks against its Native neighbors around the eastern Great Lakes. These campaigns were rooted in the economic, epidemic, and cultural forces at the heart of the shatter zone. The Haudenosaunees sought to bolster their position in the colonial fur trade by asserting control over hunting territories and trade routes. With their communities decimated by smallpox, they were also looking for captives for adoption to strengthen their fledging numbers. Within a decade the Iroquois crushed the Hurons, Petuns, Neutrals, and Eries and absorbed the remnants of these peoples into their own ranks. In the 1660s and 1670s they extended their raids to the western Great Lakes and the Ohio Valley. Southern slavers likewise infested the Ohio Country.[30]

Cut off from familiar exchange networks and engulfed by violence, the Shawnees and other Ohioans faced terrifying times. With few or no firearms, they found it impossible to resist the invaders well supplied with guns by their Dutch and English trading partners. Years later a Pekowi man remembered with dread the painful times when "upon our Return from hunting, We found our Town surprized and our women and children taken prisoners by our Enemies." In this maelstrom of violence, the Ohio communities fragmented and fled. Whole towns abandoned their homelands in search of what one Shawnee called "a Countrey at Peace." Some sought safety by crossing the Mississippi River. Others moved closer to European trading centers for trade and protection. By 1680 the Ohio Valley had become almost entirely depopulated. Often, the escape became a journey to oblivion. In the last decades of the seventeenth century most of the Ohioan groups named in the early French documents simply vanish from colonial records. Some communities may have been destroyed or enslaved by their enemies. Some perhaps succumbed to disease. Most, more likely, simply moved away and amalgamated into the new multiethnic coalescent societies that were emerging throughout the East, as diverse survivors from epidemics, fragments of disintegrated Mississippian chiefdoms, and refugees from slave raids joined together for security.[31]

The Shawnees, too, left their homes on the Ohio. During the 1670s and 1680s they scattered across the East in dozens of bands that adopted a highly mobile way of life in order to escape the violence and look for new trading opportunities. As generations of scholars have come to find out, the Shawnee dispersal was so complex, rapid, and poorly documented that it is very difficult to trace in detail. But perplexing as the individual movements of the Shawnee groups often are, it is possible to investigate the development and consequences of their diaspora in broader strokes. By situating the Shawnee dispersal in the context of the shatter zone, Atlantic economy, and Shawnee social structures, three pivotal patterns emerge. First, the Shawnee migrations were driven not by some innate wanderlust but by warfare and trade, both rooted in the political economy of the shatter zone. Second, without belittling the suffering, pain, and grief they must have felt, it is important that we do not reduce the Shawnee refugees to passive victims, crushed by unstoppable forces of colonialism. The diaspora, while certainly painful, was also a Shawnee strategy to survive, even flourish, in a world out of joint. It created a web of widespread communities connected by kinship and alliance, and Shawnees quickly learned to use this web to their advantage. Their connections allowed individuals and families to navigate across enormous distances of troubled landscape according to their interests and needs. Such a network of communication and contact provided each Shawnee community and kin group with various political and economic alternatives in their efforts to survive in the harsh world of warfare and epidemics. As historian Alan Gallay has argued, the Shawnees "found strength in diaspora." Finally, the diaspora did not mean a total breakdown of the old political order. On the contrary, the dispersal followed enduring Shawnee social structures. It was the old networks of interconnected towns and clans, as well as persisting town identities, that empowered the Shawnees to scatter, create far-reaching connections, and survive as *Shawnees*.[32]

The Shawnee groups that dispersed from the Ohio toward the Great Lakes, the Southeast, and the mid-Atlantic had divergent interests and pursued differing strategies to survive the crisis. Many moved, not so much pushed by the Haudenosaunees and the southern slavers as pulled by colonial trade. The first Shawnees to leave the Ohio drainage migrated to the Savannah River and settled in the neighborhood of Charles Town, the center of the Atlantic deerskin trade, in the 1670s. At least some of these migrants and traders were Thawikilas, for British colonists later called their descendants "Asswikales" and "Shaweygiras." Some of them had probably already traded with the Spanish settlements in Florida. Their migration to the Savannah, then, was an effort by experienced merchants to solidify their position in the productive colonial commercial networks of the Southeast at a time when many established trade routes in the Ohio Valley were crumbling. Other Shawnees, too, headed south from the Ohio. Around 1675 some groups, probably including at least some Kishpokos, settled on the Tallapoosa River where they created close political and ritual alliances with the local Muskogean-speaking Tallapoosas, Abihkas, and Alabamas, who were in the process of forming a multitown coalition that the English would later call the Upper Creek confederacy. A third major group of Shawnees looked for trade and military protection in the northwest. In the 1680s some seven hundred Pekowis, Mekoches, and possibly other Shawnees made their way to the Illinois River, where the French explorers had just established Fort St. Louis. Hundreds of other Algonquian refugees from the upper Mississippi and western Great Lakes also fled Haudenosaunee warriors to the fort, making it the center of French-Indian trade and diplomacy and the heart of a powerful anti-Iroquois coalition.[33]

Most of these places offered no safe haven in the turmoil of the shatter zone. The Savannah River Shawnees were quickly embroiled in the burgeoning Indian slave trade centered in Charles Town. With Carolinian assistance, they raided neighboring communities, making some profits and many enemies. But they soon found Carolina a fickle ally, as the English did not shy away from enslaving their allies as well as their enemies. As early as 1707 many Shawnees fled north from the Savannah, settling on the Potomac and Susquehanna rivers. Eight years later the remaining Savannah people joined their Yamasee, Apalachee, and Creek neighbors in the Yamasee War against the exploitative Carolinian slave regime. After months of devastating violence, they escaped colonial retribution to the Chattahoochee River on the modern Alabama-Georgia border. There, the Savannah Shawnees settled among the various Muskogean communities that were gradually forging a loose intertown alliance network known to the English as the Lower Creek confederacy. The Shawnees at Fort St. Louis, in turn, fell out with their French and Algonquian neighbors. Harassed by the local Miamis, they abandoned Fort St. Louis in the early 1690s. One group of Pekowis and perhaps others trekked across much of the East and finally settled on the lower Susquehanna River. Others, including some Mekoches, migrated from the Illinois to the Delaware River at the invitation of the local Lenapes and Munsees in 1694.[34]

By 1710 most Shawnees lived in the mid-Atlantic region, scattered in numerous towns stretching from the Potomac to the Delaware River. The Tallapoosa and Chattahoochee rivers likewise formed important foci for Shawnee populations. Smaller groups remained dispersed from the Mississippi to the Hudson River. Moreover, individuals, families, and whole towns kept moving between these far-flung population centers. Confusing as these constant migrations and regroupings seem, it is essential to abolish the deep-seated image of the Shawnee migrations as chaotic wanderings. When Shawnees and other Late Fort Ancient groups abandoned their Ohio homelands, they generally moved to regions and settled among peoples to whom they were bound by long-standing exchange relations and political alliances. Even when Shawnee bands migrated to entirely unknown lands, colonial documents show, they always prepared their journeys carefully, contacted the local Indians and colonists for permission to enter the region, and sent scouting parties to reconnoiter the distant lands. The fact that most Shawnees time after time moved close to new colonial trading centers such as Fort St. Louis, Charles Town, and Philadelphia also testifies to the planning that clearly preceded most migrations.[35] Such careful preparations suggest that most Shawnee migrations were not desperate flights of badly destroyed communities. Instead, they were well-planned efforts by intact towns to find safer homes and more lucrative trading opportunities when their homelands turned into war zones disconnected from major exchange routes.

Precontact networks helped Shawnee communities to navigate the troubled landscapes of violence and disease and often shaped their migration patterns. New alliances likewise proved crucial for the migrants. By the late seventeenth century several powerful, antagonistic coalitions of Natives and Europeans had emerged in the East to compete for military and diplomatic supremacy, land,

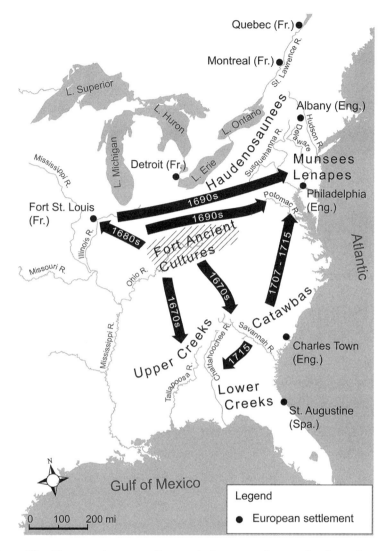

Map 1. The Shawnee diaspora, 1680–1715 (information from Callender, "Shawnee,"
623). Map drawn by Terhi Tanska.

and trade. The Haudenosaunees asserted their position militarily and economically around the lower Great Lakes with the help of first Dutch and then
English colonies. In the western Great Lakes various mostly Algonquian peoples
allied with the French to stop the Iroquois incursions to the region. In the
South diverse Mississippian refugees and splinter groups consolidated into the
Creek, Choctaw, Cherokee, and Chickasaw confederacies, which allied variously with the Spanish, French, and English colonies. Amidst these competing

and powerful coalitions small refugee groups such as the diasporic Shawnees could survive only with the help of allies. "Weary of the warrs," outnumbered, and outgunned, they desperately needed allies to gain protection, land for cultivation, and access to trade with the Europeans.[36]

Everywhere they went, the Shawnee bands eagerly sought to ally with local Indians and Europeans. They always established common settlements with other refugees and survivors from warfare and epidemics. One Pennsylvanian official, for example, reported that the diverse Shawnee groups moving into the Susquehanna Valley in the 1690s "had two or three towns of their own but they scattered into divers places . . . living promiscuously & intermarrying with" the local Susquehannocks (Conestogas), Lenapes, Munsees, Conoys, and others. Often living in diasporas of their own, such displaced splinter groups were eager to bolster their security and trade connections by allying with the Shawnees and sharing land with them. But such multiethnic refugee communities still remained vulnerable to more populous and better-armed neighbors. Thus it became crucial for the Shawnees to forge ties with the major diplomatic, military, and economic powers of their new homelands. Accordingly, in the 1690s the Pekowis, Mekoches, and others settling along the Susquehanna and Delaware rivers negotiated a peace with their Haudenosaunee enemies. They likewise forged alliances with the English colonies of Pennsylvania, Maryland, and New York. In the South the Kishpokos, Thawikilas, and other Shawnees living on the Tallapoosa and Chattahoochee fostered close ties with the powerful Upper and Lower Creek confederacies. Fundamentally, it was these alliances with the regionally powerful Haudenosaunees, English, and Creeks that allowed the Shawnee refugees to carve relatively permanent homes for themselves in the river valleys of the mid-Atlantic and the South.[37] These alliances ingrained the refugees into the regional networks of exchange, sharing, and protection that provided them with a measure of safety and stability in the shatter zone.

Alliances between the diasporic Shawnee communities and their Indian neighbors were woven of political, social, and spiritual threads. In the mid-Atlantic, for example, the Pekowis who settled on the lower Susquehanna River regularly joined their Susquehannock, Lenape, and Conoy neighbors in negotiations with the Pennsylvania and Maryland authorities. In colonial treaties these peoples "upon Susquehannagh" were often represented by a single orator, who spoke "in the Name & on the Behalf of all the Indians present."[38] This collaboration was based on much more than mere political expediency. Intermarriages between Shawnees and their neighbors bound individuals with diverse ethnic and linguistic backgrounds together as families. Elite Shawnee women played a major role in constructing such networks. One such woman was Weenepeeweytah, a "Cousin" of a lower Susquehanna Shawnee headman known as Savannah. She married a noted Seneca man named Sawantaeny whose networks extended from the Potomac River to Iroquoia. Weenepeeweeyah's marriage thus gave her whole community relatives and friends among the far-flung and powerful Haudenosaunees. It is likely that leading Shawnee families actively sought to marry their daughters to elite men in surrounding communities to foster peace and cooperation among the neighbors. Marriages between notable Shawnee women and influential Haudenosaunee, Lenape, and Susquehannock men attached diasporic Shawnee communities to the social landscape of their new homelands. At the same time, the new ties of kinship and obligation connected individual Shawnee bands and families more closely to their Lenape, Conestoga, and Creek neighbors than to other Shawnees and would for decades shape their politics far more than the opinions and actions of other Shawnees.[39]

Alliances had a strong spiritual dimension. For Shawnees, the world was full of powerful other-than-human-beings, known as *manetowi*. Young boys and girls eagerly sought personal allies from among these beings. During puberty they undertook a vision quest to find their own guardian spirit, known as a *hopawaaka*, who would bestow them with a special form of sacred power, also called hopawaaka. This power enabled a human to perform miraculous deeds in some special area of life. The survival and success of an individual depended on the support of a guardian spirit, whose power he or she could mobilize for personal benefit. It was exactly this kind of alliance that Shawnees looked for when they allied with more powerful Indian and colonial communities. In negotiations with English and Haudenosaunee leaders the Shawnee diplomats regularly approached them like a youth seeking a hopawaaka would approach the manetowi: by offering tobacco and asking for pity and assistance. Colonists interpreted such rituals as signs of political submission. In fact, however, the Shawnees sought hopawaaka-like protectors whose power they could tap for communal benefit.[40]

When Shawnees scattered throughout eastern North America and allied and settled with Susquehannocks, Lenapes, Conoys, Munsees, Tallapoosas, and Alabamas, they defied many modern assumptions about ethnicity, identity, and community. To modern scholars, bred in an era of territorially intact nation-states, one of the most puzzling questions concerning the Shawnee diaspora has long been how the Shawnees managed to remain *Shawnees* through decades of dispersal, especially when most of their Ohioan neighbors assimilated into larger coalescent societies. This question is partially based on anachronistic notions of community and identity. Like most Indigenous confederacies that were forged just before and after the European contact, the early Shawnee confederacy was not a unified political or ethnic entity but a loose alliance network of towns and kin groups, designed to cultivate goodwill and cooperation among its members. It was only one of the many overlapping networks of alliance, exchange, and kinship that clans and local communities had been building with both neighbors and distant exchange partners for hundreds of years. When they faced the turmoil of the late seventeenth century, Shawnee kin groups and towns were able to rely selectively and flexibly on many of these older networks for allies and assistance. Often, it made more sense for a clan or a town to seek an asylum among its old exchange partners and relatives among the Tallapoosas or Susquehannocks than to try to fight off the Haudenosaunees with other Shawnees. Rather than signaling a dramatic unraveling of a cohesive Shawnee people, the Shawnee dispersal thus demonstrates the persistent importance of old clan, town, and divisional identities, interaction networks, and strategies.[41] When the confederacy fragmented under tremendous pressure, these older structures remained.

Shawnee divisions and towns exhibited particular endurance through the diaspora. Many of the major migrations seem to have been town-based. Divisional town names, such as Pequa (Pekowi) and Chillisquaque (Chalaakaatha) on the Susquehanna, testify to the enduring importance of the divisions. Clearly, one's division and its sacred bundle, as well as one's town and its spiritual and political center, the council house, constituted two fundamental foci for individual identities and political loyalties that persisted despite violence and migration. A town and its mšikamekwi were not place-bound but could always be rebuilt wherever the community moved. Similarly, the divisional sacred bundle moved with the people; in 1832 a U.S. Indian agent described how a Mekoche community moving from Ohio to Kansas was led by "their 'high priest' in front, bearing on his shoulders 'the ark of covenant,' which consisted of a large gourd and the bones of a deer's leg tied to its neck." As movable sources of spiritual power and identity, the council house and sacred bundle provided Shawnees with a sense of stability in a world in turmoil.[42]

But given the importance of town and divisional identities, why and how did the collective Shawnee identity persist among the diasporic groups scattered from the Illinois River to the Savannah? Such persistence is most powerfully demonstrated by the fact that both Shawnee towns and families regularly migrated to regions where other Shawnees had already settled, often across remarkable distances. In the 1690s, for instance, one group of Pekowis traveled from Fort St. Louis to their kinspeople living on the Savannah River. A few years later the Pekowis moved north and settled on the lower Susquehanna. In 1707 they got a chance to repay the generosity they had experienced on the Savannah when a large group of Savannah Shawnees escaped a combined attack by Catawbas and Carolinians to the Susquehanna. Individuals as well as communities traveled. When one Susquehanna Pekowi man was suspected of killing a colonist from Maryland, he left his home and fled "to Messasippi." In

1743 an Englishwoman, captured and adopted by Shawnees "in their Carolina Warr's," was living on Great Island on the Susquehanna's West Branch.[43]

It is unlikely that such extensive travels would have been undertaken if people had not had a relatively detailed idea where they would find relatives and friends. This hints that even when Shawnees dispersed across the East, they remained in contact with one another and people from widely scattered communities continued to visit each other for social, ritual, and political purposes. Diasporic Shawnee families and individuals often traversed long distances from one community to another, following the lines of kinship that radiated from each town outward toward relatives near and far. In a very intimate way, this constant movement of kinspeople kept alive the most fundamental bond among the dispersed Shawnee communities: kinship.[44]

Clans formed the most important web of kinship that the Shawnees utilized to travel between communities and localities. M'shoma membership tied widespread people together, and even a stranger could expect hospitality from clan relatives upon entering an unknown community. Some evidence suggests that new kinds of interclan ties may have emerged during the Shawnee diaspora. In 1824 the Kishpoko prophet Tenskwatawa claimed that the Shawnees had "anciently" had no fewer than thirty-four clans. Compared with such neighboring peoples as the Haudenosaunees and Cherokees, who had from three to seven clans, this is an astonishingly high figure, especially considering that both the Cherokees and Haudenosaunees were far more populous than the Shawnees. The Shawnee clans must have been very small compared with those of the Haudenosaunees and Cherokees, with an average size of at best a little more than one hundred members. One possible explanation for this unusually high number of unusually small clans is that in the turmoil of the seventeenth-century migrations Shawnee clans divided repeatedly, as smaller groups separated from the main body in order to seek their fortunes in new lands. In such cases a particularly close relationship would have continued to link the main clan and its splinter group, thus building a bridge of kinship between people separated by wide geographical distances.[45]

When the Shawnees scattered from their Ohio homelands throughout the East, they thus learned to conceptualize the vast lands surrounding and separating them not as an insurmountable wilderness, but as a "kinscape." This was a landscape in which widespread groups of Shawnee relatives constituted anchorlike nodes, connected by networks of paths and rivers. Through decades, individual towns, clans, and families navigated this network in search of security, trading partners, and assistance. This network, and the safety it provided, fostered a sense of common identity among the scattered communities. One powerful symbol of such an identity became deeply ingrained even in the meager colonial documents. Throughout their diaspora the scattered Shawnee groups consistently introduced themselves to Native and colonial outsiders as "Shawnees," rather than as Pekowis, Chalaakaathas, Mekoches, Kishpokos, or Thawikilas.[46] Portraying one's community to strangers as a part of a larger whole was undoubtedly a sensible security strategy for groups wandering in often unknown lands and among unknown peoples, but it also demonstrates that the Shawnees continued to envision themselves as a distinct people, no matter how dispersed and mixed with outsiders. Their sense of peoplehood was not tied to collective homelands or to a shared political leadership. Instead, it hinged on kinship and memories of common origins.

STRUGGLING FOR POWER IN THE SHATTER ZONE

In the dangerous shatter zone, alliances with stronger Native and colonial neighbors formed an important source of power and security for the diasporic Shawnee communities. But alliances could also turn dangerous. Many of the powerful peoples the Shawnees tried to enlist as hopawaaka-like protectors had grand ambitions for regional political and economic dominance. While willing to ally with Shawnees and other smaller Native groups to realize such plans, they conceptualized alliances in far more hierarchical terms than Shawnees and constantly sought to impose their will on their allies in order to promote their ascendancy. Through the first quarter of the eighteenth century the Shawnee communities had to protect their autonomy constantly against such overbearing allies and defend their notions of more egalitarian alliances. Often, these conflicts sparked intracommunity strife in Shawnee towns, when the locals debated how to best cope with the threatening outsiders.

The Shawnees who settled in the mid-Atlantic region along the Susquehanna, Delaware, and Potomac rivers between 1690 and 1710 found themselves particularly dependent on, and vulnerable to, powerful neighbors. The mid-Atlantic was a volatile region where many peoples, frontiers, and interests met, mixed, and occasionally clashed. The country between the Delaware and Potomac was a home to Conestogas, Lenapes, Munsees, and other Indian peoples shaken by epidemics and warfare. Numerous Native refugees from the south and west also crowded to the region to escape wars, land loss, and disease in their homelands. Three English colonies, Pennsylvania, New York, and Maryland, were likewise rapidly growing and claiming land in the area. Competition over land, resources, and trade was rampant among these diverse locals and newcomers. Every community needed allies to defend its position in this rivalry.[47]

Allies were vital to the small Shawnee bands that began settling the mid-Atlantic river valleys in the 1690s. Eager to find a safe place in a world of turmoil, the Shawnees quickly forged diplomatic and trading ties with the three English provinces. The Shawnees consistently sought to characterize these alliances as egalitarian kinship relations. A 1701 treaty between the Pekowi settlers on the lower Susquehanna and Pennsylvania, for example, stated that the colonists should become "true ffriends & Brothers" of the Indians and "at all times readily do Justice, & perform all Acts & Offices of friendship & Good will" to them. The English, however, viewed alliances with the Natives from a more hierarchical viewpoint based on a belief of European cultural superiority and a long legacy of feudalism. In exchange for protection, trade, and permission to settle on lands claimed by the English, the colonists expected Shawnee obedience. They recognized the Indians as independent communities living under their own governments but insisted that the colony, and ultimately the Crown, held a final sovereignty over the Natives. As Pennsylvanian officials often put it, the Shawnee and other Indian allies of a colony "belong[ed]" to the province.[48]

In the early eighteenth century the Iroquois Confederacy, too, grew interested in the mid-Atlantic region. In 1701, after half a century of aggressive expansion around the Great Lakes, military defeats and population decline forced the Haudenosaunees to make peace with New France and its Algonquian allies. To restore their fledging power in the Northeast many Iroquois turned their attention southward and began forging new political and economic ties with the Europeans and Indians settling in what is now Pennsylvania. While they sought new diplomatic and trading partners from the colonists, they hoped to transform the region's diverse Native communities into "props" that could be mobilized to support the Five Nations in diplomacy and warfare. The Haudenosaunees employed various strategies to exert control over the Shawnees, Lenapes, Conestogas, and other Indian communities in the mid-Atlantic. They laid claims on the Susquehanna Valley where many Shawnees lived and sought colonial recognition for these claims. They sent delegates to councils between Shawnees and Pennsylvanians to monitor the land transactions, trade pacts, and other issues discussed in the meetings. The Haudenosaunees even tried to force the Shawnees to remove to the Iroquois country where they could be more easily controlled. During the first decade of the eighteenth century the Shawnees relied on English support to counteract Iroquois efforts of domination. Pennsylvanians in particular saw the Shawnees as important trading partners and potential allies against the French and were willing to lend diplomatic muscle to protect them from overbearing Haudenosaunee interference. This, however, made the Shawnee communities increasingly dependent on the English.[49]

How Shawnees responded to such external threats had important repercussions for power and politics in their own communities. Since Late Fort Ancient times Shawnee leadership had been decentralized, collective, and clan-based. The town councils had long formed a forum where the hokimas, war leaders, and Peace and War Women of the various m'shomas met to discuss communal affairs and make consensual, collective decisions. In the early eighteenth century town councils sometimes appointed one of the local clan leaders as the ceremonial hokima or "peace chief" of the entire community. His duty was to cultivate peace between his town and surrounding peoples by negotiating, mediating conflicts, and promoting goodwill. In 1720 one leader of the Susquehanna Shawnees explained that his town had for years had "no Chief, therefore some of them applied to him to take that Charge upon him." This implies that some representatives of the community, probably the council, ceremonially asked a particularly respected person to become the town "Chief." When selecting a town hokima, the council most likely chose a person who was a persuasive speaker, was skilled in creating consensus, and had wide kin and marital ties to the various clans and leaders of the community. Town hokimas had little personal authority. They wielded no coercive power but had to construct consensus and defuse conflicts "only by fair words." Indeed, rather than powerful decision-makers, they served as speakers for the town council where decisions continued to be made collectively.[50]

A man named Opessa played such a role in Pequa, a town established by the Pekowis on the lower Susquehanna River in the 1690s. From 1700 to 1711 Opessa represented Pequa in almost every diplomatic encounter with the English, Haudenosaunees, and other neighboring peoples. At such meetings Opessa "spoke in behalf of the youth of his Town," usually praising the blessings of peace, and exchanged ceremonial gifts with the leaders of other communities to seal alliances and cultivate good relations. His role as a ceremonial speaker is underlined by the fact that in colonial treaty minutes he almost always appears in the company of many other leaders, sometimes styled "his great Men." Opessa also fostered social harmony inside Pequa. One fall, for instance, Opessa "and his young people (who were then going a hunting), were in Council" in "his Cabin." This suggests that Opessa was advising younger people of proper behavior and communal hunting plans before families dispersed "to the Woods" for the winter hunting season. It is revealing that even here Opessa seems to have been most concerned about how his townspeople behaved outside their community, in "the Woods" where they were likely to meet neighboring Haudenosaunee, Lenape, Conestoga, and English hunters.[51]

English colonists, coming from a highly hierarchical state society, often seriously misunderstood Shawnee leadership. Although they realized that no Shawnee leader possessed anything like royal authority, they dubbed the Native headmen "kings" and assumed that they wielded centralized, communitywide power in their towns. In the early eighteenth century Pennsylvanians repeatedly demanded that Shawnee leaders live up to such expectations and rule their communities according to colonial orders. This ignited heated disputes in Shawnee towns, as people argued about the boundaries of legitimate authority, often under intense pressure from the colonists.

These debates surfaced dramatically in Pequa in 1711. When some "young people" from the town killed an indentured servant of a Maryland fur trader, Governor Charles Gookin of Pennsylvania demanded satisfaction from Opessa. Eager to impress the Pequa Shawnees with colonial power, Gookin declared "that the Laws of England are such, that whosoever Kill'd a man must run the same fate." Either he was trying to pressure Opessa to deliver the killers to Pennsylvanian justice or expected that the Shawnees themselves would execute them. Opessa evaded such demands by claiming that the culprits had died, except one who had moved away. This was an absolutely necessary move. Among the Shawnees, influential local hokimas could mediate intracommunity killings between the m'shomas of the victim and the perpetrator. In the end it was nevertheless up to the victim's clan relatives to decide whether they would accept a ritual gift of condolence that would atone the crime or extract revenge on the killer or his or her clan members. As a town hokima Opessa had no authority to require the arrest, let alone execution, of men belonging to clans other than his own. Fortunately, Gookin wanted to avoid trouble with his Indian neighbors and accepted Opessa's explanations. He promised to forgive the killing but threatened that next time he would "Do Justice" just like he had now "shewed you mercy." Shocked by the threat, Opessa replied that if any of his townspeople killed colonists in the future, "he himself would be the Executioner, & Burn them that should dare to Do it."[52]

That was an astonishing promise. That a clan leader, even one appointed as a town hokima, would use violence to impose his will on his townspeople was unheard of. Even more disturbingly, Opessa had made his promise without consulting other leaders. Such behavior was not tolerated in Pequa. Some years later another Shawnee leader explained to Pennsylvanian officials that "their King who was then living, Opessah, took the Government upon him, but the people differed with him; he left them." This suggests that the other leaders and clans in Pequa had withdrawn their support from Opessa and forced him out of the town. His downfall demonstrates dramatically the eagerness and power of Shawnee clans to guard decentralized community leadership. After Opessa's forced removal, no single leader acted as Pequa's town hokima. One historian has interpreted this as evidence that the town reverted to "anarchy." More likely, the local clans deliberately rotated several individuals from different kin groups as the community's spokesperson in order to hinder the rise of too powerful leaders threatening to "Burn" their townspeople.[53]

But the crisis was not over. Next the Haudenosaunees stepped in to exploit the delicate situation. In 1714 a delegation of Iroquois visited Philadelphia, where they informed Pennsylvanian authorities that since Opessa had moved away, they had appointed an Oneida named Cakundawanna "as the new Elected King of the Shawanois." It looks like the Five Nations wanted to

persuade the Pennsylvanians to recognize one of their own leaders as an over-
seer of the Shawnee communities on the Susquehanna River. The people of
Pequa were not as easy to control as the Haudenosaunees had hoped, however.
Even though Pennsylvanian leadership officially recognized Cakundawanna as
the new Shawnee "king," the Shawnees simply ignored him. Ultimately, even
colonial officials preferred to deal with actual Shawnee leaders, and
Cakundawanna never reappears in the English documents as a representative,
let alone a ruler, of the Shawnees. Opessa's downfall demonstrates well the
constant pressure the Shawnee communities in the mid-Atlantic region felt
from both the English and the Iroquois; yet it also shows that in the 1710s the
Shawnees were still able to defend their autonomy and maintain relatively egalitarian alliances with the colonists and the Haudenosaunees, even if this was
becoming increasingly difficult.[54]

During the late 1710s, however, the alliances the mid-Atlantic Shawnee
communities had constructed with the neighboring English colonies and the
Haudenosaunees turned from a successful safety network into a threat that
eroded Shawnee autonomy. This shift was connected to a major geopolitical
reorganization of the entire region. Before, the English colonists had been
somewhat wary of the distant Iroquois Confederacy and had shielded their
Shawnee and other nearby Indian allies from Haudenosaunee domination.
Gradually, however, the diplomatic and trade relations between Pennsylvania
and the Five Nations grew closer, and many Pennsylvanian leaders came to see
the Haudenosaunees as more important allies than the Shawnees, Conestogas,
Lenapes, and other smaller groups of Native peoples living across the mid-
Atlantic region. Many colonial officials calculated that the Haudenosaunees
might help them to control the other Indians more effectively. The collusion of
the British and the Iroquois left the Shawnees and their neighbors in a vulnerable position.[55]

In the late 1710s mounting pressure from the English and the Haudenosaunees
created a new crisis in the Susquehanna Shawnee towns, threatening their
autonomy and internal stability. At the heart of the crisis was the warfare that
the Iroquois had waged against the Catawbas, Tutelos, Cherokees, and other
"Southern Indians" living south of the Potomac River since the 1670s.[56] When
Shawnees began settling along the Susquehanna, many of their young men
eagerly joined the Haudenosaunee raids to the south. Many did so for personal
motives; as one Pennsylvanian colonist observed, "Young men love to go sometimes to War to shew their manhood." But Shawnees also had more communal
reasons to harass the Southerners. The Savannah River Shawnees had fought
the Catawbas for decades, and both groups had raided the other for slaves. In
the early 1700s Catawba attacks had forced many Shawnees to flee from the
Savannah to the Susquehanna, and growing numbers of Shawnees there felt it

their duty to revenge their slain kinspeople. Moreover, many Susquehanna Shawnees hunted and fished on the Potomac River, which sparked conflicts over local resources with the Indians living south of the river.[57]

British colonists resented the warfare between the Northern and Southern Indians. Because all Natives involved in the fighting were allies of one British colony or another, many English feared that their warfare would fatally weaken the buffer of Indian allies that the colonies needed against potential French incursions from New France and Louisiana. In 1717 the governor of Pennsylvania, William Keith, launched an aggressive campaign to stop the Indian allies of his province from joining the Haudenosaunee raids to the south. For the next five years he tried alternatively to cajole and coerce the Shawnees, Conestogas, and Lenapes to make peace with the Southern Indians. Portraying the English as the feudal lords of their Indian vassals, Keith explained that each colony "had Nations of Indians under their protection" who "Belonged" to the colony and were subject to the same "Great King & Emperour" as the British. An attack against any such Indian community offended its colonial ally and, ultimately, the king. From this hierarchical position of power, Keith simply ordered Pennsylvania's Indian allies to stop fighting the Southerners and promised that in case of further troubles "this Governmt., on your Complaint, will Endeavour to procure Satisfaction from the English Governmt. to which such Indians belong." In other words, he told Shawnees and their neighbors to leave a major part of their sovereignty to British hands.[58]

Shawnees and their Indian neighbors showed little enthusiasm to follow Keith's bombastic orders. They had sound reasons for fighting the Southerners and could not understand what business the British had to interfere in the matter. When the warfare continued unabated, the infuriated Keith threatened his recalcitrant allies with trade embargos and colonial displeasure. In particular, he admonished Indian diplomats, whom he identified as "kings" or "chiefs," to end the fighting without realizing that these men were clan leaders with very limited power in their towns. Shawnee headmen's responses to Keith's threats are instructive. They blamed the persistent warfare on their "Young men who lived under no Government." But rather than enforcing "Government" upon these youngsters, as Keith demanded, the leaders patiently explained that such a course was impossible and undesirable in their noncoercive and decentralized political system. As one hokima put it in 1720, "he counselled [the young men], but they would not obey; therefore he cannot answer for them."[59]

Historians have often followed the language of the Shawnee leaders and argued that a generational conflict between young warriors and old chiefs rocked their communities in the early eighteenth century. It seems more likely, however, that the leaders blamed the constant raiding on the youngsters to keep powerful Pennsylvanians ignorant of the fact that the warfare actually enjoyed much wider support in their towns. Peace Women in particular possessed considerable authority to stop war parties "not countenanced by the nation." They could admonish war leaders to give up military expeditions that the women of the community considered unsound. War Women, in turn, played a key role in encouraging the men of their clan to revenge the death of their kinspeople killed in warfare.[60] The persistence of the fighting suggests that these powerful women, as well as the warriors and neenawtoomas of many clans and communities, endorsed the raids against the Southerners. No single clan or town hokima, no matter how committed to peace personally, had the authority to override such a powerful coalition. Most importantly, no one even tried. Even under constant British pressure the Shawnee hokimas employed only traditional "fair words" to influence their communities and flatly rejected the role of coercive ruler that Keith tried to thrust upon them. Perhaps they had learned from Opessa.

Frustrated, the British finally decided to end the Southern wars with the help of the very people who were the most active participants in the fighting, the Five Nations. In 1722 Keith and the governors of New York and Virginia invited Haudenosaunee leaders to a treaty at Albany and made them a lucrative offer. The governors suggested that a permanent boundary should be drawn to separate the inveterate Northern and Southern Indians from one another. They promised that the Southerners would not venture north of the Potomac River and west of the Appalachian Mountains. In exchange, the governors requested that Haudenosaunee warriors would no longer enter the area south of the Potomac and east of the Appalachians. Significantly, the colonists also asked the Iroquois to make a similar promise on behalf of "the Indians belonging to and depending on the 5 Nations." The Haudenosaunee leaders recognized this as a chance to assert Iroquois authority over Shawnees and their neighbors. They calculated that if they accepted the responsibility for the actions of these peoples, the British would help them to control these communities. Accordingly, the Five Nations headmen promised that neither their own warriors nor those from the Shawnee, Conestoga, and several small Iroquoian communities on the Susquehanna River would violate the Potomac-Appalachian border.[61]

The Albany Treaty of 1722 represented an unprecedented British and Iroquois attack against the autonomy of the Shawnee communities on the Susquehanna, Potomac, and Delaware rivers. After the colonists and Haudenosaunees had imposed both a peace and a boundary on the Shawnees, Governor Keith simply sent messengers to inform them and their neighbors of the matter. He also told the Shawnees that any Indian violating the new boundary without a passport from his or her colonial ally would suffer the penalty of death or slavery. Alarmed, the Shawnee, Conestoga, Lenape, and Conoy leaders replied cautiously that although the Potomac boundary would interfere with their hunting, they would abide by the treaty. Sweet words aside, they were afraid of angering the powerful coalition of the three English colonies and the Five Nations. The situation must have felt particularly threatening to the Shawnees. During the previous fifty years they had learned to rely on widespread mobility and contacts to survive and flourish in the dangerous shatter zone. Now the English and Haudenosaunees threatened to curtail that mobility and cut their contacts with their far-flung allies, relatives, and tribespeople.[62]

The diaspora of the late seventeenth and early eighteenth centuries left deep legacies in Shawnee communities. When warfare, epidemics, and economic turmoil dispersed Shawnees across eastern North America, they sought security by allying with a wide variety of Indian and European peoples. Yet, as the Albany Treaty demonstrates, these alliances could sometimes turn dangerous and make Shawnee communities vulnerable to domination by stronger allies. In the 1720s Shawnees drew differing conclusions from these experiences. Many communities from the Susquehanna, Delaware, and Potomac valleys began a new migration toward their ancestral homelands on the Ohio River. There they would construct new forms of intercommunity cooperation and seek unity to defend themselves against overbearing outsiders. Other Shawnees, in turn, continued to rely on mobility and multiethnic alliance networks, navigating the troubled times among their Creek, Lenape, and Iroquois kinspeople and friends. From the violence of the shatter zone emerged two divergent security strategies and understandings of community.

"THE SHEYNARS IN GENERAL"

Unity and Diversity on Imperial Borderlands, 1725–1755

In March 1738 more than one hundred Shawnees from three neighboring towns located on the Allegheny River some twenty miles upriver from modern Pittsburgh met in a large council at one of their settlements. After long and deliberate discussions, three headmen, ceremonial orator Nucheconner, hokima Laypareawah, and "Chief Councellor" Coyacolinne, dictated a letter to Pennsylvanian provincial authorities to explain the results of the meeting. "The Sheynars in general," reported the headmen, had agreed to "Gether two Gather and make a strong Towne."[1]

Following the lives of Nucheconner, Laypareawah, Coyacolinne, and their allies allows us to explore how the Shawnees reconceptualized and rebuilt their diasporic nation in the second quarter of the eighteenth century. From the mid-1720s on, hundreds of Shawnees fled colonial encroachment and loss of autonomy in the mid-Atlantic region to the Ohio Valley. There they began to gather together in new ways, physically, socially, and politically. This was a response to the dangerous geopolitics of the region. The Ohio Valley was a volatile borderland between the French and British colonies. To turn this borderland into a homeland, the Shawnees strengthened intercommunity cooperation and devised new diplomatic strategies that enabled them to ally with both the British and the French, yet curtailed the influence of both empires on the Ohio. In the South, several hundred Shawnees likewise gathered on the Tallapoosa and Alabama rivers. They too sought trade and alliance from the French and the British alike, while also seeking to keep both at arm's length. As the Shawnees balanced between the rival European powers, they had to reconcile long-standing local autonomy with political collaboration. They mixed nascent unity with traditional diversity by sharing power and constructing institutions of collective decision-making. In the 1750s Shawnee unity threatened to erode, however, as eastern North America transformed into an Anglo-French battleground and Native communities had to choose their course between the two hostile empires.[2]

RECLAIMING THE OHIO HOMELANDS

In May 1723 leaders of the Pekowi Shawnees, Conestogas, Lenapes, and Conoys (Ganawese) from several neighboring towns dotting the banks of the lower Susquehanna River gathered together to send a message to the government of Pennsylvania. Among the headmen may have been both Nucheconner and Laypareawah, whose roots can be traced to the Susquehanna Shawnee communities. Concerned about the escalating immigration of German and Scotch-Irish settlers in the Susquehanna Valley, the Native leaders pleaded that "the English may not be suffered to straiten or pinch the Ganawese or Shawannaoes to make them remove further off, but to consider them as Brethren." They also added "by way of Complaint" something that the colonial authorities were not willing to enter into the public records documenting the provincial Indian affairs. Quite likely it was a further remonstrance against colonial encroachment on Shawnee and Conoy lands.[3]

The Indian leaders' message captures well the spiraling political and economic problems the Shawnees and their neighbors living on the Susquehanna, Delaware, and Potomac rivers faced in the 1720s. When the Shawnees had settled in the region thirty years earlier, the local English colonists had offered them trade and protection. By the 1720s, however, the rapidly growing colonies found landed expansion far more interesting than Indian allies. Pennsylvania in particular had grown explosively. Between 1690 and 1730 its population jumped from eighty-eight hundred to forty-nine thousand. Most of the settlers became engaged in commercial agriculture and were eager to expand their landholdings. Increasingly involved in profitable land speculation, Pennsylvanian authorities pressured Lenapes, Conestogas, and other local Indians to sell more and more land. Many new settlers simply squatted unceremoniously on Native lands. Shawnees were particularly vulnerable to dispossession. Provincial leadership insisted that Shawnees were mere visitors in the region and lived on Haudenosaunee, Conestoga, and Lenape lands on the sufferance of their hosts. Their claims to the soil were "without any manner of Foundation." Nucheconner's and Laypareawah's community, the lower Susquehanna Pekowis, was particularly hard-hit by colonial expansion. From the 1710s through the 1730s they were forced to move their towns upriver several times, as Palatine and Scotch-Irish settlers flooded the Susquehanna Valley. Other Shawnee communities faced similar encroachments. On the Delaware River, for example, the local Mekoches retreated from their town at Pechoquealin north to the Wyoming Valley, located on the North Branch of the Susquehanna.[4]

Dispossession meant much more than simple relocation. Often, it went hand in hand with hunger. Repeated migrations forced Shawnees to clear new fields year after year, which inevitably disturbed agriculture. Even when fields stayed put, the colonial presence endangered Shawnee crops. The colonists usually let their cattle and hogs graze freely and find their own food, and all too often the animals found it in the unfenced fields of neighboring Indian settlements. In 1718 the Conestogas, Shawnees, and Conoys of the lower Susquehanna asked the Pennsylvanian government to run lines around their land "that they might not be Disturbed by the Cattle of any persons settling near them." Throughout the 1720s poor harvests led to recurrent famines among the Susquehanna Indians. Hunting and trade suffered too, when the Albany Treaty shut the Shawnees and their neighbors out of important winter hunting grounds south of the Potomac.[5]

Land loss and hunger were exacerbated by the loss of autonomy. After the Albany Treaty the Pennsylvanian government viewed the Shawnees more as vassals than as allies. Colonial authorities increasingly relied on their new Iroquois partners to control the smaller Native groups on the Susquehanna and Delaware rivers. The Six Nations, as the Haudenosaunees were known after the Tuscaroras joined their confederacy, willingly colluded with the English to expand their authority over their Indian neighbors. In 1728 they sent an Oneida diplomat named Shickellamy to the Susquehanna "to preside over the Shawanese" and advised the Pennsylvanians to negotiate all matters pertaining to the Shawnees with this man. Most disturbingly, the Haudenosaunees helped the colony to appropriate even more land from the Shawnees, Lenapes, Conestogas, and their neighbors. The Pennsylvanian government recognized dubious Iroquois claims to the Susquehanna Valley and then bought these lands directly from Haudenosaunee leaders. Local Indians were left to watch helplessly as their homes were sold away by distant headmen claiming to be their overlords.[6] With their lands and independence under attack, the Shawnees living across the mid-Atlantic region were quickly becoming landless clients of the British and the Haudenosaunees.

The Shawnees' response to these mounting threats was a familiar one: migration out of harm's way. But instead of scattering across the East, as they had done during the crisis of the late seventeenth century, most Shawnee communities on the Susquehanna, Delaware, and Potomac now began a gradual movement toward their ancestral lands in the Ohio Valley. When the lower Susquehanna Pekowis still tried to persuade Pennsylvanian authorities to respect their land rights in May 1723, Ocowellos, the "King of the upper Shawnees," led a community of Chalaakaathas from the West Brach of the

Susquehanna west to Conemaugh Creek, a tributary of the Allegheny River in what is now western Pennsylvania. Other Shawnees soon followed. During the late 1720s Nucheconner, Laypareawah, and others who had been "pinched" too hard by the British and the Haudenosaunees crossed the Appalachian mountain range through the valleys of the Susquehanna's West Branch, Juniata, Youghiogheny, and Monongahela rivers and settled on the Allegheny and its eastern tributaries. In 1728 French agents reported that more than 150 Shawnee men "with their families" were building towns in the region. Three years later close to one thousand Pekowis from the lower Susquehanna, Chalaakaathas from the upper Susquehanna, and other Shawnee migrants had settled in three communities on Conemaugh Creek. Several hundred Thawikilas from the Potomac lived nearby on the Youghiogheny River, and a headman named Kishacoquillas established a fifth town, Ohesson, a little eastward on the Juniata River. As the 1730s wore on, these and new migrants from the east pushed even farther west, settling along the upper and central Ohio.[7]

Many factors attracted Shawnees to the Allegheny and Ohio valleys. Because the region had been almost entirely depopulated in the late seventeenth century, its game-rich woods and fertile river bottoms lay open for newcomers. But Shawnees hardly viewed themselves as mere newcomers in a vacant land. Although they had been driven from the Ohio fifty years earlier, they still recognized the valley as their ancient homeland or, as one headman evocatively put it, "his Land at the Ohio, where he was born." In fact, for decades Shawnee families living on the Susquehanna had regularly gone "a hunting . . . towards the branches of the Wabash and Ohio, which they commonly do in the fall of the year, and do not return before the month of May following." Hunting, fishing, and gathering for months every autumn and winter in the Ohio Valley, they had kept alive their economic, spiritual, and emotional ties to the land. For most Shawnees, the migration to the west meant a return to home.[8]

It was a homecoming made possible by shifting geopolitics. The Yamasee War (1715–1717) had ended Indian slaving in the South. The Iroquois Confederacy, plagued by internal factionalism and British and French pressure, was no longer able to engage in large-scale military campaigns to control the distant Ohio Valley. The Trans-Appalachian interior also lay beyond the reach of the English colonies on the Atlantic seaboard. By moving west, the Shawnees not only reclaimed their ancestral homelands, but also asserted their independence from their British and Haudenosaunee oppressors. Pennsylvanians and Iroquois tried in vain to stem the Shawnees' migration, for it threatened to rob them of valuable political clients and trading partners. They worried that on the Ohio the Shawnees might forge commercial and military ties to New France, a rival and enemy of the British and the Iroquois alike. To prevent this, Pennsylvania and the Haudenosaunees joined forces in 1732 and ordered the

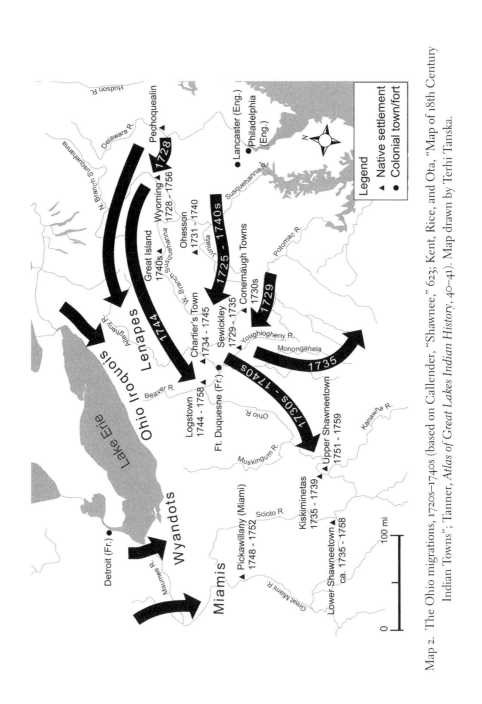

Map 2. The Ohio migrations, 1720s–1740s (based on Callender, "Shawnee," 623; Kent, Rice, and Ota, "Map of 18th Century Indian Towns"; Tanner, *Atlas of Great Lakes Indian History*, 40–41). Map drawn by Terhi Tanska.

western Shawnees to return to the Susquehanna. No Shawnee obeyed. Offended, the Six Nations sent emissaries to further insist on the matter. This time a Seneca headman "pressed" the Youghiogheny Thawikilas "so closely that they took a great Dislike to him," and angered warriors "seized on him & murdered him cruelly." What happened next expresses well how the Ohio migrations had melted Haudenosaunee power over the Shawnees into thin air. The Thawikilas fled Iroquois retaliation south to their relatives living among the Upper Creeks, while the Six Nations could merely complain about the incident to Pennsylvanians. The colonists were equally baffled by the novel Shawnee independence. James Logan, the secretary of the provincial council, now realized "how little it is in our Power to deal with those people."[9]

Migration to the Allegheny-Ohio Valley was also an important economic strategy for the Shawnees from the mid-Atlantic communities. When colonial hogs ate their crops and the Albany Treaty limited their hunting grounds, the Ohio Country offered the Susquehanna, Delaware, and Potomac Shawnees prime farmland and woods teeming with deer. The western migration gave a major boost to the commercial pursuits of the Shawnees, too. Since the 1690s they had traded profitably with Pennsylvanian merchants, exchanging animal furs and skins for guns, textiles, iron knives, copper pots, glass beads, and rum. When Shawnees moved west in the 1720s, their Pennsylvanian trading partners quickly followed them, at first making seasonal visits to the Indian country, then establishing permanent warehouses in Native towns. The trade soon flourished on the Ohio. In 1730 some of the most prominent Pennsylvanian merchants boasted that they had "Gott Larger quantityes of Skins and furrs and Dissposed of more Goods than had been for many years before to ye Greatt advantage of ye Trade." The Shawnees prospered as well. Years later Alexander McKee, a British Indian agent with a mixed Shawnee-Irish parentage, reminisced how in his youth in the 1740s "the [Shawnee] Warriors, the best Hunters, in their grand Dances frequently changed their dresses eight or ten times a night." According to McKee, such festive outfits, consisting of silver ear bobs, nose rings, and arm bands, ruffled shirts, and laced hats, as well as Native finery, were "worth forty or fifty pounds per Man." Clearly, hunting and trading on the Ohio brought rising material well-being to the Shawnee settlers.[10]

Shawnees were not the only ones attracted by the rich floodplains and woodlands along the Allegheny and Ohio. From the 1720s through the 1750s thousands of other Native migrants from east, west, and north made their way to the Ohio Country. Many of them faced political and economic predicaments similar to those experienced by the Shawnees. From eastern Pennsylvania came the Shawnees' long-time Lenape allies who were equally distressed by colonial expansion and Haudenosaunee hegemony. The Miamis, Weas, and Piankashaws expanded from the southern side of Lake Michigan to the Maumee, Wabash, and Little and Great Miami rivers in search of new hunting lands. Wyandots escaped intracommunity strife in Detroit to the Sandusky River in the late 1730s. Small Ottawa and Ojibwe groups from the Great Lakes settled on the south side of Lake Erie. Finally, after 1740 many Haudenosaunees, especially Senecas, began moving from their homes in present-day upstate New York to the Cuyahoga and upper Allegheny rivers. There, these Ohio Iroquois, or "Mingos," formed vibrant communities that gradually distanced themselves politically from the Six Nations Confederacy. As these diverse peoples built their homes in the Ohio Country, the once-uninhabited region quickly turned into a colorful multiethnic population center. By the late 1740s some three thousand to four thousand people lived in the area between the Allegheny and Scioto rivers alone.[11]

When so many peoples, including many former enemies, rushed to the same lands, there was a high risk for a violent explosion. Yet nothing of the sort ever occurred. Instead of fighting for the Ohio lands, the migrants relied on diplomacy and alliances to share them. They negotiated complex arrangements that gave various groups rights to the region. Sometimes these alliances gave one group an exclusive claim to a specific area, but more often they allowed several communities to enjoy overlapping but not necessarily identical rights to the same lands. Such land sharing had long been common among many Native peoples of eastern North America. For them, sharing the land and its resources gave birth to a deeply spiritual tie between individual communities and turned them into allies with reciprocal obligations of mutual aid, protection, and gift-giving. Negotiations over land always involved the creation of ceremonial kinship relations, and soon networks of ritual kinship covered the Ohio Country like a giant spider's web, linking diverse settler communities intimately to one another. This diplomacy constitutes such a stark contrast to the bitter violence of the late seventeenth century that it seems probable that the Shawnees, Haudenosaunees, Miamis, Lenapes, Wyandots, and others moving to the Ohio Valley deliberately tried to avoid creating a new shatter zone there. Migrating in small family and town groups, they hoped that negotiations, alliances, and kinship could save them from the violence of the previous generation and guarantee them safer homes on the Ohio.[12]

Shawnees, too, mobilized diplomacy to assert their ancestral claims to the Ohio Valley. Most importantly, they negotiated a series of alliances and land agreements with the powerful Wyandots, Miamis, and Weas who were expanding to the region from the north and west. In 1732 these western nations adopted the Shawnees as their "brothers" and recognized their right to the lands south and east of the Ohio and Allegheny. Although the Wyandots worried that further Shawnee expansion north of the Ohio "would hurt their hunting ground," only a year later the Miamis invited their new Shawnee brothers to share this land with them. Over the next several years Shawnees continued to negotiate with the Wyandots, too, until they likewise accepted the Shawnee presence on the northern and western side of the Allegheny-Ohio. By the late 1730s two large Shawnee towns had accordingly appeared on the northern bank of the Ohio River.[13] These negotiations with the western Indians reveal a well-planned Shawnee strategy for reclaiming their old homelands.

Shawnees also built close ties to many other Native peoples moving to the Allegheny and Ohio. They cemented especially their old connections with the Lenapes. Shawnees and Lenapes from the Susquehanna often moved west together and established common or closely neighboring towns on the Allegheny and Ohio. Kinship and friendship bound Shawnee and Lenape families and communities together. The Shawnee military leader Lawachkamicky (Pride), for example, was "a Relation to" the Lenape headman Hopocan (Pipe). The prestigious Lenape war chief Shingas, in turn, occasionally stayed at Nucheconner's town on the Allegheny. Haudenosaunee migrants too settled in the Allegheny Shawnee communities, and Miami and Ojibwe hunters and warriors visited these towns regularly.[14] In very fundamental ways, people with differing ethnic, political, and linguistic backgrounds came together in the Ohio Country, sharing space, work, fun, rituals, and beds. There was nothing new in such multiethnic interaction and mingling. Shawnees had always lived in a world where kinship, marriages, and exchange bound diverse peoples together. The alliances attached the Shawnee settlers to the social landscape of the Ohio Country and provided them with new kinspeople on whose assistance they could rely in future crises.

Allies were crucial for the Shawnees, for they also faced enemies in the new western lands. When settling on the Ohio, the Shawnees intensified their hunting on the south side of the river, especially in the region we now call Kentucky. There they ran into the hunting bands of their old Southern enemies, the Catawbas and Cherokees. In the 1730s old animosities flared into renewed warfare over the Kentucky hunting grounds. The conflict was further aggravated by Iroquois aggression. Haudenosaunee warriors regularly traveled through the Shawnee and Lenape towns on the Allegheny on their way to raid the Southerners. Often, angry Catawba warriors pursued the attackers to the Allegheny where they struck the local communities rather than following the Haudenosaunees farther north. Allies were essential for Shawnees in repulsing such attacks and staking their claims in Kentucky. In 1736, for example, one town on the Allegheny was able to defeat a large Catawba war party with the help of warriors from a neighboring Lenape community.[15]

The Ohio migration remade the geopolitical landscape of the Shawnees. When the Shawnee settlers began building their homes along the Allegheny-Ohio waterway, they placed themselves directly between two formidable colonial systems, New France in the north and west and the British colonies in the east. The western migration of the Shawnees drew the attention of both French and British officials to the Ohio Valley and wakened them to the immense strategic importance of the region. The colonists realized that control of the Ohio-Mississippi river system offered the key to the mastery of the entire interior of North America. Dreams of dominance aside, in the 1720s and 1730s neither Great Britain nor France was able to assert direct military or political control in the Ohio Country that lay far from metropolitan centers and was populated by thousands of Indians. Instead, both empires sought to extend their influence to the region by attempting to draw the local Natives into their political and commercial orbit through alliances. The British and the French were especially interested in the Shawnees whose towns on the Allegheny and upper Ohio controlled access to the Ohio River from the east and the north.[16]

Shawnees were equally interested in the colonial empires. They knew well that Europeans were valuable trading partners and powerful military allies. But from bitter experience they were also painfully aware of the threats the colonists could pose to Native land rights and autonomy. In the Ohio Country the Shawnees devised a new diplomatic strategy designed to bring them the benefits of European alliances, while neutralizing the colonial threats. Like many Indian peoples on imperial borderlands throughout North America, the Ohio Shawnees learned that living between two rival colonial powers could be turned into a source of strength and independence. Surrounded and courted by two European empires, the Shawnees "in between" sought to ally with both. Their goal was to draw trade, gifts, and protection from the British and the French alike in exchange for their friendship. Relying on two antagonistic empires, the Shawnees hoped, would protect them from becoming commercially or politically dependent on, or dominated by, either one.[17]

During their migrations over the previous half century the Shawnees had seen many Indian peoples, especially the Haudenosaunees and Creeks, play rival colonies against one another in such a fashion. These examples probably inspired Shawnee leaders to try a similar strategy in the Ohio Valley. The Shawnees' new diplomatic strategy also sprang from their realization that the English colonies and New France offered different benefits and posed different problems. While the British were commercially powerful and carried useful and relatively cheap trade goods to Shawnee towns, French traders were less interested in buying the deer hides the Shawnees had to offer, for their customers in France preferred more exotic northern furs. On the other hand, the Shawnees had seen the rapid growth and expansion of British colonies up close. In contrast, New France did not seem to covet land as much as political and military alliances with the Ohio Indians. Identifying such differences between the

Europeans, the Ohio Shawnee leaders forged different kinds of alliances with the British and the French.[18]

Shawnee leaders began to visit Montreal in 1723, when the Chalaakaatha headman Ocowellos traveled there from the West Branch of the Susquehanna River. In Montreal he ritually adopted the governor of New France as his "Father." Such an intimate kin connection was vital, because it bound the French to Shawnee webs of kinship and brought very specific obligations to the colonists. In the Shawnee scheme of things, a father was not a stern patriarchal authority, but a kind and lenient protector of and provider for his children. Accordingly, Ocowellos and other Shawnee leaders who traveled to Montreal during the following two decades ceremonially begged their French Father to give them gifts, send gunsmiths to their towns, and defend them against the hostile Catawbas and the domineering Haudenosaunees. They also complained to the governor that "they were unhappy alongside the English" and assured him that "we all have no other will than yours." Yet these same Shawnee leaders continued to visit Philadelphia and correspond with the Pennsylvanian government. They promised that they "had no Intention to leave their Brethren the English, or turn their Backs upon them" and welcomed Pennsylvanian traders to their towns, against the express orders of their Father. Herein lies the core of the new diplomatic strategy of the Ohio Shawnees. They sought to mold the French into a protective Father and the British into a trading Brother. Such complementary alliances would nicely balance one another, fulfill different Shawnee needs, and play the colonists against one another.[19]

Historians have called this Native strategy "neutrality"; however, they often deny that neutralist Native strategies between rival European empires resulted from deliberate Indian plans. Rather, many scholars argue, in politically decentralized Indian societies individual leaders and factions pursued alliances with different colonial powers according to their sectional interests. Since the consensual political system gave no group the ability to coerce others to adopt its diplomatic agendas, Native communities divided into rival "Francophile" and "Anglophile" factions. Indian factionalism, in effect, unintentionally produced neutrality, for it guaranteed that in each nation, even in each town, some people always supported an alliance with Britain while others favored a friendship with France. This interpretation undoubtedly fits the situation in many Indian communities, but it underestimates Native agency and foresight. Among the Allegheny and Ohio Shawnees the evidence strongly suggests that Indian leaders cultivated complementary alliances with Pennsylvania and New France perfectly intentionally. The strongest proof for this is the fact that many prominent Shawnee headmen personally fostered close contacts with *both* colonies. Ocowellos may have been the first Shawnee to visit Montreal, but he also saw himself as such a good friend of the

Pennsylvanians that he was the first to inform them of his trip. Another headman, Paguasse, signed letters that the Allegheny leaders sent to Pennsylvanian authorities, yet he also hoisted the French flag in front of his house to show his friendship with New France. Nucheconner was especially active in fostering alliances with the British and the French. Although he corresponded regularly with Pennsylvanian and Virginian authorities and visited Philadelphia, his settlement on the Allegheny was known as the "French Town." This implies that it was an important base for visiting agents, traders, and gunsmiths from Canada. Clearly, Shawnee leaders deliberately sought to link their towns to both a French Father and a British Brother.[20]

Cultivating the complementary British and French alliances did not factionalize the Ohio Shawnees; it drew them into closer collaboration. Whereas the scattered Shawnee towns had previously negotiated with the colonies independently of one another, in the late 1720s communities on the Allegheny and Ohio began sending common delegations to conferences in Philadelphia and Montreal. In 1729 three leaders representing towns east of the Allegheny traveled to Montreal to treat with the French. Three years later a Shawnee delegation to Philadelphia included a Thawikila headman from the Youghiogheny River, leaders from the towns on the Allegheny, and a Mekoche diplomat from the Wyoming Valley. In 1739 Nucheconner joined forces with two other Ohio leaders, Missemediqueety (Big Hominy) and Tamany Buck, Kishacoquillas and others from the Juniata River, and Kakewatchiky, a Mekoche hokima from Wyoming, to meet with the provincial authorities in Philadelphia. Each time, a single orator spoke for these multicommunity delegations in their councils with the colonists. This suggests that the leaders representing the different towns had agreed on a common position before meeting the Europeans. The delegates also honored their diversity. At one point in the 1739 Philadelphia council, for example, Nucheconner underlined that he was speaking only for the Shawnees "scattered far abroad from the Great Island [on Susquehanna's West Branch] to Alleghenny." Significantly, this left out Kakewatchiky's community in the Wyoming Valley, which had apparently joined in the earlier part of Nucheconner's talk. Though allies, the Ohio and Wyoming Shawnees made it clear that they did not always share the same concerns and opinions.[21]

The growing cooperation of the Allegheny and Ohio communities is also evidenced by the correspondence between the local Shawnee headmen and British colonial officials. Between 1732 and 1738 Nucheconner, Paguasse, and other leaders from the Allegheny and Conemaugh towns joined together to send at least six letters to Pennsylvanian and Virginian authorities. Written down from Native dictation by British traders, these messages addressed issues that were important to many western Shawnee communities, especially their trade with the English. The Shawnee signatories repeatedly emphasized that the letters were composed collectively by several local leaders "att Our Councill." This implies that in the 1730s leaders of the Allegheny and Conemaugh communities began to meet at regional councils to discuss common concerns. Modeled after traditional town councils, these meetings were open to all interested communities, clans, and leaders. As in town councils, decision-making was based on discussion, compromise, and consensus. The governor of New France, Charles de la Boische, marquis de Beauharnois, explained that the Shawnee leaders would "have frequent talks together, and nothing is terminated among them until after divers interviews." Creatively combining unity with diversity, Nucheconner and other Allegheny and Conemaugh leaders built an institution that facilitated increasing cooperation among their communities but simultaneously protected long-standing clan and town autonomy.[22]

By 1738 the local leaders meeting in joint councils had appointed one of their number, Coyacolinne, as the "Chefe Counciler" of the intertown meetings. Very little is known of this man except that he seems to have been a skillful diplomat with extensive connections among the Shawnees. His title suggests that he acted as a ceremonial head of the regional councils. The emergence of such a role indicates that the Shawnees perceived their cooperation as a permanent arrangement and created new structures and rituals to organize it. Nucheconner too played a crucial role in the councils. He was either a cosigner or the sole signatory in all of the letters the Allegheny and Conemaugh towns sent to colonial leaders. Impressed by what they took as signs of Nucheconner's lofty standing, the British dubbed him the "King of the Shawanas." Clearly, they perceived him as the central leader of an increasingly united Shawnee nation. Nucheconner was not a powerful ruler, however. More likely, he was a *maumeesemaukāātar*, a ceremonial orator, who voiced in public the decisions hammered out by clan hokimas, matrons, and war leaders in town and regional councils. His emergence as the collective spokesman for several of the western Shawnee towns powerfully demonstrates that the once-scattered communities were now careful to portray themselves to outsiders as a strong, united front.[23]

Nucheconner provides a key to understanding why the Allegheny and Ohio Shawnees began to seek unity and cooperation in the 1720s and 1730s. As a Pekowi originally from the lower Susquehanna River, Nucheconner had spent much of his life in a small community constantly pushed around by the British and the Haudenosaunees. When they moved west, he and other Pekowis were eager to strengthen themselves by fostering collaboration with other Shawnee groups, many of whom shared similar experiences of diasporic hardship and oppression. It is also possible that their successful efforts to reclaim the old Ohio homelands reminded the Shawnees of memories and stories from the times when the different divisions had first united to settle the land at the center of the

Earth given them by the Creator. For many Shawnees, unity and cooperation had profound sacred and historical, as well as strategic, connotations.

How Shawnees constructed and conceptualized unity stemmed from traditional foundations. Kinship remained of utmost importance. Nucheconner, for example, was closely associated with, and possibly related to, the younger Pekowi leader Laypareawah. Known as "the young Shawano King" among the British, Laypareawah was the son of Opessa, the early-eighteenth-century hokima of Pequa. The young man probably had relatives among the Shawnee migrants from the lower Susquehanna as well as among those from the Potomac, where his father had settled after abandoning Pequa in 1711. Through marriage Laypareawah also became the brother-in-law of the war chief Lawachkamicky, "a noted man . . . and a great Warrior." Only faint traces of such kin connections among the Shawnee settlers survive in the colonial records. Sparse as they are, they nevertheless give us a vague idea of the intimate ways in which Shawnee leaders and their families cultivated unity and connections between their communities. Marriages between high-status women and men from different clans and towns built bridges between long-separated groups. Such unions created intimate reciprocal obligations and made it easier for allied leaders related through marriage to muster broad-based political support in several communities. Marriages between people from different towns also led to very concrete mixing. A 1737 census of three towns on the Allegheny, compiled by a Pennsylvanian fur trader, lists "Obocketoy" and "Obockater Junr" as living in different towns. Since these men were probably father and son, this suggests that multiple social ties spread even the members of single families to several communities and thus created new links between the Shawnee communities.[24]

In the late 1730s a group of leaders from the Allegheny towns took measures to bring the Shawnee consolidation to a new level. In March 1738 Nucheconner, Coyacolinne, and Laypareawah informed Pennsylvanian officials that several neighboring Shawnee communities had agreed to "Gether two Gather and make a strong Towne." By the next year they had established a new settlement, known as Lower Shawneetown, or Sonontio, farther west, at the confluence of the Ohio and Scioto rivers. Once again, Nucheconner and his allies probably had security in mind when encouraging diverse Shawnee bands to gather at the new community. Less than a year before its founding, Catawba warriors had twice raided the Shawnee and Lenape settlements on the upper Ohio and Allegheny. In Sonontio numbers brought security against enemies. But more was involved in the founding of the town. Controlling the meeting point of the Ohio and Scioto, Lower Shawneetown was located strategically at the crossroads of several Native and colonial trade routes. Its founders clearly sought to gain a prominent role in the profitable Ohio fur trade. As they may have calculated, many Pennsylvanian and Virginian merchants soon built their warehouses at Sonontio, laying the foundation for a brisk trade. This helped to attract an astonishing number of inhabitants to the town. By 1751 some twelve hundred to fifteen hundred Shawnees, Lenapes, and Ohio Iroquois lived at Lower Shawneetown, far more than in any previous or contemporary Shawnee settlement.[25]

Recognizing the diplomatic and military advantages of unity, Nucheconner and other local leaders deliberately encouraged newcomers to move to Sonontio. In order to advertise the spiritual and political power of their community they built a massive council house, some ninety feet long, at the center of the town. Housing local and regional councils, the mšikamekwi was an invitation for new groups to settle at Lower Shawneetown and participate in the wide-ranging decision-making carried out there. The town's leadership also took steps to regulate communal life in novel ways. In the late 1730s Nucheconner, Coyacolinne, Laypareawah, and their allies banned rum trade in Lower Shawneetown, fearing the violence and social disturbances that excess drinking often caused in Indian communities. They even "Oppointed four men to Stave all the Rum or strong Lickquors" brought to the town. Although the rum ban proved impossible to enforce, Lower Shawneetown gained a reputation as a center of chiefly power among the Ohio Shawnees. In the early 1750s Pennsylvanians referred to it as "the Place of Residence of the principal Men of that Nation."[26]

The growth of Lower Shawneetown reveals new political ideas and fault lines among the Ohio Shawnees. While Nucheconner and other Sonontio leaders sought to gather together in the town as many Shawnees as possible and regulate their communal life, all Shawnees did not welcome such endeavors. The communities in the Wyoming Valley and on the Juniata collaborated with Lower Shawneetown regularly but clearly maintained a distinct political identity, as evidenced by Nucheconner's careful choice of words in the Philadelphia council in 1739. Other Shawnee bands remained more distant from the supporters of consolidation and cooperation. One community from the Susquehanna planned to move to Detroit, rather than to Lower Shawneetown. Others migrated to the Cumberland River, a region they identified as "the lands where we were born." Throughout the 1730s the Haudenosaunees and the British distinguished the Thawikilas from other Shawnees by referring to them with their divisional name.[27] Despite the interest of Nucheconner and his allies to collect their people together for common defense, diplomacy, and social order, Shawnee groups retained divergent identities and ties to the land. The Shawnee social universe remained localized, and long-standing divisional, town, and clan identities continued to shape patterns of migration, cooperation, and diplomacy.

MIGRATION AND ALLIANCES IN THE SOUTH

The largest and most important group of Shawnees that did not join their relatives in the Ohio Country consisted of those Kishpokos, Thawikilas, and others who had settled along the Tallapoosa and Chattahoochee rivers in the Deep South after the 1670s. Over the decades these southern Shawnees had created intimate social, political, and ritual ties to the local Cowetas, Tallapoosas, Alabamas, Abihkas, and other Muskogean peoples, known to the British collectively as the Creeks. Although the Tallapoosa and Chattahoochee Shawnees had come to view the South as their home, they remained connected to their kinspeople on the Ohio and maintained a distinct linguistic and political identity that set them apart from their Muskogean hosts. Beginning in the 1720s they faced challenges very similar to those experienced by their northern relatives at the same time. Just like in the Ohio Valley, European imperial interest in the Shawnee homelands grew when British, French, and Spanish officials sought to extend their influence to the interior South through military and commercial alliances with the local Indians. And just like in the North, the southern Shawnees tried to secure their position between the competing empires by gathering together and forging complementary alliances with several rival colonies. The Shawnees in the South likewise strove to build alliances with the surrounding Indian peoples. In the 1730s they began advocating a general peace among the Native peoples of the Deep South, Ohio Country, and Illinois.

When British expansion and Haudenosaunee domination drove Shawnees from the Susquehanna, Delaware, and Potomac rivers to the Ohio Valley, the southern Shawnees too experienced dangerous transformations in their political landscape and relied on migration and consolidation to address these new problems. In 1715 the Shawnees living on the Savannah River had joined their Yamasee, Apalachee, and Lower Creek neighbors to rise against the abusive South Carolinian traders and slavers in the Yamasee War. After harassing the English settlements for almost a year, the allies had retreated west to the Chattahoochee River. Although the Creeks and South Carolina concluded a peace and reopened trade in 1717, conditions on the Chattahoochee remained tense. Many Lower Creeks were suspicious of their former English enemies and forged closer ties to Spanish Florida and French Louisiana. When some Chattahoochee Shawnees allowed Carolinian traders to build a warehouse in their town in 1725, a French agent enticed Creek warriors from the nearby Coweta to burn it down. Relations between the Lower Creeks and South Carolina soured even more when the English accused the Creeks of harboring hostile Yamasees. After 1723 South Carolinians tried to bend the recalcitrant Chattahoochee Creeks to colonial will with the help of repeated trade embargos. In 1728 the English even planned a military expedition against the Lower

Creeks. Although the campaign never materialized, the Carolinians did destroy several Yamasee towns in Florida.[28]

These simmering tensions disturbed the Shawnees living on the Chattahoochee, and by 1729 they had finally had enough. Several Shawnee communities now moved farther west and settled in the Upper Creek country, close to where the Tallapoosa and Coosa rivers join to form the Alabama River. The migrants had relatives in the area, for Kishpokos had lived among the Upper Creeks for decades. They were also quick to forge new ties to the local Muskogean communities. Jean-Baptiste Martin Diron d'Artaguette, the French commander of Mobile, reported that in "several councils . . . the Indians of these quarters" had agreed that the Koasatis would "place [the Shawnees] to where they judge proper." Eventually the Koasatis and the closely allied Alabamas gave the Shawnee newcomers land near the Coosa-Tallapoosa junction. Sharing land created an intimate alliance among the three groups.[29]

Something beyond old relatives and new allies attracted the Chattahoochee Shawnees to the Tallapoosa-Coosa region. During the Yamasee War the small French colony of Louisiana, huddled along the lower Mississippi River, had taken advantage of English defeats to gain influence among the Indians of the Deep South. In 1717 the French had built Fort Toulouse at the strategically critical Coosa-Tallapoosa confluence. Far from an imposing military stronghold, the fort was essentially a center for French trade, diplomacy, and gift-giving at the heart of the Upper Creek homelands. It was built not to intimidate the Indians, but to benefit them and draw them into an alliance with France. When the Chattahoochee Shawnees moved to the Coosa-Tallapoosa region, they immediately settled close to the French outpost. Initially, the French were deeply suspicious of them. One officer claimed that the Shawnees were "completely devoted to the English." He feared that the Shawnee settlements would form a beachhead for Carolinian merchants eager to expand their trading activities west toward Louisiana. There were some grounds for such suspicions, as the Shawnees welcomed British traders to their towns. One local headman, probably a war leader with close ties to peddlers from Carolina, was even known as "the red English captain of the Shawnees." His town formed an important way-station on the trading path that ran from Charles Town to such western Indian nations as the Choctaws and Chickasaws. But the Shawnees, just like their Alabama, Tallapoosa, and Koasati neighbors, also wanted to retain Fort Toulouse in their country. When Abihkas planned to destroy the fort in 1748, the local Shawnees boldly stopped them, declaring that "they were friends of the French and that they did not wish to do them any harm." Like their Ohio kinspeople, the southern Shawnees saw the advantages of having two rival colonies competing for their business and friendship.[30]

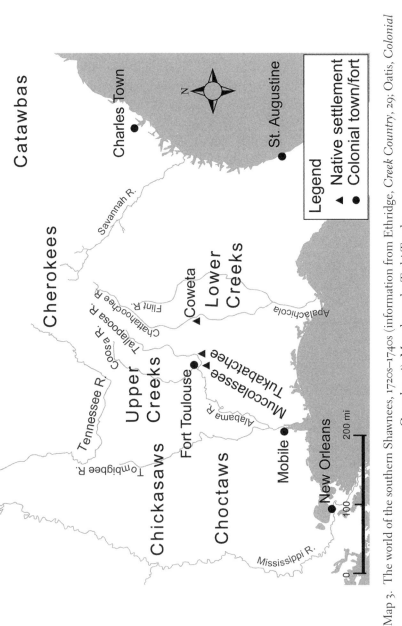

Map 3. The world of the southern Shawnees, 1720s–1740s (information from Ethridge, *Creek Country*, 29; Oatis, *Colonial Complex*, xi). Map drawn by Terhi Tanska.

Neither the British nor the French trusted the southern Shawnees balancing between Louisiana and South Carolina. French officials in New Orleans and Mobile constantly fretted over the eagerness of the Shawnees to trade with the English. Ironically, British agents in Charles Town were equally suspicious that the Shawnees were "intirely in the French interest." All colonists nevertheless agreed that the Tallapoosa Shawnees, though numbering fewer than one thousand people, occupied such a strategic position in the interior South that their friendship was essential for imperial interests. Officials of Louisiana and South Carolina alike worked hard to cultivate an alliance with the Shawnees. Through the 1740s the governor of Louisiana, Pierre de Rigaud de Vaudreuil, time and again requested his superiors in France to send him textiles "in the English style," for the Shawnees were so accustomed to trading with the British that they would not accept any other kind. When more Shawnees from the Ohio Valley migrated to the Tallapoosa River in 1748, the governor of South Carolina in turn quickly sent messengers to invite their headmen to a council in Charles Town.[31]

A small, diasporic people surrounded by several far more powerful Native and colonial neighbors, the Tallapoosa Shawnees depended on alliances and diplomacy to retain their space in the contested South. Their repeated dispersals and migrations since the 1670s had made them remarkably well connected. They had relatives, allies, and friends living in dozens of diverse communities throughout the South, the Ohio Country, and the Mississippi Valley. Their own communities were multiethnic, too. While some Shawnees built their own towns along the Tallapoosa, others settled in preexisting Muskogean communities, especially in Muccolassee and Tukabatchee. In 1731 the Tallapoosa Shawnees gave shelter to forty Chickasaw refugee families driven from their homes on the Mississippi by the French and the Choctaws. Marriages between Shawnee hosts and Chickasaw guests were common, and some years later about sixty Shawnees moved west to the Chickasaw lands. Others settled among the Cherokees.[32]

Such connections were nothing new to the Shawnees, who had always had wide networks of allies and trading partners. In the 1730s and 1740s the Tallapoosa Shawnees began utilizing their connections for a new goal, however. When they visited their kinspeople among the Cherokees and those living on the Ohio and renewed their alliances with their Creek, Chickasaw, and Choctaw neighbors, they began to talk about a general peace among all Indian peoples. Only vague rumors of the Shawnee diplomacy ever reached literate colonial officials, but even the meager documents tell of brisk diplomatic activity. In 1737 the French heard that the Shawnees were mediating a peace between the Alabamas and the Cherokees, who had been at war for twenty years. During the next ten years more news of "the project of the general peace that the Shawnees have proposed" trickled to New Orleans and Charles Town. Shawnee diplomats initiated and led peace talks among the Cherokees, Creeks, and Chickasaws and even approached their bitter Catawba enemies. In their most impressive feat, the Shawnees helped to negotiate a truce between the Cherokees and the Algonquian peoples living on the Wabash River, long inveterate enemies.[33]

To imperial officials any Native peace that excluded Europeans seemed ominous. Both the British and the French worried that "the general peace" advocated by the Shawnees might transform into a pan-tribal military alliance against their colonies. There is little evidence that the Shawnees' peace project was primarily anti-imperial, however. Rather, it was grounded in the social networks, history, and political landscapes of the southern Shawnees. Having relatives in most Native communities throughout the South, the Shawnees saw little point in intertribal warfare. Moreover, their traumatic experiences of slave raids and the Yamasee War had taught them how vulnerable small, diasporic communities could be on contested borderlands. The very mobility of their life made the southern Shawnees advocate peace, too. Shawnee individuals, families, and towns were constantly moving back and forth between the Tallapoosa River and the Shawnee communities scattered throughout the Ohio Valley and the Southeast. Peace guaranteed them a safe passage to their friends and relatives and made possible the migrations that had formed an essential part of Shawnee life for more than half a century.[34]

The southern Shawnees remained in close contact with their kinspeople on the Ohio. Some colonial documents hint that the Tallapoosa and Ohio Shawnees may have collaborated in mediating the hostilities between the Cherokees and the Wabash tribes. Movement between the two groups continued through the 1730s and 1740s. In 1735 the Thawikilas who had killed the overbearing Haudenosaunee diplomat on the Youghiogheny River fled "to the Southward . . . from where they first came, which is below Carolina." Nine years later about eighty Shawnees from "Canada" (probably the Ohio Valley) migrated to the Alabama River and settled among the local Alabamas. In 1746 one hundred more joined "the people of their village" who had previously settled upriver from Fort Toulouse. Some of these newcomers explained to suspicious Carolinians that "they only wanted to *return to their own Lands.*" This suggests that they had previously lived in the South, then moved to the Ohio, and were now returning back to the Tallapoosa once more. Clearly, their ancestral homelands and kinspeople on the Ohio meant less to these travelers than their lands, relatives, and allies along the Tallapoosa. At a time when Nucheconner and his allies encouraged Shawnees to "Gether two Gather" at Lower Shawneetown, these migrants testify that local and kin-based identities among the scattered Shawnees remained strong.[35]

LETHAL PLACES

In colonial America imperial borderlands could be places of political opportunity and independence for Native peoples, but they could also turn into
"lethal places" when European empires asserted their power. Through the 1720s
and 1730s the efforts of the Ohio and Alabama Shawnees to protect their lands
and autonomy by cultivating complementary alliances with the French and the
British had been facilitated by the so-called long peace between the two empires
that had followed a series of colonial wars between 1689 and 1713. In 1744 the
outbreak of King George's War shattered the imperial peace and transformed
the Ohio Valley and the Deep South into militarized "zones of international
friction." Especially in the Ohio Valley, the Anglo-French competition intensified dangerously over the next decade. Both New France and the British colonies tried to pressure the Ohio Indians to become loyal imperial allies rather
than independent politicians playing the European empires against one another.
Under such conditions the Ohio Shawnees found it difficult to maintain alliances with their French Father and British Brother alike. While many communities tried to continue this time-tested strategy, others gravitated toward one or
the other colonial empire on the basis of local and kin-based concerns. The
escalating imperial conflict threatened the webs of cooperation the Shawnees
had weaved during the previous two decades. By the mid-1750s Shawnee towns,
factions, and clans espoused various contrasting strategies to survive, avoid, or
benefit from the Anglo-French confrontation. Yet they also continued to collaborate and communicate over wide distances. Although such a combination of
diversity and unity often appears confusing to modern scholars, Shawnees saw
no contradiction in thinking and acting both locally and nationally at the same
time. After all, that had been the essence of being Shawnee for a long time.[36]

The Ohio Country had originally offered a safe haven for the Shawnee
settlers. In the early 1740s, however, dark clouds gathered above the region.
Rumors of an alleged Shawnee-organized Indian uprising in Maryland cooled
Shawnee-British relations in 1742. The next year warriors from Great Island on
the Susquehanna's West Branch threw oil on the flames when they robbed a
Pennsylvanian trader. According to Pennsylvania's frustrated governor, George
Thomas, the Shawnees "are known . . . to be a perfidious people, and to have
render'd themselves justly to be suspected by their Behaviour in many
Instances." Shawnee relations with the Six Nations were even more strained.
Ever since the Ohio migrations, the Haudenosaunees had resented the inde-
pendence of the western Shawnees. They also remembered bitterly how the
Thawikilas had killed the Seneca diplomat in 1735. Pennsylvanians believed
that "the Six Nations and the Shawonese are far from being on Good Terms."
Worse was to come. In 1744 dynastic rivalries in Europe sparked King George's

War in America. Although no large-scale military campaigns took place in the Ohio Country, the war seriously narrowed the local Indians' room for maneuver between the British and the French and widened internal fault lines in many Native communities.[37]

Such fault lines surfaced dramatically among the Shawnees in 1745. In April Peter Chartier, a Shawnee-French trader living on the Allegheny River, robbed several Pennsylvanian merchants, apparently with the help of some of his Shawnee kinsmen. He then led a number of Shawnees to the Wabash River where they expected to trade with and receive protection from the French. Chartier's motives remain unclear. He had lived in Pennsylvania all his life, but heavy debts and quarrels with the provincial leadership may have prompted him to look for a brighter future among the French. Whatever Chartier's goals, his Shawnee allies certainly were not interested in fighting for the French. They apparently moved to the Wabash simply to put more distance between them and the recently threatening British and Haudenosaunees and to enjoy the "great Things" that "the French promis'd" them. Nevertheless, the episode plunged all Shawnees in danger. Although many prominent headmen such as Kakewatchiky from the Wyoming Valley and Missemediqueety and Lawachkamicky from Lower Shawneetown "protested against [Chartier's] proceedings," the enraged Pennsylvanians blamed all Shawnees for the hostilities. Colonial authorities even asked the Iroquois to "Chastize Nuecheconno," believing that as the "King" of the Shawnees he was responsible for Chartier's "defection." To make matters worse, on the Wabash Chartier's band quickly "offended" the neighboring Weas, Piankashaws, and Illinois. Soon, both Lower Shawneetown and the Tallapoosa Shawnees were also embroiled in violence with these peoples. Within a year, Chartier's rash, independent actions had seriously disrupted the complex networks of alliances the Shawnee leaders on the Ohio and in the interior South had been building for two decades.[38]

The Ohio Shawnee communities responded to the crisis in two contrasting ways that reflected their differing identities and interests. Chartier's Shawnees fled the turmoil on the Wabash to the South. In 1748 they settled among their tribespeople in the neighborhood of Fort Toulouse. Many of Chartier's followers had personal ties to the Deep South. Carolinian agents, for instance, reported that "Shartie's Wife is an Apalatchee Woman." This indicates that at least some of Chartier's people had previously lived on the Savannah and Chattahoochee rivers together with the local Apalachees and were now returning home from the increasingly dangerous Ohio. The band proved a destabilizing factor in the South. Although Chartier assured Louisiana's officials that his people were "entirely devoted" to France, some of his followers suspected that the French had had a hand in rousing the Wabash tribes against them. In retaliation, they took revenge not only on their enemies on the Wabash, but also on the

Choctaws, long-time allies of Louisiana. The "general peace" advocated by the southern Shawnees began to crumble, as their communities became entangled in Chartier's conflicts. However, even Chartier refused to take sides in the ongoing Anglo-French rivalry in the Deep South. "The Shawnees have not betrayed up to the present the neutrality that they have always observed," reported Governor Vaudreuil in 1749. Indeed, most southern Shawnees continued to trade with both South Carolina and Louisiana. Their distance from colonial centers of power protected them and allowed them to play the British and the French against one another.[39]

In the Ohio Valley, in contrast, safe distance from imperial power was shrinking fast, and the local Shawnees had to calibrate their strategies to survive in the region. Surrounded by the threatening British to the east, the Haudenosaunees to the northeast, and the Wabash peoples to the west, the Lower Shawneetown leadership intensified their efforts to gather the Shawnees together for security. In 1744 Nucheconner and his allies invited Kakewatchiky's Mekoches from the Wyoming Valley to the Ohio. Disturbed by English and Iroquois belligerence, the Mekoches moved to the upper Ohio where they established a new community, Logstown. Like the flight of Chartier's Shawnees to Alabama, the migration of the Wyoming Mekoches to the Ohio was based on kinship networks and shared histories. Leaders of Lower Shawneetown and Logstown traced their family histories to the Susquehanna and Delaware valleys. There, they and their parents had been neighbors and allies for decades. Even during the Ohio migrations the western Shawnees had regularly joined forces with the Wyoming Mekoches in colonial diplomacy, testifying that strong bonds continued to link these far removed groups. Other Shawnees from the Susquehanna Valley, too, continued to join Lower Shawneetown. In 1742, for example, a headman named Ossoghqua participated in negotiations over the lower Susquehanna lands at Philadelphia, suggesting that he still lived in the area. Six years later he visited the Pennsylvanian frontier town Lancaster with two Lower Shawneetown leaders. Apparently, Ossoghqua had moved west in the face of ongoing Pennsylvanian expansion on the Susquehanna. Gathering together remained the response of the Lower Shawneetown leadership to the growing dangers of the Ohio Valley.[40]

Shawnees were not the only people in the Ohio Country who were forced by King George's War to rethink their political alignments and strategies. Indians throughout the entire Pays d'en Haut region between the Ohio River and the Great Lakes adopted new diplomatic and commercial alliances designed for a world full of new opportunities and dangers. The roots of this turmoil went deep into the region's history. In the late seventeenth and early eighteenth centuries New France had built a string of forts, missions, and trading posts around the Upper Great Lakes and claimed the largely depopulated Ohio

Country as its own on the basis that French explorers had allegedly "discovered" the region. The Pays d'en Haut soon became critical for French imperial ambitions in North America. Fur trade in the Great Lakes sustained New France economically, while the lakes and the Ohio River formed a lifeline connecting the French settlements in Canada, Illinois, and Louisiana. Yet the French presence in the Pays d'en Haut was entirely dependent on local Indian allies who traded with the French and fought with them against their common Haudenosaunee enemies. The migration of Shawnees, Lenapes, and Iroquois to the Ohio Country after the 1720s threatened New France's delicate position in the west. While these settlers were eager to join France's alliance network, they also had older political and commercial ties to the British that they were not willing to sever. Most disturbingly for the French, the Shawnees and Lenapes drew hordes of Pennsylvanian and Virginian traders to the Ohio. Lured by the cheap merchandise offered by the British, many old French Indian allies welcomed English traders to their towns, especially when the British naval blockade of Canada strangled French trade in the Pays d'en Haut during King George's War. To the French authorities this looked like an English invasion of French territory. Seeing their vital system of alliances unraveling before their eyes, officials in New France resorted to harsh measures and urged the Great Lakes and Ohio Indians to drive the British traders off the Pays d'en Haut.[41]

With both the French and the British behaving increasingly aggressively, the Ohio Shawnees sought to warm their relations with the Haudenosaunees. Most importantly, Nucheconner, Kakewatchiky, and their allies began forging an alliance with the Seneca, Onondaga, and Cayuga emigrants who were settling on the upper Ohio and the southern shores of Lake Erie. These Ohio Iroquois were a powerful ally with a grand vision for retaining the Ohio Country in Native control. Imitating the Six Nations Confederacy, they planned to unite all Ohio Indians into a strong coalition under Haudenosaunee leadership. Together, they believed, the Natives would be strong enough to assert their autonomy between the warring French and British empires. The Ohio Iroquois resented the French efforts to curtail their flourishing trade with the Pennsylvanians and Virginians. In 1747 they showed their resentment graphically by killing and scalping Canadian traders and declaring war on New France. To strengthen their position, the Ohio Iroquois sought military and material support from Pennsylvania. In November 1747 their leaders traveled to Philadelphia, where they explained that they "had concluded to kindle a Fire in their Town, and had invited all the Indians at a considerable Distance round about them to come to their Fire." The headmen stressed that this nascent Indian coalition was staunchly anti-French and needed British assistance to survive. Eager to strengthen their political and commercial influence in the Ohio Country, Pennsylvanian authorities sent the provincial Indian agent Conrad Weiser with a large present to meet the Ohio Iroquois and their allies in their own country. The next August, Weiser held a large council with the Ohio Iroquois, Lower Shawneetown and Logstown Shawnees, Lenapes, Wyandots, Mahicans, and Mississaugas at Logstown. There, he ceremonially recognized the Ohio coalition as an independent political force and Pennsylvania's ally.[42]

The Ohio Iroquois proved a valuable ally to the Lower Shawneetown and Logstown Shawnees. In 1748 the Iroquois persuaded Pennsylvanian authorities to accept the Shawnees' ritual apologies for Chartier's raid and normalize the Shawnee-British relations. When the French-allied Weas killed a Lower Shawneetown man and captured his family two years later, the Ohio Iroquois informed the French officers in Illinois that "we look upon the Chaouanons as our children" and demanded the French to arrange the return of the prisoners. Iroquois-brokered rapprochement with Pennsylvania brought growing numbers of British traders to the Shawnee towns. French authorities reported with concern that Lower Shawneetown had "been joined by a considerable number of savages of all nations, forming a sort of republic dominated by some Iroquois of the Five Nations who form part of it, and that . . . the English almost entirely supply their needs." The Shawnees had once more found a hopawaaka-like protector. But it came with a price. Pennsylvanian authorities again saw the Iroquois as a convenient tool for controlling the all too independent western Shawnees. Indeed, the colonists agreed to forgive Chartier's defection only after the Shawnees had given the Ohio Iroquois "the strongest assurances of their better behavior for the future." Afterwards, Pennsylvanians insisted on treating with the Shawnees through Iroquois mediation. The familiar specter of British-Haudenosaunee domination had returned to haunt the Shawnees.[43]

The Treaty of Aix-la-Chapelle ended King George's War in 1748. A peace negotiated in Europe did nothing to pacify the Ohio Country, however. Quite the contrary, imperial rivalry over the region intensified behind a façade of nominal peace. Traditional French Indian allies throughout the Pays d'en Haut continued to join the Ohio Iroquois coalition and welcome British traders to their towns. Utilizing their strategic location and wide contacts, Lower Shawneetown and Logstown leaders helped to establish links between these western nations and the Ohio Iroquois–Pennsylvania alliance network. Nucheconner and Kakewatchiky introduced a group of Wyandots from Detroit to Pennsylvanians in 1747. A year later they helped Miamis from Pickawillany, located on the Great Miami River, to establish commercial ties with the Quaker colony. Despite the European peace, government officials in New France relied on aggressive measures to stop such activities. In 1749 Captain Pierre-Joseph Céleron de Blainville led a strong military expedition from New France down the Ohio River to assert Louis XV's claims to the country and awe the local Indians back into the French alliance. When the warriors of Lower Shawneetown fired on Céleron's troops and the British traders ignored his orders to leave the Ohio, the French lost all patience. Over the next two years Canadians and their remaining Indian allies robbed several English traders on the Ohio and occasionally harassed the local Native communities.[44]

Lower Shawneetown was a particular irritation to the French. The governor of New France, Pierre Jacques de Taffanel, marquis de La Jonquière, seethed that "it would be in our interest to destroy those Chaouanons by getting the nations to wage war against them." The leaders of Lower Shawneetown were also ready for war. In February 1752 Missemediqueety, Lawachkamicky, Laypareawah, and Nickiphock appealed to Pennsylvania for assistance, declaring that they would "not suffer ourselves to be insulted any more by our deceitful Fathers." The Quaker-led Pennsylvania Assembly, however, refused to sanction any military action in a time of peace. The French had no such scruples. In June 1752 a French-Algonquian raiding party sacked Pickawillany, the westernmost center of British trade. A year later French-allied Ottawas killed a Shawnee close to Lower Shawneetown. For the locals, the large town they had once built to protect them against enemies had become "a Place where we are always in fear."[45]

Unfortunately, the Shawnees' fears were multiplied by their British and Ohio Iroquois allies. In 1747 a group of wealthy Virginian planters had formed a land speculation organization, the Ohio Company. The Crown gave the company an enormous land grant of half a million acres in the Ohio Valley on the condition that the speculators would settle the area in seven years. When the company's surveyors began to explore the Ohio Country, the Shawnees and Lenapes remembered how they had lost their homes in the East to colonial settlers two decades earlier. Their worst fears were confirmed when Virginian and Pennsylvanian squatters pushed to their hunting grounds in the western Appalachians. By the early 1750s many Ohio Indians felt increasingly trapped between a French hammer and a British anvil. Mixing stinging sarcasm with their concern, Lenape headmen Tamaqua (Beaver) and Oppamylucah asked an Ohio Company agent "where the Indians' Land lay, for that the French claimed all the land in one Side the River Ohio and the English on the other Side." For Shawnees who had for thirty years labored to assert their rights in the Ohio Country, this situation must have been deeply disturbing. Protecting their lands now became their leading goal.[46]

Protection was indeed needed. In June 1752 Virginia invited the Ohio Indians to a treaty at Logstown to discuss the land claims of the Ohio Company. In a private meeting, the colonists pressured, threatened, and bribed an Ohio Seneca headman named Tanaghrisson (Half King), until he allegedly acknowledged the company's claims and gave the Virginians permission to construct a fort at the forks of the Ohio. No Shawnee or Lenape was consulted in the matter. For them, the Treaty of Logstown revived bitter memories of Haudenosaunees selling away their lands to Pennsylvania. When two Virginian diplomats visited Lower Shawneetown two months later, some of the locals insulted them by hoisting "a suit of French colors, which the French had given to Nucheconner." Next year Nucheconner returned to Virginian officials the Union Jack they had given to the Shawnee delegates at the Logstown meeting. These were powerful symbolic messages that some of the Lower Shawneetown people were renouncing their alliance with the land-hungry Britons.[47]

Shawnee relations with both the Ohio Iroquois and the British hit rock bottom in 1753. That summer six Lower Shawneetown warriors were imprisoned in South Carolina when on their way to raid their Catawba enemies. The warriors had committed no crime; they were arrested simply because unidentified "Northern Indians" had recently killed a local colonist. To make matters worse, the leader of the war party was Lawachkamicky, the influential headman with relatives and in-laws in many prominent Shawnee and Lenape families. In September and October Nucheconner appealed to Virginia and Pennsylvania for help in restoring the prisoners. The Ohio Iroquois, however, were enraged over such an independent initiative. Oneida headman Scarouady instructed the colonists not to take any action in the matter. Claiming that "the Chiefs of the Shawanesse had no Power, without consulting and having Leave from the Six Nations, to transact any publick Business," he explained that he intended "to take his own Method" to have the prisoners freed. Both Scarouady and the British evidently saw the situation as an opportunity to tighten Ohio Iroquois and colonial authority over the Shawnees. Thus no one acted, and Lawachkamicky died unexpectedly in prison. Outraged, many Shawnees accused the British of breaking their alliance.[48]

News of Lawachkamicky's imprisonment and death reached the Shawnee towns on the Ohio at a critical moment. In April 1753 the new governor-general of New France, Agne de Menneville, marquis Duquesne, had dispatched an enormous army of two thousand men from Montreal toward Lake Erie to do what diplomacy and raiding parties had not been able to accomplish: take definite possession of the contested Ohio Country. The French plan was to drive the Pennsylvanian and Virginian traders from the area and stop further British encroachments by building a chain of forts from Presque Isle, located on the southern shore of Lake Erie, to the forks of the Ohio River, at the site of modern Pittsburgh. No such show of imperial force had ever been seen on the Ohio. The French invasion threw both the local Indians and the English into confusion. British traders fled from the Ohio Country, while Pennsylvania and Virginia proved unable to mount effective countermeasures against the French army.[49]

Squeezed between the aggressive French, the land-grabbing British, and the domineering Iroquois, the Shawnees were divided. Since Lower Shawneetown had for years had a tense relationship with New France, many locals were terrified by the invasion and sought British and Haudenosaunee aid against it. In contrast, many smaller Shawnee communities spread along the upper Ohio felt more threatened by the English and the Iroquois. With the Ohio Company eyeing their lands greedily, these "Upper Shawnees" viewed the French invaders as a potential counterforce against the British-Iroquois threat. In September 1753 a delegation of the Upper Shawnees accompanied Tanaghrisson to meet the French army. Tanaghrisson planned to give the invaders a final warning to withdraw from the Ohio and believed the Shawnees would back him. However, after the Seneca had ordered the French to retreat, the Shawnees welcomed them to the Ohio, declaring that "we shall be as glad to see you in our villages as you seem to be to hear us speak." William Trent, the Ohio Company agent based at the forks of the Ohio, correctly noted that the Upper Shawnees used the French army to protect their independence from the Haudenosaunees. He explained that "while the French are at a Distance, the Six Nations will oblige the Shawness [*sic*] & Delawares to act as they please; But if the Army moves this Way I think the Shawnesse and Delawares will pay little Regard to 6 Nations."[50]

Some Shawnees went even further. In 1754 an unidentified group of warriors raided the frontier settlements of South Carolina. Most likely they were kinsmen of Lawachkamicky, out to avenge the death of their relative. But most Shawnees shunned such extreme measures. According to Shawnee legal traditions, it was possible to compensate a murder with ritual gifts of wampum, valuable and sacred beads made of marine shells. Lawachkamicky's brother and brother-in-law Laypareawah accepted Pennsylvanian gifts of condolence and assured the British that the war leader's "Death will by no means occasion a Breach of Friendship between Us and You." In the Deep South the local Shawnees were as cautious as their kinspeople on the Ohio. In 1754 Governor Vaudreuil warned the Tallapoosa Shawnees and their Creek neighbors that the English were going to send an army against them. A Shawnee messenger from the Ohio also tried to persuade the Creeks to take up arms against the British. Most of the southern Shawnees nevertheless declared that they wished "to live in Peace and Quietness with all People."[51]

This plurality of local and factional strategies might suggest that diversity once again overshadowed unity in the Shawnee world. But even when choosing contrasting paths in the imperial crisis, the Shawnee communities in the Ohio Valley continued to work together. Although some groups sought rapprochement with the French and others with the British and Ohio Iroquois, the Shawnees did not divide into clear-cut "British" and "French" factions. Rather, most leaders, communities, and kin groups experimented tentatively with alternative strategies, kept open lines of communication with both empires, and avoided committing themselves strongly to any one course of action. They clung to neutrality even when the French army reached the forks of the Ohio and established Fort Duquesne to guard this strategic location in the summer of 1754. The French invited Shawnee leaders to a council at the fort and gave them "large Presents, desiring them to stand their Friends or Neuter." Instead, the Shawnees "made them no answer at all" and sent a large delegation led by Laypareawah to "see their Brethren the English" in Pennsylvania. Meeting with Pennsylvanian officials at Aughwick, the Shawnees merely assured them that "we are still your Friends and Brethren as We always have been." The Britons complained that the Shawnees and other Ohio Indians took such a neutral stance opportunistically, to extort presents and concessions from both the French and the British. Most Shawnees, however, simply had no wish to become embroiled in what they perceived as an impending and dangerous imperial war on their homelands. Forty years later some Mekoche headmen reminisced that "when the French with his big foot which the Great Spirit had given him, came to this Island" and "thought himself master of all this Country," the Mekoches begged both him and the English "not to fight in this Our Country but rather in their own & on the Great Lake, as by fighting here they might trample on some of our Children." They understood all too well the danger of being crushed between two warring empires.[52]

Eventually, the efforts of the Ohio Shawnees to stay out of the escalating Anglo-French conflict failed. In the summer of 1755 the British sent a massive army under General Edward Braddock to seize Fort Duquesne and bring the Ohio Valley under British control. Deeply concerned for their lands, the leaders of the Shawnees, Lenapes, and Ohio Iroquois met twice with Braddock. Both times the headmen promised to assist the redcoats against the French, if Braddock only guaranteed that the Indians could retain at least *some* lands on the Ohio. Instead, the general bluntly declared "that No Savage Should Inherit the Land." The French officers at Fort Duquesne showed a far greater appreciation of the military importance of Indian allies. They warned visiting Shawnee and Lenape leaders that the British army was "coming against you, to take your Lands." According to the testimony of the Lenape war leader Shingas, this was enough to convert a part of the enraged Ohio Indians into French allies, but "the Greater Part remained neuter till they saw How Things wou'd go Between Braddock and the French in their Engagement." That decisive moment came on July 9. On the Monongahela River, about ten miles south of Fort Duquesne, an army of Great Lakes Indians together with a small French force and some Shawnees and Lenapes attacked Braddock's troops as they marched toward the French strong-hold. The combined Native-French force crushed the Britons. Within hours, two-thirds of the redcoats were dead or wounded, including Braddock himself.

With panic spreading through the columns, the British army quickly fled back
to its base in Virginia.[53]

Braddock's defeat was a momentous event. It convinced most Shawnees,
Lenapes, and other Ohio Indians that with French assistance they could throw
the land-hungry British settlements back to the Atlantic seaboard and secure
the Ohio Country for the Indians. Some even calculated that once the populous British colonies were defeated with French help, the Indians would have
little trouble in dislodging the isolated French garrisons from the Ohio. Many
Shawnees now agreed that they should use military force to defend the homelands they had carved for themselves on the Ohio during the previous thirty
years. In October 1755 most Ohio Shawnees accordingly joined Lenapes and
other warriors from the Ohio and Great Lakes and launched a series of devastating military campaigns against the frontier settlements of Virginia,
Pennsylvania, and Maryland. But even now some groups refused to fight. In
1795 Mekoche leaders recalled that "notwithstanding all we could do to prevent
the Indians interfereing in the Quarrell [between France and Great Britain] the
French gained their point with our younger Brothers the Shawanoes & the
other Nations & prevailed upon them to take the Hatchet against the English,"
but "we Makujays have always endeavored to bury these matters." The war
continued to divide, as well as unite, the Shawnees.[54]

In 1756 the Anglo-French confrontation on the Ohio helped to trigger a global
imperial conflict that would soon spread to Europe, India, and the Caribbean.
In time, Europeans came to know this bloody showdown as the Seven Years'
War. From the perspective of the Shawnees and their Native neighbors, the
name is a gross misnomer. The French and their allies had threatened Lower
Shawneetown since 1750, and most Ohio communities would continue to fight
against foreign invaders well beyond 1763, when the Treaty of Paris ended the
war between Great Britain and France. The Shawnee warriors who descended
on Pennsylvanian, Virginian, and Maryland settlements in the fall of 1755 and
the Mekoche diplomats who tried to preserve the peace certainly became entangled in a global war, but they did so for diverse local, kin-based, and factional
reasons. Out of this familiar diversity, the long war would create new developments toward unity. The decision of most Shawnees to defend their lands with
arms marked a dramatic break from their century-old strategy of migration and
dispersal in the face of an enemy invasion. It was the land itself that kept the
Shawnees on the Ohio and made them choose fighting instead of retreating.
"The God Who made all things gave us this Country and brought us through
this Ground," explained the orator Missiweakiwa in 1760. He underlined how
intimately the Shawnees had come to identify with their homelands on the
Ohio. Missiweakiwa's words suggest that an increasingly strong Shawnee iden-

tity, the "us," was emerging side by side with a notion of common Shawnee homelands, "this Country." Indeed, when defending their lands, the Shawnees—despite their contrasting strategies—continued to work together and struggled to create unity that would protect them during these dangerous times. From this cooperation would emerge a new vision of a Shawnee nation.[55]

3

"The Chief of All the Tribes"

Nation and Empire, 1755–1775

The Seven Years' War has been called the "the most important event to occur in eighteenth-century North America." It destroyed French colonial power in North America and gave birth to a greatly enlarged British empire that stretched, at least on paper, from the Atlantic seaboard to the Mississippi River. In standard narratives of U.S. history this geopolitical upheaval forms the backdrop for the American Revolution. The efforts of the British government to impose centralized order on the vast new empire after the war, so this interpretation goes, sparked angry protests among the American colonists, who claimed that their traditional rights as British subjects were threatened. Debates over taxation and representation escalated during the decade after the Seven Years' War and finally exploded into a revolution that split a new American nation from the empire.[1]

The violent emergence of the British empire set in motion processes of nation-building also across the Indian country. Forty years after the outbreak of the Seven Years' War, in February 1795, Mekoche headmen Catahecassa (Black Hoof), Biaseka (Wolf), and Red-Faced Fellow recounted the history of the Shawnees to British officers at Fort Miamis, in what later became the state of Ohio. They too portrayed the war as a momentous event with revolutionary repercussions. Yet the Mekoches looked at the war from a vantage point far different from the perspectives of officials in London and Paris or colonists in Philadelphia and Montreal. Indian peoples throughout eastern North America had powerful reasons of their own to view the outcome of the Seven Years' War as tremendously dramatic. The fall of New France to British hands in 1760 at one stroke made obsolete the time-tested Native security strategy of playing the rival English and French colonies against each another. It left the Indians alone to face the largest empire they had ever seen—an empire, moreover, that clearly coveted Native lands. Throughout the Indian country, Indigenous communities had to find new sources of diplomatic, military, and spiritual power to defend themselves. Many Shawnees, like neighboring Creeks, Lenapes, and others, came to view national consolidation as the best response to the new imperial threat. During the two decades following 1755, diverse Shawnee groups from the Ohio, Susquehanna, Tallapoosa, and elsewhere gathered in the central Ohio Valley to stand up to the British empire together. They defined their nationhood by building institutions of collective leadership, drawing national boundaries, and rethinking the relations among the five Shawnee divisions. In 1795 Catahecassa, Biaseka, and Red-Faced Fellow reminisced that other Shawnees had recognized the Mekoches as the leaders of this national consolidation, as "the Chief of all the Tribes." Not all Shawnees shared such a memory, however. In fact, through the 1760s and early 1770s the efforts of the Mekoches and their allies to gather all Shawnees behind a collective leadership divided as well as united Shawnees. Many towns, clans, warriors, and women opposed what they perceived as a threat to traditional local and kin group autonomy. In the new imperial landscape, political consolidation offered security to Native communities but also sparked divisive social conflicts.[2]

IMPERIAL WAR AND SHAWNEE CONSOLIDATION

The story of the Seven Years' War in the Ohio Valley is well known. From 1755 to 1758 the local Shawnees, Lenapes, and Ohio Iroquois, often with French and Great Lakes Indian allies, waged a successful and devastating war against Pennsylvania, Virginia, and Maryland in an effort to neutralize the colonial threat against their ownership of the Ohio Country. In three years the Ohio warriors killed between fifteen hundred and two thousand colonists, captured about one thousand more, and destroyed both military forts and civilian farms. In terror, surviving Anglo-Americans abandoned extensive areas of settlement on the disputed borderlands in present-day western Pennsylvania and Virginia. With the backcountry society near the breaking point, the British were ready for major concessions by 1758. That October Pennsylvania grudgingly concluded the Treaty of Easton with the eastern Lenapes of the Susquehanna Valley. The provincial leadership returned to Indians a large tract of land between the Allegheny Mountains and the Susquehanna River that had been bought from the Haudenosaunees under fraudulent circumstances in Albany four years earlier. The colonists also pledged that no European settlers would be permitted west of the Appalachians before Crown officers and Six Nations leaders had established a permanent boundary between Native and British lands.[3]

When news of the Easton Treaty spread to the Ohio Country, many local Shawnees and Lenapes felt that the British promises guaranteed their territorial integrity and fulfilled their principal war aims. Accordingly, they cautiously opened their own peace negotiations with the English. Exhausted by the long war and short of military supplies, the Ohio Indians even stood back when a new British army under General John Forbes marched to the forks of the Ohio and evicted the French from Fort Duquesne in November 1758. But when the redcoats built their own Fort Pitt at the forks, the Shawnees and their neighbors grew concerned. They remained eager to conclude a peace with the British but feared new encroachments on their lands and warned Forbes to retreat speedily from their territory. Because the remaining French posts on the Allegheny River still posed a serious threat to Forbes's beachhead on the Ohio, British officers were eager to mollify the powerful Natives. They promised that as soon as the French were driven entirely out of the region, they would return to the east side of the Appalachians and leave the Ohio Country to the Indians.[4]

For the next four years the Ohio Indians and the British tried painstakingly to build a lasting peace. Unfortunately, they disagreed over a fundamental issue: who would rule the Trans-Appalachian West—independent Native nations or the British empire? In British eyes, the British success against France answered this question. In 1759 English and Haudenosaunee forces took Fort Niagara, forcing the French to evacuate their remaining posts in the Ohio Country. Later that same year Quebec fell to the redcoats. The next year the British captured Montreal, and New France capitulated. With the French all but eliminated from the continent, the British began to tighten their grip on the Ohio Valley and the Great Lakes. Instead of abandoning Fort Pitt, the redcoats occupied twelve old French posts across the Pays d'en Haut. Under strict orders from London to economize after the enormously expensive war, military officers terminated the traditional custom of giving diplomatic gifts to the Natives whose lands they were unilaterally occupying. The Indians saw this as a sign of utter disrespect. This was, indeed, the message the British high command wished to convey: the empire had come to the west to rule, not to curry Indian friendship. Topping all other insults and injuries, early in 1763 Shawnees and their neighbors heard that France and Great Britain had concluded a peace treaty in Paris, bringing the imperial war to an end. As a part of the treaty, France had ceded all the territory between the Appalachians and the Mississippi River to Britain. No Indians had been consulted, a dramatic sign that neither empire respected the Native ownership of these lands.[5]

That was too much. In the spring and summer of 1763 Shawnees, Lenapes, Senecas, Ottawas, Ojibwes, Potawatomis, Wyandots, and other Natives throughout the Great Lakes and Ohio Country again took up arms against the British in what has become known as Pontiac's War. Within months, the Indians captured eight of the new Trans-Appalachian British forts, devastated Pennsylvanian and Virginian frontier settlements once more, and routed the redcoats during several encounters. The British nevertheless managed to hold on to three crucial strongholds in the west: Fort Pitt, Niagara, and Detroit. After more than a year of exhausting warfare, both sides finally admitted that they were unable to vanquish the other and again opened peace negotiations. When the Shawnees and their neighbors realized they could not dislodge the British entirely from the Ohio Country, they sought to build a new, mutually beneficial relationship with the empire. In 1765 the Shawnees, Lenapes, and Ohio Iroquois adopted King George III as their ceremonial Father in the place of the defeated French. They allowed the British to retain forts in the Indian country but insisted that in exchange "our Father will . . . take better care of his Children than has heretofore been done." This meant protecting Native land rights and opening trade with the impoverished Indians. Deeply disturbed by the devastating and costly Indian wars, Crown officials were equally ready to compromise. Already two years before, the British government had issued the Royal Proclamation of 1763 to address Native grievances about land. The proclamation made the Appalachian Mountains the boundary between Indian and British territories. For Shawnees, this was their major accomplishment in the two wars. Twenty years later the Mekoche headmen would proudly remember how King George had "drawn the Line" with them. A decade of violence had finally secured their homelands in the Ohio Valley.[6]

While it is easy to follow the military and diplomatic outlines of the ten years of Shawnee-British warfare with the help of colonial documents, it is much harder to grasp how the Natives experienced this tumultuous era and what lessons they drew from it. To understand Shawnee responses to the warfare and the new imperial landscape it created it is necessary to try to look beyond the standard diplomatic-military narrative and identify Native perspectives, goals, fears, and social processes. When this is done, one fundamental fact becomes immediately clear: the Shawnees had never experienced a war as total, sustained, and destructive as the one they fought against the British from 1755 to 1765. The warfare left its mark on every aspect of their communities, from demography to economy and spiritual life. Although Shawnees reaped great success on battlefields and were able to keep British and provincial troops at arm's length from their homes, they lost warriors and headmen in the violence. The warfare also disrupted normal subsistence activities so badly that "Starving Conditions" became all too familiar in Shawnee towns. The French could offer little help. In 1758 a British naval blockade of Canada once again all but ended French trade in the Ohio Valley and made the local Indians "a poor people," as one Shawnee admitted in 1760. The wartime privations and wide-ranging armies formed a potent combination for the spread of deadly epidemics. Smallpox ravaged the Great Lakes region in 1757 and then hit the Ohio Valley in 1762, when the Shawnees living along the Scioto River were "mostly Sick and some Dying every day." During Pontiac's War British officers at Fort Pitt deliberately spread the disease among their Indian enemies by giving infected blankets to visiting Native negotiators. While we will never know the exact figures, hundreds of Shawnees and their neighbors reportedly died in the epidemic that continued well into 1764. Such destruction seriously undermined the ability of local communities to feed and defend themselves. It also caused deep spiritual concern. In 1762, for example, some Shawnee elders thought that the smallpox was "sent from God upon them for they are very Proud."[7]

Shawnees came to understand these devastating, violent years as a historically decisive moment. Anglo-American colonists saw the British victory over New France as a sign of divine providence. The Shawnees, too, recognized that the Seven Years' War gave birth to a new geopolitical and spiritual order. But unlike the Anglo-Americans, who celebrated this new order and believed that it proved them to be God's chosen people, the Shawnees found the postwar world both politically and spiritually threatening. In 1760 the Ohio Shawnee orator Missiweakiwa explained at Fort Pitt that his people and their allies had taken up arms against the English five years earlier because the colonists had "[driven] us up here on the high Land; then the Indians of all Nations began to think, that our Brethren [the English] wanted to drive us entirely out of the Country." Two years later Indian agent George Croghan reported that Indians throughout the Ohio Country "begin more and more to dread our growing power." When the Shawnees heard that France had ceded their country to George III in 1763, they complained that "the English would soon be too great a People in this Country." They were echoed by Netawatwees (Newcomer), an important Lenape headman, who feared that the British had "grown too powerfull & seemd as if they would be too Strong for God himself."[8]

These words capture the urgent sense of ultimate territorial, political, and spiritual threat that the Shawnees and their neighbors felt when facing the British empire. It was a new threat that called for new solutions. Many Shawnee leaders now began to unite their numerous divisions, towns, and clans into an extensive coalition that would be strong enough to stand up to the British diplomatically and militarily. They drew on the webs of collaboration crafted by the previous generation of leaders, including Nucheconner and his allies. They also took inspiration from Native traditions that portrayed alliance and cooperation as a source of power. But the Shawnee leaders also invented new ways to bind Shawnee groups together. In the process they created a new vision of a united Shawnee nation.

The leaders of Lower Shawneetown had encouraged Shawnees to gather together since the late 1730s. When the fighting with the English broke out in the fall of 1755, they intensified these efforts. After Pennsylvanian troops destroyed Kittanning, a major Lenape town on the Allegheny River, in

September 1756, hundreds of Shawnees from Logstown and other vulnerable upper Ohio communities moved to the relative safety of Lower Shawneetown and its vicinity on the Scioto River. Two years later the headmen of the Ohio Shawnees "sent to bring all their people who have lived several years amongst the Creeks, home." Many Kishpokos moved from the Tallapoosa River to the Scioto, disturbed by their growing insecurity on the imperial borderlands of the Deep South. Lower Shawneetown leaders also sent similar messages to diasporic Shawnee communities living on the west side of the Mississippi, hoping to draw them to the Scioto. Shawnees kept coming from the east, too. When General Forbes's army was gathering in Pennsylvania in 1758, a small community of neutral Mekoches that had remained in the Wyoming Valley on the Susquehanna River fled to the Muskingum River under their hokima, Paxinosa. There they coalesced with many Upper Shawnee refugees, forming a new town called Wakatomika. By 1762 more than fifteen hundred Shawnees from various directions had congregated at two settlement clusters in the central Ohio Valley: the "lower" towns along the Scioto and the "upper" towns on the Muskingum. Violence, then, hammered disparate communities and kin groups physically together. Old alliances, kinship networks, and histories shaped the formation of these communities. The core of the Lower Shawnees, for example, descended from groups that had in the late seventeenth century settled on the Susquehanna and Delaware rivers and then congregated at Lower Shawneetown in the 1740s. In contrast, at least a portion of the people who founded Wakatomika traced their roots to the Potomac River.[9]

Regardless of their disparate backgrounds, the various Lower and Upper communities intensified their cooperation during the war against the British. Initially, it was military collaboration that drew them together. In their previous wars against Indian enemies the Shawnees' war parties had been small groups of ten to twelve warriors. Even though the Shawnees continued to rely largely on small-scale hit-and-run tactics against the English, they did occasionally collect much larger forces to strike major military targets. In 1756, for example, about two hundred Shawnees, Miamis, Wyandots, and Potawatomis captured Ephraim Vause's Fort in Virginia after an eight-hour firefight. In 1763 many Shawnees participated in the unsuccessful siege of Fort Pitt, as well as in a two-day battle with British regulars at Bushy Run. The next year they attacked Fort Dinwiddie in Virginia. The Shawnee forces in these encounters were so large that they must have consisted of men from several towns, clans, and divisions. Organizing and leading such military operations required considerable skill and effort. During the decade of warfare charismatic military leaders who were able to draw together men from several communities to fight the common British enemy emerged in the Shawnee towns. Men like the "Chief Captain" Miskapalathy (Red Hawk) gained wide popularity by demonstrating their spiritual power, bravery, and leadership abilities on the battlefield. In 1764 one British officer even claimed that "the Chiefs of their Warriors . . . have the principal authority" among the Shawnees. This was an exaggeration based on a lopsided British interest in the military organization of their Indian enemies, but Shawnee war leaders did muster considerable influence. During the war they led the discussions in town and tribal councils, where they sat in places of honor in the first row in front of hokimas. Moreover, the close social and emotional bonds forged on military expeditions between war leaders and warriors led one British agent to observe that "ye Warrers are Lead Intierly by what they [the war chiefs] Say."[10]

The collaboration of the Shawnees deepened when they tried to forge a peace with the British during the tense years from 1759 to 1763. Initially, the various Shawnee towns and factions sent their own delegations to negotiate with the Crown's officers at Fort Pitt. However, when the British assumed an increasingly domineering position in the negotiations after the fall of Niagara and Quebec, the Shawnee peace delegations grew in size, as several communities and factions joined together to impress the English with their strength. Envoys also began to evoke symbols of national unity and speak in the name of *all* Shawnees. For example, in April 1760 some 130 Shawnee men and women, by far the largest delegation thus far, visited Fort Pitt where the Mekoche orator Missiweakiwa claimed to speak "in behalf of all my nation."[11]

Intertown councils again played a key role in the widening Shawnee cooperation. By the early 1760s increasing numbers of Shawnees agreed that peace and war with the British were such critical issues that they should be decided collectively by all local and kin groups in joint meetings. Thus, when "the Principal Shawnee Warriors" negotiated with George Croghan at Fort Pitt in March 1761, they explained that they could make no binding answers to his talks before "taking your Speeches to our Towns and laying them before our Council." Two years later the Mekoche hokima Kisinoutha (Hardman) and two other headmen, Dominiska and Leaguisicka, promised that they would discuss the latest British peace proposals in "a gineral Councel of all our Nations." Clearly, the Shawnees sought to unite as many leaders, clans, towns, and divisions as possible behind collective decisions. In the early 1760s making a lasting peace with the threatening empire became a common goal that drew the various groups together.[12]

The widening Shawnee cooperation in the peace negotiations was organized by a new generation of hokimas. Nucheconner, Laypareawah, Kakewatchiky, Paxinosa, Kishacoquillas, and several other prominent prewar headmen had died during the conflict. They were succeeded by a cohort of younger leaders, often their direct descendants. Kisinoutha, a Mekoche headman who had taken a prominent position in the peace process by 1759, was the son of Kakewatchiky, the old hokima who had first led the Mekoches from the Wyoming Valley to the Ohio. Kisinoutha often joined forces with Nimwha and Colesquo (Cornstalk), who were the sons or grandsons of Paxinosa, another headman originally from the Wyoming Valley. When organizing the peace talks with the Crown officers, these young hokimas collaborated closely with Miskapalathy and other popular military leaders. From 1759 to 1765 Shawnee peace delegations usually consisted of both hokimas and war chiefs. Because these groups of leaders had differing social roles, their followings were probably somewhat different. As aggressive defenders of their communities, the military leaders enjoyed most support from young men for whom warfare formed an important part of masculine identity and a path to social prestige. Hokimas, in turn, were expected to cultivate good relations with outsiders calmly and patiently. Therefore, their leadership may have appealed to groups that felt more vulnerable than warriors in the turmoil of war, such as women and old men. The cooperation of hokimas and war chiefs from different towns thus drew together various communities and kin groups, the men and the women, as well as the young and the old. In Shawnee eyes, such broad support greatly strengthened the legitimacy of any diplomatic embassy. The collaboration also reflected the Shawnee belief that decisions as important as peace-making required the consent of all social groups: old men, young men, and women. Unity was possible only by building consensus among different kinds of people.[13]

The new Shawnee leaders remained first and foremost clan leaders and conceived themselves as such. In 1765, for instance, Shawnee delegates in a council at Johnson Hall signed a peace treaty with the British with pictures of their clan eponyms. Yet the Shawnee leaders also constructed new political roles to organize their growing cooperation. Most dramatically, they nominated one of their number, Kisinoutha, to be the ceremonial head of the entire Shawnee nation. Kisinoutha was a Mekoche, the hokima of Raccoon clan. His roots went back to the Wyoming Valley and Logstown, but by the time he rose to prominence he lived in the lower towns on the Scioto. In the early 1760s Kisinoutha became the leading Shawnee diplomat in the negotiations with the British. Impressed by what they mistook as his great personal power, the colonists dubbed him the "King" of Shawnees, just as they had done to Nucheconner twenty-five years earlier. Kisinoutha was, of course, no more a monarch than Nucheconner had been, but he seems to have been something more than a tribal orator. For the next fifteen years he would lead Shawnee delegations in treaties with Anglo-Americans, speak (or claim to speak) on behalf of all Shawnees, and call national council meetings at his home town on the Scioto. It appears that after 1760 several Shawnee communities acknowledged Kisinoutha as their collective hokima, a leader who would represent them to outsiders and ritually cultivate peace between them and the British. Many towns and clans grouped behind him to demonstrate their unity to the British. Kisinoutha was certainly a good choice for such a role. As a hereditary hokima he had a strong claim to legitimate authority. Through his father he had extensive kinship connections among the Scioto, Logstown, Wyoming Valley, and Wakatomika Shawnees. This made him well placed to unite the Upper and Lower Shawnees. Finally, because Kakewatchiky and the Mekoches had always maintained friendly relations with Pennsylvanians, it was easy for Kisinoutha to take a symbolic lead in the peace negotiations with the British and convince the Crown's officers of the goodwill of his followers.[14]

Kisinoutha's new status combined tradition and innovation. Even when heading delegations that drew together Shawnees from the Scioto, Muskingum, Logstown, and Wyoming Valley, he portrayed himself as a traditional hokima who simply built consensus among clan leaders, war chiefs, women, and elders and voiced their unanimous decisions to outsiders. Rather than claiming any personal authority, he once explained that he spoke for "our great men." Kisinoutha relied heavily on his wide kinship networks to foster unity among disparate communities. In colonial documents he appears consistently in the company of other prestigious Mekoche leaders, especially the war chiefs Miskapalathy and Oweeconnee (Shade) and Paxinosa's descendant Nimwha. As Mekoches, all of these men were closely connected, and some of them probably shared even more intimate clan and family ties. The support of such powerful relatives, each with followers of his own, helped Kisinoutha to unite people and promote consensus in council discussions.[15]

Even though Shawnee cooperation was deeply based on kinship and Native traditions of collective decision-making, it was also driven by British pressure. When Kisinoutha and other leaders tried to negotiate a peace with the Crown officers in the early 1760s, the English insisted on treating them like the central government of a hierarchical, unified nation. Desperate to end the expensive Indian war, colonial officials longed to locate a clear nexus of power among the unruly Shawnee communities. They wanted to find a national leadership that would conclude a peace on behalf of the nation and then enforce it among the Shawnees. Time and again military officers and Indian agents demanded that Shawnee diplomats make binding promises and sign treaties "for themselves & the whole of their Nation." They took hostages and placed trade embargos to force all towns and warriors to abide by the treaties negotiated by individual headmen. When Kisinoutha together with Lenape and Seneca diplomats explained in 1764 that they could only persuade, not command, their people to accept British peace terms, Colonel Henry Bouquet thundered, "it is your duty to chastize them when they do wrong, & not suffer yourselves to be directed by them." Shawnee chiefs balked at such demands. They continued to understand leadership as persuasion, not as coercion. But Shawnee leaders also understood that they needed to persuade all their people to comply with reasonable English peace conditions, for otherwise the aggressive empire might take indiscriminate revenge on all Shawnees. British pressure thus shaped Shawnee unification, even though the colonists did not dictate the process.[16]

Colonial policies forced Shawnee leaders to try to assert collective national leadership in issues that had been traditionally regarded as local and clan affairs. This sparked divisive conflicts over legitimate power in the Native communities. The most serious of these surrounded the colonial captives the Shawnees took during the Seven Years' and Pontiac's wars from the border settlements of Virginia and Pennsylvania. Between 1755 and 1764 warriors captured as many as 285 colonists, mainly women and children. Although some of the prisoners were killed, sold to other tribes or the French, or kept as slaves, most were adopted into Shawnee clans, often to replace recently deceased clan members. Whether slaves or adoptees, all captives were considered "a property of the Familys they live with." Elderly Shawnee women wielded most power over the fate of the captives. When warriors brought new prisoners into a town, it was the local hokima wiikwes who decided whether they should be adopted or killed ritually. The older women of a clan probably also selected captives for adoption and introduced them into their new webs of relatives.[17]

Although many adopted captives, especially young children, became so fully enculturated into the Shawnee communities that they were unwilling to return to their old homes even when given the chance, British officials made the delivery of all "prisoners" a principal condition of peace in the early 1760s. In order to keep the difficult peace process alive and to shield their people from British retaliation, Shawnee leaders like Kisinoutha and Miskapalathy time and again promised that they would return all captives, even though they knew perfectly well that they had no power to force clans and clan matrons to "free" adoptees who were seen as "our own Flesh and Blood." When the headmen tried to persuade their tribespeople to hand in the captives, bitter arguments broke out in Shawnee towns. In 1761 George Croghan reported that the communities on the Muskingum River were "in the utmost Confusion about our prisnors." Two years later Shawnee leaders, desperate to keep the ailing peace process alive, "pleaded Exceedingly in Councils for Delivering up ye Prisoners, telling the Indians they were Blind & Stupified & [k]new nothing hardly." Clearly, constructing collective leadership for traditionally autonomous clans and towns caused what some war chiefs described as "some Confusion in our own affairs." Shawnees needed to determine how autonomous, egalitarian kin and local groups could make collective decisions on difficult, deeply divisive issues without sacrificing their ideal of power as persuasion.[18]

As so often before, Shawnees relied on sharing power, collective decision-making, and compromises. Leaders strove to unite disparate towns, clans, and factions by actively encouraging compromises that were so flexible that even groups with radically divergent opinions could at least temporarily join together to support them. Similarly, they allowed dissenting groups and leaders to try out opposing strategies, whose merits were then compared and debated in tribal councils until one strategy emerged as the most successful one and most leaders, clans, and communities were prepared to embrace it. This could take months or even years, leading many scholars to view Shawnee politics in terms of permanent and disruptive factionalism rather than as a slow but consistent quest for consensus. For Shawnees, national consolidation did not mean the creation of a powerful central government that would impose its will on the people. Rather, it meant that the local and kin groups maintained a façade of unity against outsiders and kept up intensive communication with one another, constantly seeking unity through discussion and compromises.

Shawnee strategies for constructing unity in dangerous circumstances surfaced most vividly in the difficult negotiations in 1764 and 1765 that finally ended Pontiac's War. In the summer of 1764 two large British armies, in total almost twenty-five hundred troops commanded by Colonel Henry Bouquet and Colonel John Bradstreet, prepared to invade the Ohio Country in an effort to crush the hostile Indians. Divided, the Shawnees deployed two contrasting strategies to survive the invasion. In July sixty Shawnees and Lenapes, led by a fervently anti-British leader known as Charlot Kaské, traveled first to Fort de Chartres on the Mississippi River and then to New Orleans to plead military assistance from the French, who still occupied these locations. Four months later, when this delegation was still on its way, Kisinoutha led another envoy, composed predominantly of his Mekoche kinsmen, to negotiate with Bouquet, who had led his army to the gates of the Shawnee country on the Muskingum River. Feigning submission, the Mekoches succeeded in negotiating a truce with Bouquet without making any substantial concessions to the English. Although they delivered about forty captives and some hostages to the colonel, they promised only vaguely that the rest of their hundred or so prisoners would be returned "as soon as we can carry them." In private, Bouquet cursed the Shawnees for being "very Obstinate," but approaching winter and dwindling supplies left him little choice but to accept the Mekoches' token symbols of goodwill and return to Fort Pitt.[19]

Bouquet took the Shawnee "obstinacy" as a sign of their persistent hostility. In fact, it only reflected the normal process of Shawnee national decision-making. Although Kisinoutha's Mekoche embassy had negotiated a truce with Bouquet, they could not impose it on other communities without consulting them. They were especially "unwilling to take so much upon them" before hearing the results of Charlot Kaské's visit to the French. This finally happened in early 1765, when some of Kaské's companions returned to the Scioto. Now armed with more information on the various options open for their people, the Shawnee leaders "called a Council of their whole Nation" to discuss the alternative courses of action with one another and their Lenape, Seneca, and Wyandot allies. There they "determined that the measures entered into with Colonel Bouquet should be performed on their part provided the English on their part would open a Trade with them and convince them by their future Conduct of their Sincerity."[20] Once again, groups with differing opinions had been allowed to experiment with divergent strategies. Once again, local and clan leaders had finally united behind what seemed like the most promising course of action after a long round of comparison, debate, and compromise. And once again, the decision hammered out in the tribal council was such a flexible compromise—a conditional peace whose future depended on British conduct—that Shawnees with widely differing opinions could for the moment join to support it.

The final peace between the Ohio Indians and Great Britain was concluded formally in two large conferences in Fort Pitt and Johnson Hall (on the Mohawk River in what is now upstate New York) in May and July 1765. On both occasions Shawnee diplomats did their best to demonstrate the unity of their nation to the British. The Shawnee delegations that traveled to Fort Pitt and Johnson Hall consisted of leaders representing several clans, communities, and factions who emphasized their unity by speaking to the British through a single orator. At Fort Pitt the Shawnee embassy of more than one hundred headmen, women, warriors, and children "came over the [Ohio] River" to the fort "beating a Drum and singing their peace song, agreeable to the Ancient Custom of their Nation, which they continued till they entered the Council House." Although more detailed descriptions of this ceremonial procession do not exist, later evidence suggests that it was led by Kisinoutha, other important hokimas, and ceremonial dancers. They were followed by war leaders and warriors, while women and children, led by the most prominent Peace Women, brought up the rear. Afterwards, the Shawnee speaker Lawoughgua gave the British a large wampum belt "with a figure of our Father, the King of Great Britain, at one end, and the Chief of our Nation at the other . . . holding the Chain of Friendship." A single ceremonial procession, a single peace belt, and a figure of a single "Chief" now symbolized all allied Shawnee clans, towns, and divisions.[21]

Cooperation and symbols did not magically transform Shawnees into a united nation in 1765; many divisions remained, both old and new. Charlot Kaské, for example, declared that "he will never love [the English] nor make a peace with them." The recalcitrant headman moved across the Mississippi to Spanish-claimed territory where he continued to encourage local Indians and French settlers against British efforts to occupy Illinois. The divisive conflict between tribal leaders and clans over the English captives was never settled; it merely ceased to be an issue when the war-weary Crown officers simply closed their eyes to the fact that Shawnees continued to hold at least fifty of their adopted prisoners even after 1765.[22] But despite the many enduring fault lines among the Shawnees, most of their leaders were now committed to political consolidation. As they saw it, only unity could preserve them from the formidable empire that shadowed their country.

IMAGINING THE SHAWNEE NATION

Political cooperation alone does not transform a group of people into a "nation." Instead, people have to *imagine* themselves as a nation: they must create symbolic expressions of unity that link them together, bestow a common identity on them, and define other groups as outsiders.[23] This is precisely what the Shawnees did during the 1760s. As the symbols of unity the Shawnee diplomats mobilized at the Fort Pitt conference in May 1765 suggest, the growing Shawnee cooperation was not simply a desperate response to a geopolitical crisis. On the contrary, political consolidation represented a creative Native reinterpretation of what made the various Mekoche, Chalaakaatha, Pekowi, Thawikila, and Kishpoko communities the Shawnee people and what being a Shawnee meant. Consolidation was certainly a crucial survival strategy in the new imperial landscape, but it stemmed from Indigenous initiative and culture. In the 1760s and early 1770s Shawnee leaders redefined Shawnee nationhood by rethinking three key issues: the relations among the five Shawnee divisions, national history, and Shawnee relations to land.

The relationships among the Mekoches, Chalaakaathas, Pekowis, Kishpokos, and Thawikilas constitute one of the most perplexing problems of Shawnee politics during this period. It is clear that people from all five divisions gathered together in the central Ohio Valley and engaged in extensive military and diplomatic collaboration during the 1760s. Yet we know very little about how the divisions organized their cooperation. Colonial documents seldom even mention the divisions, let alone discuss their relations with one another. A careful analysis of the family backgrounds and kinship relations of Shawnee leaders nevertheless reveals that most of the headmen who led the Shawnees' peace negotiations with the British and later strove most vigorously to uphold the peace were Mekoches. In addition to Kisinoutha, such Mekoche leaders and diplomats included at least Nimwha, Colesquo, Miskapalathy, Missiweakiwa, and Oweeconnee. From the 1770s on, Mekoche headmen often appear in colonial records to claim that the Mekoches were the "Principal Tribe" or the "King Tribe" of the Shawnees. Well into the nineteenth century they insisted that they had the right to lead the entire Shawnee nation. In 1795 Catahecassa, Biaseka, and Red-Faced Fellow even explained to British officers that just like the fact that only an heir of George III could become the king of Great Britain, "none but a person of our Tribe could be king" among the Shawnees.[24]

This evidence seems to suggest that hierarchical relations evolved among the Shawnee divisions during the 1760s, with the Mekoches assuming the leadership of the consolidating nation. Yet when the colonial treaties, correspondence, and other papers describe actual Shawnee politics during this period, they paint a picture of egalitarian cooperation among the various communities that continued to share power and make consensual decisions in collective councils. To solve this apparent contradiction one must turn to Native oral histories. In the 1920s Thomas Wildcat Alford, a tribal official at the Pekowi-Kishpoko-Thawikila community in Oklahoma, wrote down oral histories he had learned from elders several decades before. One of these histories tells about the dark and dangerous times during the Seven Years' and Pontiac's wars. According to Alford, the two devastating wars "led to secret councils among the chiefs of the several clans, or septs [divisions], composing the tribe or nation, and to consulting the meaning of the *Meesawmi* which each clan [division] possessed. . . . These secret councils lasted several years, and finally grew into general councils of the tribes in which discussions were made as to what should be done for their future welfare, in order to survive."[25]

This account resembles Shawnee origin legends in which the Mekoches, Chalaakaathas, Pekowis, Kishpokos, and Thawikilas ally and determine their relationships, rights, and duties on the basis of the specific nature of their respective miišaamis. Alford's history suggests that when the British empire threatened Shawnee lands and autonomy in the early 1760s, Native leaders drew inspiration from traditional origin stories and tried to bind their divisions together by the reciprocal sharing of miišaami. For Shawnees, sharing sacred power through ritual formed an established way for uniting disparate communities. In the crisis of the early 1760s the miišaami of the Mekoches seems to have looked especially valuable to many Shawnees. Several nineteenth-century ethnographies associate the Mekoche miišaami with purification, health, and the color white. These were all sacred activities and attributes that both Shawnees and other eastern Indians considered essential for peace-making. In the dire geopolitical, territorial, and spiritual predicament the Shawnees united behind the Mekoches and expected them to mobilize their sacred power to neutralize the threat of the British empire by negotiating a peace for all Shawnees. This arrangement continued the traditional ideal of the Shawnee people as a confederacy whose members used their miišaamis to benefit one another. Moreover, the role of peace-maker made sense to important Mekoche leaders like Kisinoutha and Nimwha, partly because of divisional traditions but also because their families had a long history of accommodation with Pennsylvanians.[26]

Peace-making clearly did not make Mekoches "kings" in any European sense. Since the Mekoches' role as the collective peace-makers of the Shawnee nation nevertheless certainly underlies their subsequent claims to national leadership, it is essential to analyze how the Mekoches understood this role. This was best explained by Catahecassa, Biaseka, and Red-Faced Fellow when they recounted Shawnee history to British officers in 1795. The three headmen based the Mekoche claims to political prominence on spiritual power. They began their history by narrating how the Creator had long ago given the Mekoche ancestors a spiritually powerful "Kings song." This almost certainly refers to miišaami, for Shawnee traditions describe singing as an integral part of the rituals where miišaami is mobilized. According to Catahecassa, Biaseka, and Red-Faced Fellow, the "Kings song" made the Mekoches "the Chief of all the Tribes & King over the other nations." The translation is ambiguous, however. It is not clear which words the headmen used for such critical concepts as "King" and "Chief" or what they meant by distinguishing "Tribes" from "nations." Therefore, it is instructive to see how Catahecassa, Biaseka, and Red-Faced Fellow later in the narrative detailed what being "the Chief of all the Tribes" entailed. Sounding much less like monarchists now, they explained that in the peace-making in the early 1760s the Mekoches had become "the people whom [King George] depended upon" to guard the Royal Proclamation boundary between the Shawnees and the British empire. It was their duty to "push . . . gently back" all Anglo-Americans who might try to cross the border and "speak mildly to them to preserve peace." Rather than kings, the Mekoches portrayed themselves as the protectors of the Shawnee-British peace. Their task was to take care of the alliance with the threatening empire on behalf of the entire nation. In effect, they acted like national hokimas.[27]

It is understandable that colonial officials coming from a centralized and hierarchical kingdom may have easily mistaken the Mekoches' role as national peace-makers for "kingship." But it is undeniable that Mekoches sometimes jealously guarded their prerogative to negotiate with the British and insisted that other Shawnees should follow their leadership in colonial affairs. Cultivating peace with an aggressive and expansionist empire forced the Mekoches to assume a domineering position among the Shawnees. To keep the peace they had to argue, like Catahecassa and his companions reminisced, that "Our Warriors which the Great Spirit has given us must listen to our advice." As the bitter arguments over the return of the colonial captives show, the Mekoches had to interfere in matters that had long been deemed clan or town affairs. To validate their right to do so, Mekoche leaders evoked both their divisional miišaami and age, claiming to be "very ancient" and "the first born" of the Shawnee divisions. Other divisions often challenged such interpretations. While they accepted the Mekoche leadership in the peace negotiations in the

1760s, they continued to conceive the Shawnee nation as an egalitarian alliance of the five divisions, bound together by kinship and sacred power. The Chalaakaathas in particular contested the Mekoche claims of seniority, instead insisting that they were the "grandfathers" of the other divisions. In the 1770s some colonial visitors also described the main Chalaakaatha community on the Scioto River as "the chief town" of the Shawnees. Paradoxically, the dispute between the Chalaakaathas and Mekoches demonstrates that both groups agreed that the Shawnees formed a single nation. They simply disagreed about who held the legitimate right to collective national leadership.[28]

Evolving notions of Shawnee nationhood are also evident in the ways in which Shawnees stored historical documents in the latter half of the eighteenth century. Ever since the sixteenth century the exchange of wampum belts and strings, made of interwoven marine shell beads, had formed an integral element of Indian diplomacy across northeastern North America. In international meetings a speaker would always give a belt or a string of wampum to his audience after each major point of his talk. Each belt or string thus represented a particular speech, proposition, or agreement made between two groups and served to remind the recipient of it. As sacred objects, wampum beads testified to the sincerity of the speaker and legitimated treaties. Native leaders stored the belts and strings they had received in a special "Council Bag," sometimes called a "public treasury" by Euroamericans. Among many peoples, such as the Haudenosaunees and Lenapes, this collection was under the care of a designated wampum keeper, a chief "noted for his memory and upright character who . . . could 'read' the belts and teach ongoing generations." When leaders wanted to remind themselves, their followers, or other communities of an agreement made in the past, they took the belts embodying that agreement out of the council bag and publicly "read" them, that is, recounted the talks attached to each belt. When European colonists introduced paper documents in Indian diplomacy, these too soon found their way to Native council bags. Indian leaders began to display treaties and letters in international conferences to remind all parties of their message.[29]

It is not known who kept the historical archives in Shawnee communities before the 1760s. Given the independence of the widely scattered Shawnee towns during the diaspora of the late seventeenth and early eighteenth centuries, it is likely that each town had its own wampum keeper or a place, possibly in the council house, where the locals gathered all the belts and other documents that the town's various leaders had received in negotiations with outsiders.[30] When political cooperation among the Shawnee groups intensified in the early 1760s, leaders began collecting the historical records of several communities under the care of Mekoche headmen. When Kisinoutha and other Mekoche leaders opened peace talks with Colonel Bouquet on the

Muskingum River in November 1764, their speaker Miskapalathy displayed an impressive collection of historical documents. Hoping to remind Bouquet of the long history of friendship between the Shawnees and the English, Miskapalathy showed him "A Treaty held with them in April 21th, 1711 [1701]; A Message from Governor Gordon, December 4th, 1750; A Letter from Thomas Penn, Jany. 18th, 1732; [and] Another Letter from Governor Thomas, 15th August, 1742."[31]

These papers represented a collection of documents from many Shawnee communities. The first was a treaty concluded by the Pekowis of Pequa with Pennsylvania; the second had been sent to the Chalaakaatha, Thawikila, and other headmen living on Conemaugh Creek (in 1731 rather than 1750); and the fourth had been addressed collectively to Nucheconner, the Pekowi speaker of the Ohio Shawnees, and Kakewatchiky, the hokima of the Wyoming Mekoches. By 1764, then, Mekoche headmen kept, or at least had an access to, the archives of several divisions and towns. The wampum belts that the British officers gave to the Shawnees when the final peace treaty was made in 1765 also found their way to the possession of the Mekoche headmen. The Mekoches' role as the guardians of the Shawnees' new alliance with the British empire meant that past and present documents recording this alliance were collected under their care. This certainly strengthened Mekoche authority in Shawnee politics. The Shawnee term for wampum was *hogema betswagi*, or "Chief beads." The name implies that Shawnees associated wampum and the possession of belts with political leadership. Even more importantly, gathering wampum belts, letters, and paper treaties from various communities to one place demonstrates that the Shawnees had begun to conceptualize the individual histories of the different towns and divisions as a collective national story.[32]

In addition to history, in the 1760s land became a crucial symbol and a spiritual and material resource that bound Shawnees together. By 1765 the Shawnees had fought for their Ohio homelands for a decade. During the warfare numerous Shawnee groups, scattered across eastern North America since their late-seventeenth-century dispersal, had gathered together in the region lying between the Scioto and Muskingum rivers. This process continued after the Shawnees had concluded the peace with the British. In 1769 messengers from the Ohio Valley traveled east to the Susquehanna River and invited the few remaining eastern Shawnee communities to move west with them. Threatened by a recent Haudenosaunee cession of their homelands on the Susquehanna, most of the easterners took up the offer and made their way to the Ohio. Other groups moved to the central Ohio Valley from the Deep South. At least one Thawikila band apparently settled on the Scioto. All migrants did not come to stay. In 1774 the Irish-Shawnee Indian agent Alexander McKee met a Shawnee headman from the Deep South in Fort Pitt. The chief explained that he was "only upon a Visit from the Creek Country which is my home and where I intend to return in a short time." But even though many diasporic communities remained in the South and elsewhere, most Shawnees now conceived the central Ohio Valley as their collective homeland.[33]

The Shawnees had not experienced such spatial concentration for almost a century. They identified with the country between the Scioto and Muskingum rivers both spiritually and politically. During the 1760s and 1770s Shawnee orators repeatedly explained to Anglo-Americans that the Creator had given them this land and that it had to be clearly separated from British territory. "God Who made all things gave us this Country and brought us through this Ground, he gave you a Country beyond the Great Water," declared Missiweakiwa at Fort Pitt in 1760. "This Country . . . is the Property of us Indians," continued Nimwha eight years later. In 1776 Colesquo elaborated that Shawnees "esteem[ed]" "our Lands" as "our heart." This was not a mere emotional metaphor. Shawnee creation myths told that the Creator had put the Shawnees at "the centre of this Island . . . for the heart of the Earth" to "hold [the world] steady." Even the Shawnee headman visiting the Ohio Valley from the Creek country observed that "the Great God who made us all gave them [the Ohio Shawnees] this Country, so that it is natural for them to endeavor to take Care of it." A profound spiritual bond attached Shawnees to the Ohio land.[34]

Missiweakiwa's and Nimwha's words reveal a growing Shawnee interest in national borders. When the British empire claimed the territory between the Atlantic and the Mississippi after the Seven Years' War, Shawnees and other Indian peoples throughout the East began drawing boundaries of their own. Time and again Shawnee diplomats argued that a sacred boundary—what the Mekoche headmen would call "the Line" in 1795—separated Native country from British territory. The Shawnees also had clear notions of borders between them and the other Indian nations. They claimed the land between the Muskingum and Scioto as "the whole Shawanese Country," even if they were willing to share the resources of the land with their allies, especially the Lenapes and Ohio Iroquois. Many colonists were aware of these borders. When Moravian missionary David Zeisberger traveled from the Lenape towns on the Tuscarawas River to the Shawnee communities on the Muskingum, he recorded in his diary how the small hamlets spread across the landscape gradually changed from predominantly Lenape villages to predominantly Shawnee ones. At the main Shawnee settlement on the Muskingum Zeisberger remarked that he had "reached the *Shawnee* border now, because their *District* begins here." According to him, between the Muskingum and the Scioto there were "many other *Towns*, all *Shawnee*." This was an exaggeration, for many of the settlements were actually multiethnic communities where Lenapes, Ohio Iroquois, and other Indians lived together with Shawnees. Nevertheless, for Zeisberger all these towns fell under Shawnee authority because they were located on Shawnee lands.[35]

In the late seventeenth century the diasporic Shawnees had conceptualized North America as a vast "kinscape" crisscrossed by kinship networks that connected far-flung communities and individuals. In the 1760s the Shawnees gathering in the central Ohio Valley envisioned a "bordered land," where an explicit "Line" divided their sacred country from the British empire. Their views of landscape, as well as history, were increasingly oriented toward the nation.[36]

CHALLENGING THE EMPIRE

In 1765 most Shawnees agreed that broad intertown and interdivisional cooperation offered the best security against the British empire. Within just a few years, however, they came to disagree whether diplomacy or military resistance was the most efficient method for dealing with the continuing imperial threat. Many Shawnees also began to suspect the particular forms their national consolidation was taking. Some felt uncomfortable with the Mekoche claims to leadership. Others were troubled when men and women claiming national leadership tried to assert power regarding issues that traditionally had been under town and clan control. From the late 1760s through 1775 fierce political debates divided Shawnee communities, threatening their new unity. At stake was not only the nation's relationship with the empire, but also political order among the Shawnee people.

These debates rose from the particular dilemmas facing the Shawnees after 1765, but they were rooted in profound long-term social and economic transformations in Shawnee communities that obstructed the efforts of Kisinoutha and his allies to unite the various clans and communities behind a collective leadership. The most important of these changes was the dispersal of two large Shawnee communities, Lower Shawneetown and Wakatomika. During the Seven Years' War these towns had constituted the foci for the physical gathering of the diverse Shawnee bands. Long the major center for Shawnees and Shawnee cooperation, Lower Shawneetown reportedly had more than one thousand inhabitants in 1757. This undoubtedly put strong pressure on such critical local resources as firewood and farmland. The next year the large town was abandoned because the locals feared that its location on the Ohio made the settlement too exposed to English attacks. The people now moved higher up on the Scioto River. Instead of rebuilding their massive town there, they established a number of smaller communities spread out along the river. In 1762 a visiting British officer, Thomas Hutchins, found two towns "in A very large Savannah" on the opposite sides of the Scioto, "about A Mile" apart.

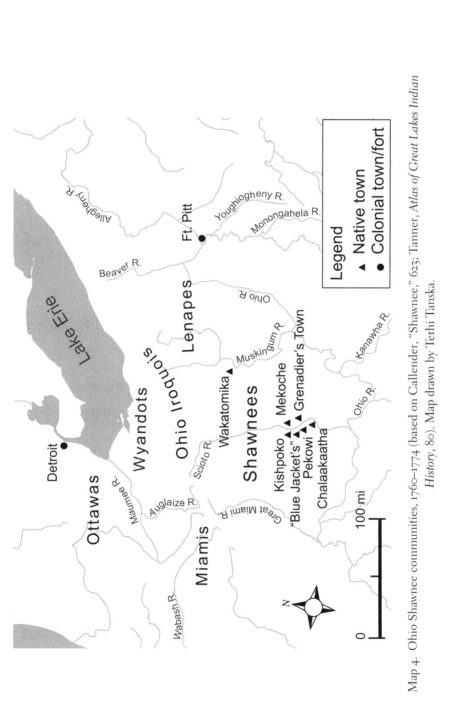

Map 4. Ohio Shawnee communities, 1760–1774 (based on Callender, "Shawnee," 623; Tanner, *Atlas of Great Lakes Indian History*, 80). Map drawn by Terhi Tanska.

Eleven years later there were at least five Shawnee towns on the Scioto and its tributaries. Many of the new communities, such as "Pickaweeke" and "Chillicaathee," bore divisional names, which makes it likely that Lower Shawneetown had first fragmented along divisional lines. With time, even some of the division-based settlements had broken up, as smaller groups of kinspeople had left to establish new villages, often around a charismatic or wealthy leader. Similar fragmentation occurred along the Muskingum. In 1762 Hutchins described a single Shawnee town, Wakatomika, on the river, but by 1774 there were six much smaller communities in the region. Most of the new settlements consisted of only four or five houses. By the early 1770s numerous tiny Shawnee hamlets also dotted the countryside between the Scioto and Muskingum.[37]

While the war had pushed the Shawnees to settle together, the peace with Great Britain contributed to the settlement fission after 1765. Many of the new small communities were established by people who were successful in exploiting trade and other new economic opportunities created by the peace. Several of them were women. In 1764 "Grenadier Squaw," the sister of the Mekoche headmen Nimwha and Colesquo, had her own town on the Scioto where she engaged in cattle-raising and rum traffic. Nine years later on the Muskingum, missionary David Jones visited "a small town consisting of Delawares and Shawannees," where "the chief is a Shawannee woman, who is esteemed very rich." This woman, probably a Mekoche named Anipassicowa, owned African American slaves and a "large stock" and specialized in provisioning travelers with milk and corn at what Jones considered "a very expensive price." Back on the Scioto a young Pekowi trader and war leader, Sepettekenathé (Blue Jacket), founded a new community outside Pickaweeke. The Shawnee relatives of the Indian agent Alexander McKee also lived in a community of their own, called Wockachaalli, where they prospered in cattle-raising. Many women and young men, then, relied on trade and new livelihoods to construct autonomous spaces for themselves and their kin. The very existence of their prosperous towns posed a challenge to the efforts by Kisinoutha and his allies to unify the Shawnees. Communities like Wockachaalli and Sepettekenathé's town provided competing foci for political allegiances and personal identities and fostered the development of disparate localized interests. They likewise separated the most prominent Shawnee leaders physically from some of their supposed followers. This was crucial in an oral society, where leaders influenced people principally with the help of "fair words" and personal example. Such strategies needed constant face-to-face interaction to be effective.[38]

Divergent interests and identities led to divergent opinions about the proper relations among the numerous Shawnee towns. The Scioto and Muskingum communities in particular disagreed about Shawnee consolidation and the political relations it entailed. Ever since the founding of Lower Shawneetown in the late 1730s, its leaders had sought to gather Shawnees together. Following the old prewar pattern, in the 1760s most of the men advocating Shawnee unity and claiming national leadership hailed from the lower towns on the Scioto. In contrast, many inhabitants of Wakatomika and other Muskingum settlements were more ambiguous about national consolidation. They were happy to collaborate with the Lower Shawnees in diplomacy and warfare but insisted that they retained the right to make their own decisions. Most importantly, the Upper Shawnees claimed the right to deal with the British independently. Twice in a critical situation during the peace-making, in 1762 and 1764, Wakatomika's headmen carefully explained to the English that their followers were distinct from the people of the lower towns and that they, unlike the Scioto Shawnees, were willing to make peace and return their captives. In 1774 Wakatomikans attacked the Scioto headmen even more dramatically. This time they claimed to Sir William Johnson, the British superintendent of Indian affairs, that the Lower Shawnees were planning a war against the English. In his report of the incident Johnson called the Upper Shawnees "Wakatawicks." Considering how unusual it was for Crown officers to refer to individual Shawnee groups with town or divisional names, Johnson's choice of words underlines the seriousness of the rift between the Upper and Lower Shawnees and may follow the language of the Wakatomikan leaders. The incident demonstrates a persistent fault line between the Muskingum and Scioto communities.[39]

The unity of the Shawnees was most seriously eroded by disagreements over the best policy for dealing with the threat the British empire continued to pose to their lands. In 1765 most towns, clans, warriors, and women had supported the peace negotiated by the Mekoche headmen because they were "Tired of the late War" and understood the peace treaty as strictly conditional. Within just a few years, however, it became clear that many Anglo-Americans would not abide by these conditions. The Shawnees and the British understood the peace of 1765 in fundamentally different ways. While the Natives saw the Seven Years' and Pontiac's wars as Indian victories, or at least draws that guaranteed Native ownership of the Ohio Country, most Pennsylvanians and Virginians considered themselves the victors. They saw the Indian lands as conquered territory and ignored the Royal Proclamation boundary in a rush to stake claims to the Trans-Appalachian country. By the late 1760s thousands of hunters, squatters, and land speculators, especially from Virginia, had surged to Fort Pitt, the Monongahela River, and present-day Kentucky—all important Shawnee, Lenape, and Ohio Iroquois hunting lands.[40]

Shawnees disagreed on how they should handle the dangerous situation. Many saw peaceful diplomacy as the only sensible way to contain the British threat. Others pointed out that the Shawnees and their Indian allies had already twice beaten the encroaching colonists to a standstill and advocated military resistance. We do not know exactly who composed these accommodationist and militant factions. As the guardians of the Shawnee-British peace and boundary, the Mekoche headmen Kisinoutha, Miskapalathy, Nimwha, and Colesquo consistently advocated diplomacy. Although British documents are largely silent on Shawnee headwomen, tantalizing bits of evidence suggest that many Peace Women also supported the peace with the empire. Given their authority to stop war parties, Peace Women must have played a central role already in the Shawnee-British peace process in 1759–1765. Scattered references to elderly women protecting Anglo-American visitors in Shawnee towns, speaking for peace in councils, and maintaining a friendly correspondence with colonial agents testify that such support continued after 1765. One who benefited from the Peace Women's efforts was David Jones, a Presbyterian preacher who visited the Scioto towns in 1773. After the arrogant Jones had promptly infuriated his hosts by insisting that "God gave us the right way," his life was saved by Shawnee women at least twice. On the second occasion, an enraged warrior threatened to kill Jones, when "a very noted person of this nation, called the *Blinking* Woman" and "two or three squaas" stepped in and "said something in [Jones's] favour," in terms strong enough to send the warrior packing in "apprehension" that he might be "roughly treated" by these women. Less dramatically but just as importantly, Cawechile, the "head woman of the Mequache Tribe," cultivated friendly relations with Pennsylvanian traders and officials.[41]

It is less clear who constituted the militant element in the Shawnee communities. The Mekoche headmen often derailed more militant Shawnees as "young men." Historians should not take such claims at face value, however. Shawnees associated youth with inexperience and rashness; young men were thought to be "foolish," "rash," and "unthinking." However, the Shawnee word for a young man, *mayaanileni*, was also used as a metaphor for "a common Indian," that is, a person who was not a leader. Rather than denoting simply biological age, mayaanileni was a politically loaded term. Calling someone a young man meant claiming authority over him and questioning his ability to make responsible decisions. When Kisinoutha and his Mekoche allies claimed that their militant opponents were "foolish young men," we should not assume that they were necessarily biologically young. It is more likely that many of the militant Shawnees were war leaders and warriors. Even more importantly, by the mid-1770s the divide between the militants and the accommodationists largely followed the lines between the five Shawnee divisions. Although earlier colonial documents are silent on the divisional composition of the factions, it is likely that from the start divisional and clan membership played a part in determining how individuals aligned in the arguments over the British alliance.[42]

Whatever the exact composition of the Shawnee factions, in the late 1760s they still strove to co-operate to minimize the British threat to their homelands. The Mekoche leaders in particular tried to keep the Shawnees united by coordinating the actions of the accommodationists and militants. This is most evident in the Shawnees' new western policy in the Mississippi Valley. After the fall of New France, the Scioto and Muskingum Shawnees established contacts with French officers and traders in Illinois and Louisiana in order to retain some French support against the British. In 1762 and 1763 a series of European treaties transferred France's claims west of the Mississippi River to Spain and those east of the river to Great Britain. Many French colonists fled the new British rule from Illinois to the Spanish dominion across the Mississippi. Several French officials even took up positions in Spanish service. Throughout the late 1760s Shawnees from the central Ohio Valley continued to visit their French friends on both sides of the Mississippi. While colonial records reveal very little of what went on between the Shawnee visitors and their hosts, it is clear that Shawnees wanted to keep open lines of communication to a European empire that might offer a commercial and military counterweight against the British. Shawnees probably realized that the small Spanish garrisons and French settlements in the Mississippi Valley were far too weak to challenge the English. Some of them nevertheless hoped that one day the Catholic powers would again gain strength and assist the Shawnees once more to check British encroachments.[43]

English officers and agents suspected that the Shawnees who visited the Mississippi Valley were dangerous militants looking for French military support. Although some Shawnees may well have harbored such hopes, not all visitors were die-hard militants. In 1766 one delegation visiting the Illinois Country was led by Colesquo, the Mekoche headman closely associated with Kisinoutha and Nimwha. Mekoches likewise took the lead in trying to discourage the British from occupying Illinois. In 1766 Miskapalathy warned Crown officers that the western nations would resent the English presence on their lands. Two years later Nimwha was even blunter. When visiting Fort Pitt, the Mekoche headman observed that the British were preparing an expedition down the Ohio River to Illinois: "We see you now about making Batteaux and we make no doubt you intend going down the River again, which we now tell you is disagreeable to all Nations of Indians; and now desire you to sit still at this Place." The Shawnees undoubtedly worried about being surrounded by the British to the east and west. As the guardians of the Shawnee-British border, the Mekoches sought to stop colonial invasion into the Indian country. Their willingness to keep up contacts with the French and the Spanish in the Mississippi Valley suggests that they, too, wanted to retain a potential counterweight against the British and tried to harmonize the wishes of the Shawnees supporting peace with the empire and those advocating armed resistance.[44]

Despite Shawnee warnings the British army proceeded to occupy Illinois in the late 1760s. In the east the redcoats initially tried to stop colonial encroachments on the Indian lands on the west side of the Royal Proclamation line. Unfortunately, Crown officials soon had to admit that they lacked the power to enforce the border. Their solution was to open negotiations to push the boundary between Indian and colonial lands farther west. At the Treaty of Fort Stanwix in November 1768 Sir William Johnson bought from the Six Nations an enormous tract of land extending from the Mohawk River to the Cherokee River and covering virtually all of modern Kentucky. The sale was highly dubious. Not only did Johnson exceed his orders from the ministers in London and buy more Native territory than instructed in order to serve his land-speculating business partners, but the Haudenosaunees had little or no right to most of the lands they sold. Kentucky in particular was used and claimed by Shawnees, Lenapes, and Cherokees. The Treaty of Fort Stanwix was based merely on the old British-Iroquois fiction that the Six Nations held power over these peoples. Only a small delegation of Shawnees and Lenapes was present at Fort Stanwix, and Johnson actively marginalized them from the actual negotiations. He even hid the true nature of the land transactions from the Ohioans, admitting later that he had said "Every thing that could possibly occur to me" to keep them happy.[45]

The treaty set Shawnees and their neighbors "in a rage." They "complained much of the Conduct of the Six Nations giving up so much of the Country to the English without asking their Consent & Approbation." Disputing the validity of the cession, Shawnees continued to claim the Kentucky lands as their own. Leaders explained to Crown officers that "the Six Nations have no more right to sell the Country than we have" and insisted that "we cannot Sell it [because] god has given us this Land to Live on." The Treaty of Fort Stanwix and the Anglo-American onslaught to Kentucky shook the fragile peace dangerously. Shawnee headmen explained that when their "young men" were "dissapointed in their hunting and find the Woods cover'd with white people & their Horses where they used to find their Game, they are foolish enough to make Reprisals without waiting to apply to the Great Men that shou'd redress their Complaints and regulate the Conduct of their white Brethren towards them." Some Shawnee hunters simply confiscated the guns, skins, and other property of the Anglo hunters and settlers they met in Kentucky and warned them off the land. But sometimes such encounters turned bloody. By the late 1760s small-scale violence between Shawnee hunters and colonial settlers had become commonplace in Kentucky.[46]

Shawnees were not the only ones breeding this violence. Most of the colonists encroaching on Native lands were embittered by memories of the recent bloody wars. In their eyes the killing of any Indian was a heroic feat. Historian

David Preston has calculated that from 1760 to 1774 (excluding Pontiac's War) approximately one hundred Indians and Euroamericans were killed in a series of interethnic murders on the contested Ohio borderlands. Among the victims were close to twenty Shawnees, while Shawnees were suspected of killing roughly ten colonists.[47] Both Crown officers and many Shawnee leaders were terrified that the violence might spark a new war. Amidst the escalating bloodshed the two elite groups joined forces to control their respective "young men" and preserve the peace. Following Indigenous rather than British legal customs, they organized elaborate condolence rituals where the dead were symbolically buried, as the leaders of the killer's people gave soothing ceremonial gifts to the bereaved nation and apologized for the evil deeds of their followers. These ceremonies were expected to, as it was expressed, bury the bones of the dead, wipe away the tears of the living, and calm everybody's feelings. Both Shawnee and British leaders also took pains to assure one another, as well as their own followers, that the killings were merely "unhappy accidents" caused by individual "foolish young Men" and that they should be quickly forgotten.[48]

Even though these rituals conformed to Shawnee customs, they reflected new tensions among the Natives. In Shawnee towns local hokimas often mediated intracommunity violence. They could even help the relatives of a killer to collect and give ritual gifts of wampum to the clan of the victim to compensate the crime. The fact that the leaders of several m'shomas cooperated in the mediation probably put considerable social pressure on the victim's kin to accept the condolence presents rather than pursue revenge. Yet the final decision rested on the victim's clan. Women, who as mothers maintained the life of their clan, and young men, who as warriors defended their kinspeople, were especially influential in these decisions. As hokima Ethanakeessthe pointed out in 1766, rituals and gifts of condolence were needed precisely to make "young men & womens hearts perfectly Easy." When violence with the British escalated, some Shawnees grew unsatisfied with the power of gifts and rituals to atone for the deaths of their loved ones. In May 1766 the headmen warned Crown officers that if the killings continued, they would not be able to control "their young People." Four years later Miskapalathy insisted that the violence "involves our Chiefs in difficulties," as they tried to restrain "some of our rash unthinking young Men" from taking revenge.[49] Once again, maintaining the peace with the British forced the headmen claiming national leadership to assert increasing authority in an area that had traditionally been under the control of clans, women, and warriors. The peace of 1765 was quickly degenerating into an alliance between Shawnee and British leaders, both of whom had trouble controlling their "young people."

British encroachments and violence undermined the collaboration between Shawnee accommodationists and militants. Debates between the two factions became increasingly divisive. In 1769 Alexander McKee reported that "ye Cheaffs of the Shawnas & Dalloways are against" a new war and "has tould thire Warreres that itt wold End in there Ruin Butt the Worrars Say they May as well Dey Like Men as be Kicked about Like Doggs." Sparse documentation makes it difficult to determine how most Shawnees felt about the issue. Since arguments about the peace, colonial encroachments, and violence dragged on for years, it is likely that the majority were more willing to monitor British actions than to rush into a new war. When the militant Shawnees found their support in their own communities thin, they started to look for followers elsewhere. Ever since they had dispersed across eastern North America in the late seventeenth century, the Shawnees had settled with, befriended, and married diverse Native peoples from the Gulf Coast to the Great Lakes and from the Atlantic seaboard to the Mississippi Valley. During the Seven Years' and Pontiac's wars they had drawn on these wide networks of kin and allies to challenge the British. Fighting against the colonists with a wide coalition of Native allies had taught the Shawnees that military collaboration of diverse Indian peoples could have terrifying efficiency. The wartime cooperation had also strengthened old webs of alliance, kinship, and friendship between Shawnee warriors and Indians from the Great Lakes, Illinois, and the Southeast.[50]

In the late 1760s the militant Shawnees evoked these relationships to challenge the British empire again. Enraged over the Treaty of Fort Stanwix, they began constructing an extensive Indian confederacy "to Defend themselves against any Enemy." In a highly ambitious plan, the Shawnee militants sought to unite the Native peoples of the Ohio Valley, the Great Lakes, the Wabash-Illinois region, and the South. This was a daunting task, for these peoples spoke dozens of unrelated languages and often had a long history of antagonistic relations. But Shawnees were well placed to carry out such a plan. In the Ohio Valley they were literally in the middle of the diverse Northern, Western, and Southern peoples. Kinship networks, marriages, exchange relations, and political alliances tied them to all of the surrounding nations and allowed them to build bridges between distant and often hostile groups. Moreover, Shawnee diplomats had mediated truces between the Southern and Western nations already in the 1740s and therefore could draw on previous experiences and contacts. After Pontiac's War many Shawnees labored tirelessly to unite their neighbors near and far behind the common cause of protecting Indian lands. From 1767 to 1775 they organized a series of multitribal conferences in the Scioto towns, where representatives from all surrounding nations assembled to discuss the Anglo-American invasion on Indian lands and plan diplomatic and military solutions to the threat. Militant Shawnees also visited Creek, Wyandot, Illinois, Cherokee, and other Indigenous communities in the South, Illinois, and the Great Lakes region. In 1770 they accomplished a major feat when the Ohio,

Great Lakes, and Wabash-Illinois peoples agreed to a peace with their long-time enemies, the Cherokees and other Southern Indians. One deeply concerned British Indian agent reported that the Shawnees were now "at the head of the Western confederacy which is formed upon the principle of maintaining their property in the lands obtained from the Six Nations at Fort Stanwix."[51]

The confederacy of the militant Shawnees was much more fragile than Crown officers feared, however. In the late 1760s and early 1770s the Shawnee diplomats drew together diverse peoples across the East to talk, but they were unable to unite the nations into a military coalition. Moreover, while the Shawnee diplomacy united likeminded militants from many communities, it bred divisions within those communities between militant and accommodationist factions. Among the Shawnees, too, the extensive intertribal cooperation of the militants undermined on several levels the national consolidation advocated by Kisinoutha, Miskapalathy, Nimwha, and other tribal leaders. Most obviously, it contested the peace policy of the national leadership. More fundamentally, it gave rise to an alternative societal vision, one that was based on multiethnic ties of loyalty and questioned the importance of Shawnee unity. Finally, the cooperation strengthened old networks of multiethnic ties and loyalties, as peoples with varying tribal backgrounds married one another and settled together. Large numbers of Ohio Senecas and Cayugas, for example, settled among the Shawnees on the Scioto and Muskingum rivers. Men claiming collective Shawnee leadership soon realized that controlling these Iroquoians was even more difficult than controlling their own "young men."[52]

By the early 1770s British authorities were so anxious over the mounting violence on the Ohio frontier that they constantly pressed Shawnee headmen to restrain their "young men," reminding them that it was their duty as the caretakers of the alliance. Yet Kisinoutha and others had to admit that this was increasingly "out of [their] power." When explaining this to the English, they drew attention to what they saw as a radical difference between Shawnee and colonial methods of social control. "Ignorant of Laws to govern them," some leaders explained in 1766, they "could do nothing with their young Warriors but by persuasion." Four years later Miskapalathy pointed out that "the English have Laws amongst them to guide the folly of their young people and Govern the Wicked minded. This is an advantage we have not." The Shawnees used the word "law" to describe coercive methods of social control that they perceived as typical to the British. Decades of intimate interaction with the colonists had made Shawnees familiar with such methods. They had seen soldiers flogged in Fort Pitt, African American slaves kept in chains, and criminals hanged. The words of Miskapalathy and other Shawnee headmen reveal that they understood that the centralized and hierarchical political order of the British society was based on such brutal use of force. They likewise recognized that "law" would greatly facilitate their own efforts to consolidate autonomous kin groups, towns, warriors, and women under their leadership. But Shawnee headmen never tried to institute "law" in their communities. Instead, they continued to lead their people "only by fair words."[53] Their understanding of power and leadership continued to be grounded in Shawnee culture. Even when they promoted Shawnee consolidation, they sought to create not a centralized, hierarchical nation of the European imagination, but a united people bound together by spiritual power and kinship.

The British may have had law, but in the early 1770s the empire all but gave up enforcing it on the contested Ohio borderlands. For years the British government, chafing under the staggering debts left by the Seven Years' War, had tried to force the American colonists to pay their share of the costs of the new empire. Yet every new tax levied by Parliament had sparked protests and riots through the colonies. As the situation grew increasingly tense in the early 1770s, the ministers in London transferred redcoats and resources from the empire's western frontier to police the mutinous cities on the Atlantic Coast. After the king's troops abandoned Fort Pitt in 1772, no one was left to guard the British side of the Indian-British boundary in the Ohio Valley. Virginians and Pennsylvanians continued to settle in growing numbers on the upper Ohio River and in Kentucky, disturbing Native peoples across the region. Interethnic violence intensified, but with few Crown officers left in the West, there was no one with whom Shawnee and other Indian leaders could have organized proper rituals of condolence.[54]

In 1774 the parallel crises within the Shawnee nation and the British empire finally deteriorated into a full-scale war. In April Virginian settlers murdered some fifteen Ohio Haudenosaunees, Lenapes, and Wakatomika Shawnees along the upper Ohio. The violence tore apart Shawnee unity and exposed long-standing factional, localized, and kin-based rifts. The Scioto Shawnee headmen tried once more to mediate the killings with colonial authorities. This time, however, Wakatomikan clans asserted their customary right to retaliation and raided Virginian settlements together with their Ohio Iroquois relatives. Virginia's royal lieutenant governor, John Murray, Lord Dunmore, seized the opportunity to strengthen his colony's claims to the contested Kentucky lands and declared a general war on the Shawnees. In August Virginian troops razed Wakatomika and other Upper Shawnee towns on the Muskingum. In October they defeated the badly outnumbered Shawnees at the Battle of Point Pleasant and marched within striking distance of the Lower Shawnee towns on the Scioto. With his soldiers threatening Shawnee homes, women, and children, Dunmore forced Kisinoutha, Colesquo, and a handful of other Mekoche leaders to acknowledge Virginia's claims to Kentucky in the Treaty of Camp Charlotte.[55] Yet it is highly questionable whether other Shawnee communities, factions, and kin groups endorsed the treaty. It was equally questionable whether they would again gather together behind the Mekoche leadership.

By 1775 both Shawnee and Anglo-American communities were divided by debates over legitimate authority, centralized power, and local autonomy. As the British empire disintegrated into a civil war, the Shawnee towns, divisions, kin groups, and factions that had for twenty years sought unity to defend themselves against that very empire adopted contrasting strategies to navigate the new and dangerous situation. Some, especially among Mekoches, continued to cultivate the unity of the Shawnee nation. Others built multitribal alliance networks or asserted local independence. All Shawnees continued to foster the multiple ties of kinship, spiritual power, and alliance that bound them to one another. These ties continued to connect the various communities through the two decades of violence that followed.

"A Struggle with Death"

The Twenty Years' War, 1775–1795

In April 1775 colonial militia and British troops clashed in Lexington and Concord, Massachusetts. The bloody encounter began a conflict that for some colonists became a war for independence, for others a war to save the British empire, and for yet others a war to conquer the Trans-Appalachian Indian lands no longer protected by royal proclamations and troops. For the Shawnees and their Native neighbors facing this assault, the American Revolution became the first act in a violent struggle over the Ohio Valley. Now known as the Twenty Years' War, the conflict would outlast the Revolutionary War and continue until 1795, when the U.S. military finally forced the Ohio Indians to cede most of the present-day state of Ohio and southern Indiana to the United States. The War of Independence gave birth to the United States; the Twenty Years' War began the relentless westward expansion of the new nation.[1]

The two decades of violence intimately linked the fates of the warring Shawnee and American societies together. The birth of the expansionist republic hammered the Native communities on its borders. "The Americans," Shawnees and their allies lamented in 1784, "put us out of our lands . . . [and] treat us as their cruelest enemies are treated, so that today hunger and the impetuous torrent of war . . . have brought our villages to a struggle with death."[2] Such devastation shattered the unity of the Shawnee nation, as hundreds of tribespeople fled the bloodshed from the Ohio Valley to the Trans-Mississippi West. In a like manner, the military campaigns of the Shawnees and their Haudenosaunee, Lenape, Cherokee, and other allies against the American settlements in Kentucky and along the Ohio River threatened the fragile unity of the newborn United States, as frontier citizens complained that the nascent national government in the East did not do enough to defend them against the Indians. On both sides the violence also pushed people together. It forced the

American settlers in the West to seek the protection of the remote federal government and the federal government to assert its military power in the distant Ohio Valley. The war compelled the Shawnees to cultivate and rethink the kin connections and ritual ties that bound their communities together. Many leaders struggled to keep groups with conflicting opinions together, yet others abandoned shared homelands and collective leaders to escape the violence. In the 1780s and 1790s militant Shawnees also drew on their extensive webs of kinship and alliance across the Native East to construct a powerful Indian Confederacy that challenged the United States for control of the Ohio Country. The Twenty Years' War, then, broke old societies and created new ones throughout eastern North America.

THE WAR FOR KENTUCKY

In June 1775 two French traders arrived in the Shawnee towns on the Scioto River carrying a message from Captain Richard Lernoult, the British commander of Detroit. When the locals gathered to hear their words, the Frenchmen announced that a war had broken out between the king of Great Britain and some of his American "children." They warned their hosts that Virginian rebels, the very people who had seized Kentucky in Dunmore's War less than a year before, now planned to invade the Indian lands north of the Ohio River. Scarcely a month after this dramatic news had reached the Scioto Shawnees, a Virginian messenger named James Wood visited them to explain the American Revolution from the colonists' perspective. In a meeting with Kisinoutha and other leaders, Wood claimed that the colonists wished no war with the Indians. Indeed, Virginians only wanted "to Confirm the Peace agreed upon last fall between Lord Dunmore and the Shawanese." Wood also promised that the colony would "do every thing in our power to prevent" Anglo-Americans from crossing the Ohio River to the Indian side.[3]

Shawnees must have been utterly surprised to hear that the English were suddenly fighting among themselves. The conflicting British and colonial news of this civil war worried the tribespeople. In 1775 the Shawnees still mourned for the thirty-odd men who had died at Point Pleasant. Moreover, they were suffering from a severe famine, for they had not been able to plant, harvest, or hunt properly during the violence of the previous year. In such a situation the prospect of a new imperial war seemed dreadful. An Anglo trader living among the Shawnees reported that "the Indians were Constantly Counseling and . . . the Women all seemed very uneasy in Expectations that there would be War." As farmers, Shawnee women feared that renewed violence might cost them another year's crop, a loss that could prove fatal to their families. It is likely that many Peace Women of the clans spoke against any involvement in the British civil war. Shawnee women assured Wood that when the messengers from Detroit had offered the Shawnees wampum belts to invite them to ally with the king, "the Shawanese had dug a hole in the Ground and buried [the belts] never to rise again."[4]

Similar uneasiness spread through Native and colonial America during the spring and summer of 1775. The localized violence that flared at Lexington and Concord in April quickly grew into a full-scale war, when twelve other British colonies on the Atlantic seaboard joined to assist Massachusetts against the redcoats and the fighting spread to Boston and Canada. As the warfare escalated, British subjects throughout North America were forced to rethink their loyalties and choose their sides. Many communities divided into "Patriot" and "Loyalist" factions and disintegrated into civil wars of their own that were often as rooted in local disputes over land and power as in disagreements over colonial liberties and royal authority. The fragmentation of the empire spread "division and confusion" also in Indian communities from the Great Lakes to the Gulf Coast. Twelve years after the Treaty of Paris had ended the long Anglo-French conflict and left the Native peoples to face the British empire alone, the English "family quarrel," as many Indians called the Revolutionary War, once more placed the Indians of eastern North America in a critical position between two warring Euroamerican powers: the British Canada and the thirteen rebel colonies. Indian communities could again try to further their own territorial and defensive agendas by allying with one Euroamerican belligerent against the other. But Native societies also divided, when towns, clans, factions, and leaders disagreed over which alliance would best serve their interests. Just like in colonial communities, such disputes were often grounded in much older local political rivalries and tensions. Now such old fault lines were torn wider by the Americans and the British, who pressured and cajoled the Indians to pick sides in the imperial conflict. A group of Iroquois captured the experiences of many Indians when they confessed that "they never knew a debate so warm & contention so fierce to have happened" among the Haudenosaunees.[5]

In the Ohio Country, too, the British civil war fused quickly with older local conflicts. It heightened tensions between Indians and Anglo-Americans, as well as disputes within Native communities. Among the Shawnees these conflicts were intertwined. Shawnees had struggled with Virginians over Kentucky for more than a decade. From the start, militant and accommodationist tribespeople had disagreed over how to best defend their lands from colonial expansion. The cycle of violence that spiraled from Lexington across eastern North America exacerbated both of these conflicts because it bound them to a broader imperial war. The colonial rebellion against the king made the Shawnee-Virginian struggle over Kentucky crucial not only to Shawnees and

Anglo-American settlers, but also to Continental leaders in Philadelphia and British policymakers in London. Initially, both Crown and colonial officials were circumspect in their dealings with the Ohio Indians. Governor Guy Carleton of Canada despised the idea of mobilizing Indian allies against the Crown's colonial subjects, however rebellious they might be. Americans, in turn, had little reason to hope that the Natives would support their war effort after two decades of land disputes and frontier violence. Through 1775 and 1776 both belligerents sought mainly to guarantee Indian neutrality on the Ohio, rather than to win active military support from the tribes. In order to protect their interests in the Trans-Appalachian West, British and Americans alike nevertheless had to expend more resources in the land conflict between Shawnees and Virginians that had previously seemed distant to imperial and colonial centers of power. In 1776 the Continental Congress decided to garrison Pittsburgh, Wheeling, and Fort Randolph on the upper Ohio to defend the Kentucky settlements. British officers at Detroit, in turn, sent powder to militant warriors in the Ohio Indian communities. Such state intervention aggravated factional disputes in Native communities. As Crown officers began supporting militant Indian leaders with presents and promises of future assistance and Continental agents sought out accommodationist tribespeople for similar favors, it became increasingly difficult for Native factions to find common ground in town and tribal councils.[6]

In the Shawnee country the Revolutionary War bore little resemblance to the conflict on the Atlantic Coast. While the Anglo-Americans in the East debated over taxation and representation, only one thing mattered to the Shawnees: their land. They were especially concerned over their principal hunting ground in Kentucky. By 1775 some three hundred colonists had settled there. All Shawnees resented this invasion. Even the Mekoche leaders who had conceded to the Treaty of Camp Charlotte under duress in October 1774 disputed the forced cession of Kentucky by the next summer. When James Wood visited the Scioto towns in August 1775, Kisinoutha complained that "Virginians . . . were now settling in Great Numbers in the Midst of their Hunting Grounds on the Kentucke River and that many . . . Crossed the Ohio [and] killed and drove off their Game." Other headmen blamed Virginians for "coming in the Middle of us like Crazey People . . . to shove us of our Land entirely." They pleaded that the colonists must "not come further on our Land but let us live in friendship." When Shawnees heard of the British civil war, their primary concern was how it would affect their land rights.[7]

In the confusion of 1775 the Mekoches continued to rely on diplomacy to protect Shawnee lands. During the next two years the hokimas Kisinoutha and Nimwha, military leaders Colesquo and Oweeconnee, Peace Woman Cawechile, and other Mekoche leaders forged a strategy of neutrality that was designed to keep the nation out of the British war and restore Kentucky to the Shawnees. In tribal councils the Mekoche leaders tirelessly argued that warriors must "sit still" and not get involved in the English civil war. When Henry Hamilton, the British lieutenant governor of Detroit, offered a war belt to Colesquo and Kisinoutha in August 1776, the chiefs staunchly declined it. Kisinoutha commented that "it was not in [Hamilton's] power to make them" fight the colonists. Traveling "Constantly Backward's and forward's" between their homes on the Scioto, the Continental outpost at Pittsburgh, and the British forts at Detroit and Niagara, the Mekoche leaders sought to persuade both Anglo-American belligerents that their "heart was good toward" "all . . . white Brothers." At the same time Kisinoutha and his allies mobilized friendly persuasion to keep Anglo-Americans away from the lands the peace of 1765 had guaranteed to the Shawnees. Time and again they asked Continental officials to remove the Virginians from Kentucky, explaining that continuing colonial settlement of the area would inevitably lead to bloodshed. The Mekoches also allied with Allegheny Seneca, Lenape, and Wyandot leaders to demand that both the British and the colonists keep their armies away from the country north of the Ohio River.[8]

The Mekoches' commitment to diplomacy demonstrates that they continued to view themselves as the guardians of the Shawnee-British alliance and border. Moreover, they continued to conduct negotiations with the Anglo-Americans in the name of all Shawnees, firmly believing that the nation could withstand the crisis only if united. Some Shawnees, however, challenged both the leadership of the Mekoches and their policy of neutrality. Throughout 1775 and 1776 small parties of Ohio Iroquois, Wyandots, and Ottawas harassed the Virginian settlements in Kentucky. Although the Iroquois occasionally received powder from the British officers at Detroit and distributed it among their allies, these raids initially had little to do with the Revolutionary War. They simply continued the old land dispute and cycle of revenge between Ohio Indians and Virginians. The prime mover in the fighting was a small group of Ohio Iroquois living on the Scioto River above the Shawnee towns. Led by a formidable war chief named Pluggy, these Iroquois were bitter over the death of their kinspeople in Dunmore's War. They raided Virginians relentlessly and encouraged men from neighboring communities to join them. A few Shawnees did. Most of them were related to Pluggy's people and had their own scores to settle with the Virginians. Some were ambitious young men looking for military glory. Their numbers remained small, however, and no notable leaders joined them. In May 1776 trader John Gibson still opined that "the Shanese & Delawares does not seem to have any Hostile Intention against" the Americans. After the destruction of Dunmore's War, most Shawnees were reluctant to rush headlong into a new war.[9]

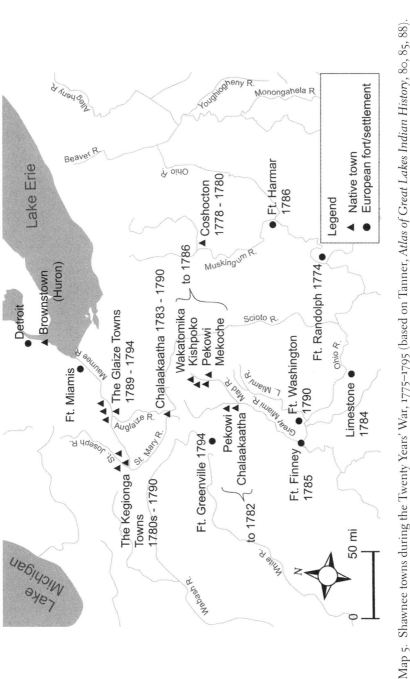

Map 5. Shawnee towns during the Twenty Years' War, 1775–1795 (based on Tanner, *Atlas of Great Lakes Indian History*, 80, 85, 88). Map drawn by Terhi Tanska.

But the rift between neutral and militant Shawnees was growing deeper. Most disruptive for the unity of the nation, this factional division increasingly followed the lines between the five Shawnee divisions. When Pennsylvanian diplomat Richard Butler visited the Scioto towns in September 1775 to invite the Shawnees to a meeting with Continental representatives, Peace Woman Cawechile drew him aside for a private chat. She revealed that "there is a Division amongst" the Shawnees, for the Chalaakaathas and Pekowis were "Not yet Reconciled to" the Virginians after Dunmore's War. According to Cawechile, these two divisions had accepted a war belt from the Ohio Iroquois and Wyandots and had charged that the Mekoches had "weded the white people." When Kisinoutha later summoned the national council to hear Butler's message, Chalaakaatha and Pekowi leaders refused to attend, explaining sarcastically that "it was them the Mequashes that had that bussiness to do & No Others had any Buisiness" with the Americans.[10]

Soon both Continental and British officers learned to associate the Shawnee divisions with contrasting political agendas. In 1777 General Edward Hand reported at Pittsburgh that "two Tribes of the Shawanese declare for us, two are against us." Never before had the Shawnee divisions appeared so often in colonial documents than in the early years of the Revolutionary War. Anglo-Americans, at least, perceived the political differences among the five divisions as more important and visible than before. In the dangerous world unsettled by the English family quarrel, Shawnees relied increasingly on their divisional people. It would be misleading to claim that the escalating Revolutionary War broke the nation neatly into militant and neutral divisions, however. In addition to divisional membership, personal kinship networks, political interests, and economic connections also influenced the choices individuals and families made during these difficult years. Two prestigious Pekowi war leaders, Aquitsica (Wryneck) and Sepettekenathé (Blue Jacket), for example, continued to support the Mekoche policy of neutrality until 1777 despite the militancy of many other Pekowis. Although we cannot be certain of their motives, ties of kinship and marriage may have connected Sepettekenathé and Aquitsica to Mekoche leaders. Kisinoutha himself had a small log house in Sepettekenathé's town, and some evidence suggests that Sepettekenathé may have lived among the Mekoches as a child. Moreover, Sepettekenathé was a prosperous merchant with trading partners in both Detroit and Pittsburgh. For him, war was a bad business proposition.[11]

Ultimately, the Mekoche strategy of neutrality and diplomacy failed. Pointing to the treaties of Fort Stanwix and Camp Charlotte, the colonists denied time after time that Shawnees could have any claims to Kentucky. As more settlers from Virginia and North Carolina followed "long hunters" and surveyors like Daniel Boone to the Bluegrass Region, increasing numbers of

Shawnees began to see war as the only option to defend their hunting lands. The year 1777 marked the rising tide of Shawnee militancy. In February more than twenty warriors joined the Ohio Iroquois to raid Kentuckian settlements. A month later a Chalaakaatha war leader known as Black Fish mustered enough men to attack the fortified settlements of Boonesborough and Harrodsburg. The ranks of the militants continued to swell during the summer. In part this was due to broader international developments. The British government had overcome its reluctance against recruiting Indian warriors in offensive operations against the rebels. It now instructed commanders in North America to mobilize their Native allies in guerrilla warfare against colonial targets. In June Lieutenant Governor Hamilton assembled a massive council of Great Lakes and Ohio Indians at Detroit and encouraged them to attack the frontiers of Kentucky, Virginia, and Pennsylvania, promising them abundant material support. Many Shawnees who had shunned Hamilton's request a year before were only too willing to join him now. They did not turn into British pawns, however. When the Mekoche diplomacy with the colonists led nowhere, British support made war seem like an increasingly feasible strategy to protect Shawnee land rights in Kentucky. Militant Shawnees recognized that British guns, ammunition, and manpower could help them to drive the invaders out of their hunting grounds. For them, George III was simply a convenient ally in their war for Kentucky, which had begun long before a single shot had been fired at Lexington.[12]

As growing numbers of Shawnees moved toward a full-scale war in 1777, tensions between militant and neutral tribespeople skyrocketed. Mekoche headmen denounced the militants as "foolish young Shawanese." When warriors returned home from raids with stolen horses and captives, Mekoche leaders sometimes returned such plunder to American officers. Colesquo's sister, Grenadier Squaw, even warned Fort Randolph of impending raids. Enraged, militant Shawnees and their Iroquois allies derided the Mekoche headmen as "Virginians." Colesquo, one of the most prominent Mekoche spokesmen for peace, feared for his life when the militants questioned his Shawnee identity. He lamented that "his people would not listen to him, but had threatened to do away with him." Such an unprecedented vehemence reveals dramatically how deep the division between the militants and neutralists had become.[13]

When disputes rose to such a pitch, the Shawnees resorted to an old strategy of relieving intracommunity strife: they split. During 1777 more than one thousand Chalaakaathas, Pekowis, Kishpokos, and Wakatomikans abandoned their homes on the Scioto and moved west to the Little Miami, Great Miami, and Mad rivers. Although many of these people still wished to stay clear of the Anglo-American war, they saw little common future with the encroaching colonists. They sought security by migrating farther from the Virginians and closer to their western Indian allies, especially the Miamis. The Mekoches, in contrast, still tried to maintain peace with the colonists. Their task was growing more dangerous, however. In November 1777 Colesquo, his son, and two other Mekoche diplomats were visiting Fort Randolph when Ohio Iroquois warriors killed an American militiaman just outside the fort. In revenge, the victim's comrades murdered the four Mekoches. But even this atrocity did not destroy the Mekoches' commitment to peace. During the winter Kisinoutha and Colesquo's brother Nimwha led more than two hundred Mekoches from the Scioto east to the Muskingum River. There they settled near Coshocton, a large town of neutral Lenapes where many Mekoches had kinspeople. Together the Lenapes and Mekoches continued to labor for peace.[14]

Many Shawnees were shocked by the division of the nation and lamented that they could "not see the necessity of this Separation." But the "Separation" did occur, and it forced everyone literally to choose their camp. Both kinship networks and strategic calculations shaped such decisions. Although the Pekowi headmen Aquitsica and Sepettekenathé had hitherto supported the neutralist agenda of the Mekoche leadership, they now followed their Pekowi relatives to the Mad River. There, both of them soon emerged as the leading war chiefs of the western Shawnees. Apparently, they had abandoned all hope of a diplomatic solution to the land dispute in Kentucky. In addition, Sepettekenathé was related through marriage to several British Indian agents and French traders in Detroit. Such contacts likely influenced his actions, too.[15]

After 1777 the western Shawnees, led by Black Fish, Aquitsica, Sepettekenathé, and other war chiefs, pursued their warfare against the Kentucky settlements with growing vigor. During the spring of 1778 several Shawnee delegations visited Detroit where they formally accepted British war belts from Lieutenant Governor Hamilton. In September three hundred warriors again attacked Boonesborough, the main colonial settlement in Kentucky. Armed with British guns and occasionally accompanied by British rangers, Shawnees and their Lenape, Ohio Iroquois, Wyandot, Ottawa, and other Native allies raided forts, harassed work parties, cut communications, and destroyed infrastructure throughout Kentucky. Militant Shawnee leaders took pains to deepen their vital alliance with King George III. Shawnee women, many of them from chiefly families, married influential agents of Detroit's Indian Department, including Alexander McKee, Matthew Elliott, and Louis Lorimier. Such ties bound the agents to the Shawnee communities and Native webs of reciprocal kinship obligations. This gave Indian leaders more leverage to demand military assistance and supplies from their Father.[16]

The western Shawnees also continued their efforts to unite Indians throughout the East in a common fight against the intruders in Kentucky.

Their towns on the two Miami and Mad rivers became centers for militant Natives who had decided to fight the encroaching colonists despite the efforts of their tribal leaders to maintain peace. Militant Lenapes, Chickamauga Cherokees, and Ohio Iroquois all settled among the western Shawnees. Shawnee messengers also toured Native towns around the Great Lakes, in Illinois, and in the South in search of allies. In 1776 Shawnee, Mohawk, and Ottawa diplomats visited the important Cherokee town Chota in Tennessee, where they "sung the warsong" and incited the local warriors to attack the frontiers of Virginia and North Carolina. Other Shawnees settled among the Chickamaugas on the Tennessee River and used the strategic location to organize cooperation between Northern and Southern Indians. In 1780 more than seven hundred Shawnee, Haudenosaunee, Ojibwe, Ottawa, and Potawatomi warriors invaded Kentucky together with a detachment of British rangers. With the help of British ordnance, this formidable multiethnic army seized three American forts and captured more than three hundred colonists.[17]

The Shawnees' division and successful military alliances with Indians across the East transformed American understandings of Native societies. When the militant Chalaakaathas, Pekowis, Kishpokos, and Wakatomikans broke away from the promises of peace and neutrality made by the Mekoche leaders, colonial authorities denounced them as treacherous rebels. In 1780 Colonel Daniel Brodhead, the Continental commander at Pittsburgh, disdainfully described the allied Native peoples on the two Miami and Mad rivers as "renegadoes from the different Indian nations . . . collected at the Shawanese towns." A few years later another American official called them "banditti of Savages," while yet another officer contrasted them with "the regular tribes." During the war the Americans began conceptualizing friendly Indian leaders as legitimate tribal chiefs and dismissed hostile factions as unauthorized secessionists. Ironically, even as the colonists rebelled against their own king, they insisted that Native peoples must remain centralized under the leadership of unpopular tribal governments. Americans were particularly hostile to multiethnic communities, such as those on the Little and Great Miami and Mad rivers. These settlements seemed to be under no kind of centralized authority, and no single tribal chief could be held accountable for their actions. Even more seriously, the military strength of the allied Indians scared American officers and agents.[18]

While the militant western Shawnees built new communities and collaborated with new allies, old relationships and identities remained powerful, too. Even the bitter "Separation" of the militants and the Mekoches could not break the numerous overlapping kinship networks based on divisional, clan, and marital ties that connected individuals, families, and communities to one another across factional boundaries and reminded everyone that, despite everything, they were all Shawnees. In 1778, only a year after the dramatic split, the Mekoche headman Nimwha toured the western Shawnee towns, probably to discuss the progress of the war with the militant leaders and mend relations with them. Many western Shawnees, in turn, visited the Mekoches on the Muskingum to ask for corn during a famine and to persuade their relatives to move west with them.[19]

Such connections became vital for the Mekoches when they realized that the war-torn upper Ohio Valley was no place for neutrals. Throughout the late 1770s the British, the militant Indians, and the Continental officers all tried to bully the Mekoches and Lenapes of Coshocton to join the war. Finally, in September 1779 Colonel Brodhead bluntly informed the Mekoches that they had to demonstrate their friendship to the Americans by taking up arms against the English and their Indian allies. This was too much for the Mekoches. When Kisinoutha and Nimwha, the two most vocal advocates of peace, died during the following winter, their people moved to the Mad River and settled once more among the other Shawnees. Convinced that neutrality was no longer an option, most Mekoches now reluctantly joined their tribespeople's war against the Americans. Following Shawnee traditions, the Mekoche hokimas acknowledged that during wartime the leadership of the nation should be placed in the hands of military leaders. The Pekowi war chief Aquitsica, their old ally, played a crucial role in attaching the Mekoches again to the more militant western Shawnees. In 1781 Mekoche leaders followed Aquitsica to Detroit, where the Mekoche war chief Oweeconnee deferentially called him "our Chief" and joined him in asking British assistance against the Americans. Enduring bonds of kinship and alliance thus continued to link divisions and towns together, while American aggression pushed former neutrals to take up the hatchet against Kentuckians.[20]

In the early 1780s the Shawnees' war for Kentucky became ever more destructive. Despite recurrent Indian attacks, the colonial population of Kentucky had swelled to eight thousand by 1782. Shawnees complained that new fortified settlements now "surrounded the Indian Hunting ground." In fact, constant fighting left warriors so little time and powder to hunt that communal subsistence economies and trade suffered severely.[21] Worst, the rapid growth of the Kentuckian settlements made them strong enough to carry the war to the Shawnees' home front. The colonial militia adopted a devastating new military strategy against the Ohio Indians aimed at breaking the economic backbone of the Native communities. The troops crossed the Ohio in late summer just before harvest time, marched quickly to the Shawnee towns, and hit them with a cavalry attack, sometimes supported by artillery. If the militia succeeded in routing the Indians, the soldiers quickly destroyed their fields, houses, and agricultural stores and then retreated back to Kentucky. In the first of such raids in June 1779 Kentuckians burned the Chalaakaatha town on the Little Miami and wounded Black Fish mortally. In August 1780 General George Rogers Clark's troops destroyed four Shawnee towns on the Great Miami and Mad rivers. Two years later Clark laid five more towns to waste. Each time, Shawnees evacuated the attacked communities quickly and lost few lives in the destruction. Yet their material losses were severe. The Kentuckians burned their homes, stole their property, and, most seriously, stripped their cornfields and sacked their agricultural stores. In August 1780 alone Clark's men "destroyed upwards of 800 acres of corn, besides great quantities of vegetables."[22]

Such destruction left the Shawnees in pain. "Our Women & Children," lamented the headmen after Clark's attack in 1780, "are left now destitute of Shelter in the Woods or Food to subsist upon. Our Warriors have not now even the Ammunition to Hunt for, or defend them." In despair, the Shawnees turned to their British allies. After each invasion "wretched women and children" flocked to Detroit in search of food. They were followed by delegations of leaders who pressed their Father "very importunate[ly] for Ammunition and Provisions." The British sorely needed their Indian allies in the western war and had no choice but to yield to the Shawnee demands. In 1779 the British Indian Department at Detroit began furnishing the Crown's Native allies with large annual presents of provisions, arms, ammunition, tools, clothes, textiles, ornaments, and alcohol. The gifts were delivered to Indian leaders each fall, usually at Alexander McKee's trading post on the Maumee River. These presents became crucial for Shawnee survival. As American invasions, declining hunting, and loss of trade shattered the economy of their communities, the Shawnees and many of their Native neighbors became dependent on British material assistance.[23]

Yet despite destruction and dependence, Shawnees remained undefeated. "They are not cast down, but . . . still hold up their Heads and are determined to revenge themselves upon the Enemy," declared Aquitsica in 1781. In the early 1780s the Shawnees and their allies indeed more than held their own in the war. In June 1782 they routed Colonel William Crawford's troops at Sandusky. Two months later they crushed Kentuckian militia at Blue Licks. Then, surprisingly, it was the British who seemed to lose their spirit to fight. In the fall of 1782 the redcoats halted their offensive operations. Even the annual presents to the Indians were delayed. Shawnees and their allies grew suspicious, as they began "to fear they are to be the dupes of the War." Their fears were well founded. In early 1783 news reached them that Great Britain and the United States had concluded a preliminary peace in Paris on November 30, 1782. Not a single Indian had been consulted in the negotiations.[24]

SHAWNEE STRATEGIES BETWEEN WAR AND PEACE

In the words of one British officer, news of the Treaty of Paris left Indians "thunderstruck." Native peoples throughout the East were astonished that the British and Americans had negotiated a peace without even informing them. But they were far more shocked when they learned what the peace entailed. In the treaty Great Britain, just like France twenty years before, had ceded all the lands lying east of the Mississippi, north of Florida, and south of the Great Lakes to the United States. Enraged Indians denounced the English "Conduct to them as treacherous and Cruel" and marveled how the "King could pretend to Cede to America What was not his own to give or that the Americans would accept from him What he had no right to grant." The United States had no scruples about accepting the cession. The new republic was heavily in debt after eight long years of war, and the government saw the sale of the Trans-Appalachian Indian lands to settlers as a vital source of revenue. According to the American interpretation, the Indians had lost the war with their British allies, and their lands belonged to the victors. Shawnees found such claims preposterous. After all, they had not been defeated in battle, even if the redcoats had. "You seem to grow proud, because you have thrown down the King of England," Kekewepelethy (Captain Johnny), a young military leader from Wakatomika, told American diplomats. Neither he nor his tribespeople were ready to give away their land just because George III had signed a piece of paper across the ocean.[25]

Yet Shawnees were uncertain about how to protect their country. The ambiguous policies of their unreliable British allies added to their confusion in the years following the Treaty of Paris. In 1783 an American officer gloated to Shawnee peace negotiators that the king had "neglected" his Shawnee children "like Bastards." When some Shawnees wanted to keep on fighting for Kentucky despite the British-U.S. treaty, English officers warned them that the redcoats would offer them no more assistance. On the other hand, many British Indian agents, who were intimately connected to Shawnee communities by marriage, kinship, and trade relations, assured the Natives that the king remained their caring Father. They argued that the Treaty of Paris did not alter the 1768 Treaty of Fort Stanwix, which had designated the Ohio River as the boundary between the Indians and the Anglo-American colonists. Moreover, within a year of the peace British officials in Quebec and London began to fear that the Treaty of Paris exposed Upper Canada to American invasion. Citing U.S. failure to fulfill all peace conditions as an excuse, the ministers in London authorized British troops to remain at the strategic posts of Detroit, Niagara, and Michilimackinac in defiance of the treaty in order to retain the western Great Lakes under British control. They also advised the Indian Department to mend the bruised alliance with the Natives of the Ohio and Great Lakes country, for a bulwark of Indian allies would effectively shield Upper Canada from American aggression. Soon, British goods again flowed to the Shawnee and neighboring communities from Detroit, while Alexander McKee and other Crown agents married to Shawnee women advised the Indians to hold fast the Ohio boundary. Yet the British messages were so mixed that it was difficult for the Natives to determine how far the king would go to help them protect their lands.[26]

In the confusing conditions following the Treaty of Paris, familiar divisions and disputes resurfaced among Shawnees. When news of the treaty spread through the Indian country in the spring of 1783, the Mekoches once again prepared to begin peace talks with the United States. In the summer Colesquo's son Biaseka (Wolf) visited Louisville, Kentucky, to open negotiations with the local Virginian officials. Even though Virginian militia had murdered his father and brother six years earlier, Biaseka remained committed to the peaceful ideals of his division. He apparently saw it as his duty as a hereditary Mekoche hokima to use his miišaami to end the bloody war. In Louisville Biaseka assured the Virginian authorities that "he hoped all would be peace." He was backed by other Mekoche leaders, especially Moluntha, who seems to have succeeded Kisinoutha as the ceremonial hokima of the Shawnee nation. Over the following year Biaseka and Moluntha kept up a friendly correspondence with U.S. officials and prepared the ground for serious negotiations. To steer the Shawnees toward peace they also returned a number of British war belts to Detroit. During the war Crown officers had offered these dark-colored wampum belts to Shawnee headmen as ceremonial invitations to join the king against the rebellious colonists. After the Shawnees had accepted the belts, they served as symbolic reminders of their military alliance with George III. By returning the belts Biaseka and Moluntha essentially ended this alliance. Their action was also a powerful symbol of authority among the Shawnees. It demonstrated that the Mekoches were the wampum keepers of the nation and had the right to seek peace in the name of all Shawnees.[27]

Familiar opponents quickly denounced the return of the belts. The most vocal center of opposition was Wakatomika, the mixed Shawnee–Ohio Iroquois town that had relocated from the Muskingum to the Mad River after Dunmore's War. The Wakatomikans had for years had an ambiguous relationship with the Scioto Shawnee headmen claiming national leadership. By the early 1780s the multiethnic community had acquired such a distinct identity and reputation for stubborn independence that British officers often differentiated the locals from other Shawnees, calling them "Wakitumikée Indians." Embittered by old memories of Virginian encroachments and Dunmore's War, the Wakatomikans remained the most militant of all Shawnees. When Crown agents tried to persuade the Shawnees to suspend military operations in the spring of 1783, "some difficulty at first arose with the Wakitamikie Tribe and the Mingoes." After the Mekoches returned the British war belts to Detroit in 1784, Wakatomika's military leaders Kekewepelethy, Chiaxey, and the brothers Peteusha (Snake) and Shemanetoo (Black Snake) demanded the belts back so "that they may be put to their intended use, if occasion requires it." Even though the Wakatomikans were prepared to try negotiations with the Americans, they wanted to maintain the military alliance with the redcoats in case a reasonable peace proved impossible.[28]

While the Mekoches tried to open peace negotiations and the Wakatomikans remained ready for war, many Pekowis, Kishpokos, and Thawikilas selected a third road. Tired of violence, yet certain that the Americans would not let them live in the Ohio Valley in peace, they left their homes to search for a brighter future on the west side of the Mississippi River, in what is now eastern Missouri. For a century Shawnees harassed by enemies had taken refuge in this area. In the 1680s some tribespeople had fled Iroquois attacks there, and after Pontiac's War militants suspicious of the British empire had settled in the Spanish-claimed central Mississippi Valley. In the turmoil of the 1780s hundreds of Shawnees, Haudenosaunees, Cherokees, Choctaws, Lenapes, and other eastern Indians saw the Trans-Mississippi country as a refuge from endless violence and began migrating to the area. In 1782 and 1784 multitribal delegations visited the Spanish authorities in St. Louis, asking for land, protection, and alliance. Spain claimed an enormous territory west of the Mississippi, but along the great river the empire was weak and constantly threatened by its American, British, and Osage neighbors. Desperate for allies, Spanish officers welcomed the Shawnees and other eastern Indian refugees to the central Mississippi Valley and tried to secure the assistance of these newcomers through generous treatment. As news of Spanish land grants, gifts, and trade spread to the Ohio Valley during the 1780s, growing numbers of Shawnees shunned both accommodation and war with the United States and migrated west instead. A new Shawnee diaspora had begun.[29]

When the Americans coveted their land, their British allies wavered, and their tribespeople fled across the Mississippi, many Ohio Shawnees intensified their collaboration with other Native peoples who shared their predicament. Decades of multitribal diplomacy and years of common war against the United States had fostered a sense of common destiny among the diverse Indian communities across the East. The disastrous Treaty of Paris further strengthened their conviction that only unity could save them. In September 1783 hundreds of Shawnees, Haudenosaunees, Wyandots, Lenapes, Ottawas, Ojibwes, Potawatomis, Creeks, and Cherokees assembled at Sandusky to plan a common response to the threat the Treaty of Paris posed to their territorial rights. Shawnee military leaders took an active role in the council. Led by

Aquitsica, they admonished all Indians "to join in the Defence of their Country." The influential Mohawk headman Joseph Brant (Theyendanegea) also spoke strongly for Native cooperation. There must "be never hereafter a Separation between us," Brant declared; "let there be Peace or War, it shall never disunite us, for our Interests are alike nor Should any Thing ever be done but by the Voice of the whole." Inspired by such arguments, the leaders collected at Sandusky agreed that all Indians should join together into a grand confederacy to defend their lands against the United States. They formulated two radical decisions that became the backbone for widespread Native collaboration for the next twelve years. First, they agreed that all decisions concerning peace and war with the Americans had to be made unanimously by all of the allied Indians. Second, they decided that only this Indian Confederacy as a whole had the authority to cede any Indian land to the United States. While it must have been painful to the Shawnees, the assembled leaders conceded the loss of Kentucky, whose American population simply seemed too great to be dislodged. But with British backing, the Indians evoked the Treaty of Fort Stanwix and insisted that the Ohio River formed the legitimate boundary between the Indians and the United States. The land north of the Ohio was to be shared by all Natives, and it could be ceded only by their collective decision.[30]

Many disparate Shawnee groups initially united behind the resolutions of the Sandusky council. In March 1784 the Mekoches Moluntha and Biaseka joined forces with the Wakatomikan Kekewepelethy and informed U.S. peace envoys that although Shawnees wanted peace, the matter could be decided only collectively by all Indians at their "Great Council fire." Americans, however, refused to recognize the Indian Confederacy as a legitimate negotiating partner. Afraid of the strength of the united Natives, they insisted that peace and borders must be negotiated separately with individual nations. This strategy of divide and rule would form the cornerstone of U.S. Indian policy for decades to come. U.S. peace commissioners initiated it in 1784 when they pressured a small group of Iroquois leaders to cede a large part of the Haudenosaunee country to the new republic at the Treaty of Fort Stanwix, even though the Iroquois negotiators lacked authorization from the Indian Confederacy, as well as from their own Six Nations Confederacy. The next year U.S. diplomats forced a handful of Wyandot and Lenape headmen at Fort McIntosh to relinquish the southern half of what is now the state of Ohio, again without the sanction of the confederacy. The Shawnees were shocked. Kekewepelethy and other Wakatomikans protested that the Treaty of Fort McIntosh gave to the United States "the whole Shawanese Country," even though the Shawnees had not even attended the negotiations. Kekewepelethy informed U.S. officials that the Indians would never accept any border other than the Ohio River. Defiantly, he warned the Americans that "you will find all the People of our Colour in this

Island Strong, unanimous, and determined to act as One Man in defence" of their country.[31]

But American pressure and the threat of violence was already aggravating factional divisions even among the Shawnees. Unfortunately, Aquitsica died during this critical moment in 1784. Respected by the accommodationist Mekoches and the Shawnee militants alike, and connected to both factions through kinship, Aquitsica had been crucial in binding together Shawnees with disparate political opinions. After his death disputes among the Shawnees intensified. When the Americans invited Shawnees to peace talks in the fall of 1785, it became clear that the nation was seriously divided. Kishpokos declared that they were "determined not to go [to the treaty], let the Consequence be what it will," because "all the Brown Skins" had determined to defend their lands together "to the last Man." At Wakatomika Peteusha likewise refused to negotiate without the participation of the entire Indian Confederacy and informed Americans that "nothing can be done by us but by General consent" of all Natives. Mekoche leaders, however, were willing to negotiate. In January 1786 Moluntha, Oweeconnee, and Cawechile led some 220 Mekoches to meet the U.S. commissioners at Fort Finney, located at the confluence of the Great Miami and Ohio rivers.[32]

The Mekoches had multiple reasons for negotiating with the Americans. Clearly, they took their spiritually sanctioned role as peacemakers seriously. They explained that they wished to "go on with the good work of peace" and put their relations with the United States "on the same footing as before the war." Despite the treaties of Fort Stanwix and Fort McIntosh, the Mekoches believed that they would not have "to enter into any Engagements respecting Lands." It is also likely that the inability of the Indian Confederacy to stop the Fort Stanwix and McIntosh treaties had convinced Moluntha and his allies that they could more efficiently search for peace and American recognition of Shawnee territorial rights by themselves. But opening independent negotiations with the United States was also a Mekoche strategy to assert their fledging position as the leaders of the Shawnee nation. Since 1777 the militant Shawnees had largely disregarded Mekoche claims to national leadership. Moreover, during the war patterns of leadership had developed in divergent directions among the Mekoches and the militants. Stephen Ruddell, a Kentuckian youth who lived among the Shawnees as an adopted captive from 1780 to 1795, later reminisced that the Mekoches had "a king over them whose authority was hereditary," but among the other divisions "the chiefs owed their power & authority to their merit." Indeed, after old Mekoche headmen such as Kisinoutha, Nimwha, and Colesquo had died by 1780, their relatives Moluntha, Biaseka, Oweeconnee, and Cawechile continued to lead the division. Nehinissica, "a young chief" whom the Mekoches "value[d] highly," was known as "the Young Prince" among the

Americans, implying that his lofty status was hereditary. In other Shawnee communities, in contrast, the influence of military leaders like Aquitsica, Sepettekenathé, and Kekewepelethy had grown considerably since the beginning of the war. The authority of these men was based on their personal hopawaaka power, military prowess, and the consequent respect of warriors and other community members. They would not easily agree that the miišaami of the Mekoches, while certainly powerful, gave that division any right to lead all Shawnees. It was therefore extremely important for the Mekoche leaders to demonstrate their authority by negotiating a peace with the United States that would protect the Shawnee country.[33]

Unfortunately, the negotiations at Fort Finney proved a disaster for the Mekoches. The U.S. peace commissioners Richard Butler and George Rogers Clark bluntly told the chiefs that the Shawnees had lost their lands in the Revolutionary War. Unless the Mekoches accepted this, the United States would commence new hostilities against their people after eight days. Surrounded by U.S. soldiers, there was little Moluntha, Oweeconnee, and Cawechile could do. "Through fear" they "were obliged to sign" a treaty that gave away most of the remaining Shawnee country and left the nation only a small reservation between the Great Miami and Wabash rivers. It was a catastrophic conclusion to a genuine diplomatic effort to bring peace to the Ohio country. The treaty infuriated Shawnees and destroyed whatever support the Mekoches had enjoyed among the other divisions. The Chalaakaathas protested that "their king and sachems have sold both land and warriors" and declared that they were "determined not to agree to what has been done." By the summer of 1786 warriors from Wakatomika joined Wabash Indians and Chickamauga Cherokees in attacking American settlers on the Ohio River and in Kentucky. So did many Ohio Iroquois living among the Shawnees. But even now the Mekoches continued to strive for peace. Although Moluntha was personally shocked by the treatment he had received at Fort Finney, he still worked to unite all Shawnees behind the peace and Mekoche leadership. In June he explained to a U.S. military officer that even though the Shawnees were "very much scattered," the Mekoches would eventually bring their "young men" "under subjection."[34]

U.S. officials had trouble deciding how to cope with the growing threat of the Shawnees and their allies. While frontier citizens demanded protection against the Indian raids, the weak confederation government simply lacked the resources to wage a full-scale Indian war. Many policymakers in the East favored a more accommodating Indian policy and hoped to negotiate a new treaty with the Shawnees and other western nations. Frustrated with such inaction, the Kentuckian settlers decided to take matters into their own hands. In October 1786 Colonel Benjamin Logan raised the local militia and marched against the Shawnee towns on the Great Miami and Mad rivers without official

authorization. Warned of the militia's approach, the Shawnees quickly evacuated their settlements. Only Moluntha and a few other Mekoches remained at
home when Logan's troops rode into their town. Moluntha raised the American
flag, hoping to negotiate with the invaders, but a militia officer struck him dead
with a tomahawk. The Kentuckians then proceeded to burn four Shawnee
towns to the ground.[35]

Logan's raid hit the Shawnees hard. Most left the smoldering ruins of their
homes and retreated north. In the waning months of 1786 about one thousand
Chalaakaathas, Mekoches, Pekowis, Kishpokos, and Wakatomikans built new
towns on the Maumee and St. Mary's rivers, closer to their Miami and British
allies. Others had had enough of the bloodshed. Hundreds of Kishpokos and
Pekowis fled the escalating violence across the Mississippi where they joined
previous Shawnee refugees. The mass migration to the west began to split the
Shawnees into what one French traveler would later call "two tribes," the
eastern Shawnees, who were still willing to fight together for their Ohio
lands, and the western Shawnees, who saw migration, dispersal, and accommodation with the Spanish and French colonists across the Mississippi as a more
viable strategy for survival. Even divisions and towns split when people debated
what to do with the war that never seemed to end. Speaking on behalf of the
Mekoche leaders, Kekewepelethy explained in 1787 that "all my town is for
peace, the one half of the Picaway town, and the half of Chilocotha Town, the
half of Cespico town also, and the half of Wacatomica."[36] The violence that had
first fragmented the Shawnee nation was now infiltrating even more intimate
layers of the social fabric.

THE INDIAN CONFEDERACY

Even when the intensifying violence ripped apart old social networks and
political alliances, the eastern Shawnees built new ones. The Shawnees who
fled Kentuckian violence to the Maumee River became the co-creators of a
new, thriving multiethnic world where diverse Native peoples mixed with
British Indian agents and Canadian traders. Located close to Detroit, the bastion
of British military power and trade in the Great Lakes region, the Maumee
River attracted thousands of Indian refugees fleeing in the face of U.S. expansion in the late 1780s. Miamis established several large towns at Kekionga,
where the St. Mary's and St. Joseph's rivers meet to form the Maumee. After
Logan's raid they were joined by Pekowi, Mekoche, and Chalaakaatha refugees,
whose ties to the Miamis dated back at least to the 1680s. The Shawnees' old
Lenape allies built their own towns next to the Shawnee and Miami settlements. Other Shawnees and Lenapes built more communities downriver at the
confluence of the Maumee and Auglaize rivers, a place known as the Glaize.

More Native refugees and migrants came from all corners of eastern North America. Ohio Iroquois and Chickamauga Cherokees settled at Kekionga and the Glaize. From the north came bands of Ottawas and from the east Mohawk families. Small groups of Mahicans and Abenakis migrated to the Maumee from the distant Atlantic seaboard. Even Creeks from Alabama regularly visited the Maumee towns to talk about the shared predicament of all Indians. As the violent expansion of the United States drove these diverse peoples from their homelands, it pushed them together physically, politically, and spiritually.[37]

British support was equally important in drawing Native refugees to the Maumee. Crown officers continued to distribute annual presents and other supplies to the Indians at McKee's post, just downriver from the Glaize. As they delivered guns, powder, food, and tools to the Natives, the agents encouraged the Indians to defend the Ohio boundary and promised that the redcoats would soon again assist the warriors. And even if the king's troops remained huddled in Detroit, British and French traders flocked to the Maumee communities. Despite the ongoing violence, trade flourished once more.[38]

On the Maumee the Shawnees intensified their efforts to unite the Native peoples against the United States. After the Sandusky council in 1783 the Indian Confederacy had laid largely dormant. Although especially Shawnee, Haudenosaunee, and Cherokee leaders had met regularly to renew the resolutions made at Sandusky, they had been unable to stop the treaties made at forts Stanwix, McIntosh, and Finney. Neither had they been able to agree whether the Indians should respond to the threat of these treaties with words or weapons. In 1786 the accelerating violence convinced Native communities across the Ohio and Great Lakes country to put aside their differences and find again a collective voice. In December Shawnee leaders from the new Maumee settlements traveled to Brownstown, a Wyandot community just outside Detroit, where they met delegates from the Haudenosaunees, Wyandots, Ottawas, Miamis, Lenapes, Ojibwes, Cherokees, Potawatomis, and Wabash Indians. Gathered around "our Confederated Council Fire," the assembled leaders wrote a letter to the Congress of the United States in which they explained their view of the crisis that had begun with the Treaty of Paris and outlined their proposition for ending the hostilities. They denounced the Fort Stanwix, McIntosh, and Finney treaties as illegitimate and insisted that Congress rene-gotiate them with the entire Indian Confederacy. "All treaties carried on with the United States," explained the Natives, "should be with the general voice of the whole confederacy." If the Americans continued to ignore this demand, the confederacy would go to war.[39]

It was a bold ultimatum. That the leaders collected at Brownstown were willing to lay down the law to the United States in such plain terms demon-strates their growing belief in the power of the united Indians. Yet Indian unity was still a process in the making. What colonial observers, many Natives, and most historians have called "the Indian Confederacy" was in reality a series of overlapping alliances and kinship networks linking dozens of autonomous towns, clans, families, and leaders loosely together. The confederacy had no permanent decision-making structures or leaders of its own. As an organization, it came to life only at massive conferences like those held at Sandusky and Brownstown, where hundreds, sometimes thousands, of Indigenous men, women, and children collected to discuss their common concerns and participate in shared rituals. It was at such meetings that leaders renewed alliances among communities, fostered a sense of unity, and organized collective military and diplomatic campaigns.

Cultivating unity among dozens of towns and kin groups that spoke several mutually unintelligible languages and had divergent local interests was a daunting task. But the Shawnees had a long experience of it, and they soon emerged as the principal architects of the Indian Confederacy. They relied on both political arguments and spiritual symbols to convince Miamis, Lenapes, Wyandots, Ottawas, Ojibwes, Potawatomis, Sauks, Cherokees, Haudenosaunees, and other Natives to make a common stand against U.S. expansion. In a series of confederacy conferences from the mid-1780s through the early 1790s Shawnee leaders argued that all Indians formed a single people united by common interests, spirituality, and race. On the most straightforward level, they insisted that defending every inch of land north of the Ohio River was in the interest of all Indians. Even though the land immediately north of the Ohio was claimed by the Shawnees, Lenapes, Ohio Iroquois, and Miamis, more distant peoples such as the Ottawas, Potawatomis, and Ojibwes from the Great Lakes should also join in its defense. This was so, the Shawnees and their allies explained, because if the Americans ever conquered the northern shore of the Ohio River, they would inevitably continue their expansion northward and westward and invade the country of the Lake Indians and the western nations. Shawnee leaders recognized that sooner or later the insatiable American hunger for land was a threat to all Indians, for the Americans "never will rest until they have got the whole country." Now was the time for the Natives to unite and halt the expansion at the Ohio River.[40]

Political collaboration among the diverse Native communities was facilitated by the fact that the Shawnees modeled the Indian Confederacy on time-tested practices of collective and consensual decision-making. Just as their Fort Ancient ancestors had united disparate villagers into larger towns and their grandparents and parents had consolidated autonomous towns into regional and national coalitions, the Shawnee leaders built the Indian Confederacy by encouraging people from various nations, towns, and kin groups to gather at common council meetings where they could discuss shared problems and construct collective policies through negotiation and compromise. Just like Shawnee town and national councils, the confederacy meetings recognized only unanimous decisions and possessed no coercive power to enforce decisions. Although this often impeded quick action and supported factionalism, most Indians found the egalitarian structure of the confederacy attractive, for it facilitated cooperation without endangering long-standing communal autonomy. The confederacy conformed well with fundamental political philosophies of the Ohio Valley and Great Lakes Indians. For Shawnees and their neighbors, incorporating new groups into collective decision-making bodies had for centuries been the established way to build broad-based unity and collaboration.

On spiritual terms, Shawnee leaders drew on a long tradition of prophetic nativism among the Indians of eastern North America to envision and encourage Native unity. Following the teachings of several Lenape visionaries influential around the middle of the century, they argued that all Indians were the children of the same Creator and thus one people despite their diverse tribal and linguistic backgrounds. Such arguments had circulated throughout the East since the 1730s and resonated with many Native peoples. In the hands of the militant Shawnee headmen the idea of the spiritual unity of the Indians acquired increasingly racial dimensions. In 1785 Kekewepelethy called Indians "the people of one Colour." A Kishpoko speaker termed them "Brown Skins." Others connected skin color to spirituality. In a massive council at the Glaize in 1792 the Mekoche orator Musquaconocah (Red Pole) spoke of "all nations of our Colour" and assured his audience that the Creator looked at them "with as much or perhaps more compassion than those of a fairer complexion."[41]

During the second half of the eighteenth century eastern Indians had begun to use racial categories to order the social universe. Like contemporary Europeans, they focused increasingly on skin color to describe and explain the cultural differences that distinguished them from Europeans and Africans. Shawnee leaders did not invent racial categorization, but they gave it powerful political currency by equating shared skin color with a shared spiritual identity and shared political interests. For Kekewepelethy, Musquaconocah, and other Shawnee advocates of Native collaboration, skin color became a potent symbol for the argument that all Indians must unite to protect the country north of the Ohio.[42]

Beneath such symbols of unity the world of the Shawnees and their Indian allies remained town- and kin-centric. Even the Shawnees continued to debate how the allied Indians should deal with the United States. Initially, the Shawnees most active in building the Indian Confederacy were war leaders who saw Native military cooperation as the most efficient way of resisting U.S. expansion to the north side of the Ohio. At the Sandusky council in 1783 the

Shawnee delegation was led by Aquitsica, the renowned Pekowi war chief. When he died the next year, his close ally Sepettekenathé, now known as Waweyapiersenwaw, and the Wakatomikans Kekewepelethy and Peteusha took the lead in advocating the military collaboration of the Indian nations. All three men boasted prominent military careers. The most famous of the trio, Waweyapiersenwaw, or Blue Jacket, had led several expeditions against the Kentucky settlements during the Revolutionary War. In 1784 the British Indian Department had ceremonially granted him a commission that recognized him as a "War Chief." Peteusha had led Shawnee warriors in the defeat of Colonel William Crawford's troops in 1782. Later, he had specialized in raiding the boats of American settlers on the Ohio River. Kekewepelethy was a ceremonial orator as well as a military leader. He had participated in the disastrous Treaty of Fort Finney, but unlike the Mekoche headmen, he had publicly denounced the American demands for land there. This had gained him a reputation as a brave defender of Indian rights.[43]

Gradually, other Shawnee leaders joined these war chiefs to cultivate Indian unity. Most importantly, after the double disaster of the Fort Finney Treaty and Logan's raid in 1786 many Mekoches again endorsed Native cooperation. Biaseka and Musquaconocah became particularly active in organizing confederacy councils and collaboration. Kin ties played an essential role in connecting these men to the confederacy. Biaseka had a close relationship with Peteusha, who was apparently a Mekoche himself. In 1790 the two men joined together to establish a new town at Kekionga, where they wished "to gather all our straggling nation." Waweyapiersenwaw and Musquaconocah, in turn, were either half-brothers or cousins. Kekewepelethy was probably of Mekoche descent. Early in his career he had acted as an orator and "an *aid*" for Moluntha and other Mekoche chiefs. Despite their later disagreements, this background created intimate bonds between Kekewepelethy and the Mekoche leadership. During the late 1780s, then, the Shawnee military leaders successfully mobilized their kinship networks to muster support for the Indian Confederacy among the Mekoches who had just a few years before ignored Native unity to negotiate alone with the United States. Among the Shawnees, the confederacy grew horizontally as a series of interlocking alliances between leaders, kin groups, and towns.[44]

Collaboration among the diverse Shawnee leaders and groups was far from harmonious. Even when the Mekoche hokimas recognized the importance of Native cooperation for the defense of Shawnee lands, their views of the proper order of the Shawnee society differed from those of the war leaders. The Mekoches still claimed national leadership, which caused frequent friction between the two groups. In 1794, for example, Mekoche headmen demanded wampum beads that Crown officers had given to Waweyapiersenwaw "for his own purpose." The Pekowi war chief refused. This was no minor disagreement. Any leader needed wampum belts to present his agendas in international conferences. At stake, then, was whether Waweyapiersenwaw's or the Mekoches' voice would be heard among the neighboring Indians. Such factional disputes between the Mekoches and the war leaders continued to be grounded in divisional identities. Throughout the 1790s the papers of British officers and traders constantly referred to Shawnee towns and war parties as "Maycoché," "Pickeardé," "Chilicothe," and "Kiskapoo." This testifies to the enduring importance of the divisions in Shawnee communal life and politics.[45]

U.S. officials did their best to exacerbate frictions within the Indian Confederacy. Convinced that individual tribes would be easier to control than an extensive and strong coalition of Indian peoples, they took every opportunity to undermine Native unity. But the United States was hardly able to divide and rule the Indians at will. After the Revolutionary War the republic was weak and in constant danger of breaking up. In 1787 bleak economic realities forced Congress to admit that the United States simply could not afford a war against the Shawnees and their allies. When the Brownstown council threatened the Americans with a pan-Indian war, Congress finally accepted the Indian Confederacy as the legitimate representative of the Natives north of the Ohio and agreed to negotiate a new treaty with the leaders of the allied Indians. But even now congressional officials instructed the U.S. peace commissioner, Governor Arthur St. Clair of the Northwest Territory, to make "every exertion . . . to defeat all confederations and combinations among the tribes." Worse still, even before the peace talks began, St. Clair informed the Indians that the treaties of Fort Stanwix, McIntosh, and Finney would not be renegotiated. Congress merely wished to confirm these treaties with the Indian Confederacy and give the Natives additional gifts for the lands they had allegedly already ceded. Frustrated, Shawnees, Miamis, and their western allies along the Wabash River refused even to attend the new negotiations. Only a small group of Lenapes, Wyandots, Senecas, Ottawas, Ojibwes, and Sauks met with St. Clair at Fort Harmar on the Muskingum River in January 1789. Although the Natives again lacked authorization from the Indian Confederacy, St. Clair bullied them into signing a new treaty that confirmed the earlier land cessions. After the negotiations the governor gloated that the Indians' "general confederacy is entirely broken."[46]

St. Clair's joy was premature, however. American arrogance at the Treaty of Fort Harmar convinced more and more Indians across the Ohio and Great Lakes country to take up arms in defense of their lands. Indian attacks against the new American settlements in southern Ohio and Kentucky became so severe that they threatened the fragile unity of the United States. With a weak central government and myriads of localized identities and interests, the new republic had tottered on the brink of fragmentation since the end of the Revolutionary War. Many of its western citizens, especially in Kentucky, accused the eastern elites of neglecting them. Some planned to secede from the Union and join the Spanish empire or form an independent republic of their own. When the Indian Confederacy threatened to devastate the western settlements, the newly formed federal government of the United States had to take firm action to show its own citizens, the Natives, and the surrounding British and Spanish empires that it was both willing and able to protect its people and territory, even in the distant Ohio Valley. Accordingly, in October 1790 Colonel Josiah Harmar led nearly fifteen hundred troops toward the Maumee towns to subdue the Indian Confederacy. The Americans advanced as far as Kekionga, but there the united Shawnee, Miami, Potawatomi, Ottawa, Lenape, Sauk, and Meskwaki warriors routed them in a series of fierce battles. A year later the United States tried again. This time Governor St. Clair himself marched with sixteen hundred regulars, levies, and militiamen against the Maumee communities. At dawn on November 4, 1791, Waweyapiersenwaw, the Miami war chief Mishikinakwa (Little Turtle), and other military leaders attacked the U.S. camp on the Wabash River with more than one thousand warriors. After three hours of severe fighting the U.S. army fled in panic, and more than six hundred Americans lay dead on the battleground. Another three hundred had been wounded. It was the worst defeat the United States would ever suffer in Indian wars. The Indian Confederacy had shown that it was a force not to be taken lightly.[47]

But Shawnees and their allies paid a high price for their victories. By 1791 the Shawnees had been fighting the United States for sixteen years, during which their towns and fields had been laid to waste up to five times. The loss of Kentucky and the expansion of American settlements to the north side of the Ohio had diminished Shawnee hunting grounds drastically. Although Anglo-American visitors often admired the size and prosperity of the Shawnee, Miami, and Lenape cornfields on the Maumee River, periodic famines were common in these communities. Deteriorating economic conditions deepened Shawnee dependence on their British allies. Increasingly, it was British goods and supplies that enabled the Indians to carry on their war successfully. Women and children needed British provisions when warriors were away on military campaigns; men needed British powder, ball, and guns to fight the Americans and hunt for their families. English presents took on a central role in the everyday life of the Shawnee communities. Survival without a steady supply of Euroamerican goods was more and more difficult.[48]

Paradoxically, the impressive Indian victories over Harmar and St. Clair also eroded the unity of the Natives. After the shocking defeats the United States was ready to reopen negotiations with the confederacy. Many Ojibwes, Ottawas,

Potawatomis, and Haudenosaunees were now prepared to back down from the confederacy's original demand of the Ohio boundary in case the Americans, too, would make some territorial concessions. Local perspectives explain their position. The Lake Indians doubted that American settlements in southern Ohio threatened their lands farther north. The Iroquois communities in New York, on the other hand, were so exposed to American aggression that their leaders wished to bring the war to a speedy end. The Haudenosaunees and Lake Indians proposed that the Natives should cede the lands east of the Muskingum River to the United States as a compromise that would guarantee peace. Shawnee war leaders would hear none of that, however. Together with their Miami and Lenape allies they insisted on the Ohio boundary. Through 1792 and 1793 bitter arguments over the border wrecked the delicate unity of the allied Indians. Even the Shawnees split. In 1793 an American Quaker embassy reported that "the young Shawnese were high, and rough in their dispositions, especially warriors," while official U.S. peace commissioners learned that "near one half" of Shawnees "were for peace." Ironically, arguing about the Muskingum boundary was a moot point. The United States had no intention of giving up the populous settlements already established on the west side of the Muskingum.[49]

The decisive moment in the Twenty Years' War came in 1794. When the peace negotiations proved fruitless, General Anthony Wayne led a new U.S. army toward the Maumee towns. At the same time, long-running tensions between Great Britain and the United States reached a critical point. Guy Carleton, the governor of Canada, assured the Indians that the English would soon join them in a common war against the Americans. In May British troops from Detroit constructed a small outpost, Fort Miamis, on the Maumee just below the Glaize. Hopes of determined British aid breathed new life into the fledging Indian Confederacy. During the summer hundreds of warriors assembled on the Maumee, as the Shawnees, Lenapes, Miamis, Wyandots, Ojibwes, Ottawas, and Potawatomis put aside their differences to face Wayne's army together. But their unity remained fragile. After an initial clash with the Americans in June, most Lake Indians returned home, satisfied that they had done their part for the confederacy.[50]

But the Indians had not halted Wayne's advance. As the Native forces diminished, the Americans marched on to the Maumee. Shawnees, Miamis, and Lenapes evacuated their towns. Women and children fled downriver to Swan Creek, located in the protective shadow of Fort Miamis and its guns. The remaining warriors, now badly outnumbered, confronted Wayne's troops at Fallen Timbers just above the Glaize on August 20. After a fierce fight, they were forced to retreat downriver. The Indians still had one hope left: the British troops at Fort Miamis. But when the retreating warriors reached the fort, its gates remained shut. Unwilling to risk a war against the United States without explicit orders, the British commander refused to let the warriors take refuge inside the fort. The Natives had to give up the battle and flee to Swan Creek. Wayne did not pursue them; instead, his men destroyed the evacuated Indian towns and cornfields along the Maumee. Some Shawnees experienced such devastation for the sixth time since 1779. This time they could not even return to rebuild their homes, for Wayne erected two strong-holds, Fort Wayne and Fort Defiance, on the ruins of Kekionga and the Glaize. The United States now had a strong military beachhead in the heart of the Indian country.[51]

During the winter of 1794–1795 hunger, military defeat, and British betrayal broke the Indian Confederacy. Convinced that further resistance against the United States was futile, many leaders opened peace negotiations with General Wayne without waiting for collective confederacy resolutions. By December Wayne boasted that he had "succeeded in dividing & distracting the councils of the Hostile Indians." Heated disputes over leadership broke out among the Natives, as various factions and communities tried to come to terms with the Americans. Twenty years of war had scattered nations and eroded old structures of authority. There was little agreement over who had the right to lead which of the dozens of autonomous, multiethnic local communities. Among the Shawnees the war-weary Waweyapiersenwaw joined the Mekoches to negotiate a preliminary peace treaty with Wayne in the name of the nation in February 1795. Those Shawnees who still wanted to continue the war were furious. Even Waweyapiersenwaw and the Mekoches quickly fell out. Biaseka and the Mekoche military leader Catahecassa (Black Hoof) charged that Waweyapiersenwaw had taken "more upon him than he has right to" in the peace talks by claiming leadership over all Shawnees. The Mekoches argued that "none but a person of our Tribe could be king" and insisted that as their "Younger Brothers" the Pekowis and other Shawnee divisions must follow their leadership.[52]

As the Indian Confederacy disintegrated, the U.S. government sought to assert its vision of proper Native political organization. Federal Indian policy had long aimed at undermining pan-Indian collaboration and cultivating distinct, politically centralized tribes. American policymakers calculated that the leaders of such isolated and weak tribes could easily be made pliable through bribery, economic dependence, and threats. In 1787, for example, Congress had instructed U.S. peace commissioners that it was important to "select out carefully the chief and respectable men" "in the tribes" and "attach [them] to the United States by every means."[53] The confusing and dangerous landscape of independent Native towns, mobile kin groups, and complex multi-ethnic alliances was to be destroyed and replaced by an ordered world of centralized nations, their leaders under tight American control. When preparing the final peace treaty with the Ohio and Great Lakes Indians, federal officials were determined to finally fulfill these plans.

In July and August 1795 hundreds of Shawnees, Miamis, Wyandots, Lenapes, Ojibwes, Ottawas, Potawatomis, Ohio Iroquois, Eel Rivers, Kaskaskias, Piankashaws, and Kickapoos gathered at General Wayne's headquarters at Fort Greenville, in what is now west-central Ohio, to negotiate a conclusive treaty of peace. Shawnees remained extremely divided. Despite their disagreements, Waweyapiersenwaw, Catahecassa, and Musquaconocah led 143 Mekoches, Pekowis, and Chalaakaathas to the conference. Many important leaders and communities stayed away, however, including Kekewepelethy and his Wakatomikans. Similar divisions plagued many other Indian nations. Those groups that did go to Greenville found themselves in a very weak position for negotiating. U.S. soldiers now occupied forts throughout the Indian country. Moreover, in November 1794 Great Britain and the United States had buried their lingering differences in Jay's Treaty, removing any possibility that the redcoats would rush to aid the Indians. Most dramatically for the Natives, the British had agreed to hand Detroit, Niagara, and Michilimackinac over to the United States and retreat to their side of the international border as defined by the Treaty of Paris twelve years before. With all the aces in his hands, Wayne simply forced the Indians to cede most of present-day Ohio and southeastern Indiana to the United States. In addition, the Natives had to allow U.S. troops to occupy a series of forts even on the lands that remained in Indian possession. The United States now gained a tight military grip over the region south of the Great Lakes.[54]

The Indian Confederacy was a mere shadow at Greenville. The radical idea that the confederacy had collective custody of all Indian lands north of the Ohio melted into thin air when the Natives realized that they had little power to prevent the United States from taking all the lands it wanted. Individual leaders and tribes claimed exclusive rights to particular territories in order to guarantee that they would receive at least some compensation if the Americans took the land. The United States was in fact willing to pay for the lands it wrested from the Indians, with the payments forming an integral part in the federal effort to break the confederacy and support the rise of politically centralized tribes. The government agreed to pay one thousand dollars in "useful goods" annually to the Shawnees, Wyandots, Lenapes, Miamis, Ottawas, Ojibwes, and Potawatomis each, as well as five hundred dollars to the smaller tribes.[55] In the middle of the dire economic crisis wrought by the two decades of warfare, these annuities made Native nations crucial economic units. Moreover, the annual payments were to be made to men recognized by the Americans as legitimate tribal leaders. U.S. officials hoped that such economic support would strengthen centralized tribal governments and make it easier for federal agents to control Native leaders and communities.

U.S. authorities realized that the less than full Indian attendance at Greenville left the treaty on shaky ground. Secretary of War Timothy Pickering admitted to President George Washington that "the chiefs who signed the treaty are not numerous" but hastened to add that they included such notables as "Blue Jacket [Waweyapiersenwaw], the great Warrior of the Shawanoes" and "Misqua-coo-na-caw [Musquaconocah] their great speaker." It now became a matter of American self-interest to support the signatories of the treaty so that its legitimacy could not be questioned. Federal officials showered leaders like Waweyapiersenwaw with gifts of provisions, trade goods, silver medals, gorgets, and chiefly commissions, hoping that such generosity and respect would encourage the impoverished Natives to rally around these men. During the winter of 1796–1797 the Americans even took Waweyapiersenwaw, Musquaconocah, and a group of Ojibwe, Potawatomi, and Miami leaders to Philadelphia to meet President Washington.[56]

But despite American hopes, pressure and presents did not magically turn the divided Shawnees into a centralized nation. Instead, the Treaty of Greenville left a bitter legacy of conflict and dispersal. After the defeat at Fallen Timbers and the catastrophic treaty, many Shawnees again crossed the Mississippi into Spanish-claimed territory, where they joined their Kishpoko, Pekowi, and Thawikila kinspeople. When British troops evacuated Detroit in 1796, Kekewepelethy followed them to the Canadian side of the Detroit River and settled near the new English stronghold, Amherstburg. Many Kishpokos resentful of the Greenville Treaty migrated southwest to the Whitewater River in what is now Indiana. On the Maumee, political debates spilled into open violence like never before. When Musquaconocah died on his way back from Philadelphia in 1797, his relatives suspected witchcraft and killed the alleged sorcerer. In the cycle of revenge that followed, two more Shawnees lost their lives, including the venerable Mekoche war chief Oweeconnee. We can never know in detail what complex motives and interpersonal animosities led to this outburst of violence. The premature death of two prominent Mekoche headmen nevertheless suggests that disputes connected to the Greenville Treaty may well have been involved beneath the witchcraft accusations. If so, this is the first recorded case of Shawnees killing one another in a political dispute.[57]

By the late 1790s twenty years of vicious violence had dispersed and impoverished the Shawnees worse than ever since their diaspora in the late seventeenth century. The violence had driven them from the lands they had first united to defend and scattered the nation from the Maumee River to the central

Mississippi Valley. It had factionalized divisions and towns alike. Years later an aging war leader named Nenessica (Blackbeard) described the Twenty Years' War as a "great disturbance" that "put us in confusion."[58] Yet we should not see the Shawnees only as passive victims of colonial violence. Through the long war they had mobilized kinship networks, political alliances, and migrations to survive, defend their lands, and build new communities on the ruins of the old. After the Treaty of Greenville many leaders would again combine kinship webs, sacred power, and new economic strategies to once more draw the dispersed Shawnees together and ensure the survival of the nation in a world greatly transformed.

"BECOME AN INDEPENDENT PEOPLE"

Rebuilding the Nation, 1795–1833

In April 1809 eight Shawnee leaders visited a model farm operated by a Quaker named William Kirk in the outskirts of Wapakoneta, a large Shawnee town in what is now northern Ohio. There, the spokesman of the delegation, the Mekoche headman Catahecassa, recounted in grateful tones how Kirk had arrived at Wapakoneta two years earlier and admonished the Shawnees to take up "farming Buisness" and "raising Cattle & hogs," because "the game would be very scarce in a short time." Kirk's mission was part of the new federal Indian policy launched in the last years of the eighteenth century. Known as the "civilization program," the government's plan was to assimilate the Native peoples peacefully into American society by teaching them American economic and cultural practices such as commercial agriculture and Christianity. The Wapakonetan Shawnees had welcomed the government's economic and technological assistance. Yet they were not interested in assimilation. Instead, Catahecassa explained that Shawnees must adopt American innovations because these would help "our Nation [to] increas" and "become an independant people."[1]

While it initially sounded like a celebration of the federal civilization program, Catahecassa's speech actually outlined an equally ambitious rival project: the Mekoche leadership's plan to rebuild the scattered and impoverished Shawnee nation after the Twenty Years' War. After the Treaty of Greenville the Shawnees were rapidly encapsulated by the expanding United States. Increasingly a minority within the new republic, they had to imagine new strategies to retain their nationhood and autonomy. At Wapakoneta, Catahecassa and a group of other Mekoche leaders crafted a policy of national rebuilding that had three goals: gathering all Shawnees together on shared homelands, defending the sovereignty of the nation, and restoring the nation's economic self-sufficiency. As before, such a quest for unity sparked conflicts among the Shawnees. Some tribespeople denied the Mekoches' right to national leadership. Others argued that the Mekoches' willingness to adopt features of American culture endangered traditional Shawnee lifeways. In the first years of the nineteenth century these disputes became more violent than ever, as cultural and ideological fault lines between disparate Shawnee groups widened into open rifts. It was, however, the Americans who most resented the efforts of the Mekoches to build a sovereign Shawnee nation within the United States. In the 1820s they claimed that such an *imperium in imperio* threatened the sovereignty of their republic and took ruthless measures to dismantle the Shawnee nation.

FROM DEPENDENCY TO SOVEREIGNTY

The years following the Treaty of Greenville were hard for the Shawnees, as factional conflicts and economic problems troubled them. The leaders who had attended the Treaty of Greenville had been forced to cede most of their old Ohio homelands to the United States. The Maumee country where the Shawnees had taken refuge during the Twenty Years' War was claimed by the Miamis and Wyandots, and no one knew how long these hosts would allow the Shawnees to remain there now that American expansion made land scarce for all Indians. In the unsettled conditions many Shawnees hesitated to expend resources on building new permanent settlements and clearing new fields to replace those destroyed by General Wayne in 1794. Hunting and fur trade suffered as well. The Treaty of Greenville had transferred most of the old Shawnee hunting grounds to the United States. Although the treaty guaranteed Indians the right to hunt on the U.S. side of the new border, the rapid growth of the American population soon made Native hunting there difficult. In fact, Americans regularly crossed the Greenville line to hunt illegally on Indian lands. In 1802 Catahecassa complained that they "kill more than we do" and explained that "the little game that remains is very dear to us." With their agriculture, hunting, and trade in shambles, Shawnees often went hungry. American and British presents of provisions and supplies became essential for survival. Even then, according to Catahecassa, "our women and children [are] distressed for want of clothing and by hunger."[2]

Through these troubled times the Mekoche leaders retained their old vision of a united Shawnee nation. They still believed that unity formed the best defense of Shawnee lands and sovereignty in the transformed political landscape. After 1795 the Mekoches launched an ambitious program to gather the scattered nation together once more. Mekoche leaders identified two things essential for their success. First, only economic prosperity would make their people truly independent of American and British interference and allow their impoverished bands to collect together. Second, only sacred power could empower the nation to conquer the devastating legacy of poverty and faction- alism left by the Twenty Years' War. In 1796–1797 the Mekoche headmen Biaseka and Catahecassa founded a new town, Wapakoneta, on the upper reaches of the Auglaize River, in the heart of the territory where the Shawnees had lived for the previous twenty years. They soon began inviting Shawnees from places as distant as the Trans-Mississippi West to move to their town. As one Mekoche spokesman declared, "at present we shall live in one place and never move, and I hope everyone will look on us as formerly. We shall then believe the great spirit above will preserve all our nation."[3]

Mekoche leaders were willing to experiment with cultural innovations to achieve their goals. They quickly recognized that they could utilize the eager- ness of U.S. officials to "civilize" the Indians for their own purposes. In the 1780s U.S. authorities, most notably Secretary of War Henry Knox and President George Washington, had begun to worry about the mounting costs of the endless Indian wars and the damage that the violent dispossession of the Native peoples would do to the national honor of the new republic. As a remedy, Knox suggested that instead of destroying the Indians, the United States should civi- lize them. Evoking popular Enlightenment notions of cultural evolution, he argued that it was the duty of the republic to raise the "savage" Natives to the level of American civilization and transform them from barbarian foes into useful citizens through education. In the 1790s this "civilization mission" became the central tenet of the federal Indian policy. Government agents and missionaries were sent to Native communities across the East to guide the Indians toward what the Americans understood as civilized life. The most important step on this evolutionary ladder, as the Americans saw it, was to trans- form the economic foundation of the Native societies. Ignoring the fact that Algonquian women had taught maize farming to the first English settlers on the Atlantic Coast in the seventeenth century, U.S. officials and missionaries insisted that Indians were hunters who roamed in the wilderness hungry and impoverished. The key to civilizing them was to teach them agriculture. Even when some Americans grudgingly admitted that Indian women did in fact farm, they belittled Native agriculture. For Knox, Washington, and their compatriots, agriculture was efficient when it utilized heavy plows able to break and turn the ground properly. This, they insisted, was men's work, far too strenuous for women. Moreover, they believed that a farmer reached his best productivity when cultivating a private field of his own where he was the master of his fortune. Americans who saw eastern Indian women tilling communal fields with simple hoes could not comprehend how such farming could ever produce sufficient food. According to them, their mode of agriculture was better in every way. Not only productive, it was based on the proper patriarchal family structure and encouraged private enterprise. When Americans offered to teach farming to the Indians, they thus sought to impose their version of family, gender relations, and property on the Natives as well.[4]

Despite its lofty goals, the civilization program constituted a ruthless attack against Indian sovereignty and landownership. American policymakers hoped that the proliferation of private family farms would erode the unity of Native nations and assimilate the Indians into U.S. society. They believed that when the Indians changed their wandering hunting way of life to that of settled farmers, they would need only a fraction of their lands and would gladly sell the surplus to the United States. As President Thomas Jefferson wrote in 1803, "when [the Indians] withdraw themselves to the culture of a small piece of land, they will perceive how useless to them are their extensive forests, and will be willing to pare them off from time to time in exchange for necessaries for their families & farms."[5]

The Treaty of Greenville opened the civilization mission in the Old Northwest, encouraging Indians to explore American agriculture by making the new tribal annuities payable "in domestic animals, implements of Husbandry . . . & in compensation to useful Artificers who may reside with or near [the Indians], & be employed for their benefit." The Mekoche leaders of Wapakoneta were interested in such offers. In 1801 they requested "some Farming tools" from the government. The next year Catahecassa led a delegation of headmen to Washington, where he asked President Jefferson for "all necessary Farming tools & those for building houses," as well as "some domestick Animals." The Mekoches did not have acculturation in mind, however. On the contrary, Catahecassa and other leaders recognized that American technology could help them to achieve their own goals of economic self-sufficiency, political sovereignty, and national unification. They argued that new Euroamerican agricultural strategies and technologies would make the Shawnees of Wapakoneta prosperous enough to be able "to act without depending on the will or caprice of other people." Their prosperity would then draw their scattered tribespeople from the Maumee, Wabash, Canada, and Trans-Mississippi West to Wapakoneta. "We make no doubt," declared Catahecassa in 1807, "but all that we can get here will do well for themselves, their women & Children." For the Mekoche leaders, the federal civilization mission was a useful tool for restoring what they considered the traditional political order.[6]

The economic program of the Wapakonetan leaders got a promising start. When two Quakers visited the town in 1804, they noted approvingly that the local Shawnees owned "40 head of Cattle & make Butter & Cheese." The Friends regarded this as a sign that the Wapakonetans were "making some progress in Civilization." Three years later Secretary of War Henry Dearborn

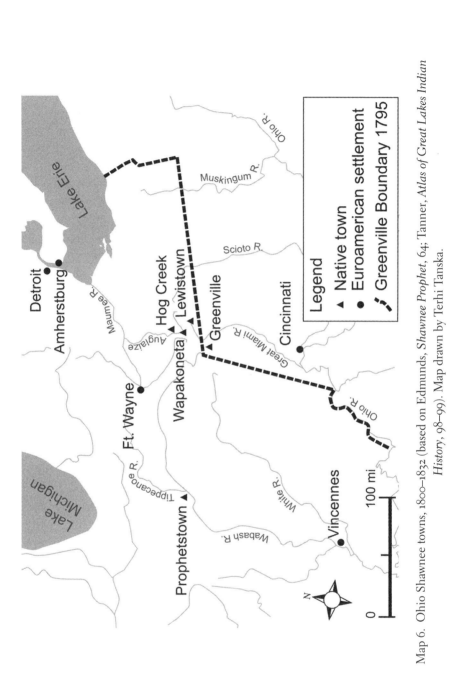

Map 6. Ohio Shawnee towns, 1800–1832 (based on Edmunds, *Shawnee Prophet*, 64; Tanner, *Atlas of Great Lakes Indian History*, 98–99). Map drawn by Terhi Tanska.

appointed another Quaker, William Kirk, to establish a model farm in Wapakoneta to assist the Shawnees in their efforts to adopt American agriculture. Kirk and several hired hands worked in the town for eighteen months with government funding. With their assistance the locals cleared new fields; planted new cultigens such as potatoes, cabbage, and turnips; and experimented with plow farming. They also "built Comfortable houses of hewd logs with chimneys" and fenced their fields. In 1808 Kirk hired a blacksmith to work in Wapakoneta and began constructing a sawmill and a gristmill. By that fall the Wapakonetans had "at least 500 acres of [land] grown in corn & Vegetables." They also owned "a plentiful Stock of Cattle & hogs."[7]

Many neighboring American settlers were genuinely impressed by "the advances made" in Wapakoneta "since Mr. Kirk has been here." Yet revolutionary as farming and stock-raising Indians living in log houses may have seemed to Americans with little previous knowledge of Native communities, the developments in Wapakoneta remained firmly rooted in Shawnee culture. Kirk often penned self-serving reports to his funders in the War Department, claiming that the Shawnees were rapidly abandoning communal fields in favor of private farms and that Native men were taking over the agricultural work. There is little independent evidence for such claims. Some Wapakonetan men may have assumed a more active role in farm work than had been common before. John Norton, a traveler of mixed Cherokee, English, and Mohawk background, visited Wapakoneta in 1810 and wrote that "the Men here are never prevented, by a vain pride, from taking upon them a part of the Labours of the Corn field, when free from other engagements." Yet the only tasks Norton described men performing in the fields were clearing and fencing the land, and both of these were traditional duties of Shawnee men. Other visitors depicted Wapakonetan agriculture in highly traditional terms, with women farming communal fields and small household gardens.[8] The townspeople clearly fitted Kirk's instructions to their own culture and goals.

The secretary of war terminated Kirk's mission at the end of 1808, when the Quaker was suspected (wrongly) of mishandling government money. Even then his assistance had greatly advanced the goals of the Mekoche leaders. As Wapakoneta began to prosper, many impoverished Shawnee bands made their way to the town. In addition to the Mekoches, the settlers included at least Chalaakaathas and possibly some Kishpokos. By 1809 Wapakoneta's population had risen to five hundred, making it the largest Shawnee community since Lower Shawneetown in the 1750s.[9] Three other settlements were also founded close by. Almost four hundred Shawnees and Senecas built Lewistown on the headwaters of the Great Miami River. The mixed Shawnee-Haudenosaunee heritage of this group suggests that at least some of its inhabitants may have traced their roots to Wakatomika, the old and stubbornly independent community of Shawnees and Ohio Iroquois. A smaller settlement known as Captain Johnny's Town stood within two miles of Lewistown, while Chalaakaathas established the hamlet of Hog Creek on the Auglaize just down-river from Wapakoneta.[10] Not since the Treaty of Greenville had so many Shawnees gathered together. Most significantly, now groups like the Mekoches, Chalaakaathas, and Wakatomikans who had often quarreled bitterly during the Twenty Years' War were willing to live and work together.

The federal government supported forcefully such consolidation of Native peoples. William Wells, the U.S. Indian agent at Fort Wayne, explained that "each nation should be collected together and some regular system of government established among them." To create centralized Indian nations, federal officials relied on annuities. They hoped that yearly deliveries of money, provisions, clothes, and tools to a few prominent tribal chiefs would encourage scattered Indians to gather around these men, whose own status would depend on the continued economic support of the United States. This would greatly facilitate the federal control of the Natives. Each fall the Shawnees, too, received one thousand dollars' worth of goods and money in accordance with the Treaty of Greenville. The leaders of Wapakoneta quickly persuaded U.S. offi-cials that they were entitled to receive the whole Shawnee annuity on behalf of the nation. It is not clear how they argued their case. Most likely they reminded the Americans of their prominent role in the Greenville negotiations and emphasized their support for the civilization program. Hundreds of Shawnees collected each fall at Detroit or Fort Wayne for the annuity payment, but offi-cials always gave the goods to Catahecassa, Biaseka, and other Wapakonetan headmen. The chiefs then distributed the supplies to their people. In the tight times following the Twenty Years' War the ability to funnel the much-needed annuities to their community helped the Wapakonetan chiefs to validate their leadership, strengthen their authority, and attract more Shawnees to their town. With annuities, the control and redistribution of material resources became increasingly important for the leaders. Impoverished by the long war, common men and women found themselves dependent on the American goods procured by Catahecassa, Biaseka, and other chiefs. For the first time, Shawnee leaders commanded direct control over the material well-being of their people.[11]

Yet important as the annuities were, one should not overemphasize their significance. Unlike some historians have claimed, Catahecassa and his allies were not "government chiefs" who simply used their access to American resources to force other Shawnees under their leadership. In fact, the annuity of one thousand dollars was so small that when it was divided among the Shawnees, "none of us get more then a Blankett, a Shirt or a Axe, and the greater part of us nothing at all," as Catahecassa once complained. Something more than American supplies attracted Shawnees to Wapakoneta. This was spiritual power. In 1795, just before they began building Wapakoneta, Biaseka and Catahecassa declared that the Creator had long ago placed the Mekoches "in the middle of" the world "to hold it steady" and given them a powerful miišaami to maintain the correct order of the universe. If all Shawnees gathered together at Wapakoneta, they could once more put their trust on the Mekoches' spiritual power in a world out of joint. The federal Indian agent John Johnston explained that the Mekoches had "the priesthood [among the Shawnees].— They perform the sacrifices and all the religious ceremonies of the nation." In other words, the Mekoches again mobilized their miišaami to benefit all the Shawnees gathered at Wapakoneta. Oral histories collected by Charles Trowbridge in the 1820s also associate the Mekoches with great spiritual power. In one narrative the ancestor of the division is described as covered with white paint as a sign of his ritual purity.[12] The Wapakonetan Mekoches thus funneled both spiritual blessings and federal annuities to their people. For Shawnees, political unity and leadership continued to be grounded in sacred power. Like their ancestors had done several times since the sixteenth century, the people who gathered at Wapakoneta, Lewistown, Captain Johnny's Town, and Hog Creek came together to share not only economic resources, but also miišaami.

Shawnee consolidation remained likewise rooted in old ideas of kinship and collective decision-making. Catahecassa once described the five Shawnee divisions as "the different families of our nation." His own status illuminates well the egalitarian structure of the nation he helped to build. Catahecassa had first gained renown as a war leader in the 1780s and 1790s, but after the Treaty of Greenville he became a skillful negotiator with U.S. officials and missionaries. Americans often called him "the Principal Chief of the nation," but this reflected their own notions of centralized national structures rather than Shawnee political realities. Instead, Catahecassa was the spokesman of the national council, just like Nucheconner, Kisinoutha, and Moluntha before him.[13] In the early years of the nineteenth century local and clan leaders from Wapakoneta, Lewistown, Captain Johnny's Town, and Hog Creek began meeting at the council house of Wapakoneta to discuss their common concerns. Although Catahecassa, Biaseka, and other Mekoches played a prominent role in these councils, it is possible to identify representatives of other groups, too, including Shemanetoo, whose roots went to Wakatomika and who may have been a Kishpoko; the Pekowi leader Pemthala (John Perry); and Lewistown's headman Quitewepea (Lewis). In one thoroughly documented council meeting in 1825 each division and at least one clan had its own speaker who stated the opinions of his group to the whole council before the assembled leaders attempted to forge a collective decision.[14]

The persistence of such collective decision-making is remarkable, for U.S. officials sought to centralize power in Indian communities in the hands of pliable individual headmen with the help of annuities, presents, and bribes. "When an Indian chief becomes an obstacle in our way," wrote Johnston, "he should be let down and others raised in his place and this I know can be done with proper management on the part of the public agents." Many historians, too, have argued that decentralized Native political structures, "traditionally committed to consensus decision making, were ill-equipped to stand up to the federal pressures." Shawnee evidence, however, points to exactly opposite conclusions. The national council at Wapakoneta remained both able and willing to hinder the centralization of power to any one chief. When Lewistown's headman Quitewepea, for example, secretly visited Washington to curry the favor of federal officials, he was sharply rebuked by other Shawnee leaders and quickly lost much of his influence in national affairs. Collective decision-making remained a strength for the Shawnees, for it made it impossible for federal officials to control the nation by bribing or pressuring individual headmen. Council work also became an effective means to assert cooperation among the diverse groups collecting at and near Wapakoneta. Leaders quickly noticed that stubborn dissenters would be marginalized from decision-making and lose their power to influence such critical matters as annuity distributions and land cessions.[15]

One of the main goals of the Wapakoneta council was to create a collective homeland for all Shawnees in northern Ohio. The Treaty of Greenville had guaranteed that all Indian land not ceded in the treaty would remain in Native possession "so long as [the Indians] please." Less than a decade after the treaty federal officials nevertheless began a campaign of relentless territorial expansion in the Old Northwest. Between 1803 and 1809 Governor William Henry Harrison of the Indiana Territory and Governor William Hull of the Michigan Territory concluded a total of fifteen treaties with the local Indians in which the Natives sold virtually all of present-day Illinois, half of Indiana, and large parts of Michigan and Wisconsin to the United States. Legally, the treaties were highly dubious. Harrison in particular arbitrarily designated one or two Indian nations as the "true" owners of any piece of land the government wished to buy and then bullied or bribed a handful of selected headmen to sell it. To facilitate cessions he knowingly bought land from tribes that had no right to sell it and ignored those communities that he suspected might be averse to selling.[16] This ruthless land grabbing put the Shawnees in a particularly vulnerable position. Living on the Auglaize and Great Miami rivers as the guests of the Miamis and Wyandots, they were justly concerned that someone might easily sell the very ground on which they had built their homes. After all, this had happened time and again during the past century, from the Haudenosaunee-Pennsylvania land sales to the treaties of Fort Stanwix and Fort McIntosh.

In February 1802 a delegation of Wapakoneta and Lewistown leaders traveled to Washington with a contingent of Lenape headmen. The Lenapes shared the Shawnees' predicament. Diasporic refugees originally from the mid-Atlantic seaboard, they had often had to defend their land rights in the Ohio Country against other Native nations as well as the Americans. The Twenty Years' War had once again forced the Lenapes to retreat to new homelands on the White River in modern Indiana, and now they wished to solidify their claims to this country. In Washington Catahecassa spoke for the Shawnee and Lenape delegations and asked President Jefferson and Secretary of War Dearborn to "give us a good piece of land." He explained that the federal authorities should recognize Shawnee and Lenape ownership of a territory whose eastern boundary ran from the headwaters of the Mad River to the Auglaize and its tributary, the Blanchard River, and down these rivers to the Glaize. From there the border turned west, followed the Maumee River, and crossed the portage to the Wabash. Finally, the boundary ran south along the Wabash to the Greenville treaty line that formed the southern border of the Shawnee and Lenape country. The Mekoches had long spoken of a collective Shawnee homeland, but never before had they defined its borders in such detail. The growing territorial pressure of the American republic forced both Shawnee and Lenape leaders to imagine their people increasingly as territorial nations. As Catahecassa explained to Dearborn, "We wish . . . that you would give us under your hand a Deed that nobody shall take any advantage of us." Unfortunately, federal officials were reluctant to strengthen any Indian claims to the soil. Dearborn refused giving the delegation a deed for their lands, explaining that "the President does not consider himself authorized to divide the Lands of his red children or to make any particular grants to any." Disappointed, the Wapakonetan leaders nevertheless continued their efforts to persuade neighboring Indians to acknowledge their rights to the lands along the Auglaize. In the following years they often discussed with the Lenapes, Miamis, and Wyandots "the propotial of deviding the Lands" into bounded national territories.[17]

All Shawnees agreed on the importance of guaranteeing tribal land rights. But many recognized disturbingly centralist tendencies in the efforts of the Wapakonetan leadership to collect the nation together on common homelands. In the lean years after the Twenty Years' War, the Wapakonetan leaders sought to strengthen national unity by taking a harder line against dissenter groups that refused to settle at or near Wapakoneta. In particular, they tightened their grip on two crucial scarce resources—land and annuities—and claimed that these constituted national property that should be under the control of the national council rather than individual local or clan leaders. During the first decade of the nineteenth century the control of land and annuities became a source of bitter disputes between the national leadership at Wapakoneta and dissident groups elsewhere.

The first clash occurred in 1805, when the U.S. government wanted to buy Indian lands between the Sandusky and Cuyahoga rivers in northern Ohio. Marginal to most Shawnees, the country belonged to the Wyandots living on the Sandusky. However, about thirty Shawnees had settled among the Wyandots. Their representatives participated with Wyandot leaders in the land cession negotiations with federal officials at Fort Industry. Catahecassa, too, attended the treaty. Eventually, both Catahecassa and a Sandusky Shawnee leader signed the land cession together with Wyandot, Lenape, Munsee, Ottawa, Ojibwe, and Potawatomi headmen. This suggests that Shawnees considered the consent of both local leaders and the national council a prerequisite for valid land cessions. But the Shawnees did not agree who had the primary right to the new annuity rising from the land sale. The Treaty of Fort Industry promised a collective annuity of one thousand dollars to all the Indians involved in the treaty. It clearly stated that the Shawnees' portion of this sum was intended for the Sandusky Shawnees who had actually used the ceded lands. Yet only two years after the treaty Catahecassa complained that the Wapakonetans "have received none" of the money. Later the Mekoches persuaded Agent Johnston to pay the entire annuity at Wapakoneta. Johnston regarded the Wapakonetan leadership as the national government of the Shawnees and saw nothing odd in their request to control what they claimed was national revenue. This time it was the Sandusky Wyandots' turn to complain. They argued that "the Shawnees of Wacpockanata is not intitled to any of the money of Swan Creek Treaty but there is some Individuals familys who reside amoung us who is intitled to a Share." Economic hardships thus pushed Indian leaders across the Great Lakes region to compete for land and money.[18]

In 1806 the Wapakonetan leadership was embroiled in a new dispute over national resources. This time they faced the aging Pekowi war chief Waweyapiersenwaw. Although Waweyapiersenwaw had often collaborated with the Mekoches in the past, their relationship had long been tense. After the Treaty of Greenville the Pekowi headman had refused to settle at Wapakoneta and had instead established a town of his own near Detroit. In 1806 he joined forces with a group of dissident Kishpokos who had settled in Greenville, Ohio, and openly accused the Mekoche chiefs at Wapakoneta of misusing power. When famine threatened the Greenville Kishpokos and Pekowis that fall, Waweyapiersenwaw persuaded Michigan's Governor Hull to hand over a sizable portion of the Shawnee annuity to them. The Wapakonetans were enraged. "We think it is not right," complained Catahecassa, "as there is not half as many of our Nation lives there [in Greenville] as there is here and none of our principal Chiefs there, but

Bluejacket [Waweyapiersenwaw] who we do not consider as a Chief as he does not come to our Council."[19]

Catahecassa's outburst highlights a pivotal development in the Mekoche leaders' image of Shawnee nationhood. When they struggled to unite the Shawnees on common homelands and to secure centralized control over such critical resources as land and annuities in politically and economically precarious circumstances, Catahecassa, Biaseka, and their allies defined the Shawnee nation in increasingly narrow terms. They now argued that those Shawnees who refused to move to the tribal homelands surrounding Wapakoneta and take part in the national council at that town lost their right to share the national resources or to be considered "Chiefs." Many Shawnees who cherished old ideas of local autonomy resented this centralized vision of nationhood. By 1805 some of them were ready for a rebellion.

THE REBELLION OF TENSKWATAWA AND TECUMSEH

In the spring of 1805 some two hundred Kishpokos, settled on the White River in what is now eastern Indiana, were suffering from a deadly sickness that may have been either influenza or smallpox. At a time when most Ohio Shawnees were gathering at Wapakoneta and its neighborhood, these Kishpokos harbored no such plans. A long history of diaspora and dissent separated them from the Mekoches urging national consolidation. When the Haudenosaunee attacks had dispersed the Shawnees from the Ohio Valley in the late seventeenth century, many Kishpokos had taken refuge among the Upper Creeks in Alabama. Throughout the eighteenth century Kishpoko bands had continued to move back and forth between the Creek country and the Shawnee lands on the Ohio. In the 1780s hundreds had migrated to the central Mississippi Valley, while others had settled among the Chickamauga Cherokees on the Tennessee River. Even those Kishpokos who had eventually joined their tribespeople on the Maumee River in the early 1790s had refused to participate in the Treaty of Greenville. After the treaty they had shunned Wapakoneta and settled instead among their Lenape allies on the White River.[20] Mobility, multiethnic kinship networks, and local autonomy had thus shaped the lives of the White River Kishpokos and their ancestors for well over a century.

As the epidemic harassed the Kishpokos in the spring of 1805, a healer named Lalawéthika succumbed to a deathlike trance. His family was already preparing for his funeral when he suddenly came back to life. Lalawéthika had an astonishing story to tell. He explained that during his trance he had traveled on a mysterious path to a place "where it forked." There, spirit beings had told him that this was where "people were convicted of sin." Lalawéthika had then met Meteelemelakwe, the Creator, who had warned him that Indians were on a path to destruction. They had abandoned many of their sacred traditions and adopted White habits instead, even though the Creator had specifically given "different manners, customs, animals, vegetables &c." to the Indians and the Whites. They had married White people, although Meteelemelakwe had marked Indians and Europeans "with different colours, that they might be a separate people." Indians had also allowed Whites to settle on the lands that the Creator had made solely for them. Finally, they had learned countless "sins" from the Whites, "such as stealing [and] getting drunk," that were ripping apart the moral fabric of their communities. The Creator sternly told Lalawéthika that unless the Indians renounced White customs, revived their own traditions, and rejected their vices, they "would be destroyed from the face of the earth."[21]

Inspired by his vision Lalawéthika began preaching a "nativist gospel" to Indians near and far. He adopted a new name, Tenskwatawa, or Open Door, to emphasize his sacred duty to lead the Natives to a better future. Many people came to know him simply as the Prophet. Tenskwatawa's doctrine constituted what anthropologists today term a revitalization movement. Common among colonized peoples around the globe, revitalization movements call for spiritual and social reform in order to restore the autonomy and traditional culture of a people threatened by foreign invaders. This was Tenskwatawa's goal, too. He taught that Indians must give up drinking and other sins learned from the Whites. They also had to throw away "all kind of White people's dress" and again wear "Skins or Leather of your own dressing." Those married to Euroamericans must leave their spouses and mixed-blood children. Condemning centuries of economic and cultural coexistence between Natives and newcomers, the Prophet demanded the Indians quit the fur trade with the Euroamericans. He explained that killing animals "for their Skins only" made the Creator angry. Like many previous Indian prophets in the eighteenth century, Tenskwatawa also feared that the trade made the Natives dependent on Euroamerican goods. In a radical spiritual critique of the civilization program, he further declared that Indians must not acquire or even eat cattle, hogs, sheep, or chickens, for these animals Meteelemelakwe had made solely for the White people. Whereas the Mekoches of Wapakoneta sought to protect Shawnee independence within the United States by cautiously adopting some features of American economy, Tenskwatawa saw a total cultural, economic, and political separation from the Americans as the only viable path to Native autonomy.[22]

Tenskwatawa addressed his gospel to all Indians. When both federal officials and Wapakonetan leaders sought to consolidate Native peoples under distinct tribal governments, the Prophet claimed that it was not important whether one was a Shawnee or an Ottawa. The essential thing was to be an Indian. Drawing from the teachings of the eighteenth-century prophets and the leaders of the

Figure 1. *Ten-squat-a-way, The Open Door, Known as The Prophet, Brother of Tecumseh*, by George Catlin. When George Catlin painted this portrait of Tenskwatawa at the Shawnee reservation in Kansas in 1830, the aged prophet chose to pose with some of the most potent instruments of his spiritual power, including the "medicine fire" in his right hand and the sacred beads in his left. Both had played a central role in Tenskwatawa's rituals twenty years earlier. © Smithsonian American Art Museum, Gift of Mrs. Joseph Harrison Jr.

Indian Confederacy, Tenskwatawa argued that all Native peoples were spiritually and racially united: they shared the same Creator and the same skin color. Echoing Kekewepelethy, Musquaconocah, and other Shawnee advocates of Indian unity in the 1780s and 1790s, the Prophet admonished the Indians to "cultivate peace between your different Tribes that they may become one great people." It was a vision that struck at the heart of the Mekoche plan to collect all Shawnees together and separate their homeland from the lands of the neighboring Native peoples.[23]

Tenskwatawa's teachings quickly electrified political debates in Shawnee communities. His condemnation of the civilization program constituted a direct attack against the Wapakonetan leaders who advocated the adoption of American farming technologies, cattle, and mills. Resentful of William Kirk's efforts to build a model farm in Wapakoneta and to teach the local men to farm, Tenskwatawa claimed that the goal of the civilization program was "to make Slaves of us & git our lands." In 1806 he led his Kishpokos from the White River to Greenville, where they established a new town close to the site where the fateful peace treaty had been negotiated eleven years before. The Prophet invited other Shawnees to abandon the Mekoche leaders and gather at Greenville. Attacking the Mekoches' claims to sacred authority, he accused Catahecassa and three other Wapakonetan headmen of actually possessing "Poisonous Medicine" used for witchcraft and threatened that "if they would not give it up," his followers would "kill them."[24]

Tenskwatawa's threat demonstrates in a chilling way the growing virulence of political debates among the Shawnees. Since the Treaty of Greenville disputes over power and social order had turned increasingly nasty, as evidenced by the witchcraft accusations and intranational killings in 1797. This virulence stemmed from many roots. Throughout the East many Indians had since the early eighteenth century distrusted traditional leaders and their sacred power, which seemed inefficient against the onslaught of colonialism. Prophets preaching Native cultural revitalization had occasionally even accused chiefs willing to collaborate with colonists of witchcraft. The new racial worldview advocated by the Shawnee leaders of the Indian Confederacy in the 1780s and 1790s, and later adopted by Tenskwatawa, added a new edge to such suspicions. When the supporters of Native unity argued that Indians formed a single spiritual, cultural, and racial body, they called into question the identity and loyalty of those tribespeople who showed any interest in accommodating the Euroamericans or adopting Euroamerican technologies or customs. This shifted the rules in intranational disputes. Previously, political adversaries had recognized one another as Shawnee kin and avoided violence, even in bitter disputes. But when the advocates of Native unity equated their accommodationist opponents with "Whites," they defined such people as non-kin and were prepared to treat them as such. Already during the Revolutionary War militant Shawnees had threatened the life of the Mekoche headman Colesquo and his allies, whom they "esteemed Virginians."[25]

Tenskwatawa made no idle threats. In March 1806 he had helped the White River Lenapes to identify and execute several witches. Revealingly, all of the alleged sorcerers had been either acculturated Lenapes with close ties to Moravian missionaries or chiefs who had sold Lenape land to the United States and advocated cooperation with the Americans. When two Wapakonetans were killed in the spring of 1807, the townspeople accused Tenskwatawa's followers. For a moment the Shawnees seemed to be on the brink of a civil war. Fortunately, moderate minds prevailed. In June the Wapakonetans and the Prophet's people buried the killings and witchcraft accusations. The relations between the two groups remained tense, however. "That part of our nation that reside at Greenville," complained the Wapakonetan leaders, "will not listen to us."[26]

Hard hearing went both ways. In fact, relatively few Shawnees listened to Tenskwatawa's teachings. Many tribespeople were disturbed by his virulent attack against the Wapakonetan leaders; others questioned his views of what constituted legitimate Shawnee traditions. Like many revitalization leaders, Tenskwatawa chose some traditions for revival but discarded others as "sinful." Most dramatically, he banned personal "medicine bags" in which people carried spiritually powerful objects associated with their personal guardian spirit. According to the Prophet, evil people abused their personal sacred power for witchcraft; therefore, it was essential to destroy the medicine bags. Such reinterpretations of traditions caused considerable opposition among the Shawnees. Indeed, Tenskwatawa won followers among mainly his kinspeople and other long-time opponents of the Mekoche leadership. His most important ally outside his own Kishpoko community was Waweyapiersenwaw. A staunch opponent of the Mekoches and a leader of the old Indian Confederacy, the aged Pekowi headman found Tenskwatawa's call for pan-Indian cooperation appealing. Moreover, ties of kinship may have connected him to Tenskwatawa, whose mother was a Pekowi. Waweyapiersenwaw was soon "considered the friend and principal adviser of the Prophet."[27]

Tenskwatawa found more eager audiences elsewhere. Throughout the Old Northwest Indian peoples anxious over the expansion of the United States, the growing scarcity of game, and the social disruption caused by heavy drinking embraced his gospel of social and spiritual reform. For many, it offered a better solution to their mounting problems than the civilization program championed by federal agents and some tribal leaders. Hundreds of Indians across the Great Lakes country traveled to Greenville to learn more of this new message of hope. At first, most visitors came from the neighboring

Shawnee, Lenape, and Wyandot towns, but in 1807 scores of more distant pilgrims made their way to the Prophet. Ojibwes and Ottawas came from the shores of Lakes Michigan and Superior; Potawatomis from Wisconsin, Michigan, and Illinois; Kickapoos from central Illinois; Menominees from Green Bay; Ho-Chunks (Winnebagos) from southern Wisconsin; and Sauks and Meskwakis from northern Illinois. "Indians have continued to flock to Greenville," complained Agent Wells in August 1807, when travelers from "the Lakes near Mackincac" passed Fort Wayne on their way to meet Tenskwatawa.[28]

Such a collection of Indians threw U.S. officials and settlers into a panic. Many interpreted Tenskwatawa's call for Native unity as evidence that he wanted to rouse all the tribes to a common war against the United States. Such fears were unfounded. Although some of Tenskwatawa's followers berated the Americans as the "Scum of the great water," the children of the evil Underworld monsters, the Prophet himself did not advocate military resistance against the United States. There was no need to. Tenskwatawa believed that once the Indians had reformed their sinful ways, the Creator would simply destroy the Americans. But many Americans expected a more immediate showdown. When maritime quarrels brought the United States and Great Britain to the brink of a new war in the summer of 1807, terrified federal officials became convinced that Tenskwatawa was "an Engine set to work by the British." Wells in particular flooded his superiors with caustic reports accusing the Prophet of hostile plans and insisting that it was "absolutely necessary that the Shawnees at green vill Should be sent from that place." Like other federal officials, Wells was afraid of Tenskwatawa's multi-ethnic town because it was not under the control of the tribal chiefs recognized by the U.S. government. The "assemblage of vagabond Indians at Greenville composed of parts of all the Tribes in this Country" threatened the very system of centralized nations that federal officers had been constructing since the Treaty of Greenville.[29]

Many Native leaders across the Old Northwest likewise saw Tenskwatawa as a disruptive force. When especially younger men left their homes to join the Prophet at Greenville, older and more established leaders felt that their authority and the unity of their communities were endangered. In 1810 a large gathering of Wyandot, Ottawa, Ojibwe, Potawatomi, Shawnee, Lenape, Munsee, and Haudenosaunee leaders sent a pointed message to Tenskwatawa, asking "why have you invited the young men of the Old Nations to your Councils and influenced them to measures contrary to the customs of the nations to which they belong?" They insisted that the Wyandot settlement of Brownstown remained the only legitimate meeting place for pan-Indian councils and argued that it was "improper" for the Prophet to kindle a rival council fire "at any other place except for your nation alone."[30] Tribal leaders who strove to control tribal annuities and lands feared Tenskwatawa's growing multitribal community almost as much as federal officials.

Despite the opposition, Tenskwatawa's gospel continued to spread. He won adherents especially among such western Indians as the Potawatomis, Kickapoos, Ho-Chunks, and Sauks, whose communities stretched from the upper Mississippi River to Lake Michigan. The westerners resented the expansion of the United States bitterly. In 1804 Governor Harrison had deprived them of seven million acres of land in the fraudulent Treaty of St. Louis. The next year Sauks had begun building a multitribal confederacy to stem the American invasion. They and other militant western Indians received with great enthusiasm Tenskwatawa's message of the brotherhood of all Natives. In the autumn of 1807 the renowned Potawatomi war leader Main Poc visited Greenville. In an effort to unite the militant westerners and the Prophet's followers, he invited Tenskwatawa to move west to the Wabash River. Threatened by suspicious Americans and hostile tribal leaders, the Kishpoko preacher was happy to accept the invitation. Early in 1808 his followers abandoned Greenville and established a new settlement, Prophetstown, at the mouth of the Tippecanoe River, a tributary of the Wabash.[31]

The migration to the Wabash and the alliance with the western militants mark an important shift in Tenskwatawa's movement. Previously the Prophet had focused on cultural revitalization and social reformation. On the Wabash he and his brother, a war leader named Tecumseh, began speaking more and more about the need of the Indians to unite politically to defend their lands against American encroachments. In April 1808 Tenskwatawa announced that "the Indians in america" planned to unite at Prophetstown where "they would then be able to watch the Boundry Line between the Indians and white people—and if a white man put his foot over it . . . the warriors could Easly put him back." A few months later Tecumseh added that his brother wanted to "collect the different nations to form one settlement on the Wabash . . . in order to preserve their country from all encroachments." The endless land cessions demanded by governors Harrison and Hull had convinced Tenskwatawa and Tecumseh that U.S. expansion was the root cause of all Native problems. The brothers continued to seek spiritual redemption for the Indians, but they saw that they also needed a political and military response to the American invasion. Tecumseh took a prominent role in uniting "the Indians in america." Like countless Shawnee diplomats before him, he began traveling to Native communities across the Old Northwest, Midwest, and South and admonished all Indians to join forces against the American threat. The Indian Confederacy that had been destroyed in the Treaty of Greenville was suddenly coming back to life.[32]

When they called for a united defense of Indian lands, Tenskwatawa and Tecumseh attacked one of the fundamental tenets of both federal and Native constructions of Indian nationhood: tribal territories. They revived the old idea of collective Native landownership championed by the Indian Confederacy of the 1780s and 1790s. Tecumseh denied vehemently the right of federal agents and tribal leaders to draw boundaries between Indian communities and sell or buy Indian land. He argued that national borders bred "jealousies," "distinctions," and "distractions" among the Natives and impeded their unity. Accordingly, when Miami leaders protested that Prophetstown stood on their land, Tenskwatawa retorted that the settlement had been "sanctioned by the Great spirit." It was the Creator's wish that all lands north and west of the Greenville Treaty line belong collectively to all Indian peoples.[33]

U.S. officials were infuriated by such claims. Governor Harrison blustered that the Kishpokos' idea of collective Indian lands was "so absurd, and so new, too, that it could never be accepted." Harrison claimed that it was the duty of the federal government to protect the land rights of individual tribes allied with the United States. In reality he was more worried about the future of American expansion than any Indian rights. Just like the Kishpoko brothers, Harrison understood that united Indians would be far more difficult to bully into enormous land cessions than isolated tribal leaders. "Once admit an Indian confederacy founded on an acknowledged community of Interest," explained Lewis Cass, the governor of Michigan Territory, a few years later, "and we . . . should never procure another acre of land." Harrison and his superiors would have none of that. Despite mounting tensions between Tenskwatawa's followers and Americans, in September 1809 Harrison pressured a group of Miami, Lenape, and Potawatomi leaders to sell three million acres of land in present-day Illinois and Indiana at the Treaty of Fort Wayne. Although the Prophet's people regularly hunted in the ceded territory, the Kishpoko brothers were not even invited to the negotiations. Harrison explained that there was no reason to do so, because "the Prophet is not a chief of a tribe to which he belongs." Furthermore, the governor had previously defined the Miamis as the "true" owners of the lands in question, obliterating any need to consult the "vagabond" Shawnees about the cession.[34]

The Treaty of Fort Wayne enraged Tenskwatawa and Tecumseh. The brothers warned Americans not to settle on the ceded lands and fired a broadside against tribal leaders, bitterly accusing them of selling Native lands for annuities and bribes. Tecumseh declared that since "our great Chiefs have been . . . ruining our Country . . . we the Warriors now manage the affairs of our Nation." He threatened that the warriors planned to "destroy village chiefs" if the chiefs ceded any more land.[35]

In 1811 the rising tensions led to bloodshed. First Potawatomis raided American settlers in Illinois. In November Governor Harrison retaliated by burning Prophetstown. The conflict escalated the next summer, when a war broke out between Great Britain and the United States. Tecumseh, Tenskwatawa, and their followers retreated to Amherstburg, Ontario, and allied with the English. The War of 1812 revealed the deep political and cultural divisions that ran through the Shawnee and other Indian communities across the Old Northwest. While Tecumseh and his allies led hundreds of Shawnees, Potawatomis, Wyandots, Ho-Chunks, Kickapoos, Ojibwes, Ottawas, and others in a final attempt to push the Americans back across the Ohio River, even larger numbers of their tribespeople remained neutral or supported the United States. The Shawnees of Wapakoneta, Lewistown, and Hog Creek chose the latter course. Catahecassa, Biaseka, Quitewepea, and other local leaders believed that the United States was now the dominant power in the region. Certain that even united Indians assisted by the British would have no chance of defeating the Americans, they allied with the United States.[36]

Regardless of their choices, all Shawnees suffered in the war. Tecumseh fell at the Battle of Thames in October 1813. Tenskwatawa and his Kishpokos and Pekowis had to flee the American offensive deep into Canada. British Indian allies killed the Wapakonetan leader Spemeaalapah (Logan). By 1815 the "agricultural affairs" of Wapakoneta and Lewistown were "entirely deranged," because the locals had "devoted so large a portion of their time to military pursuits" as U.S. allies. Disregarding such crucial aid, "more than once" U.S. militia "plundered [the Shawnees] when passing their Towns of their Horses, Hogs, Cattle, Corn &c. some instances of their being murdered merely because they were Indians." Catahecassa himself was shot in the face by a U.S. soldier, but survived.[37]

The Treaty of Ghent ended the War of 1812 in December 1814. The treaty is often seen as an inconclusive ending to an inconclusive conflict. Formally, it merely restored the status quo ante bellum between the United States and Great Britain. Unlike similar international treaties in the past, this one guaranteed to the Indians their continued possession of their prewar territories. However, for the Shawnees and their Native neighbors the repercussions of the Treaty of Ghent were just as revolutionary as those of the Treaties of Paris in 1763 and 1783 and the Greenville Treaty in 1795. Since the treaty restored the prewar status quo, it forced the Indians to accept the prewar land cessions against which Tenskwatawa and Tecumseh had rebelled. Moreover, while the treaty recognized the right of all refugees to return to their lands, U.S. officials controlled which Indians were allowed to return where. Determined to break up Tenskwatawa's multiethnic community, Americans insisted that the Prophet's followers who had taken refuge in Canada could return to the U.S. side of the border only if they settled in their tribal territories under their "lawfull Chiefs" and did not try "to exercise any separate government." When Tenskwatawa asked for permission to return from Canada, Governor Cass replied "that if he would agree . . . to return himself and the Shawnese who are with him to their nation upon the Auglaize and permit the Kickapoos and others to return to their respective homes so that we might know to whom we could look in the event of any difficulties, his request would be granted." The message was clear: all Indians must live in tribal territories under tribal governments loyal to the United States.[38]

Wapakonetan leaders took full advantage of the federal campaign to centralize the Indian nations. When Tenskwatawa's followers tried to collect secretly at Prophetstown in 1815, Catahecassa, Biaseka, and their allies warned U.S. officials. The headmen opined that the Prophet's Shawnees should "come back to their own people and settle in a place Near of us that we might look over their behavior." Embittered, Tenskwatawa remained in exile in Canada rather than settle among his old enemies in Wapakoneta. However, most of his Kishpoko and Pekowi followers grudgingly moved to the Mekoche town when the scarcity of British supplies made life at Amherstburg unbearable. The Treaty of Ghent, then, strongly imposed national centralization on the Shawnees. It also revolutionized the international status of the Shawnees and their neighbors. As historian Alan Taylor has argued, before the War of 1812 the British had "treated the Indians as autonomous peoples dwelling in their own country *between* the empire and the republic." After the war, U.S. officials forcefully "insisted that the natives should be their dependents living within a fixed boundary separating British from American sovereignty."[39] Both Tenskwatawa's defeated followers and the Mekoche leaders of Wapakoneta now had to find out how the Shawnees could survive as a sovereign nation within the United States.

A NATION WITHIN A NATION

New threats to Shawnee sovereignty became painfully evident quickly after the war. Emigration and natural growth increased the American population north of the Ohio River at a staggering pace. Within a decade Ohio's non-Indian population had reached 800,000 and Indiana's 150,000. Native peoples became tiny minorities in a sea of Americans. In 1825 there were only 2,350 Indians in Ohio and 11,579 more in Indiana and Illinois. Even such small Native enclaves irritated the Americans. Ohio had gained statehood in 1803; Indiana followed in 1816. In the 1820s both state politicians and common people across the United States began to resent Indian communities that lay within state limits but on unceded Native lands and therefore outside state jurisdiction. Increasingly, politicians argued that such independent Native enclaves defied the states' right to sovereignty. Businessmen and farmers complained that the Indians' "wasteful" need of large hunting territories kept prime agricultural lands underdeveloped and retarded the economic progress of their states.[40]

Americans couched their arguments in novel racial terms. After the War of 1812 a powerful ideology of race gradually replaced the older Enlightenment ideas of cultural evolution as the primary explanation of cultural differences in the United States. Increasingly, Americans saw Indians no longer as cultural inferiors who could be civilized through education but as racial inferiors who were simply incapable of ever attaining the intellectual level of the "Whites." The racial divide made Indian assimilation through the civilization program impossible. This, many Americans argued, meant that the coexistence of Indians and Whites would serve neither party. Surrounded by superior Whites, the Natives would only suffer when game vanished and their "natural" hunting lifestyle became untenable. At the same time the Indians' outmoded way of life cost the Whites valuable economic resources. Therefore, it would be better for everyone if Indians were removed from their lands in the eastern states to the vast "wilderness" that lay west of the Mississippi River. There, the Natives would be able to continue their hunting way of life until they died out peacefully or became better equipped to adopt White civilization. This forceful displacement of Native peoples was euphemistically dubbed "Indian removal." Essentially a plan for ethnic cleansing, in the 1820s removal became a catchword for those Americans who strove to create politically sovereign states and seize the monopoly over the natural resources in these states for White people.[41]

When Americans championed the separation of Whites and Indians, the Shawnees put forth an alternative vision of the relations between the two peoples. The Wapakonetan leadership argued that the Shawnees could continue to exist as a sovereign nation in their own country *within* the United States. This Shawnee nation would be politically allied to the republic and economically integrated with it yet remain both independent and self-sufficient. While most Americans rejected the idea of a Native imperium in the American imperio, the Shawnees envisioned two allied but separate nations walking their interlinked but independent paths in peace.

To ensure their future as a distinct nation the Shawnees needed to protect their land. Immediately after the War of 1812 the Wapakoneta and Lewistown leadership took up their old project of defining the boundaries of the Shawnee territory and securing federal and Native recognition for these borders. It was not an easy task. All Indian communities throughout the region felt threatened by American expansion and guarded their land claims jealously. Yet there was considerable disagreement about who held exactly what rights to which lands, for several nations and towns had shared much of the Ohio Country for a century, often enjoying overlapping rights to the same areas.

The Shawnees remained convinced that in such conditions only an exclusive, internationally recognized ownership of a bounded territory would guarantee their nation's continued existence as a landed entity. In 1815 Catahecassa, Biaseka, Quitewepea, and other leaders informed the secretary of war that "we have communicated to our Neighbours" the old Shawnee plan "for having our land divided from the other Tribes of Indians . . . and they are all willing it should be so." But, the Shawnees added, the disagreements over land rights and boundaries were so severe among the Natives that "without your assistance we never can get it done."[42]

The federal government was keenly interested in buying the remaining Indian lands in Ohio and removing the Shawnees and their neighbors west of the Mississippi. In 1817 U.S. authorities planned a new treaty with the Shawnees and other Ohio and Great Lakes Indians to discuss these plans. Before the meeting, Shawnee headmen took pains to persuade their Indian neighbors to agree to sell some of their lands. Catahecassa even collaborated with Indian agent John Johnston to persuade the reluctant Sandusky Wyandots to participate in the planned council. This created a lot of resentment among the Shawnees' neighbors. In the months before the meeting angry Potawatomi warriors prowled around Wapakoneta, while the Wyandots accused the Shawnees of wanting to sell lands to which they had no rights. Wapakonetan leadership, however, saw the negotiations with the United States as a chance to strengthen the Shawnees' claim to the lands along the upper Auglaize River where some eight hundred Shawnees now lived in Wapakoneta, Lewistown, and Hog Creek (Captain Johnny's Town had been abandoned). If they could secure federal recognition for their ownership of this area, the Wapakonetan leaders were willing to sell lands more marginal to their people.[43]

In the end the Shawnees, Wyandots, Lenapes, Senecas, Ojibwes, Potawatomis, and Ottawas sold most of the remaining Indian land in Ohio to the United States at the Treaty of Fort Meigs in September 1817. Several Shawnee, Seneca, and Wyandot communities, however, retained small reservations that the federal government now recognized as the property of these towns. The treaty created separate reservations for Wapakoneta, Hog Creek, and Lewistown. Covering some 170 square miles, these reservations constituted a far smaller land base than the one claimed by the Shawnees fifteen years before, when Catahecassa had asked in Washington for federal acknowledgment of Shawnee and Lenape borders. Even then the Shawnees could claim the treaty as a minor victory. The United States had finally recognized exclusive Shawnee ownership of clearly bounded territories. Now no other nation would be able to sell the land under Shawnee feet. Even more importantly, the Shawnees had averted the first American attempt to remove them across the Mississippi.[44]

Besides land rights, after the War of 1812 the Wapakonetan leadership again saw rebuilding the tribal economy as a crucial step toward political and economic autonomy. Much of the prosperity the Shawnees had acquired during the prewar decade had been destroyed during the three years of violence. U.S. militias and enemy Indians had razed the fields of Wapakoneta and Lewistown; robbed agricultural stores, cattle, hogs, and horses; and destroyed houses and fences. "The war took every thing from us," Catahecassa, Biaseka, Quitewepea, and their allies lamented in 1815. When peace returned, the leaders of Wapakoneta, Lewistown, and Hog Creek renewed with growing vigor the program of economic development they had begun before the war. They appealed again to federal officials and the Society of Friends, or Quakers, for assistance, explaining that "we wish to get into a way that would render our living less precarious as well as less burdensome to our friends the white people."[45] If Native requests for government and missionary funding seem incongruent with economic and political autonomy, it should be kept in mind that establishing new farms, acquiring domestic animals and novel technology such as plows, and building new infrastructure such as fences, mills, and roads required substantial initial investments that the war-torn Shawnee communities hardly could have born alone.[46] Yet autonomy remained their ultimate goal.

Both the federal Indian agent John Johnston and the Quakers responded to Shawnee requests enthusiastically. The Friends did not seek to convert the Indians to Christianity; instead, they saw economic development as the road to civilization. They reopened William Kirk's old model farm in Wapakoneta in 1817 and finished the gristmill and sawmill Kirk had begun building. Johnston hired a blacksmith to work for the Shawnees and delivered plows and other farming tools to those interested in exploring Euroamerican agricultural techniques. The postwar years were hectic among the Ohio Shawnees. When the Quakers James Ellicott and Philip Thomas visited Wapakoneta in the summer of 1816, they reported that the locals were "busily engaged in the cultivation," with 250 acres of corn growing. The people of Lewistown had planted 200 acres of corn, and many households also grew flourishing garden plots of vegetables. Many Shawnees likewise turned "their attention more and more to the raising of cattle." In 1819 alone, the Wapakonetan leaders used $1,420 of the tribal annuity to buy "cows and calves" for their people. Johnston reported that Wapakonetans owned 125 cows and 200 hogs. Lewistownians were even more prosperous with their 150 head of cattle and 300 hogs.[47]

Seeing such evidence of industry, Ellicott and Thomas deduced that the Shawnees were finally "fully convinced that they have no alternative, but to abandon their former habits and apply themselves to agriculture, or become totally extinct as a people." Such ethnocentric assessments reveal that most

Quakers and government officials did not understand the nature of the economic developments in the Shawnee communities. Unlike what they believed, the Indians were not hungry and impoverished hunters desperately trying to learn the basics of agriculture. Instead, they were experienced farmer-hunter-gatherer-traders who adapted creatively to the new political economy and ecology imposed on them by the expanding American republic. For centuries Shawnees and their ancestors had practiced swidden farming in the river valleys of the Ohio Country. However, the diminution of Native territory after the Twenty Years' War had made swidden agriculture less sustainable, because it was based on frequent field relocation and long fallow periods and thus required sizable surpluses of land. Shawnees were therefore eager to learn new farming techniques that would guarantee a secure living from a smaller land base. Many also adopted cattle and hogs to replace the wild game that was increasingly decimated by American hunters. Animal husbandry was nothing new for Shawnees, for some families had kept small numbers of cattle and hogs for decades. Domesticated animals offered not only meat and hides for domestic consumption, but also an access to American markets at a time when fur trade was in sharp decline. Like American farmers in Ohio, many Shawnees probably grew hogs for commercial purposes and sold pork to American merchants and to the growing meatpacking industry in Cincinnati. Hogs became a source of Euroamerican goods and money that Shawnees had previously acquired by selling deer hides and beaver furs to colonial merchants. The economic transformations in Wapakoneta, Hog Creek, and Lewistown signaled not an evolutionary leap from a hunting to an agricultural stage of human civilization, as missionaries and officials believed, but an adaptive Native creation of "hybrid economies of survival."[48]

Shawnee leaders played a major role in these economic transformations. It was the headmen and headwomen of Wapakoneta, Lewistown, and Hog Creek who initiated the economic changes and, in the beginning, controlled them. They appealed to government officials and missionaries for assistance and resources and channeled annuities, tools, and livestock to their communities. They took control of some of the new economic infrastructure, apparently conceptualizing it as national property. According to the Friends, "one of the Chiefs went into the mills at Waupaghkonnetta, for the purpose of obtaining instruction in the management of them, in which he succeeded, and they were placed under his charge." Likewise, the chiefs appropriated money from the annuities to purchase cattle for the nation. Finally, clan headmen and headwomen organized communal work projects. Under their leadership Shawnees cleared and fenced new fields, helped American laborers to construct the Wapakoneta mills, and blazed roads to facilitate the transportation of goods between Wapakoneta and American settlements.[49]

Leaders utilized both kinship networks and economic resources to mobilize people to labor for communal projects. Clan hokimas and hokima wiikwes could summon their younger relatives to work for communal purposes. In 1816, for example, Ellicott and Thomas reported that "the chiefs furnish promptly from day to day, any number of young men" to work at the Wapakoneta mills. Workers often expected to be paid with food or other gifts. In 1817 the Quaker missionary Joseph Rhodes witnessed how Catahecassa collected people to work on the fields of Wapakoneta by feasting them with beef. Such practices resonated with traditions. Hokima wiikwes had long organized the agricultural work of the women of their clans and towns. Male hokimas and war leaders had traditionally collected their relatives and other men for war and work parties by feasting them and giving them gifts of spiritually powerful goods, including vermillion and tobacco. Such labor mobilization took place within the framework of reciprocal obligations based on kinship and age. Older relatives, as well as widely respected communal leaders, possessed the moral authority to request younger men and women to work for communal purposes. Yet elders and chiefs were expected to repay the labor with gifts and food. Thus, while leaders asserted control over the new economy, they did so in ways that rested on deeply traditional notions of reciprocity. Even the use of the Wapakoneta mill remained free for Shawnees despite its chiefly control.[50]

It was precisely such enduring communal bonds that the Shawnees' American civilizers wished to break. In the late 1810s and 1820s the physical structure of the Shawnee towns became an important site of contest between Shawnees and U.S. officials and missionaries. Following the ideals of the civilization mission, both Johnston and the Friends encouraged Shawnees to break up their towns and move to private family farms. In order to encourage the dispersal of Wapakoneta and other Shawnee settlements, Johnston targeted the government's economic assistance of "ploughs, hoes, etc." to families that moved out of the towns. At first these endeavors reaped little success. In 1816 Johnston reported that Shawnees were "becoming more and more sensible of the necessity of scattering on farms," and a year later he claimed that "many families" were "moving out from the towns and settling on their lands." But these reports were overly optimistic. In 1819 Johnston admitted that he was still forced to use "every ascertion to induce" the Shawnees "to break up their villages." Clearly, Shawnees were far less eager to abandon their communal settlements than federal agents had believed.[51]

Gradually during the 1820s individual farms became more common. In 1826 more than two hundred Shawnees from Wapakoneta moved to a new reservation in Kansas. After their migration they applied to the federal government for compensation for the property they had had to leave behind in Wapakoneta. Their applications demonstrate that before the removal many families had lived on separate homesteads, where "good hewed log house[s]" had stood beside fenced fields, vegetable gardens, and apple and peach trees. Both Johnston and the Quakers welcomed the emergence of such family farms as a radical leap toward civilization. But once again they misunderstood this development and the Native motivations underlying it. Throughout the eighteenth century Shawnee towns had had a dispersed layout. Most settlements had consisted of scattered house clusters, each of which had been inhabited by several related families that most likely belonged to the same clan. Wapakoneta, in contrast, was built in an unusually nucleated fashion. There, according to one visitor, "the houses were near each other." Such a nucleated settlement pattern had been an adaptation to the difficult political and economic conditions following the Twenty Years' War. Land loss, poverty, and insecurity had compelled Shawnees to collect at Wapakoneta where the local leaders distributed annuities, presents, and economic assistance from the federal government to their followers. In the 1820s the new and increasingly efficient economic strategies and growing material prosperity simply allowed Shawnees to return to the older, more kin-centric and spread-out settlement pattern.[52]

Johnston and the Friends also ignored the fact that the new Shawnee homesteads hardly resembled the patriarchal nuclear family farms idealized by the civilization program. Various census records collected for government purposes show that in the late 1820s Wapakonetan households had between two and twenty members. Several households included more than one adult man and woman. This suggests that it was common for extended families or related married couples to live together in the same house. According to the property compensation applications, only some of the individuals who demanded reimbursements for a house or houses did so for farmland. This indicates that not all households owned private fields; some people probably continued to cultivate a communal town field. It is also possible that neighboring households, inhabited by relatives, shared a field of their own. Shawnee towns, then, did not break up into patriarchal nuclear family homesteads, as planned by U.S. policymakers. Instead, they dispersed into house clusters inhabited by kinspeople who shared land, resources, and labor. Shawnee kin groups proved flexible enough to adapt to changing economic circumstances and strong enough to shape the economic change.[53]

Contrary to American hopes, the dispersal of the Shawnee settlements did not destroy towns as political and spiritual communities. Towns continued to form the foundation for collective action and identity. Ties of kinship and marriage bound even the scattered households of a town together. The townspeople also remained connected to a shared ritual and political center, the town council house. Families and clans still pooled agricultural produce and meat for annual planting and harvest rituals held at the mšikamekwi. Leaders and elders from different kin groups still gathered together at the local council house to deliberate communal affairs. In the 1817 Treaty of Fort Meigs even federal officials defined Wapakoneta's council house as the center of the town and its reservation.[54]

Gendered division of labor constituted another important battleground for Shawnees and Americans. For centuries women had tended Shawnee fields, while men had hunted in the woods. Each task was crucial for communal well-being, and each was understood to be particularly fitting for the gender-specific spiritual power of women and men, respectively. Federal officials and missionaries wished to abolish such a "barbarian" work order. Believing that "women are less than men," they hoped to liberate Indian women of "the intolerable task . . . of raising their corn" and turn them instead into housewives, American style, who would spend their days cleaning, cooking, and weaving at home. Native men, in turn, had to be persuaded to take up farm work and begin "furnishing food for their families." Initially, few Shawnees showed any interest in such a radical change. During the 1820s, however, some men began working in the fields. Others took up animal husbandry, which they may have seen as a more fitting substitute for hunting than farming. There is less evidence of women's choices. It seems that most of them ignored American instructions and continued to farm together with their husbands and male relatives. Some Shawnee men rejected these changes vehemently. The Pekowi leader Pemthala declared in 1825 that he would "enjoy the game while it lasts," rather than become a farmer. Even Catahecassa, who had set in motion the economic transformations in Wapakoneta, argued that "Shawnee men have never been in the habit of assuming the dress and performing the duties of women."[55]

However culturally mediated, the economic transformations gradually created serious economic, political, and cultural rifts within the Shawnee nation. By 1830 new economic stratification was becoming visible in the Shawnee communities. A small number of families now lived on farms far more prosperous than most, forming an incipient economic upper class. According to a survey by the federal government, there were 158 farms in Wapakoneta, Lewistown, and Hog Creek in 1831. When U.S. officials estimated the value of the improvements on these farms (excluding the value of land, chattels, and domestic animals), they reported that 69 percent of the farms were worth less than one hundred dollars. Indeed, almost 40 percent were evaluated at less than fifty dollars. On the other hand, eight prosperous Shawnees owned homesteads worth between three hundred and six hundred dollars.[56] These differences in wealth pertained only to the improvements on the farms. Livestock and other property were also distributed unequally among the Shawnees. Whereas most Wapakonetans seem to have owned only one or two hogs, a headman named Walekakothe (Cornstalk) had "5 large Sows, 25 barrows . . . and a quantity of pigs." This was clearly more than needed for home consumption. It is likely that Walekakothe sold pork to American settlers and meatpackers. He also owned two houses, "1 large field," a sizable orchard of apple trees, and a large collection of agricultural and woodworking tools.[57]

The evolving economic stratification among the Shawnees was not nearly as dramatic as among the neighboring Americans or many Southern Indian peoples. The wealthiest Creeks and Cherokees, for example, owned commercial plantations, cattle herds, and slaves worth more than twenty thousand dollars, while most of their tribespeople remained as poor, in monetary terms, as most Shawnees. But even the more modest differences in wealth among the Shawnees had important ramifications for everyday life. A family like Walekakothe's that owned a field, dozens of hogs, and rare tools was not only self-sufficient, but also able to sell its produce and possibly technological skills for profit. Shawnees lacking such wealth probably did not regard themselves as poor. The Quaker missionary Henry Harvey claimed that a Shawnee was "not considered a very poor man by his people" as long as he had "a poney, a gun, tomahawk, a dog, butcher-knife, and blanket." But a Shawnee whose possessions were restricted to these items needed many Euroamerican goods and services, including plows, ammunition, textiles, and blacksmithing. To buy them he or she often had to rely on credit, especially as the decline of game in northern Ohio was making fur trade increasingly unprofitable. As a result, many Shawnees fell into debt, further compromising the self-sufficiency of their families.[58]

Why did some families prosper, while others became impoverished? It is probable that those families most eager to adopt commercialized American agricultural practices and values gradually profited from their choice and amassed more material riches than most Shawnees. Yet enthusiasm alone could not provide anyone with the initial investments needed for acquiring a plow, other agricultural tools, hogs, and cattle. It is possible that the families who were able to acquire all this and more not only were interested in the new economic strategies but had previously grown wealthy in the fur trade and thus had the wherewithal needed to shift to commercial plow agriculture and animal husbandry. Federal agents and Quakers also may have given most generous assistance to those Shawnees who seemed most enthusiastic about embracing the "civilized" American agriculture.

Unlike among many other early-nineteenth-century Indian peoples, there is no evidence that Shawnee leaders used their access to tribal annuities to benefit their own farms. Judging by their farms, most Shawnee leaders were in fact only slightly wealthier than average tribespeople. Many of the richest Shawnees instead came from outside the established leadership. For example, in 1831 Lanawytucka, or William Parks, owned a farm worth five hundred dollars at

Hog Creek. Other reports estimated his whole property worth at least two thou-
sand dollars. Yet Lanawytucka was described as "a common Indian (a young
man)." His brother, Joseph Parks (Pakahtahskahka), was even more prosperous.
A man with a colorful and often debated background, Joseph Parks was reportedly "a quarter blooded Shawnee" or the offspring of an American father and a
Shawnee mother, but he had spent part of his youth among the Wyandots.
According to some accounts, he had also lived in the household of Governor
Lewis Cass in Detroit, which had given him a chance to build valuable business contacts with American merchants and entrepreneurs. A "noble example"
in "farming and raising stock," Joseph Parks was reportedly "worth five or six
thousand dollars."[59]

The Parks brothers were not only unusually rich but also used their wealth
in strikingly new ways. Traditionally, Shawnee leaders had given goods away as
gifts in order to muster popular support and fulfill their obligation to take care
of their people. But William Parks was a "young man" and Joseph Parks may
have been viewed as an outsider among the Shawnees. Thus neither shared the
duty of the hokimas and elders to share their wealth. Since the brothers apparently had a Euroamerican father, they also may have learned his cultural ideas
about the importance of private property. In any case, they saw their material
possessions as their private property that was to be used primarily for the profit
of their families. To be sure, Joseph Parks was known as a generous man who
"always fed the hungry and ministered to the wants of the poor, the destitute,
and the afflicted." But in a radical reversal of traditions, he often demanded that
his "gifts" had to be paid back with interest. By 1831 other Shawnees owed a total
of one thousand dollars to him, and soon his debtors included many prominent
leaders.[60] Such debts signal the emergence of new kinds of power relations
among the Shawnees. Unlike older relations of authority, these were based not
on spiritual power, kinship, or age but on the material wealth of a few and the
relative poverty of the rest.

During the 1820s the widening economic, political, and cultural divisions
among the Shawnees intertwined with the ongoing efforts of the federal
government to remove the nation to the west side of the Mississippi River.
Even after the Treaty of Fort Meigs U.S. officials periodically brought up the
issue of removal in their transactions with the Shawnees. Catahecassa and other
old Mekoche leaders remained sternly opposed to moving west. They insisted
that the Ohio lands had been given to the Shawnees by the Creator; removal
would disrupt the sacred order of the universe. On the basis of their long experience with Anglo-American expansionism, the Wapakonetan chiefs also argued
that a westward migration would not long protect their people from the insatiable American land-hunger. "Go where we may your people will follow us,"
Catahecassa predicted to John Johnston, "and we will be forced to remove

again and again and finally driven to the sea on the other side of this great island."[61]

Some Shawnees disagreed with the old hokima. During the 1820s many became disheartened by the constant federal pressure for land cessions and the growing scarcity of game in Ohio. Furthermore, American settlers were not shy about stealing Shawnee property. Some beat or even killed individual Natives in order to bully the Indians to leave Ohio. Like so many times since the 1780s, some Shawnees came to see the Trans-Mississippi West as a haven from this cauldron of violence, poverty, and social disruption. These advocates of removal included both "traditionalists" who dreamed of plentiful game herds in the West and prosperous farmers who wished to develop their commercialized agriculture beyond the Mississippi safe from American encroachments. In 1825 Quitewepea, an adamant supporter of the Euroamerican-style economy, led a small group of Lewistown Shawnees and Senecas to the modern Missouri-Arkansas borderlands. That same year U.S. officials finally allowed Tenskwatawa to return from Canada to Wapakoneta. There was one condition, however: the Prophet had to persuade the remaining Ohio Shawnees to remove to a new reservation in Kansas. In 1826 Tenskwatawa took more than two hundred Wapakonetans, probably predominantly Kishpokos and Pekowis, to the West in search of a homeland free from American pressure. Quitewepea's and Tenskwatawa's migrations shared one important common denominator: both were led by men who had long had a tense relationship with the Wapakonetan Mekoches. Despite their differing cultural and political orientations, Quitewepea and Tenskwatawa saw removal to the West as a way to escape American land-hunger but also as a strategy to assert autonomy from the centralized Shawnee national leadership.[62]

Catahecassa and other national leaders feared that the westward migrations of the dissenters weakened the unity of the Shawnee nation and threatened its struggle to retain its land in Ohio. Accordingly, they took pains to discourage prospective emigrants. In 1829 they demanded of Agent Johnston that the whole Shawnee annuity should still be paid at Wapakoneta and not divided between the Ohio Shawnees and the emigrants. Tenskwatawa's followers, now in Kansas, claimed that they were entitled to three-fifths of the annuity on the basis of their numbers. They complained that the Ohio Shawnees "have been mad with us" because of the migration "and are trying to do us all the harm they can for it." This argument cut deep to the contrasting Shawnee ideas of peoplehood. According to the Wapakonetan leaders, the Shawnees were a unified nation that lived in its own country. The nation's collective leadership rightfully controlled such national resources as annuities. The emigrants following Quitewepea and Tenskwatawa, in contrast, argued that the Shawnee people consisted of local communities that were bound together by kinship, language, and rituals but remained fundamentally autonomous. Each community controlled its own share of collective resources. This was an old quarrel. As before, U.S. officials interfered in the debate. Initially, Johnston agreed with the Wapakonetans and continued to pay the entire Shawnee annuity to them. Other officials reversed his position, however, and suggested dividing the annuity between the Kansas and Ohio Shawnees on the basis of population size. For Americans, this offered one more method for undermining the unity of those Shawnees who stubbornly refused to give up their homelands in Ohio.[63]

Despite the mounting difficulties, the remaining Ohio Shawnees continued to oppose removal through the late 1820s. To keep their land, they evoked their treaty rights, reminded the federal authorities of their loyalty during the War of 1812, and emphasized their willingness to adopt the American economy. But it was all in vain. In 1830 Congress passed the Indian Removal Act, which made the removal of all eastern Indians beyond the Mississippi official government policy. The next year federal negotiators visited Wapakoneta and Lewistown once more and threatened that if the Shawnees chose to stay in Ohio, their lands would be put under state jurisdiction. This would have nullified the Shawnees' own government and made them subject to state laws and taxation without the benefits of U.S. citizenship. In effect, state jurisdiction would have spelled an end to the sovereign Shawnee nation. As many Shawnees undoubtedly knew, Georgia and Alabama had recently adopted exactly such measures against the Cherokees and Creeks who had refused to sell their lands in those states, leaving the Indians at the mercy of racial violence, looting, and land grabbing by American settlers.[64]

When Catahecassa died just before the negotiations, the younger leaders decided that they could not keep their lands against such odds. In August 1831 the Wapakoneta and Hog Creek headmen agreed to exchange their reservations in Ohio for a new one in Kansas. The removal negotiations split the Shawnees. The Lewistown Shawnees and Senecas concluded their own treaty with the United States, electing to remove to a separate reservation on the Neosho River in present-day Oklahoma. Once more, the Shawnee nation faced both forced migration and dispersal.[65]

The four decades following the Treaty of Greenville had utterly transformed the world of the Shawnees. The imperial borderland of rival colonial empires had vanished, as Shawnees and other Indians of the Ohio Country had been encapsulated within the United States. The federal government's civilization program had demanded that the Indians change their culture and assimilate into the U.S. society. Yet Shawnees had responded to these challenges successfully. They had adopted selected features of the American economy and technology to restore their self-sufficiency. They had cultivated national unity to protect their autonomy and land rights. The ruthless removal policy of the United States endangered these accomplishments and threatened the sovereignty of the Shawnee nation once more. It also raised new questions about Shawnee nationhood. When they arrived at the reservation in Kansas, the Ohio Shawnees met their tribespeople who had fled American expansion beyond the Mississippi River since the 1780s. Divided by very different histories, the eastern and western Shawnees had radically different ideas about the future.

6

"Dispersed like Turkeys"

The Odyssey of the Western Shawnees, 1782–1840

In popular imagination the history of the Trans-Mississippi West in the nine-teenth century is a story of the westward march of Anglo-American settlers. But before these newcomers crossed the Mississippi in their covered wagons, thou-sands of other pioneers from the East had already settled on the fertile lands stretching from the Arkansas River to the Missouri. These early westward emigrants were Indians: Shawnees, Lenapes, Cherokees, Choctaws, Miamis, and others driven from their homes by the violent expansion of the United States.

Shawnees and their neighbors began to move across the Mississippi in the 1780s to escape the violence and dispossession that followed the birth of the United States. When many of their tribespeople continued to fight for their ancestral lands in the East, these emigrants preferred to search for safer homes in the West. They did not find a permanent haven there. After the United States bought Louisiana from France in 1803, tens of thousands of American settlers followed the Indian pioneers across the Mississippi. Greedy for the prime agri-cultural lands settled by the emigrant Indians and convinced of the racial infe-riority of the Native peoples, the newcomers perpetuated a series of ruthless ethnic cleansings across the midcontinent between 1815 and 1840. As one Shawnee headman put it, racial violence "disperced" the western Shawnees "like Turkeys" across present-day Missouri, Arkansas, Oklahoma, and Texas. At a time when their relatives in the East were increasingly encapsulated within the American republic, the westerners scattered over the contested borderlands between the United States, Mexico, and various Native peoples and tried to find "Land we Can Call Our Own" in the cracks of no-man's-land between the rival powers.[1]

This new diaspora greatly shaped the western Shawnee communities. In contrast to the Ohio Shawnees who gathered together to a national territory to survive American expansion, the westerners fragmented both politically and geographically. They mobilized again many of the strategies their ancestors had used during the great Shawnee diaspora in the late seventeenth century, including mobility, flexible community fission, and multiethnic alliances. Their independent, mobile communities defied federal Indian policy that sought to control Native peoples by collecting them in tribal reservations under centralized tribal governments. The westerners likewise challenged the Ohio Mekoches' dream of a unified Shawnee nation living on a collective homeland. By 1831 some western Shawnees saw themselves as "entirely distinct" from their eastern relatives.[2]

SHAWNEE PIONEERS IN THE WEST

It is not known when Shawnees first ventured west of the Mississippi River. They certainly had ancient contacts to the Mississippi Valley that long predated the coming of Europeans. For centuries the Ohio River had connected the Shawnees' Fort Ancient ancestors to the various peoples living in the central Mississippi Valley. Archaeological finds attest that during the final precontact centuries both humans and trade goods moved back and forth between the chiefdoms on the middle Mississippi and the Fort Ancient towns on the Ohio. When the Haudenosaunees began raiding the Ohio Valley in the late seventeenth century, many locals relied on these ancient networks and fled to the Mississippi Valley. These refugees included some Shawnees. In the late 1600s French explorers frequently encountered Shawnee travelers on the Mississippi and realized that many of them possessed remarkable knowledge of the area. Some of the refugees may have stayed in the West permanently. In 1762 the Quaker trader James Kenny heard in Pittsburgh of Shawnees living "away over ye Missipi."[3]

Shawnee migration to the west side of the Mississippi intensified in the mid-1760s following the geopolitical upheaval of the Seven Years' War. As a part of the negotiations that ended the war, France ceded its North American claims west of the Mississippi to Spain in 1762 and those east of the river to Great Britain in 1763. Suspicious of British rule, many French settlers moved from Illinois across the Mississippi to Spain's new dominion. Shawnees were equally concerned about aggressive English officers and land-hungry settlers. During Pontiac's War they sought trade and military support from the French settlements on both sides of the Mississippi. When the Mekoche leaders finally maneuvered an uneasy peace with the British in 1764–1765, a handful of militant Shawnees led by Charlot Kaské retreated from the Scioto River to the Mississippi Valley. Some of them crossed the great river and settled in the neighborhood of the region's new French settlements such as Ste. Genevieve. Throughout the late 1760s and early 1770s Shawnee diplomats from the Scioto towns, too, continued to visit the Mississippi Valley. There, they tried to persuade the local Illinois, Osages, and Quapaws to join the great multitribal alliance network they were building to protect Native lands from British expansion.[4]

Two features characterized these early Shawnee migrations to the Mississippi Valley. First, the Shawnee migrants saw the Spanish-claimed country west of the Mississippi, known as Louisiana or Spanish Illinois, as a refuge from Anglo-American expansion. Second, most of the early western settlers were political dissenters who did not condone the emerging national consensus that supported the Mekoche-negotiated peace with the British. Rather than disturb the social harmony of their towns by constantly arguing with the majority, dissenters like Charlot Kaské simply left to establish new communities elsewhere. In the following decades the Shawnee migration to the Trans-Mississippi West would continue to be fueled both by an effort to avoid Anglo-American aggression and by factional disputes in the Shawnee communities.

The Shawnee exodus across the Mississippi River increased during the turmoil of the Twenty Years' War. Although histories of the Ohio Valley traditionally cast Shawnees as die-hard militants who fought to the last man rather than surrender their country to the Americans, by the early 1780s many Shawnees were utterly disheartened by the long war that seemed not only endless, but also impossible to win. They turned their eyes west. In 1782 forty Shawnees, Lenapes, Chickasaws, and Cherokees visited St. Louis and informed Francisco Cruzat, the Spanish lieutenant governor of Upper Louisiana, that they wished to place themselves under Spain's protection. Two years later a much larger delegation of 260 Shawnees, Haudenosaunees, Cherokees, Chickasaws, Choctaws, and Lenapes arrived in St. Louis. They complained about the violence and land-hunger of the newly independent Americans, lamenting that the Americans extended "themselves like a plague of locusts in the territories of the Ohio River which we inhabit." The decisive blow came in 1786, when the Kentucky militia destroyed four Shawnee towns on the Great Miami and Mad rivers. That convinced many Shawnees that they had no future in the Ohio Valley. Over the next three years hundreds of Kishpokos, Pekowis, Thawikilas, and Chalaakaathas fled west, crossed the Mississippi, and settled at Bois Brule, the lowlands south of Ste. Genevieve in what is now eastern Missouri.[5]

The area was a logical retreat for the Shawnees. Centuries of contact had made them familiar with the region, and some of their kinspeople already lived there. Most importantly, the country between the Missouri and Arkansas rivers seemed safely distant from American settlements. At a time when warfare and land loss disrupted Shawnee hunting in the Ohio Valley, the western lands teemed with game, and the local French traders offered a profitable market for

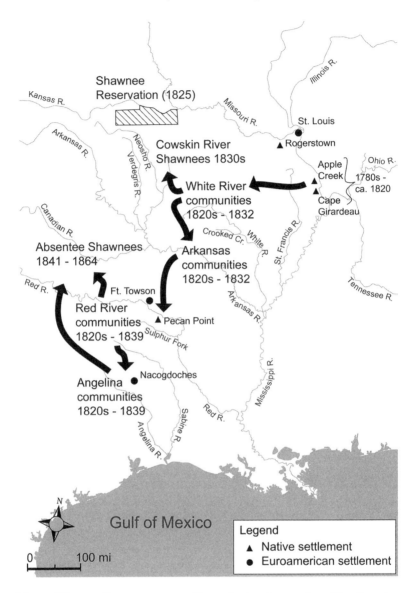

Map 7. Western Shawnee communities and migrations, 1780s–1860s (based on Callender, "Shawnee," 623; Warren, *Shawnees and Their Neighbors*, 77). Map drawn by Terhi Tanska.

the furs and skins harvested by Shawnee hunters. The Spaniards who claimed the region as a part of their empire eagerly courted the friendship of the eastern Indians. The sheer size of the Spanish empire in North America, stretching from California to Florida, easily obscures the fact that in Louisiana Spain was weak and threatened by more powerful Native and Euroamerican rivals. In the

1780s the true imperial power in the region was not Spain but the Osages. For two decades the Osages had expanded their territory at the expense of Spain's Native allies, raided Spanish and French settlements and traders with impunity, and yet forced the colonists to trade with them. In the meanwhile, the rapid expansion of the United States threatened Louisiana from the east. Many Spanish officials feared that a tidal wave of Americans would soon submerge the eastern frontier of the empire and then flood even its far more valuable core, Mexico. British Canada, too, looked menacing to the beleaguered Spaniards who had fought against Great Britain in the War of American Independence in 1778–1781. Desperate for allies, Lieutenant Governor Cruzat and other Spanish officers welcomed the Indian refugees from the East to Upper Louisiana with open arms. Hoping to create a protective buffer of Native allies against the United States, Osages, and British, they did their best to encourage Indian immigration by promising the newcomers land, trade, and protection.[6]

The Shawnees, other eastern Indian emigrants, and Spaniards shared a common predicament. All needed to gain a secure foothold in the central Mississippi Valley, and all were threatened by the Osages from the west and the Americans from the east. During the 1780s and 1790s the Indian settlers and Spain forged an alliance designed to address their mutual problems. Like so often before, the Shawnees ceremonially recognized their new European ally as their "Father" and publicly swore loyalty to Spain. They hardly turned into obedient imperial children, however. Like in their previous alliances with the British and the French, the Shawnees carefully joined only those Spanish projects they deemed advantageous for themselves and rejected participation in imperial designs that seemed dangerous or irrelevant. For example, the Shawnees firmly refused to get embroiled in a new imperial war. When rumors of an impending war between Spain, Great Britain, and the United States circulated in the Mississippi Valley in 1799, the local Shawnees made it clear that they had migrated to the region "for the purpose of living in peace & quietness & never intended to concern themselves again with the quarrels of the White People." The Shawnee independence worried Spanish officials, but they needed the Shawnees as much as the Shawnees needed them. Even if they doubted the loyalty of their new Shawnee children, the Spanish authorities had to curry Native friendship by giving gifts and land grants to the emigrant Indians. Most importantly, in January 1793 Louisiana's governor Francisco Luis Hector, baron de Carondelet, gave to the Shawnees and their Lenape allies more than six hundred square miles of land at Cape Girardeau, just above the confluence of the Mississippi and Ohio rivers, where most of the Shawnee emigrants had settled.[7]

The land grant did not guarantee the Shawnee emigrants a new homeland in the central Mississippi Valley. When the violent invasion of the United States pushed Shawnees from their Ohio homes to the Trans-Mississippi West, they became invaders too. The Osages did not look kindly at the influx of the eastern refugees into the country they claimed as their own. Previously, in the seventeenth and early eighteenth centuries when Shawnees had fled from Native or Euroamerican enemies to new lands, they had always carefully negotiated with the local Indians in advance to arrange peaceful and mutually beneficial alliances based on sharing the land and its resources. No such negotiations seem to have preceded the Shawnee migration to Upper Louisiana. Possibly the Shawnees felt that the Osages did not possess legitimate rights in the lands they wished to occupy. Perhaps previous negotiations between Shawnees and Osages in the early 1770s had taught the Shawnees that the powerful westerners were not interested in cooperation with the eastern nations. In any case, the Shawnees arrived uninvited, and the Osages would not accept it.[8]

The Osages were a fearsome enemy. Since the beginning of the eighteenth century they had aggressively built an economic and military empire across the eastern prairies from the Missouri to the Red River. They had cultivated a profitable trade in animal skins, slaves, horses, and mules with the French traders active in the Mississippi Valley and expanded their hunting grounds to the south and west at the expense of the Caddos, Wichitas, Pawnees, Kansas, and Quapaws. So powerful were the Osages that even the French and Spanish colonists could only dream of ruling them; in fact, most of the time it was the Osages who imposed their diplomatic, military, and economic agendas on the Europeans. In the 1770s and 1780s the Osages' trade with the Spaniards and French had grown exponentially. In consequence, the Osages had intensified their campaigns against their southern and western Indian neighbors, seeking to expand their hunting grounds to meet the growing market. When Shawnees and other strange Indians from the East crossed the Mississippi, the Osages saw them as a threat to their territorial and economic expansion and responded with violence.[9]

According to one Spanish officer, the emigrant Indians had "scarcely encamped when they were harassed by the Osages." "We were assaulted on all sides by the Osages," recounted Shawnees, Lenapes, Miamis, Ottawas, Potawatomis, and Peorias later, "who murdered us, [and] stole our horses." So fierce were the Osage raids in the late 1780s that some Shawnees contemplated moving back to the east side of the Mississippi and making peace with the United States. In the end, however, they decided to fight back. As one historian has noted, the Shawnee pioneers "chose what they believed to be the lesser of two evils" and challenged the Osages for control of the western lands rather than return east to face "the ongoing bloodshed and cultural changes demanded by Americans."[10]

In order to hold their ground against the Osages the Shawnees strengthened their alliances with the other emigrant Indians and Spain. In 1791 Shawnees,

Lenapes, Chickasaws, Mascoutens, Cherokees, and Sauks planned a massive meeting to discuss a common war against the Osages. The next year Shawnee leaders joined Lenape, Miami, Ottawa, Potawatomi, and Peoria delegates in St. Louis where they demanded more effective protection from their Spanish Father. Governor Carondelet was equally enraged with the Osages. Frustrated with what he saw as a continuous Osage disregard of Spanish authority, Carondelet declared a war on the Osages and instructed his post commanders throughout Louisiana to raise a massive Spanish-Indian army to destroy the Osage towns in the summer of 1793. The Cape Girardeau Shawnees and Lenapes immediately showed "a sincere zeal and a great attachment" for the plan. One hundred warriors gathered at St. Louis for the campaign. But Carondelet had overestimated Spanish power. The beleaguered colony lacked the men and resources needed for a large-scale campaign deep in Osage country. When the Spanish army failed to materialize, the emigrant Indians refused to undertake the invasion alone. In 1794 the Spanish officers, concerned over rumors of a French-American invasion of Louisiana, reluctantly normalized their relations with the Osages. Disgusted, Shawnees and their Indian allies continued their own, smaller-scale warfare. They clashed with the Osages on contested hunting grounds and fought off raiding parties harassing their settlements. While they did not succeed in defeating the Osages decisively, neither were the Osages able to force them back across the Mississippi. By 1800 it was clear that the emigrant Indians would stay in the West despite Osage resistance.[11]

Inconclusive as they were, the Osage wars had a profound effect on the western Shawnee society. When Shawnees killed and died to gain a foothold in the central Mississippi Valley, the conflict created deep emotional ties between them and the western land. Alliances with the other emigrants and the Spanish in turn bound the Shawnee settlers tightly to the evolving social landscape of the West. By the 1790s the Shawnee emigrants had settled at three major locations in the central Mississippi Valley. The largest concentration of population lay on Apple Creek, just north of Cape Girardeau, where the newcomers built two prosperous towns in a fertile upland setting. The larger of these, known variously as the "big shawneetown" and Chalaakaatha, had some 450 inhabitants, making it an exceptionally populous Shawnee community. Farther north, a former American captive, James Rogers, called Onothe by the Shawnees, and about one hundred tribespeople established a settlement known as Rogerstown on a tributary of the Missouri River. Living fewer than thirty miles from St. Louis, the vibrant center of Louisiana's Indian trade, the Rogerstown people developed flourishing fur and cattle trade with their French and Spanish neighbors. Toward the south, other Shawnees settled on the St. Francis River, a favorite hunting ground of all eastern Indian emigrants.

Over the next two decades all these communities attracted a steady stream of new settlers from the East. With time, they built new towns at Cape Girardeau, on the St. Francis, and farther to the south and west. In 1815 William Clark, the U.S. superintendent of Indian affairs at St. Louis, estimated that twelve hundred Shawnees had settled in the central Mississippi Valley.[12]

Although Shawnees escaped American violence and encroachments in the Ohio Country in often chaotic and painful circumstances, their new towns in the West were no haphazard refugee camps. Nicolas de Finiels, a French engineer in Spanish service, commented that the large Apple Creek settlements were "more systematically and solidly constructed than the usual Indian villages." Euroamerican visitors also marveled at the material prosperity of the western Shawnees. When the eastern Shawnee communities struggled with the economic ravages of the Twenty Years' War, the westerners farmed their fertile new lands, hunted the plentiful game along the St. Francis and White rivers, and traded with the local French merchants. According to Finiels, the settlers along Apple Creek "soon cleared the land, which was securely fenced in the American style in order to protect their harvests from animals." Euroamericans admired the productivity of Shawnee farming, for they cultivated "maize, pumpkins, melons, potatoes, and corn, sufficient for their support the whole year." Many westerners also intensified the small-scale animal husbandry some Shawnees had been practicing for decades and acquired large herds of cattle, hogs, and horses. When a U.S. military officer visited Upper Louisiana in 1804, he noted with approval that the Shawnee and Lenape towns on Apple Creek were "the most wealthy of any in the country." Many locals lived in substantial two-story log houses, "well furnished with decent and useful furniture." In addition, their farms included storehouses for surplus corn and "barns for the shelter of cattle and horses, with which they are well supplied."[13]

Most Shawnees moved west with old friends and allies who also wished to escape the violence, land loss, and deteriorating hunting in the East. Lenapes, close allies of the Ohio Shawnees for a century, built a town between the two Shawnee communities on Apple Creek. They had more communities on the St. Francis and in the vicinity of St. Louis, again close to the local Shawnee settlements. Miami families, the Shawnees' old comrades-in-arms from the Maumee River, settled among the Cape Girardeau Shawnees. The Shawnee emigrants likewise forged close relations with diverse emigrants from the South, especially the Cherokees, Choctaws, and Chickasaws who were settling on the St. Francis. Once again, Shawnee refugees found security in new lands from multiple multiethnic alliances.[14]

The Shawnee settlers came from various directions and had diverse backgrounds. Although most of them were refugees from the Ohio Country, some came from Alabama where they had long lived among the Creeks. When these diverse groups collected together, they used traditional political strategies and social networks to foster unity and cooperation. Webs of kinship connected settlers from different regions. Most Shawnee pioneers from Ohio and Alabama alike were Kishpokos, Pekowis, and Thawikilas and thus shared divisional identities and common ancestors. Clan membership and more intimate family ties also linked many newcomers. The Shawnee settlers used these webs of kinship to cultivate political collaboration. In 1793 some of them described one of the Apple Creek headmen as "the great chief" who met with "all the councilors" at his town. This leader was possibly a man named Metipouiosa, who seems to have had connections to both the Ohio and the Alabama Shawnees. The reference to a "great chief" meeting with "councilors" suggests that Metipouiosa was the ceremonial head and spokesman of a multitown council. His role, then, paralleled that performed by such eastern Shawnee leaders as Nucheconner, Kisinoutha, and Catahecassa. Once again, disparate Shawnee groups gathered together by sharing power and cultivating collective, egalitarian decision-making institutions.[15]

Initially, the western Shawnees maintained intimate connections to their kinspeople in the East. Even as hundreds of Shawnees retreated from the Ohio Country to the central Mississippi Valley through the 1780s and 1790s, lively contacts continued to link them to their relatives on the Maumee River. People traveled back and forth between the eastern and western communities to visit relatives, recruit allies for military and diplomatic undertakings, and persuade kinspeople to move home with them. The western migration often split families, as brothers and sisters, even parents and children, made contrasting choices about whether to stay in the Ohio Country or seek a new future in the West. A prominent woman called Pemanpich moved to Upper Louisiana with her French-Canadian-Shawnee husband Louis Lorimier, while her equally influential kinsman, the war leader Nenessica, stayed on the Maumee, lived briefly in Canada, and eventually died at the Hog Creek town in Ohio. The Thawikila war leader Kishkalwa left the Scioto towns for Alabama in 1774 and later traveled to Apple Creek, yet his cousin (or possibly half-brother) Catahecassa remained in Ohio and staunchly opposed all U.S. efforts to remove the Shawnees to the West. Such splits must often have been distressing for family members, but they also meant that most Shawnees had close relatives living in various locations from the Great Lakes to the Deep South and the Trans-Mississippi West. A kinscape of relatives continued to connect widely scattered people and provide them with allies, assistance, and asylum during a time of violent dispossession. While Euroamerican scholars have usually viewed the dispersing of Shawnees and other Native peoples as a negative process that weakened the strength of the Indian nations, for Indian communities such dispersals offered widening alliances and new opportunities for resisting colonialism. The western migrations did not suddenly destroy all feeling of unity among the Shawnees.[16]

But despite the complex webs of connections, the gap between eastern and western Shawnees inevitably widened. People continued to visit one another, but the sheer distance between the Maumee and the Mississippi limited such contacts. Time, too, weakened the emotional and political bonds between the easterners and westerners. Most importantly, differing local conditions bred differing local interests, and these gave rise to distinct local identities. This can be seen in how the western Shawnees gradually withdrew from the war their eastern kinspeople continued to fight against the United States. During the 1790s some westerners still occasionally crossed the Mississippi to raid American settlers on the Ohio and Cumberland rivers.[17] But few if any warriors traveled back to the Maumee River to help their relatives against the invading armies of Josiah Harmar, Arthur St. Clair, and Anthony Wayne. Indeed, when the eastern Shawnees were feverishly assembling their Native and British allies to stop Wayne's army in 1794, the western Shawnee leaders were more concerned by Spain's lackluster support for their campaign against the Osages. In 1795 no western Shawnee headman apparently attended the Treaty of Greenville, where their Ohio relatives were forced to cede most of the old Shawnee homeland to the United States. Even many Euroamericans recognized the expanding rift among the Shawnees. Traveling in Louisiana from 1801 to 1803, the Frenchman Perrin du Lac observed that "the Chawanons . . . are divided into two tribes very distant from each other," one west of the Mississippi, the other on the Maumee.[18]

The growing gap between the western and eastern Shawnees was based on older social and political divisions. The majority of the western settlers were Pekowis, Kishpokos, and Thawikilas, whereas most Shawnees remaining in the East were Mekoches and Chalaakaathas. Once again, the Shawnees did not split neatly along divisional lines: many Chalaakaathas moved west, too, and more than three hundred Kishpokos and Pekowis lived in the Ohio Country in 1794. But political tensions among the five divisions clearly influenced how the Shawnees dispersed during the 1780s and 1790s. When Charles Trowbridge interviewed Ohio Shawnee elders in 1824 and 1825 about tribal traditions, Tenskwatawa did not include Thawikilas in his list of Shawnee divisions, and Catahecassa claimed that they were extinct. Such statements demonstrate the growing estrangement of the eastern and western Shawnees and reveal that it largely followed long-standing divisional boundaries.[19]

It is also striking that all the western Shawnee leaders who emerge in the Spanish documents during these decades—men like Metipouiosa, Kishkalwa, and Pepiqua (Flute)—are conspicuously absent from earlier Anglo-American records. Many of them may have been rising young chiefs just achieving a status as leaders. For such men, the migration to the West would have been a way to assert their independence from older authorities back home. In fact, in the 1790s the western Shawnees emphasized very self-consciously that their migration across the Mississippi meant a political separation from the emerging national leadership in the East. In 1797 the Cape Girardeau Shawnees described to a visiting British agent how they had "left their Brothers & Country & head men."[20] At a time when the Mekoche leaders strove to collect all Shawnees to a national territory in Ohio, the westerners portrayed themselves as people who had turned their back on such consolidation and its leaders.

DISPERSAL

In the first years of the nineteenth century two pieces of paper, written far from the central Mississippi Valley and without the knowledge of either the Indian or Euroamerican inhabitants of the region, transformed the world for all of Louisiana's peoples. First, in 1800 Spain sold its unprofitable Louisiana colony to Napoleon, who dreamed of rebuilding France's North American empire. A mere three years later the emperor changed his mind and sold Louisiana to the United States, whose leaders were eager to consolidate the republic's control over the strategically and economically vital Mississippi River. The global chess of colonial diplomacy had suddenly transformed the central Mississippi Valley from a Spanish-French-American borderland into U.S. territory. The local Shawnees and other eastern Indian settlers who had fled American expansion to the area now found themselves swallowed by the United States.[21]

Massive as this geopolitical transformation was, it did not necessarily have to spell disaster for the emigrant Indians. During the 1780s and 1790s Spain had encouraged U.S. citizens from the western states to immigrate to Louisiana in order to strengthen the population base of the feeble colony. Attracted by cheap land, several hundred Americans from Kentucky and Tennessee had crossed the Mississippi and settled at Cape Girardeau and New Madrid in the vicinity of the Shawnee and Lenape towns on Apple Creek. Despite their long history of enmity and violence, the western Shawnees and Americans had learned to live together peacefully. They traded with one another, mingled socially, and shared a common fear of the Osages. After the Louisiana Purchase it initially looked like the United States would respect this history of multiethnic coexistence. The federal government promised to recognize all Spanish land grants in Louisiana, including those given by the Spanish officials to the emigrant Indians. Shawnee and American pioneers also joined forces against their common Osage enemies. For a brief moment a multiethnic "frontier of inclusion" seemed possible in the central Mississippi Valley.[22]

Unfortunately, that moment proved fleeting. As so often before, land quickly became a bone of bitter contention between Shawnees and Anglo-Americans. In 1796 the non-Indian population of Upper Louisiana had been merely three thousand. After the Louisiana Purchase, however, American settlers rushed to the area, and by 1811 the non-Indian population had already reached eleven thousand. The massive surge of newcomers presented a grave threat to Indian landownership in the central Mississippi Valley. As early as 1807 the Cape Girardeau Shawnees complained that American emigrants had settled uninvited on their Spanish land grant. While some U.S. officials took action to rectify the situation, they were defied by the squatters, who simply refused to leave Indian lands. The Shawnees grew increasingly worried, as they saw history repeating itself before their eyes. Refugees from one bloody war over land, they wanted to "provent disputes" and turned to territorial and federal officials for protection. Over the next few years western Shawnee leaders pleaded "frequently" with the federal government to give them "a permanent Tract of Country to live in; where the White people might not encroach on them."[23]

The War of 1812 made the Shawnees' position in the central Mississippi Valley increasingly insecure. Despite the prewar land disputes, the western Shawnees declined the invitation of their Kishpoko kinsmen Tecumseh and Tenskwatawa to join the war against the United States. Instead, the westerners did their best to demonstrate their willingness to live peaceably with the Americans and joined territorial ranger companies to fight the British and their Indian allies. Their bravery earned them the gratitude of many U.S. officials, but little else. The wartime bloodshed fueled a racial hatred of all Indians among the White citizens of the recently formed Missouri Territory. Many Missourians, like their compatriots throughout the republic, were also increasingly influenced by the emerging discourses of "scientific" racism that portrayed the Natives as racially inferior beings doomed to extinction. Just like in the eastern states, this led to demands to remove the Indians farther west where they would not harm, or be harmed by, the divinely ordained expansion of the United States.[24]

Worst for the western Shawnees, American migration to the central Mississippi Valley kept swelling after the war. By 1824 ninety-seven thousand Americans lived in Missouri, many of them on Shawnee lands. Coveting the fertile lands of the emigrant Indians and convinced of their own racial superiority, in the late 1810s the newcomers began a ruthless campaign to drive the Shawnees and their Native neighbors out of Missouri. Americans squatted on Indian lands, threatened the Natives with violence, and robbed their property with impunity. The prosperous Shawnee farms, whose wealth Euroamerican visitors had praised for decades, became targets of systematic looting when their owners were away during annual winter hunts. In 1815 Wabepelathy, the headman of one of the Cape Girardeau towns, complained that "early in the spring, on my return from hunting, I found my house that had been broken open, and what I had left in it was all gone." Five years later the Apple Creek leaders described how such incidents had become a grim routine: "Since several Winters our Houses have been broken open and our property robed by the Whites." They correctly recognized the motive behind the looting, explaining that "the Whites do not Steal these things merely for their value, but more to make us abandon our Land and Take it themselves." Some Shawnees faced much more than just theft. Petiethewa and "Little Captain," two brothers who owned wealthy farms near Rogerstown, were repeatedly assaulted by their American neighbors. After years of violence and threats, American settlers forcefully seized their farms in 1820.[25]

Historian John Mack Faragher has called the American assault on the emigrant Indians in Missouri an ethnic cleansing. Undoubtedly, its goal was the "forced removal of certain culturally identified groups from their land," which is how another scholar recently defined ethnic cleansing. Initially, such a violent expulsion of the Indians was not official territorial or federal policy. In contrast, some federal and territorial officials attempted to defend the rights of the emigrant Indians. In 1815 Missouri's Governor William Clark threatened to remove illegal settlers from Indian lands with military force if necessary. Unfortunately, this just angered most Missourians. The Territorial Assembly openly opposed Clark's orders and claimed that Spain had merely granted the Indian emigrants a temporary "permission to Settle and hunt" in the region, not a permanent ownership of any land. The assembly correctly observed that the Cape Girardeau Shawnees and Lenapes claimed "a Considerable portion of the richest and most fertile part" of eastern Missouri. If such lands were left to the Indians, the assemblymen argued, this would "greatly" retard "the prosperity and Population" of the territory and slow down its march toward statehood. When Missouri did gain statehood in 1822, its leading politicians, staunch supporters of slavery and states' rights, argued that the existence of the emigrant Indian communities within state boundaries but outside state jurisdiction compromised Missouri's constitutional right to sovereignty. Such clamor drowned the voices of Clark and other defenders of Indian rights. Instead of upholding the rule of law and checking the encroachments of the squatters, territorial and state officials quietly allowed, sometimes even vocally encouraged, them to settle on Indian lands. The squatters became "the club to beat the emigrant Indians" out of Missouri, when the state lacked legal means to achieve such an expulsion itself. Eager to please their western voters, most federal officeholders in the East closed their eyes to this ruthless ethnic cleansing.[26]

In the late 1810s and early 1820s the systematic racial violence and theft forced most Shawnee pioneers to abandon their homes. Like so often since the late seventeenth century, when the western Shawnees recognized that their enemy was too powerful, they chose not to fight back but moved out of harm's way "for fear of a continuation of difficulty." Most headed southwest, toward the White River and the Ozark Mountains on the Missouri-Arkansas borderland. They had long hunted in the region and knew that they would find abundant game and few American settlers there. Wabepelathy moved his community from Apple Creek southwest to the Castor River in 1815. After 1820 most Cape Girardeau Shawnees followed him and traveled farther southwest, where they "scattered on the waters of White River." Although Rogerstown and some of the St. Francis communities endured in eastern Missouri against all odds, in 1823 Indian Agent Richard Graham reported that twenty-five hundred Shawnees had fled American encroachment and violence to the White River. They were not alone. Hundreds of dispossessed Lenapes, Weas, Peorias, Piankashaws, Kickapoos, and Cherokees from eastern Missouri and elsewhere likewise gathered in and around the Ozarks in search of an asylum from U.S. expansion.[27]

Refugees once more, the Shawnees struggled to secure a permanent home on the White River. Despite the poor performance of federal authorities in protecting Shawnee land rights, the refugee leaders took their case to U.S. officials. Time and again they contacted federal Indian agents and policymakers in Washington and demanded that the government give their people land on the White River in compensation for the country robbed from them in eastern Missouri. The Shawnee leaders clearly understood that they lived in a new world, within the powerful empire of the United States, where the stream of American settlers would be unending. To survive as an independent community in that world, they needed land. And to have and hold land, they needed the federal government to recognize and protect their land rights. Unfortunately, U.S. officials were not eager to strengthen Indian rights to the soil. When Pepiqua, Kishkalwa, and other refugee leaders from Apple Creek demanded a reservation of one hundred square miles on the White River in 1820, Secretary of War John Calhoun responded that the request was extravagant. The Shawnees pointed out that the fertile Cape Girardeau lands were "worth . . . six times" the mountainous country near the Ozarks. Yet they were willing to settle with a smaller reservation of just fifty square miles, provided the government also paid them twenty thousand dollars as an additional compensation. Shocked by Indians who understood the monetary value of land, Calhoun buried the issue in Congress. Two years later Kishkalwa and Pepiqua complained that they had never heard back from the federal authorities. For them and all other western Shawnees, finding "Land we Can Call Our Own" became the ultimate goal.[28]

White River was no idyllic haven for the Shawnees. When thousands of Indian refugees crowded to the area, the once-abundant game grew scarce quickly. The "hilly and strong" ground was far from ideal for farming. By 1823 the

White River communities were reduced to "the most crying and distressfull Situation for the want of nourishment." To make matters worse, American robberies had severely taxed the Shawnees' and other emigrants' large herds of horses, cattle, and hogs, as well as their other property. Much of what had not been stolen by the Missourians the Indians had lost during their arduous migration to the White River. Within a few years the communities that had once been "the most wealthy" in the central Mississippi Valley became terribly impoverished. In 1825 Kishkalwa and two other White River headmen, Mayesweskaka and Petecaussa, lamented that their people had been reduced from "rich and happy" to "poor, indebted, and Miserable."[29]

By the early 1820s violence, impoverishment, and uncertain land rights had become harsh everyday realities for the western Shawnees. To cope with such daunting conditions the Shawnees mobilized many of the same political, social, and economic strategies their ancestors had used for more than 150 years to survive in similar circumstances. Just like during the late-seventeenth-century diaspora and the many subsequent smaller-scale dispersals, the western Shawnees dealt with deteriorating living conditions and American aggression by dividing into smaller groups and constantly moving to new locations. When the large Shawnee towns in eastern Missouri could not defend their land rights against Americans without bloodshed, their inhabitants broke into smaller bands that could more easily search for new homes among their far-flung networks of kin and allies. From the White River, bands of Shawnees dispersed to the Arkansas and Red rivers and eventually to northern and eastern Texas. Everywhere they drew on decades of intertribal diplomacy, intermarriages, and kinship relations to find land, friends, and assistance among other Indian peoples, especially their old allies the Lenapes, Cherokees, and Kickapoos. Mobility, community fission, and wide multiethnic contacts were old Shawnee strategies for surviving in a world of violence and contested lands. They did not guarantee an easy life, however, and Shawnees reminded Americans that "we are a wandering people not from inclination but from necessity."[30] Yet, incredibly, using these time-tested strategies the Shawnees not only survived but were able to build new, prosperous communities on lands ranging from the White River to eastern Texas.

The exodus of Shawnees and other Indian emigrants from eastern Missouri to the southwest took them deeper into the lands claimed by the Osages and intensified their long-standing conflict with those Indians. The game-rich lands of the Ozark Mountains and the central Arkansas Valley had long formed the economic foundation of the Osages' trading empire. For the Shawnees and other Native refugees dispossessed by the Americans, this very same country and its resources promised survival and prosperity amidst spiraling impoverishment and migration. In the late 1810s and early 1820s the two groups, both fighting for their lives, clashed over the central Arkansas Valley more violently than ever.

The Shawnees now acquired a new, powerful ally in this warfare. Since the 1780s relentless American expansion in Tennessee, Georgia, and South and North Carolina had pushed small groups of Cherokees from their homelands across the Mississippi to the St. Francis, White, and Arkansas rivers. In 1810 the federal government persuaded one thousand more Cherokees to exchange their lands in the East for a new home in the central Arkansas Valley. By 1819 about five thousand Cherokees had settled there. No one had consulted the Osages about this removal. Outraged, they took up arms against the invaders. But the Cherokees proved dangerous enemies. Populous, well-armed, and determined to secure a new home in the West, they struck back with vengeance. The Cherokees realized that many other eastern emigrant Indians likewise coveted the rich lands of the Osages. To crush Osage opposition they began building an extensive military confederacy with the Shawnees, Lenapes, and other easterners. In 1817 some Shawnees and Lenapes joined a devastating Cherokee campaign against the Osages. When most Osage men left their homes for a summer buffalo hunt, the Cherokees and their allies attacked one of the major Osage towns on the Verdigris River, killing thirty-eight people and capturing one hundred more. To show their gratitude for military support, the next year Cherokee leaders invited Shawnees and Lenapes to settle with them on the central Arkansas.[31]

Many Shawnees took up the offer. To these landless and scattered refugees the powerful Cherokees seemed like an ideal ally, a hopawaaka-like guardian who would give them land and protection. Moreover, many of the Arkansas Cherokees were the same Chickamaugas who had fought alongside the Shawnees against the United States from the 1770s to the 1790s. Now the old allies joined forces again and inflicted scathing defeats on the Osages. U.S. officials were so eager to encourage the voluntary removal of eastern Indians to the west side of the Mississippi that they willingly accepted that the victories of the Cherokees and their allies constituted a legitimate claim to the central Arkansas Valley. Federal authorities organized a series of treaties between the Cherokees and Osages in which a large portion of the Osage lands in the region was transferred to the Cherokees by 1822. "Several" Shawnees reportedly settled among their Cherokee allies on this newly conquered territory.[32]

The Cherokee alliance helped the scattered Shawnees to wrest land from the powerful Osages, but it also gave them new leverage with the negligent U.S. officials. By the early 1820s the confederacy of the dispossessed Cherokees, Shawnees, Lenapes, Kickapoos, Weas, Piankashaws, and other easterners had grown so powerful in the Missouri-Arkansas borderlands that it began to worry many Americans. In Arkansas Territory Acting Governor Robert Crittenden was terrified of the "hoards of Northern Indians" who had assembled on the northern frontier of the territory under Cherokee protection. He feared that the allied Indians would use their formidable numbers and military strength to "extort a more liberal policy from the government." This was exactly what the refugees did. Although neither the Shawnees nor their Cherokee allies had any intention of going to war against the United States, the size of their confederacy allowed the small, dispersed Shawnee bands to portray themselves to federal officials not as insignificant splinter groups that could be ignored at will but as members of a powerful multitribal coalition whose demands had to be listened to. This greatly improved the Shawnees' bargaining position with the government. In February 1825 the White River headmen Kishkalwa, Petecaussa, and Mayesweskaka finally persuaded Secretary of War Calhoun to grant them a reservation in compensation for the lands that had been robbed from them in Missouri.[33]

Unfortunately, deciding the actual location of the reservation proved yet another source of contention. Kishkalwa, Mayesweskaka, and Petecaussa had petitioned for one close to the White River where the Shawnees could unite with their Cherokee allies. Superintendent of Indian Affairs William Clark accordingly planned to locate the reservation in what is now the northeastern corner of Oklahoma. Instead, federal officials finally established it far to the north, on the south side of the Kansas River, in present-day eastern Kansas. Most Shawnees were not happy with this change of plans. A few moved reluctantly to the new reservation. Weary after two decades of American encroachment and harassment, the Rogerstown people left their homes in the neighborhood of the burgeoning St. Louis and migrated to Kansas in 1828. The aging Kishkalwa, whose travels had spanned Ohio, Alabama, and Missouri, likewise took his family there. In 1828 Tenskwatawa and his Kishpoko and Pekowi followers from Ohio joined these western Shawnees at the reservation.[34]

But hundreds of White River Shawnees refused to abandon their homes yet again. They sent scouts to reconnoiter the reservation but were disappointed to learn that winters could turn bitterly cold in Kansas and that the prairie country was nearly devoid of timber. Moreover, the White River Shawnees had little previous contact with the Native peoples surrounding the reservation and considered them "strangers." And these Prairie Indians were not the only strangers the White River people felt uneasy about. They were also estranged from many of the other Shawnees settling on the reservation, especially Tenskwatawa's people. "For the last 40 years, we have resided in Upper Louisiana, entirely distinct from that portion of our people, who are now settled on the Kanzas River," White River headmen explained to federal authorities. "While they were engaged in war against the U States, we were peaceably

Figure 2. *Pah-te-cóo-saw, Straight Man, Semicivilized*, by George Catlin, ca. 1830.
A noted war leader among the dispossessed White River Shawnees, Petecaussa played
an important role in the negotiations with federal authorities in Washington in 1825
that led to the creation of the Shawnee reservation in Kansas.
© Smithsonian American Art Museum, Gift of Mrs. Joseph Harrison Jr.

following our usual occupations for the support of our families." Moreover, they continued, "so long a period has elapsed since we separated from them, that there is now but little of a common feeling of blood & friendship existing between us and them." Reluctant to settle among strangers in an inhospitable environment, about four hundred Shawnees remained on the White River and requested that the federal government give them another reservation either there or on the nearby Verdigris River.[35]

The rapidly growing American population of the Arkansas Territory resented the presence of these Shawnees and other eastern refugee Indians within the limits of the territory. Between 1820 and 1830 the non-Indian population of Arkansas jumped from fourteen thousand to thirty thousand. Most newcomers were engaged in commercial plantation agriculture that required large areas of land for cotton cultivation. They were not pleased to discover that the Shawnees lived on "good farms on the best lands" in northern Arkansas. In the late 1820s "bickerings and jealousies" arose between the Indians and Americans. Governor John Pope and other territorial officials bombarded federal authorities with inflammatory reports of an Indian war waiting just around the corner. Shawnee leaders sent their own appeals to Little Rock and Washington, explaining that they wished only to become U.S. citizens and buy the lands they occupied on the White River. In the increasingly racialized climate of the day the policy-makers in Washington found it much easier to believe that Indians were savages preparing for a war than farmers and ranchers willing to live peacefully among Americans. In 1828 the federal government pressured the Cherokees to cede their country in Arkansas and move to the conquered Osage lands west of the territory. Bereft of their allies, the White River Shawnees held out for a few years. In 1832 they too were forced to sign a new removal treaty that ordered them to move to the Kansas reservation.[36]

But it was one thing to order the Shawnees to remove and quite another to make them do so. While some families reluctantly migrated to Kansas, more than three hundred people moved instead to the Cowskin River in the northeastern corner of modern Oklahoma, just south of the reservation that had been recently created there for the Shawnees and Senecas from Lewistown, Ohio. Long-standing contacts and kinship relations linked the White River and Lewistown Shawnees and made them willing to join forces. In contrast, the White River refugees were suspicious of the Ohio Shawnees from Wapakoneta who were now settling on the reservation in Kansas. This was not only because time and distance had gradually weakened the contacts between the western and eastern Shawnees and alienated them from one another. More was involved. The refugees from the White River were Kishpokos, Pekowis, and Thawikilas who had always questioned the efforts of the Mekoches to lead the entire Shawnee nation. They knew very well that national consolidation remained the goal of the Wapakonetan Mekoche leaders in Kansas. In 1834 the Mekoches sent messengers to the Cowskin to invite the local Shawnees to the reservation. The westerners refused, pointing out that "all the Choice spots of land on the Kanzas river were already occupied" by the Ohioans and nothing was left for them but "refuse land." But they also highlighted their political separation from the eastern Shawnees. "When we Separated Ourselves from Our Shawne Brothers, It was our Intention never to Unite with them," the refugee leaders explained. In 1835 they again appealed to federal authorities for a reservation of their own next to the Lewistown lands.[37]

U.S. officials were enraged with the stubborn western Shawnees. Ever since the 1780s U.S. authorities had forcefully supported the creation of centralized tribal governments in order to facilitate federal control of the Native peoples and acquisition of Indian land. By the 1830s the entire U.S. Indian policy rested on consolidating Indians on tribal reservations. The reluctance of the western Shawnees to settle with their tribespeople in Kansas, and the ease with which they evaded federal orders to do so, challenged not only the specific removal treaties imposed on them, but the very authority of the U.S. government over Indians. No longer a military threat, the small and mobile western Shawnee bands still managed to threaten American power with their elusiveness. Enraged, Commissioner of Indian Affairs Elbert Herring declared that outright military force should be used to compel the Shawnees from the Cowskin to the Kansas reservation. "It is so injurious to the Indians to be broken into petty little bands, without chiefs to be responsible for them," he argued, linking the physical consolidation of tribes to political control. When Indian Agent F. W. Armstrong heard of the latest Cowskin Shawnee request for a separate reservation in 1835, he raged that "if those small parties are permitted to remain out of the country assigned to them; and select particular spots; and detach themselves from their respective tribes, the Government never will be done with Treaties." For Armstrong and other federal officials, forcing dispersed and autonomous Indian communities to tribal reservations under centralized national leadership was essential for controlling the Natives and buying their land.[38]

During the 1830s relentless federal pressure, the threat of American violence, and sheer impoverishment compelled many of the Cowskin people and other scattered western Shawnees to move north and settle at the reservation in Kansas. There they could at least find some land guaranteed to them by the U.S. government, as well as get their share of tribal annuities. But even such pressure did not force all Shawnees to Kansas. Several hundred headed south instead and created new communities in the volatile Mexican-American borderland in Texas.

Figure 3. *Lay-lóo-ah-pee-ái-shee-kaw, Grass, Bush, and Blossom, Semicivilized*,
by George Catlin, ca. 1830. A leader among those western Shawnees who refused
to move to the new reservation in Kansas in 1825, Lay-lóo-ah-pee-ái-shee-kaw
corresponded and negotiated with U.S. officials to secure a land base for his people
elsewhere. When posing for George Catlin, he held a letter or a treaty in his hand,
perhaps to stress the importance he placed on this diplomacy. © Smithsonian
American Art Museum, Gift of Mrs. Joseph Harrison Jr.

SHAWNEES ON THE TEXAS BORDERLANDS

Spanish Texas had long attracted eastern Indians distressed by the expansion of the United States. Around the turn of the nineteenth century bands of Alabamas, Koasatis, Choctaws, and Chickasaws began moving from the American South to eastern Texas. As early as 1807 some of the Shawnees living among the Creeks followed them. When American assaults against the eastern emigrant Indians in Missouri and Arkansas mounted after the War of 1812, many of these Indians joined in what became a mass migration to Texas. In the late 1810s at least two hundred Arkansas Cherokees traveled south to the Great Bend of the Red River. Soon, hundreds of their Shawnee, Lenape, and Kickapoo allies from the White and Arkansas rivers and farther north followed them. Mexican independence in 1821 did nothing to stop this immigration. Perhaps as many as ten thousand Native Americans from the Midwest and South moved to Texas in search of a better future during the 1820s. Just like their parents and grandparents had done forty years earlier in Louisiana, these Indians hoped to find protection and land in a country claimed by their old Spanish, and later Mexican, allies. And once more Spanish and Mexican officers welcomed the emigrants in order to strengthen their own defense against the United States.[39]

Shawnees from the oppressed Missouri and Arkansas communities began moving across the Red River, the border between the Spanish and U.S. claims, around 1820. In 1824 fifty families from the vicinity of St. Louis settled on the Sulphur Fork, a tributary of the Red River. Fewer than two years later 170 more Shawnees and Lenapes joined them. In a few years hundreds of Shawnees, Lenapes, Piankashaws, Cherokees, and Kickapoos had established a string of allied communities immediately south of the central Red River. Most of them settled at Pecan Point, downriver from Fort Towson, a U.S. stronghold on the northern bank of the border river. In 1827 a U.S. officer at Fort Towson reported that 150 Shawnee "Warriors" lived in two towns in Pecan Point. This could indicate a total population as high as 600 to 750. Lenapes built two slightly smaller communities in the vicinity, and some Kickapoos likewise settled there. Americans also encountered several "straggling" bands of Shawnees and Lenapes "living about in Camps" in the neighborhood. Pecan Point quickly became a thriving multiethnic Native American hub. Smaller groups of Shawnees found new homes elsewhere in Texas. Many Thawikilas, for example, ventured farther south to the Sabine River and settled there with some of their Cherokee and Kickapoo allies.[40]

Texas in the early nineteenth century was a dangerous, confusing, and contested borderland coveted by several rival Euroamerican empires and Native American peoples. Strategically, the province was crucial for Spain, for it formed a buffer that protected Mexico and its silver mines from U.S.

expansion. Yet during the last years of Spain's reign vicious internal conflicts and Comanche raids left Texas "in ruins" and, especially in the east, nearly devoid of a Euroamerican population. Only two thousand colonists remained in the province in 1820. The weakness of Spanish Texas created confusion and rivalry over its borders. After the Louisiana Purchase, Spain and the United States disagreed where American Louisiana ended and Spanish Texas began. To avoid a war, in 1806 the two countries created the so-called Neutral Ground in what is now the border region between the states of Texas and Louisiana and banned settlement in the area. It was not until 1819 that further negotiations finally established the eastern boundary of Texas. Although Spaniards and Americans generally agreed that the Red River formed the northern border, even there confusion and arguments arose when settlers from the United States crossed the river to squat on lands claimed by Spain.[41]

While such circumstances appeared chaotic to Euroamerican authorities bent on consolidating national boundaries and governments, the Shawnees and other Indian emigrants recognized that imperial confusion offered them crucial openings for survival and prosperity. They saw that no Euroamerican power effectively controlled the Texas-U.S. borderlands and took advantage of the Spanish, Mexican, and U.S. weakness in the area to carve out autonomous spaces for themselves.[42] Having lived between competing Euroamerican empires since the 1720s, the Shawnees were experienced in taking advantage of such circumstances. But they also knew that living on imperial borderlands created problems of its own. The Shawnees had learned that in the long run only an unambiguous Euroamerican recognition of Native land rights would guarantee their ownership of any territory they might claim on contested borderlands. Finding a permanent home remained the fundamental goal of all Shawnee pioneers in Texas. Unfortunately, the unsettled conditions and shifting power relations in Texas that helped the Indian emigrants to settle in the province proved inimical to their efforts.

In 1824 the Pecan Point Shawnees petitioned and received a formal grant of land from the provincial authorities of the Mexican state of Coahuila y Tejas. However, even though the Mexican federal government later approved the grant, its exact location and borders were left open. This proved a fatal mistake. American emigrants from Arkansas had been settling in Pecan Point as long as Shawnees, claiming that the area lay within the bounds of the United States. In 1828 they accused their Shawnee and Lenape neighbors of crowding their land and robbing their cattle and pleaded with the governor of Arkansas to remove the Indians from the alleged limits of the territory. Governor George Izard promptly mobilized the territorial militia. The soldiers drove the Indians from their homes at gunpoint and confiscated the documents which proved that Mexican officials had granted the land to them. Even the U.S. commander of

Fort Towson was shocked by the Arkansan aggression. He protested that the Shawnee and Lenape towns were located at least fifty miles from the international border on the Mexican side. But it was all in vain. Like Shawnees, American settlers knew how to use unsettled boundaries and the weakness of the Mexican and U.S. federal governments to gain land on the contested borderlands. Yet some Shawnees persisted in Pecan Point. Others migrated south, deeper into the Mexican territory, and settled on the headwaters of the Angelina River. In 1835 four hundred Shawnees lived just north of Nacogdoches, the easternmost Mexican city in Texas. They continued to petition the Mexican government for a clear title to their land.[43]

Euroamerican officials were deeply suspicious of the mobile, independent, and multiethnic groups of Shawnees, Lenapes, Cherokees, Kickapoos, and other eastern Indians that crossed the Red River in the 1820s. U.S. authorities had always viewed the western Shawnees and other emigrant Indians distrustfully. Advocating the collection of Indians on tribal reservations, they saw the western Shawnees as "Vagabonds" living "without chiefs." U.S. officials recognized that many of the Shawnees, Cherokees, and other easterners heading to Texas represented those portions of their nations that were most opposed to the federal Indian policy and least willing to negotiate with the U.S. government. At Fort Towson the officers described the neighboring Shawnees and their allies as "generally the lawless & disaffected part of their tribe[s]." Arkansas's territorial governor, James Miller, proclaimed them "a Banditti of outlaws" and accused them of using the Mexican territory as a staging area for raiding the American settlements across the border. George Gray, the U.S. Indian agent stationed at the mouth of the Sulphur Fork in Louisiana, was downright terrified of the eastern Indians settling higher up the river. To him, the region seemed "the whirlpool that is sucking within its bosom, the restless and the disaffected, of all nations and languages; parties of broken tribes." Gray feared that the growing numbers of Indians in the region meant that "in a little time the Indians can do as they please." Both he and Miller asked federal authorities to establish military posts on the U.S. side of the Red River to control these troublesome Native pioneers.[44]

There was some truth to the claims of Gray, Miller, and their like. Many Shawnee and Cherokee emigrants to Texas were in fact dissenters who did not accept the removal treaties negotiated by some of their tribal leaders. They questioned the very idea that a small group of headmen could legitimately represent their nation in negotiations with the United States. But the emigrant communities on the Texas borderlands were hardly the hotbeds of anarchy the Americans imagined. Old, well-established social ties, identities, and lines of authority structured these communities. Long-standing alliances and kinship relations defined the relations between the Shawnees, Cherokees, Lenapes,

Kickapoos, and others. The emigrants often recognized Cherokee leaders as their collective spokespeople in diplomacy with the Euroamericans, because the Cherokees had a long history of successful collaboration with Anglo-Americans. After centuries of trade and diplomacy, many Cherokee headmen had a part-European ancestry and were fluent in English. The Shawnees and other emigrants also created close ties with the Native peoples of eastern Texas. They were especially careful to cultivate good relations with the Caddos, who were "considered the mother nation of the country." Such diplomacy with their Native hosts had helped Shawnee refugees to survive in unknown lands countless of times since the seventeenth century.[45]

Old social and political ties continued to organize also the relations between and within the Shawnee communities. Most of the Texas settlers were Pekowis, Thawikilas, and Kishpokos connected by ancient kinship bonds and political alliances. Repeated forced migrations and removals had fragmented the western Shawnee communities and scattered the members of individual divisions, towns, and families across the western landscape. Yet many overlapping kinship networks, alliances, and social institutions helped the dispersed migrant bands to reunite flexibly with other splinter groups time after time for security and cooperation. In the mid-1820s, for example, the Sulphur Fork communities represented a fusion of at least two Shawnee groups, one from the vicinity of St. Louis, the other possibly from the White River. In 1825 Tecumseh's son Paukeesaa moved from Canada to Wapakoneta, Ohio. The next year he immigrated to the reservation in Kansas with his uncle, Tenskwatawa. By 1832 he had joined the White River Shawnees. Shared divisional and clan identities united such long-separated individuals and groups. In the 1820s and 1830s the White River Shawnee leaders continued to sign their messages to U.S. authorities with pictures of their clan eponyms. This attests that clans remained an important social institution among the western Shawnees. Just like during the seventeenth-century Shawnee diaspora, divisions and clans still laid a strong foundation for intracommunity leadership and intercommunity alliances.[46]

Despite the migrations, violence, and uncertainty that followed the Texas Shawnees, they could still rely on their traditional social organization to bring order and meaning to their lives in shifting and often adverse conditions. Tradition did not imply stagnation; rather, it involved the creative use of old ideas in new situations. Tradition also allowed the rich blending of old ways with foreign innovations. Although the Texas Shawnees were wary of Anglo-American expansion, they did not seek to live in isolation. The first Shawnee settlements on the Sulphur Fork were located close to the U.S. Indian agency on the Louisiana side of the Mexico-U.S. border. At Pecan Point the Shawnee and American settlers built their homes next to each other. In Nacogdoches, too, the Shawnee and other emigrant Indian towns were "intermingled with the settlements of the Americans." Centuries of contact and cooperation had made trade and other interaction with Euroamericans an integral part of Shawnee life. The Texas Shawnees traded their agricultural produce, cattle, fowl, and animal skins in Nacogdoches and other Mexican and Anglo-American settlements and bought textiles, guns, and ammunition from the colonists. Shawnee women, like women among Cherokees, Alabamas, and other southeastern peoples, had learned to "use looms of their own construction, copied from those they have seen in the United States, to weave divers parti-colored cotton textiles for their own and their families' use." Shawnees and Cherokees used so many textiles and European-style clothing that one French visitor opined that they "look like selectmen." Many western Shawnees also spoke English.[47]

Unfortunately, the Mexican government never gave the flourishing Texas Shawnee communities an unambiguous title to their lands. To make matters worse, in 1823 Mexico opened Texas to immigration from the United States, hoping that American settlers would boost the economy and population of the languishing province. They did. American immigration tripled the colonial population of Texas in a decade, and by 1835 nearly thirty thousand Anglos lived there. Suddenly the Indians, both emigrants and Texas Natives, found themselves a minority amidst the burgeoning Anglo-Texan population. As in Arkansas, most of the newcomers were Southerners steeped in racial ideology and interested in commercial plantation agriculture and ranching; therefore, they needed land and had few scruples about taking it from the Indians, whom they viewed as racial inferiors. The Anglos quickly clashed with many Native Texas tribes; soon they became irritated also by the Shawnees, Cherokees, Lenapes, and other emigrant Indians. In 1827 one Anglo leader warned Mexican authorities that if the Indian emigrants were allowed to remain in the province, "these northern barbarians will swarm in Texas as the Goths and Vandals swarmed in Italy." Depicting Indians as warlike, violent, and treacherous by nature, he claimed that these "fierce and ungovernable people" will revert "to their pristine savage condition" and "turn their fury on their benefactors." Such hostile language that portrayed racial conflict as inevitable left no room for Shawnees trading with Anglo settlers, petitioning the government for land rights, and dressing like selectmen.[48]

With such attitudes prevalent among the Anglo-Texans, the Shawnees and other Indian emigrants were understandably concerned when the Anglos rebelled against the Mexican government in 1835. The Cherokees tried to balance between the belligerents and see which side would be willing to guarantee the emigrant Indians' land rights in exchange for military support. Most Shawnees, in contrast, remained neutral through the Texas Revolution. After the Anglo victory made Texas an independent republic in 1836, its new leadership refused to honor any previous land agreements made with the Indian settlers. Angered, some Cherokees supported Mexican efforts to reconquer

Texas over the next three years. This gave the Anglo-Texans a perfect pretext to expulse all Indian emigrants, friends and foes, from the republic. The ethnic cleansing reached its bloody climax in July 1839, when Texan troops attacked the Cherokees and a few of their Shawnee, Lenape, and Kickapoo allies on the Neches River. They killed or wounded around one hundred Indians and forced the survivors to retreat to the north side of the Red River. Although most Shawnees had judiciously kept clear of the violence, they fared no better. In August Texan diplomats forced the Shawnees to sign a removal treaty. Later that fall armed Anglo troops escorted nearly three hundred Shawnees from their homes to the Red River where they were ferried to the U.S. side.[49]

Even this latest round of dispossession and violence did not break the Texas Shawnees. North of the Red River they found themselves in the Indian Territory, a special area created by the U.S. government in modern Oklahoma, Kansas, and Nebraska for the eastern Indians removed from their homes across the Mississippi. There, the Shawnee refugees once again used their centuries-old strategies of mobility, diplomacy, and intertribal networking to establish a new home. Once again, their mobility, independence, and contacts contested U.S. Indian policy. In the plans of the federal policymakers, the Indian Territory was divided into clearly bounded tribal reservations, where tribal governments were supposed to consolidate their power. Shawnees paid little attention to such schemes. At first they settled on the lands designated to the removed Choctaws and Chickasaws. Their hosts were not happy about the uninvited guests, whom they accused of stealing cattle. In 1841 the Choctaws and Chickasaws evicted the Shawnee refugees with the help of federal troops. The Shawnees retreated north to the Canadian River and settled on lands marked for the Creek Nation. This time their choice of hosts was a more fortunate one, as the Creeks welcomed the Shawnees. Many Thawikilas, Pekowis, and Kishpokos had lived among the Creeks in Alabama at one time or another since the late seventeenth century and had relatives and friends among their new hosts. They had especially close kin and ritual ties to the old Upper Creek towns, such as Tukabatchee, which had been reestablished on the Canadian River. A U.S. officer visiting the area in 1842 learned from his Creek hosts that "the Shawnees and Tuckebatche were originally one people." On the Canadian River, Tukabatchee and other old Upper Creek towns formed the western frontier of the Creek Nation. They were dangerously exposed to raids by Comanches and other Plains Indians to the west, so the Upper Creeks saw the Shawnees not only as kinspeople, but also as crucial military allies who could help protect them from the Plains Indians.[50]

Some seven hundred Shawnee refugees found a new home on the Canadian River. Although they arrived "in a deplorable condition," they quickly took advantage of the unique economic opportunities the region offered. In a few years the Canadian Shawnees became middlemen in a flourishing trade between the removed eastern Indians to their east and the nomadic Prairie and Plains peoples to their west. Ironically, the trade formed the Shawnees' silent revenge on Texas, for many of the horses and mules they bought from the Plains Indians and then resold to the easterners had been robbed from Texas. Indeed, the Comanches, Kiowas, and other Plains tribes intensified their raiding in Texas to acquire more plunder to be sold to their new eastern neighbors through Shawnee hands.[51] Texas and the United States could do little to stop this trade. Without any formal relationship with the federal government, a reservation, or a centralized national leadership, the Canadian River Shawnees remained out of the government's reach.

By the 1850s American travelers often marveled over the prosperity of the Canadian Shawnee communities. They noted approvingly their "gardens, orchards, and fields of grain," as well as the "straight and level" roads built by the Indians between their towns. "They . . . appear to have an abundance of everything," admitted one military officer.[52] As his words testify, the Canadian River Shawnees had not only survived through decades of dispossession, racial violence, and forced removals; amazingly, they had also kept their communities intact, fused their traditions creatively with cultural innovations, built new economic systems, and retained their autonomy. Once again, they flourished.

Looking back at the past half century and more in the 1850s, the western Shawnees on the Canadian River and elsewhere could easily see that their history was quite different from that of their eastern kinspeople from Ohio. Most of the westerners had not fought against the Americans since the 1770s. The westerners had not united behind a collective national leadership like the Ohio Shawnees; neither had they sought to create a collective national territory in the West. In 1936 the western Shawnee historian Thomas Wildcat Alford wrote that the divergent histories of the easterners and westerners "finally led to their division into two tribes of the nation today." But as Alford noted, the division of the Shawnees into two groups with radically different political outlooks and historical experiences was "all nonsense to the government." Adamant that Indians must be collected on tribal reservations, in the 1850s federal officials began calling the western Shawnees "Absentees," because they still remained away from the Shawnee reservation in Kansas. Such identification through negation seemed absurd to the westerners. For them, mobility and community fission had always been part of the Shawnee way of life. Their identity as Shawnees emanated not from an adherence to a centralized national leadership or ownership of collective territory but from the networks of kinship and spiritual power that connected their far-flung communities. When the federal government nevertheless continued to push all of the disparate Shawnee groups to a single reservation, the outcome was a revolution in the Shawnee society.[53]

7

"Reunion"

Sovereignty and Centralization, 1833–1870

From the 1820s through the 1840s the U.S. government forced more than ten thousand Indians to relocate from the Old Northwest to reservations in what is now eastern Kansas and Nebraska as a part of the Indian removal program. About one thousand Shawnees from Ohio, Michigan, Missouri, Arkansas, Oklahoma, and Texas were resettled to a single reservation in Kansas. U.S. policymakers also launched a new assault on Shawnee sovereignty. They argued that Indian peoples no longer constituted independent nations; rather, they were childlike wards of the federal government, and it was the duty of the government to manage their economic and political affairs like a protective guardian. At the new reservation some Shawnee leaders strove to unite their disparate communities to defend their independence. This process climaxed in 1852, when a group of ambitious, wealthy men established the National Council, a republican institution that claimed the right to lead all Shawnees and control such national resources as the reservation land and annuities. These elite men portrayed the creation of the National Council as "a reunion" that "made the council fires [of the Shawnees] complete" after centuries of diaspora and factionalism. Many tribespeople, however, doubted that a single council could work equally for the benefit of all the diverse local and kin groups forced to share the reservation. Some argued that the National Council furthered the interests of only a wealthy, bicultural elite. Efforts to unite the Shawnee nation for the defense of Native sovereignty once again led to bitter internal conflicts over the legitimacy of political centralization. At stake was the survival of the Shawnees as a distinct, independent people.[1]

A RESERVATION DIVIDED

The Shawnee reservation in Kansas was originally created in 1825 for the dispossessed western Shawnees driven from Missouri by American squatters. From the start, U.S. officials hoped that ultimately all Shawnees would be induced to remove there. Covering 1.6 million acres on the south side of the Kansas River immediately west of the state of Missouri, the reservation was designed as a place where federal authorities could collect all the troublesome, elusive, and far too independent Shawnee communities under U.S. control. Between 1825 and 1833 officials pressured about one thousand Shawnees from the Old Northwest, Midwest, and South to move there.[2]

The Shawnee settlers in Kansas were a diverse lot. The first to arrive in 1828 was a band of Shawnees from Rogerstown, Missouri. Prominent among them were the bicultural families of James Rogers (Onothe) and William Jackson (Noma/Fish), two Americans who had been captured and adopted by the Shawnees during the Revolutionary War. Under their leadership the Rogerstown people had long engaged successfully in the evolving commercial frontier economy in Missouri as farmers, cattle and hog raisers, and lead miners. Some of the Rogerstown Shawnees had embraced Christianity and acquired an American education. A radically different group followed the Rogerstownians to the reservation, when 250 Kishpokos and Pekowis moved in from Wapakoneta under the leadership of Tenskwatawa, the Shawnee Prophet. Although many of these newcomers had adopted elements of American farming technology and material culture, they remained more committed to Native spiritual traditions and more suspicious of the Americans than the Rogerstown people. More dispossessed western Shawnees settled at the reservation when the aging Thawikila leader Kishkalwa brought in a small band of kin and followers from the White River. Driven across Missouri and Arkansas by the expanding American population for more than two decades, the Thawikilas were impoverished and wary of Tenskwatawa's people, whom they remembered as trouble-making militants from the War of 1812. Finally, in 1832 and 1833 the federal government removed about four hundred Ohio Shawnees to the reservation. Most of them came from Wapakoneta and Hog Creek, but some Lewistownians, too, elected to move to Kansas instead of their own reservation in Oklahoma. A collection of Mekoches, Chalaakaathas, and Pekowis, the Ohio Shawnees were led by headmen who had for decades struggled to bring all Shawnees together as a united nation. Ironically, this very dream set them at odds with both Tenskwatawa's followers and the western Shawnees, who had always been suspicious of national consolidation.[3]

The removal to Kansas was a harrowing experience for all Shawnees. Leaving homes, places with deep emotional and spiritual significance, was difficult.

Some Shawnees from Wapakoneta later explained that "we felt as if we were tearing ourselves from ourselves, & every thing which the Great Spirit had given to us to make us happy." The federal government had promised to supply the migrating Shawnees during their journeys to the reservation, but U.S. officials regularly neglected their duties and left the Indians to find their own food and other necessaries during the trips that covered hundreds of miles and often spanned several months. Because most removal routes went through areas populated by American settlers, hunting was impossible, and the Shawnees often went hungry. Many had to sell whatever they carried with them—cattle, hogs, even clothing—to Americans "to subsist our women and children." Because of frequent delays by U.S. officials, the removals of the Wapakoneta Shawnees were undertaken in late fall and winter under difficult circumstances. People took ill; horses died. Many Shawnees arrived at the reservation "in a wrecthed state."[4]

When finally in Kansas, the removed Shawnees set out to rebuild their homes and lives once more. While men began to build log houses and clear the timber along the Kansas River for fields, women planted corn and potatoes. Leaders debated how they could best ensure a brighter future for their people. In the mid-1830s Mekoche headmen from Wapakoneta took a lead in these discussions and once more promoted national unification vigorously. Just before their removal the Wapakonetans had lost many of their most prominent old headmen, including Catahecassa and Biaseka. The old chiefs' dream of Shawnee consolidation did not die with them, however; they were succeeded by their relatives and allies who shared their vision. A Wolf clan hokima named Lalloway (John Perry) followed Catahecassa as the speaker of the tribal council, whom the Americans often mistook for "the head chief." Catahecassa's son Quaskey (Young Blackhoof) also gained a considerable following. As the apprentices and allies of Catahecassa, Biaseka, and other old Wapakonetan leaders, Lalloway, Quaskey, and their associates were accustomed to viewing Shawnee unification as a sacred task and a sound political strategy that would best protect their people from U.S. aggression. When the Wapakonetans had been forced to sell their land in Ohio to the United States in 1831, these leaders had decided to make the best of a bad situation by gathering all Shawnees to the new reservation in Kansas. According to their former agent John Johnston, the Wapakonetan leadership had proposed "removing in the coming year" and planned "to collect the whole of their nation at this point, and endeavor again to become one people."[5]

Once in Kansas, the Wapakonetans wasted no time in putting their plans into action. In 1834 Lalloway, Quaskey, and other Wapakonetan headmen visited the western Shawnees who had escaped American violence from Cape Girardeau to the Neosho and Cowskin rivers in northeastern Oklahoma. There they suggested that the westerners "should unite with us." When the western Shawnees declined, Lalloway, Quaskey, Pamothaway (George Williams), and Walekakothe (Cornstalk) sent a long letter to Secretary of War Lewis Cass and asked his assistance in persuading the Cowskin and Neosho people to migrate to Kansas. They declared that they were "so desirous . . . to have all the Shawnees again re-united as one nation—those on the Six Bulls [Neosho], Red River, &c that we would cheerfully relinquish to those who might join us, our present improvements, for a moderate remuneration and settle ourselves in other parts of our tract."[6]

These invitations bore some fruit. In 1838–1839 two hundred dispossessed and impoverished Shawnees from the Neosho moved to the reservation. There they hoped to receive a share of the tribal annuities and economic assistance from the federal government. Most of the western Shawnees, however, chose to stay away from Kansas, collecting instead in the Creek country on the Canadian River. Even some of the Ohio Shawnees did not settle in Kansas. The federal government had provided a separate reservation for the Lewistown Shawnees and Senecas on the Neosho River in northeastern Oklahoma, next to a reservation of their old allies and relatives the Senecas from Sandusky. Many Lewistown Shawnees moved to Oklahoma. In 1832 they formally amalgamated with the two Seneca groups to form the United Nation of Senecas and Shawnees.[7] Most Lewistownians and western Shawnees felt a far closer affinity to their kinspeople and allies among the Senecas and Creeks than to the Shawnees from Wapakoneta, Hog Creek, and Rogerstown. Carrying a heritage of two centuries of diaspora and multiethnic communities, they saw more security in living among strong Native allies than in trying to consolidate the entire Shawnee nation on a single piece of land.

Uniting even those Shawnees who did gather at the Kansas reservation proved a difficult task for the Wapakonetan leadership. The western Shawnees from Missouri and the eastern Shawnees from Ohio had been separated for half a century and felt little attachment to one another. The Missouri Shawnees were suspicious of the Wapakonetan plans to consolidate the nation and questioned the claims of the Mekoches that the well-being of the entire nation depended on the Mekoche sacred bundle. Reflecting on the bitter political and spiritual debates between the eastern and western Shawnees from a Missourian perspective a century later, the Kishpoko elder James Clark explained that the Mekoche "claimed he had more [spiritual] rules than the other Shawnee, but they [the Missouri Shawnees] said he was wrong and really did not know what kind of rules he had." According to Clark, the "mekoče went broke up in Ohio, he'd sold all his land and had nothing. Then he came to Kansas to be with the rest of the Shawnee. He begged the Shawnee to let him live there with them. He gave his promise not to be appointed as any sort of businessman (a chief)

Figure 4. *Lay-láw-she-kaw, Goes Up the River, an Aged Chief,* by George Catlin, ca. 1830. A prestigious Turtle clan hokima, Lay-láw-she-kaw enjoyed great respect among the western Shawnees who had refused to move to the reservation in Kansas in 1825. After more than a decade on the Missouri-Arkansas-Oklahoma borderlands, in 1839 he finally took his people to the reservation, where they developed a tense relationship with the eastern Shawnees from Ohio. © Smithsonian American Art Museum, Gift of Mrs. Joseph Harrison Jr.

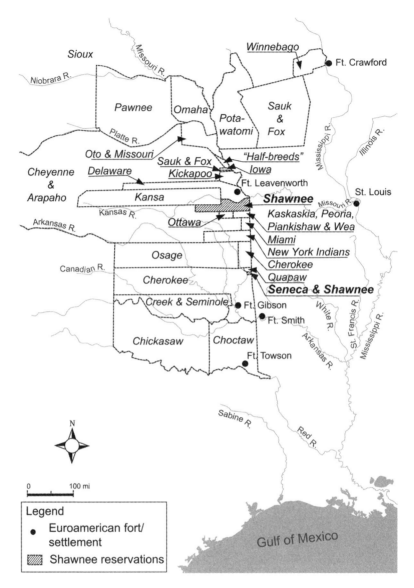

Map 8. The Shawnee and neighboring reservations, ca. 1840
(based on Andrist, *Long Death*, 11). Map drawn by Terhi Tanska.

and he promised to abide by the rules of øawikila, pekowi, kispoko, calakaaøa
and spito." For Clark and many other western Shawnees, the Wapakonetan
Mekoches looked like troublesome intruders.[8]

Control over two critical resources, the reservation land and annuities,
became particularly bitter bones of contention between the Ohio and Missouri
Shawnees in Kansas. The Shawnee reservation had been founded in the 1825

Treaty of St. Louis between federal officials and western Shawnee leaders. The treaty had specified that the reservation was meant for "the Shawnee tribe of Indians, within the State of Missouri, for themselves and for those of the same nation, now residing in Ohio, who may hereafter emigrate to the west of the Mississippi." It is, however, possible that this is not how the U.S. negotiators explained the treaty to the western Shawnee delegates in St. Louis. Many Missouri Shawnees later argued that they were the only rightful owners of the reservation and claimed that the Ohio Shawnees were mere guests there. The ambiguous language of the 1831 Wapakoneta removal treaty compounded the confusion. That treaty had promised that if there was no good land left on the Kansas reservation for the Ohio Shawnees, the federal government would provide another reservation for them *next* to the original one occupied by the Missouri Shawnees. Both Missourians and Ohioans, then, expected to receive land of their own in Kansas.[9]

Many Missourians were nevertheless willing to share the reservation with their eastern kinspeople. They only expected that the Ohioans would reciprocally share their resources with them. The western Shawnees were particularly interested in the annuities rising from the cessions of the Shawnee lands in Ohio. The Wapakonetans received three thousand dollars each year from the federal government as an annuity for cessions of Ohio lands made in 1795, 1817, and 1818. In addition, when the Wapakonetans ceded their last holdings in Ohio to the United States in the removal treaty in 1831, the federal government sold the land to American citizens and used the proceeds to create a trust fund for the future use of the Wapakonetan Shawnees. The Wapakonetans received 5 percent of this fund annually. Finally, after determined Shawnee demands, Congress granted the Wapakonetans an additional annuity of two thousand dollars in 1831 for a period of fifteen years as a further compensation for the sale of their Ohio lands. These sums were hardly large, and the federal government often neglected to pay them, but even small annuities seemed big to the impoverished Missourians, and many western Shawnees felt that they had a right to a share of the money. After all, the ceded Ohio lands had once been their home, too. Moreover, they had "provided a home for" the Wapakonetans at what they regarded as their reservation in Kansas. But no money was forthcoming from the Ohioans. "I have waited to see if my brothers would ever think of me as I did of them," complained Lewis Rogers from Rogerstown in 1838. "I stand by & see them receive the money every year for our lands [in Ohio]. While I think I am entitled to a part, they divide it among themselves & never look at me once." Many Missourians grew bitter. According to Rogers, the Ohio Shawnees "came rich and found me poor"—and did nothing about it.[10]

Shawnees were accustomed to sharing land and resources with kin and allies. What made the control of the reservation land so contentious was not the abstract question of landownership in itself, but the fact that even at the new reservation the United States kept pressing the Shawnees for more land cessions. Under constant federal pressure it became essential to determine who had what rights in the reservation land. To the chagrin of the Missouri Shawnees, the Ohio headmen assumed that as the national leaders they were entitled to negotiate with U.S. officials about further cessions. In 1836 Lalloway, Quaskey, Chawwe (George/John Francis), Oneissimo, and other Wapakoneta and Hog Creek leaders granted to the United States a right to build a road through the reservation. Five years later the federal government proposed to buy the eastern portion of the reservation and give it to the Wyandots, who were to be removed there from Sandusky. Shawnees gathered to discuss the proposition in what one eyewitness described as a "stormy" council. The Wapakonetans had close ties to the Wyandots, their old neighbors and allies in Ohio, and supported the sale, but the Missouri Shawnees opposed it vehemently. They pointed out that "the United States have land plenty—more, by far, than the Shawnees" to give to the Wyandots. When some Wapakonetans attempted to arrange the sale in secret, "very much enraged" Missourians threatened that "they would kill the chiefs who had done that act." Faced with such determined resistance, the Ohio leadership dropped the sale.[11]

The conflicts over land and annuities reflect the rough economic realities of the reservation. The removal had devastated the economy of all Shawnee bands. Forced to leave their homes, the Shawnees had had to abandon their fields, houses, orchards, mills, and heavy agricultural tools, such as plows. Many had sold their cattle and hogs rather than attempt to drive them hundreds of miles cross-country to distant Kansas. Dozens of animals also had died on the road; others had been stolen by American settlers. In the prairies of Kansas the Shawnees had to learn to farm in ecological conditions vastly different from those of the woodlands of Ohio and eastern Missouri. Hunting did not provide much relief, because there was "hardly a deer a peace for the red man" in the woods along the Kansas River, as some Ohio Shawnees complained. When a delegation of Quakers visited the reservation in 1833, they were shocked to find the newly arrived Wapakonetans on the brink of starvation. "We are living hard for the want of meat," Lalloway and others admitted a year later. In such conditions annuities, technological assistance, and shipments of relief food from the federal government became essential for survival.[12] Economic distress sharpened the conflicts among the different bands over such crucial scarce resources as land and annuities.

Conflicts over resources also characterized Shawnee relations with the United States through the 1830s. When negotiating the removal treaties, federal authorities always promised the Shawnees generous compensations for the losses they would suffer due to their relocation to Kansas. The 1825 Treaty of

St. Louis, for example, guaranteed the Missouri Shawnees fourteen thousand dollars "for the losses and inconveniences which said tribe will sustain by removal." The Wapakonetan removal treaty stipulated that the federal government would build the Ohio Shawnees a new sawmill, a grist mill, and a blacksmith's shop at the reservation. Unfortunately, U.S. officials were far faster in making such promises than in fulfilling them. When the Wapakonetans asked their agent, Richard Cummins, to have their mills constructed as soon as possible in the spring of 1834—three years after the initial promise to do so—the embarrassed Cummins realized that no one in the government bureaucracy had reserved any money for the task. The experiences of the Missouri Shawnees with federal officials were even more dispiriting. Nineteen years after the Treaty of St. Louis these western Shawnees were still waiting for nearly five thousand dollars of their removal compensation.[13]

The problem was not just bureaucratic negligence and incompetence. U.S. officials also conceptualized the relationship between the Indian peoples and the federal government in an entirely new way. Increasingly, they viewed the Natives not as sovereign nations comparable to any foreign nation, but as "domestic dependent nations." Drawing from the popular evolutionary theories of the day, federal authorities and philanthropists held Indians to be childlike savages who needed to be protected by the government. They styled the Natives as "wards" of the government and argued that the Indians and their resources had to be managed by fatherly U.S. officials. In 1835 Lalloway found out the hard way what this alleged benevolence meant in practice. As the Wapakonetans struggled to rebuild their shattered economy on the reservation, Lalloway and other leaders requested that U.S. authorities pay to them the entire trust fund that the federal government had created from the proceeds of the sale of the Wapakonetans' ceded lands in Ohio. No one answered their request. Over the years the Wapakonetans repeated their demand, without success. Federal officials had invested the trust fund in state bonds and argued that "the necessities of the tribe . . . are not so great" as to justify the loss of money that would have resulted from cashing in the stocks immediately.[14]

In the early 1830s a new group of American intruders joined federal officials to threaten Shawnee independence and resources on the reservation: Christian missionaries. Baptists, Methodists, and Quakers established missions and schools among the Shawnees to shepherd them toward a lifestyle the Americans equated with "civilization." Many Shawnees welcomed the missionaries, as both Wapakonetans and Rogerstownians shared a long history of cooperation with them. The Society of Friends, for instance, had helped the Wapakonetans to rebuild their community after the Twenty Years' War and the War of 1812. The Quakers had also lobbied for the Shawnees in Washington. Prominent Rogerstown leaders already had embraced Christianity and American education in Missouri. Even many of those Wapakonetan and Rogerstown Shawnees not interested in Christianity saw the missionaries as trustworthy allies who could assist the nation against the avaricious federal government.[15]

The arrival of the Baptists, Methodists, and Quakers, however, electrified old divisions among the diverse Shawnee bands on the reservation. The various Ohioan and Missourian communities quickly allied with different churches on the basis of their preremoval contacts and current interests. In 1830 the Rogerstown Shawnees invited Methodist missionaries from Missouri to open a school in their new community on the reservation. The Kishpokos and Pekowis who had migrated from Ohio to Kansas with Tenskwatawa in 1828 instead cooperated with the Baptists. The Wapakonetan Mekoches continued their old alliance with their Quaker friends. While relatively few Shawnees actually became members of any of these churches, denominational turf wars aggravated the already tense relations among the Shawnee communities allied with different missions. In 1833 the Methodist missionary Thomas Johnson accused the Shawnee subagent John Campbell of drunkenness and had him removed from office. The Rogerstown leader Lewis Rogers supported Johnson's claims and testified that Campbell was habitually drunk on duty. Many Ohio Shawnees in contrast suspected that Johnson's antipathy actually arose from the fact that Campbell had advised the Shawnees to send their children to the Baptist school instead of to Johnson's own Methodist establishment. The Ohio headmen considered Campbell "our friend" and accused Johnson of wishing to get rid of rival missionaries. While they had given Johnson the right to open a school in the Rogerstown community, they "don't want him to meddle with our people."[16]

The Ohio Shawnees also had deeper causes for complaint. According to them, "this man Johnston [*sic*] cultivates too much of our land and builds too many houses and cuts too much of our timber." Moreover, he "meddles himself too much about our business." The Ohioans clearly saw that missionaries, while sometimes useful allies, could become a threat to Native independence and resources. As Methodists, Baptists, and Quakers began building missions, farms, and schools on the reservation in the early 1830s, some Shawnees became increasingly concerned. In 1834 they struck back. "In full Council" an unidentified group of leaders demanded that their new subagent, Marston Clark, remove all "Missionareys Settled on their Land." Both federal officials and missionaries were alarmed. They quickly dismissed the demand as the ravings of a few discontent pagans, such as Tenskwatawa, and refused to take it seriously. The missionaries remained on the reservation. It was a powerful sign to Shawnees that they were no longer in control of their own country.[17]

Despite the problems wrought by the presence of missionaries, some Shawnees took an active interest in the religion they propagated. The missionaries never saw the kind of spectacular mass conversions they had hoped for, but the number of Christian Shawnees grew steadily, if slowly, over the first fifteen years of missionary work. By 1846, 175 Shawnees, almost a fifth of the reservation population, had converted. The Christians included many bicultural families with a mixed Native-Euroamerican lineage, such as the Rogerses and Fishes from Rogerstown, the Parkses from Hog Creek, and the Bluejackets from Michigan. Christianity had long been a part of their family heritage. But also some "full-blood" Shawnees chose Christianity. For example, the Pekowi war leader Blackfeather became an active member of the Baptist congregation in the 1830s. The spread of Christianity added one more fault line in the already divided reservation. Relations between the Christian Shawnees and those who adhered to their "national or ancient Religion" were often tense. Rituals that had for centuries united Shawnees now became a source of friction. Although some Christian Shawnees continued to participate in traditional ceremonies, others did not. The mšikamekwi ceased to be the collective spiritual heart of the community when only a part of the people gathered there for communal worship while others went instead to the Methodist, Quaker, and Baptist meetinghouses.[18]

The rift between traditionalists and Christians had important political ramifications. Traditionally, leadership in Shawnee communities had been based largely on sacred power. The Mekoches had founded their claims to national leadership on their miišaami. The authority of clan hokimas and hokima wiikwes had stemmed from their m'shoma, while the status of the war leaders had been closely connected with their personal hopawaaka. Christian converts probably doubted whether traditional spiritual power could constitute a legitimate basis for political authority. While no documents detail what the Christians thought of traditional leadership in the 1830s and 1840s, we know that by the 1860s Christian Shawnees often spoke dismissively of the old hereditary leadership. They demanded that "the best & ablest men" should be elected leaders, regardless of their divisional and clan affiliations. On the other hand, some converts gained new influence at the reservation with the help of the missionaries and federal agents. Government officials considered Christian Shawnees trustworthy forerunners of civilization and favored them in reservation politics. Agent Cummins, for example, hired educated and bilingual Christians as government smiths and interpreters at his agency, with annual salaries up to three hundred dollars. The position of an interpreter was especially important. As Cummins himself noted, interpreters worked closely with the agent "in the management of Indians" and provided him with "information that can be relied on in regard to the wishes & motives of the Indians."[19] During the 1830s and 1840s Christian Shawnees thus began to broker some of the relations between Shawnees and government agents that previously had been under the care of clan hokimas and war leaders.

No one epitomizes the skyrocketing influence of the Christians better than Joseph Parks. When the removal and the first years on the reservation brought poverty and hardship for most Shawnees, Parks was able to turn the political and economic turmoil to his advantage, largely with the help of his extensive contacts with powerful U.S. officials, missionaries, and businessmen. A Hog Creek farmer with a mixed Shawnee-American background, Parks had engaged in commercial agriculture and trade since the 1820s and grown wealthier than any Shawnee. He had spent part of his youth at the household of Governor Lewis Cass in Detroit. In 1833 Cass, now the secretary of war, had such a "full confidence in [Parks's] integrity, and also in his ability" that he appointed Parks the removal agent of the Hog Creek community. Parks had a shrewd eye for using his growing wealth. Through the difficult years of the removal and its aftermath he generously loaned money to his distressed tribespeople. Like before, however, he required that the loans must be paid back with interest. By 1835 the Wapakonetans collectively owed him two thousand dollars. To cover the debts, Lalloway and other headmen had to promise a part of Wapakoneta's annuity to Parks.[20]

Parks continued to cultivate close relations with influential Americans on the reservation. He built his house next to the Shawnee agency and made friends with the successive government agents and subagents. Richard Cummins in particular trusted Parks, hiring him as the U.S. interpreter and making Parks's African American slave the assistant blacksmith at the government smithy. Parks also reaped success in the world of business. He founded a trading firm with American merchants from Westport, Missouri, to trade with the Shawnees and other removed Indians in Kansas. This trading operation increased Parks's influence among his impoverished tribespeople. In 1837 U.S. military officers visited the reservation to hire Shawnees to fight in the Second Seminole War in Florida. Initially, Shawnees showed little interest in such an enterprise. Parks, however, distributed gifts from his trading house to those willing to join the expedition and promised that his firm would support the families of the soldiers while they were away from home. More than ninety Shawnees enlisted for the campaign, and U.S. officers appointed Parks their captain. After the Florida expedition Parks again demanded a part of the Wapakoneta annuity to cover the debts that the families of the enlisted men had run up when buying provisions and goods from his trading house on credit.[21]

Parks, then, proved very successful in diverting collective Shawnee resources to his private use. Time and again, he mobilized his wealth to fund operations that he portrayed as "national" and then demanded a part of the annuities to cover his costs, always with interest. While his assistance was invaluable to many impoverished families during the difficult years following the removal, some Shawnees suspected that he did not always live up to high ethical standards. In 1839 Wapakonetan headmen argued that Parks, acting as an interpreter, had deliberately mistranslated discussions at Wapakoneta's removal treaty eight years before to pocket some of the money due to the entire community from the sale of its land in Ohio. Such accusations did little to slow Parks's rising influence, however. Although the chiefs were "much exasperated with Capt. J. Parks," they realized that they needed the assistance of this wealthy and well-connected man in their ongoing struggles with the federal government.[22] Equally importantly, U.S. officials and missionaries remained convinced that Parks was the man to work with if they wanted to guide the Shawnees to American civilization.

THE NATIONAL COUNCIL

During the 1840s the struggles over reservation resources intensified on two fronts. On one hand, a group of rising wealthy bicultural men led by Parks asserted Shawnee sovereignty by demanding the U.S. government to allow the Shawnees to control their annuities and land free from federal interference. They argued that they formed the legitimate leadership of the Shawnee nation and claimed the right to control national resources. On the other hand, many Shawnees disputed the right of both these leaders and U.S. officials to control Shawnee land and annuities and insisted that such resources must remain under the care of kin groups and local communities. These critics of the new reservation leadership continued to envision the Shawnee people as a network of allied families and bands. They argued that the emerging wealthy elite wished to monopolize the control of crucial resources for selfish purposes, not for communal well-being. As money and land became essential for survival on the reservation, both became the nexus of bitter debates about national sovereignty and political consolidation.

These conflicts were grounded in fundamental transformations of the reservation society during the 1840s. Through their first decade in Kansas, Shawnees had struggled simply to make a living. Gradually they had learned the ways of their new homeland. Their crops of corn, potatoes, beans, and pumpkins grew bigger, their herds of cattle, horses, and hogs larger. Some families produced more meat and grain than they needed for domestic consumption and began selling their surpluses to American settlers in Missouri and to the emigrants passing through the reservation on their way to the Far West. "Their Buildings & farms are similar to those of Whites in a new-Settled Country," Agent Cummins wrote approvingly in 1842. All Shawnees lived in "Comfortable Cabins, perhaps half or more of hewn logs neatly raised." Their farms also had "Out houses, Stables, Barns &c" and were "enclosed with rail fences." Cummins proudly reported that "the Shawnees are in a prosperous condition."[23]

Hand in hand with these economic transformations the social landscape of the reservation changed drastically. Initially, the Shawnees had established small towns and villages on the reservation. But such communal settlements broke up gradually during the 1830s, as families scattered over the landscape to establish farms of their own. "The Shawnees have no town or village, each family settling where they can find a cite that pleases them," Cummins reported in 1838. Even the last communal fields vanished, as families cleared plots of their own and surrounded them with fences. Family farms and fields had been common among both Missouri and Ohio Shawnees already in the 1820s, but the families living on their own homesteads in Kansas were smaller than ever before. According to an 1842 census conducted by Cummins, more than 80 percent of the Shawnees lived in households with five members or fewer. The average family size was only 3.5 individuals.[24] The new farms, then, were occupied by small nuclear families, not by groups of related families, as had still been common in Wapakoneta twenty years earlier.

This shift signals a major change in Shawnee society: the erosion of the clan system. When nuclear families established their own farms, the m'shomas no longer constituted residential or economic units. Other social and political functions of the clans withered, too. When Charles Trowbridge had interviewed Tenskwatawa in 1824, the Prophet had described a system of more than thirty patrilineal, exogamous clans that regulated kinship, marriages, political leadership, justice, and ritual offices. When the pioneer anthropologist Lewis Henry Morgan visited the Kansas Shawnees thirty-five years later, the m'shomas had changed completely. Only thirteen of them remained. Most dramatically, the clans were no longer based on kinship. A person belonged to a m'shoma simply because he or she had received a name connected to the guardian being of that m'shoma; the members of a clan, then, were no longer united by kinship. The m'shomas did not regulate marriages or the inheritance of political offices. These changed clans, often called "name groups" by anthropologists, were essentially ritual units. Officials for such major ceremonies as the annual planting and harvest Bread Dances continued to be selected on the basis of their m'shoma membership, for Shawnees still believed that the name of a person conferred upon that person sacred m'shoma power from the guardian of the clan.[25]

Why the Shawnee clans changed so radically in such a short time is poorly understood. The clan systems of other Central Algonquian peoples removed from the Old Northwest to Kansas underwent similar transformations during the same period. This suggests that the change was rooted in the broad economic, demographic, and cultural transformations of the communities forced from their homelands to reservations where federal agents and missionaries sought to assimilate them into the American way of life. It is probable that repeated migrations, community fissions, and population decline had decreased the size, unity, and political and economic significance of the Shawnee clans since the eighteenth century. Anthropologists argue that when some m'shomas became too small to survive in the early nineteenth century, Shawnees began to combine them into larger ones. In order to guarantee that all m'shomas would remain large enough to survive, Shawnees separated clan membership from kinship and based it simply on personal names. The object of all these actions was to maintain what Shawnees saw as the most important function of the clans: their role in providing officials with specific spiritual power for communal rituals.[26] The proliferation of family farms on the reservation certainly played a role in the decline of clans. The shift from towns, communal fields, and clan-based farms to fenced homesteads operated by nuclear families strengthened the economic and political independence of small families. They, rather than m'shomas, became the focus of individual identity and loyalty.

The proliferation of family farms was also linked to a growing economic stratification of the Shawnee society. The farms the Shawnees built on the reservation varied greatly in terms of size and wealth. In 1842 Cummins reported that the smallest homesteads covered merely five acres, but the largest ones boasted more than one hundred acres. It is likely that the largest farms were most actively engaged in commercial agriculture and animal husbandry, for they were clearly bigger than needed for household production. Some of the largest Shawnee farmers even changed their work patterns dramatically to increase their production. By 1848 a "few of the more opulent," such as Joseph Parks, had purchased "negro Slaves" to labor on their farms. Although the number of slaves and slaveowners among the Shawnees remained low, the ability to buy unfree labor became one more factor dividing the Shawnees. Economically, slavery allowed the wealthiest Shawnees to produce more surpluses for commercial purposes and grow even richer. Ideologically, many other Shawnees resented slavery, and the "peculiar institution" factionalized the reservation as it did the United States.[27]

The emerging economic elite of the reservation consisted largely of families that had prospered in trade and agriculture already during preremoval times and therefore had both the means and the motive to engage in commercial production. The Parks brothers, Joseph and William, led the way, but the Bluejacket, Rogers, Fish, and Blackhoof families accumulated substantial fortunes as well. Common to most of the wealthy families was their bicultural background. Anglo-American traders and captives had married into these families over the decades, teaching their descendants American ideals of private property and commercial profit. Many of the richest Shawnees were also

Christians. Their new religion emphasized the moral, even sacred, dimensions of industriousness, work, and thrift and encouraged them to work harder to accumulate earthly possessions. Catahecassa's son Quaskey embraced such a new ideology. In 1846 he explained that "every man has his Farm and [is] trying to make them larger every year, and add to them stock of Horses, Cattle, Sheep, and Hogs, to build good houses, and live like white people." Such ideals set the wealthiest Shawnees increasingly apart from the majority of their tribespeople, who continued to value generosity and sharing more than private possessions.[28]

In the late 1840s economic stratification, erosion of clans, and federal interference in tribal affairs brought about a revolution in Shawnee politics. Until then, the new wealthy elite had remained marginal in reservation politics. While Joseph Parks and a few others had gained influence through their wealth and roles as government interpreters, official leadership positions and council meetings had been dominated by Lalloway and other more traditional leaders. This changed suddenly when devastating cholera epidemics between 1843 and 1846 swept away Lalloway, Wawillapea, Nolesimo (Henry Clay), Cottawaeothi (Black Body), and many other prominent hokimas. Their unexpected deaths created a vacuum in the reservation leadership. Parks, Paschal Fish, Lewis Rogers, Charles Bluejacket, and other wealthy men moved in quickly to fill it.[29]

The political rise of these men was actively supported by U.S. officials and missionaries. They regarded the wealthy, Christian farmers as "sensible, intelligent men" and "friend[s] to education" who would lead the Shawnees to peaceful assimilation. When reservation affairs needed to be negotiated with the Shawnees, federal authorities preferred to deal with the likes of Parks, believing that he and his associates were ultimately sympathetic to the American goals of acculturation and religious conversion. But it would be far too simple to portray Parks, Rogers, Fish, and Bluejacket as mere usurpers who seized power on the reservation with covert American assistance. Many Shawnees supported the rise of these men. They felt that the rich bicultural leaders possessed the know-how, resources, and contacts needed to defend Shawnee interests against the avaricious federal government.[30]

Indeed, in the 1840s the U.S. government seemed determined to usurp Shawnee sovereignty and resources at every turn. Officials repeatedly refused to deliver to the Shawnees the trust fund established with the sale of the Wapakonetan lands in Ohio. Other treaty monies were likewise withheld by the government seemingly indefinitely. At the same time Congress considered itself entitled to use the Shawnee annuities to pay debts that individual tribespeople allegedly owed to American traders and businessmen. In the most notorious case, a fur trader from Ohio named George Johnson claimed in 1838 that the Wapakonetan Shawnees owed him almost twenty thousand dollars and appealed to Congress to get his due from the Wapakonetans' treaty monies.

Shocked, the Wapakonetan leaders protested that their people owed, at most, a few hundred dollars to Johnson. They claimed that Johnson had bribed some headmen to sign a document acknowledging imaginary debts and the nation's collective responsibility to pay them. Despite Shawnee protests, Congress paid the money to Johnson. Soon, other shady businessmen infested the Shawnee reservation with similar schemes.[31]

Shawnees did not sit idly by while the federal government withheld and wasted their money. Time and again during the 1840s the leaders of the various reservation bands appointed collective delegations to visit Washington and demand that the treaty monies be put under Shawnee control. Wealthy bicultural Shawnees with political and business connections in American society quickly gained a leading role in these delegations. Once again, Joseph Parks led the way. Various Shawnee bands authorized him to visit the capital and negotiate over their treaty monies and other treaty rights in 1842, 1844, 1849, 1852, and 1853. Such trips, often undertaken together with a few older headmen, gave Parks tremendous influence in brokering the relations between the Shawnees and the United States. He became indispensable for the Shawnees' efforts to control their resources.[32]

In Washington, Parks and other delegates repeatedly demanded the Shawnees' treaty monies on the basis of national sovereignty. The Shawnees "are as much a *'nation'* as Great Britain," Parks, Joseph Barnett, and Chawwe declared to Commissioner of Indian Affairs Orlando Brown in 1850. Attacking the suffocating paternalism of the federal government, they asserted that they were "the *'representatives'* of a *'nation'*—not of children." "Will any body deny the right of the nation . . . to their own money?," the delegates went on to ask. If the language of the delegates sounds suspiciously Euroamerican, that is because they hired American lawyers to lobby their case in Washington.[33] Yet the argument presented by Parks and his associates was fundamentally the same that the Wapakonetan Mekoches had promoted fifty years before: even though the Shawnees lived on lands encapsulated within the United States and were connected to American society by multiple economic and political ties, they remained an independent nation. Like the Mekoche headmen in the early nineteenth century, the new bicultural reservation leadership agreed that true Native sovereignty had to be founded on economic independence. Only an independent control of the treaty monies could free the nation from the federal leash.

Back on the reservation most Shawnees heartily agreed with such arguments, but many of them were quick to ask who exactly was entitled to control and manage the national assets. Traditionally, town and clan leaders had distributed colonial gifts and American annuities in their communities. Parks and his associates hoped to monopolize this custom. They insisted that as the representatives and leaders of the Shawnee nation they had the right to receive tribal annuities and other treaty monies and use them for "national purposes." But not everyone agreed. Some critics of the new leadership claimed that the headmen all too often used collective resources for their private projects. Such accusations were not groundless. In the mid-1840s the Shawnee leaders regularly appropriated one thousand dollars out of the tribal annuity as a payment "for their Services as chiefs." Their commercially successful farms were thus partially operated with collective tribal money. Parks's actions were even more notorious. True, he struggled indefatigably against the federal efforts to pay the Shawnees' alleged debts to George Johnson out of the nation's annuity. Yet he also sought to persuade U.S. officials to use the same money to pay other debts that the Shawnees supposedly owed to his own trading firm and business partners. On the other hand, Parks and his allies also spent treaty money on legitimate communal projects. They used the annuities, for example, to pay the funeral expenses of poor people and to construct new mills and a national council house on the reservation. Neither villains nor heroes, the new leaders of the reservation, like many politicians in nineteenth-century America, appropriated collective resources for both private and public benefit.[34]

The control of the treaty monies divided the Shawnees through the 1840s. Federal legislation initially strengthened the reservation leadership's grip on national assets. The Indian Trade and Intercourse Act of 1834 stipulated that annuities and similar payments were to be paid to tribal chiefs. After accusations reached Washington that chiefs hoarded tribal money for themselves, Congress passed a new law in 1847 decreeing that federal agents must divide treaty monies among individual tribal members. The new legislation sparked a heated argument at the next year's annuity payment at the Shawnee agency. Joseph Parks and his fellow leaders still claimed twelve hundred dollars of the annuity for various national purposes. Ironically, Parks's brother William led a group of protesters who rejected the chiefs' claims and insisted that the annuity must be paid to the heads of individual families on the basis of their family size. Caught in the middle, Agent Cummins decided to solve the impasse with a vote. The chiefs won, sixty-eight votes to fifty-five, and got the money. Yet their victory left deep wounds. Joseph Parks and his allies had won the argument only with the help of a federal agent and a decision-making procedure foreign to the Shawnee culture. Their victory was based on majority opinion, not on consensus as the Shawnees traditionally required. Even that majority was questionable, for most Shawnees had refused to vote at all, possibly because they considered voting a foreign and divisive method for making communal decisions.[35]

Neither federal legislation nor Cummins's vote ended the struggles over the Shawnees' national resources. Parks and other leaders continued to lobby the government to hand over the various treaty monies retained by federal authorities.

In the early 1850s their vigorous efforts began to pay off. In 1853 the government paid to the Shawnees sixty-five thousand dollars to fulfill the obligations of the 1831 Wapakoneta removal treaty. Once again, Shawnee factions fell into a bitter argument over the control of the money. Parks and his allies among the new chiefs demanded that the entire sum ought to be paid to them for financing "national purposes." According to them, since per capita payments only "induce our young men and the trifling dishonest members among us to disregard our Council and vindicate our national acts, we shall be degraded, and our authority destroyed." The chiefs' opponents retorted that the alleged "national purposes" included paying sixteen thousand dollars of the Shawnee money to one Richard Thompson, an American lawyer and Parks's sometime business partner who had lobbied for the Shawnees in Washington. When federal officials got wind of this, they insisted on paying the money directly to individual tribal members instead of the chiefs. Enraged, Parks and his allies appointed sheriffs, called "war chiefs," to collect from each Shawnee a portion of his or her payment and hand it to the chiefs. As tensions mounted at the Shawnee agency, the new agent, Benjamin Robinson, called in troops from nearby Fort Leavenworth to oversee that the payment would proceed according to the 1847 law. Shawnee factionalism had brought U.S. soldiers to enforce U.S. legislation on the land of the Shawnee nation.[36]

Land as well as money constituted a bitterly contested collective property on the reservation. In the late 1840s the United States expanded fast toward the west. Texas joined the Union in 1845. A year later Great Britain recognized the U.S. claims to Oregon. U.S. victory in the Mexican War in 1848 extended American power across the Southwest to California. Hundreds of thousands of settlers from the East headed to the new western lands. Most joined wagon trains in Westport or Independence, Missouri, and then took the Oregon, California, or Santa Fe Trail to the west. Each of these routes ran through the Shawnee reservation, suddenly bringing immense numbers of travelers to Native lands. That spelled trouble for the Shawnees. In 1850 their leaders complained that "within the last two or three years the Troops of the United States, as well as others, emigrants, passing through their Country to and from New Mexico, California, and Oregon have from time to time committed many depredations upon their Property by taking horses, Cattle, hogs &c." Shawnees had seen this too many times before. Many feared that soon some of the pioneers passing through would decide to stay on the reservation and steal Shawnee land, too. Such concerns were well founded. Western politicians, businessmen, railroad promoters, and farmers were already demanding that the federal government open the Kansas reservations to American settlement. In 1850 the Shawnees heard disturbing rumors that the region would be organized into a new U.S. territory and the Indians compelled to remove once more.[37]

The threat of losing the reservation electrified the old dispute between the Missouri and Ohio Shawnees over the reservation land. Many Ohioans feared that the federal government might eventually recognize the Missouri Shawnees as the rightful owners of the reservation and buy the land from them. Deprived of both land and compensations for its sale, the Ohioans would "then have nothing left." The Missouri Shawnees, in turn, remained adamant that the Ohio people were merely guests in their country and demanded a share of the Ohioans' annuities as a compensation for their hospitality.[38] As factionalism threatened to divide the reservation at such a critical moment, the leading men of the new elite sought to arrange a compromise. In December 1852 Joseph Parks called prominent Ohio and Missouri leaders to an important meeting. Together, such prosperous bicultural men as Parks, Charles Bluejacket, Quaskey, and Joseph Barnett decided to establish a National Council to lead the reservation and manage the national resources collectively.[39]

No documents detail how the Ohioan and Missourian elites settled their disputes. A decade later Missourian critics of the National Council claimed that "the Ohio Shawnees, relying on their superior number and shrewdness," had "induced" a "portion" of the Missourians to found "a council elected by the two tribes." According to the critics, the goal of the Ohioans had been to ensure an equal right to sell the reservation to the United States. It is less clear what the Missourians received in exchange for recognizing the Ohio Shawnees' rights to the reservation land. Given the long-running arguments over the Ohioan treaty monies, it is likely that the Ohio Shawnees finally agreed to share these payments with the Missourians.[40]

In some ways the establishment of the National Council followed Shawnee political traditions. Like so often before, disparate communities joined in a collective decision-making body and built unity by making compromises and concessions. But despite such traditional roots, the birth of the National Council meant a true political revolution. For the first time the Missouri and Ohio Shawnees were united under a single governmental institution. The Shawnee agent Thomas Moseley Jr. celebrated this as the "union of the two Shawnee parties." Even more radically, the council was an entirely new kind of decision-making body. For centuries Shawnee leaders and elders had met at town, regional, and national councils to discuss shared concerns. Such gatherings had been large and open to all concerned clans and communities. The goal of traditional council meetings had been to unite as many groups as possible behind a common position through compromise and consensus. In contrast, the new National Council consisted of only seven officials: "1st and 2nd Chiefs, and five councilmen." They were elected without regard to their divisional or clan backgrounds—the first chief for a two-year term and everyone else for one year. Suddenly, most Shawnees did not have a relative speaking for them in national gatherings. Moreover, while traditional councils had met at a mšikamekwi, a public space at the heart of the local community, the National Council often convened at the Methodist meetinghouse or parsonage and at the homes of the council members or the federal agent. The use of private and Christian spaces shut ordinary Shawnees, particularly non-Christians, out of the meetings. Communal affairs, traditionally debated openly in large, public gatherings, were now monopolized in the hands of a small group of elected politicians. The birth of the National Council meant a radical step away from a political system based on communal consensus to one based on representative government and majority decisions.[41]

The creators of the National Council nevertheless celebrated the elections as a welcome democratic impulse. The council abolished all hereditary political offices and declared the Shawnees a "republican" people. According to Charles Bluejacket and other council members, the "civilization with its teachings overthrew the old order of things and our hereditary Chiefs bowed to the will of the people, [and] abdicated their seats from the Old hereditary chairs of State of matts and wampum." Such language appealed to Americans. Both federal agents and missionaries saw the National Council as a step toward a civilized society and supported it wholeheartedly. But many Shawnees remained suspicious. For them, sacred power, age, and kin connections constituted the proper basis for legitimate leadership. They resented the fact that the National Council was dominated by the members of the new wealthy, largely Christian elite, who lacked many of the qualities traditionally required of leaders. Joseph Parks served as the first chief of the council from its formation until his death in 1859. Over the next five years he was followed by Paschal Fish, Graham Rogers, and Charles Bluejacket. Other long-standing early council members included Charles Fish, Lewis Dougherty, and Eli Blackhoof—all prosperous bicultural men originally from the Hog Creek, Wapakoneta, Rogerstown, and Lewistown communities.[42]

The creation of the National Council solidified the rising power of the new Shawnee elite. The council became a tool for Parks and other elite men to control the reservation politics and economy. As the clans had withered during the previous three decades, they had probably become unable to perform many of their traditional social and judicial functions. The National Council took steps to fill this void. It nominated sheriffs to collect unpaid debts and punish criminals; it began administering the estates of deceased tribespeople; it took control of the annuity shares of orphans and drunkards. Many of such actions were necessary for the welfare of the reservation society at a time when older social security networks were unraveling. Yet the prominent men who controlled the council also used their power to pursue private and sectional interests. In 1854 Parks, Quaskey, and their allies compiled a constitution for the Shawnee nation that was largely designed to protect the interests and property rights of the prosperous elite. Quaskey declared that the nation needed "laws and regulations for the protection of our good citizens, and not to allow those who do not work to impose on us." The major goal of the constitution was to empower the National Council and its sheriff to collect unpaid debts—an important step for wealthy men interested in replacing traditional notions of gift-giving with new ideals of private property and credit.[43]

The rise of the National Council was rooted in the radical transformation of Shawnee society on the reservation. For centuries, clans had been powerful enough to assert their equality with one another and impede the centralization of power in the hands of a small elite. As the m'shomas changed from strong corporate groups into ritual "name groups," they were no longer able to check the emergence of a centralized, hierarchical leadership. Yet the birth of the National Council was not simply a coup by self-interested elite men seeking to seize money and power. Parks, Quaskey, Graham Rogers, and the other builders of the council feared that factionalism and disunity endangered the Shawnee efforts to assert control over the vital economic resources the federal government constantly threatened. For them, political centralization cleared the road to national sovereignty. They saw themselves as educated, civilized men who could lead the Shawnees down this road. But many others continued to disagree.

DISPOSSESSION—AND NEW BEGINNINGS

When the Wapakoneta Shawnees had agreed to sell their land in Ohio to the United States and remove to Kansas in 1831, the federal government had guaranteed that their new reservation "shall never be within the bounds of any State or territory . . . and further, that the President of the United States will cause said tribe to be protected at their intended residence, against all interruption." It took less than a quarter century for the Americans to forget these lofty promises. Inspired by the ideology of Manifest Destiny, as well as by lucrative opportunities to profit, western politicians and businessmen argued that the Kansas and Nebraska reservations posed a serious hindrance to the westward march and economic development of the United States. By 1853 they had convinced the federal government. Eager to open the reservations to American farmers and railroads, Congress authorized Commissioner of Indian Affairs George Manypenny to purchase the lands of the Shawnees and their neighbors and remove the Indians to Oklahoma. The veteran Quaker missionary Henry Harvey witnessed the shock that followed when news of the U.S. intentions reached the Shawnees. "This attempt . . . has thrown them into great commotion," Harvey wrote. Many Shawnees were "fearful that the United States will ultimately have all their country, and only have to refer back to past events to justify that fear."[44]

Manypenny toured the reservations in the fall of 1853 and tried to persuade the Indians to sell their lands. He met with determined resistance. Two generations of Shawnees, Lenapes, Kickapoos, Ottawas, and other removed easterners from the Ohio Valley and the Great Lakes had struggled to put down their roots in the new western lands; through hardship and sacrifices they had finally succeeded. They had no intention of leaving their country again. The Shawnees steadfastly informed Manypenny that they would never remove from their lands. In order to reach some sort of a compromise with the threatening federal government, they nevertheless suggested that they might sell the western part of the reservation where very few people had settled. In the following spring U.S. authorities invited the Kansas nations to send delegations to Washington for further negotiations. Eight men traveled from the Shawnee reservation to the capital in April. Divided as the Shawnees were, they sought to put away their differences and make the delegation as broad-based as possible to give all the bands a voice in the crucial meeting. Joseph Parks led the negotiators as the first chief of the National Council; Quaskey, George McDougal (Skapoawah), and George and Henry Bluejacket represented the Ohio Shawnees; Graham Rogers spoke for the Rogerstown people. More traditionalist Shawnees were represented by a Missouri Chalaakaatha hokima named Wawahchepaekar (Black Bob) and by an Ohioan headman known as Long Tail.[45]

The negotiations in Washington were tense. Despite American pressure, the Shawnee leaders remained determined that they would sell at most one million acres in the western part of the reservation. On May 10, they finally signed a treaty with Manypenny that finalized the sale. The Shawnees retained two hundred thousand acres on the eastern edge of the reservation, but there was a significant change in the status of these lands. As a part of the treaty, Manypenny insisted that the reservation land must be allotted; that is, it was to be divided to individual tribal members who would then own their plots in fee simple. For decades U.S. officials and missionaries had dreamed of breaking up communally owned tribal lands. They believed that private landownership would both break Native nations as political units and civilize the Indians by teaching them the value of private property and hard work. The Manypenny Treaty decreed that the diminished reservation of the Shawnees would be allotted to tribal members in plots of two hundred acres. The head of each family would receive the allotments of his or her family members.[46]

The allotment meant a radical cultural change from communal to private landownership. Yet many Shawnees, especially the wealthy elite, favored it. Possibly, they regarded the fee simple ownership as a more secure defense against American encroachments than the traditional communal landownership.

Prosperous families engaged in commercial agriculture also may have been interested in increasing their landholdings for commercial expansion, speculation, and other private economic ventures difficult to pursue on common lands. Parks and Quaskey spoke for allotment during the negotiations in Washington. Both received ample rewards for their efforts: the federal government granted 1,280 acres to Parks and 640 acres to Quaskey. Only the traditionalist Wawahchepaekar refused to accept allotments. Finally, Manypenny allowed his followers, known as "Black Bobs," to retain their share of the remaining Shawnee lands as a communally owned reservation.[47] The Manypenny Treaty, then, created two very different kinds of Shawnee communities in eastern Kansas: the "severalty Shawnees" living on private farms and the Black Bobs living on a communal reservation.

Like the removal treaties, the Manypenny Treaty once again guaranteed Shawnee land rights in Kansas. Unfortunately, it proved no more effective in protecting those rights than any previous treaty. Rumors that the Kansas reservations would be opened to American settlers started to circulate on the frontier in 1853, when Manypenny first visited the reservations and Congress began crafting the Kansas-Nebraska bill. Prospective squatters, settlers, and land speculators flocked toward Kansas, itching to stake their claims on the fertile Indian lands as soon as Congress formally opened the two planned new territories, Kansas and Nebraska, to American settlement. This took place on May 30, 1854, when Congress passed the Kansas-Nebraska Act. It was a huge blunder on the part of the federal government. Manypenny's negotiations with many of the Kansas Indian nations were still in progress, and even the treaties concluded so far, such as the Shawnee one, had not yet been ratified by Congress. Moreover, federal officials had planned to survey the reservations and let the Indians choose their allotments before opening the "surplus" lands to American settlers. The surveys had not even been begun by the end of May. Consequently, the final boundaries of the Indian allotments and diminished reservations were still unknown and unmarked, and "not an acre of land was legally open" to the hundreds of Americans coveting new farms and town sites in Kansas and Nebraska. Most squatters and speculators were not troubled by such legal niceties, however. In the summer of 1854 they rushed to the Shawnee and neighboring reservations, confident that the federal government would eventually recognize their claims.[48]

The rush to the Kansas reservations was extremely violent and politicized. The bitter national dispute over slavery intertwined with the land scramble and led to bloodshed. The Kansas-Nebraska Act left open the extension of slavery to the two new territories. Both free-soilers and proslavery groups hurried to Kansas to ensure their control of its future. Neither side shied away from the use of guns to guarantee that their supporters would gain more land and voting power in the new territory. Even settlers uninterested in slavery organized armed gangs to protect their land claims and to bully rival pioneers out. The territory quickly gained a notorious reputation as "Bleeding Kansas." Despite their violent divisions, one thing was common to all newcomers: they totally disregarded Native rights to the land. The Shawnees were particularly hard-hit, as their reservation stood just west of the populous western counties of Missouri. The resources of the reservation, particularly the timbered lands along the Kansas River, attracted a wave of emigrants from Missouri. Already in 1853 the Shawnee agent, Robert Miller, reported that the reservation was overrun by squatters. Some of them worked for shares on Shawnee farms, but Miller suspected that the squatters' "object seems to be ultimately obtaining a right to the soil." Some newcomers had even founded a town called Franklin on lands the Shawnees claimed to be within their diminished reservation.[49]

The Shawnees faced the crisis more disunited than ever. Political factionalism, cultural and economic divisions, and the allotment divided the people and made a determined, united response to the onslaught of American squatters impossible. "The Shawanoes are more divided among themselves than any other tribe in this region," wrote the Baptist missionary Jotham Meeker. He continued: "They are three bands the Macochas, Piquas, and Chillicothes—are again subdivided into Heathen and Christian parties—and still again into Meth[odist] North, Meth. South. Quaker and Baptists." The National Council proved unable to unite all these discordant groups into a common front. The land rush crisis revealed painfully that the interests of the prosperous elite families dominating the council differed greatly from those of the majority of Shawnees. While most Shawnees were unfamiliar with private, fee-simple landownership and found it difficult to defend their land rights against the squatters, enterprising elite men engaged in land speculation activities of their own. Soon after the Manypenny Treaty "a number of the principal men of the tribe," including Joseph Parks and Charles Bluejacket, were "buying out" the allotments of those of their people "that will sell." About half of the Shawnees planned selling their plots and escaping the turmoil in Kansas to Oklahoma where they would settle among their old allies the Cherokees. The money gained from selling the western part of the reservation also sparked familiar conflicts. Led by Parks, the National Council again sought to monopolize the money for "strictly national purposes." These purposes included paying Parks four thousand dollars for "long continued & faithful services."[50]

In March 1855 the traditionalist Wawahchepaekar and his Chalaakaathas took a stance against the National Council. The hokima visited Agent Robinson and informed him that "a majority" of the Shawnees was "opposed to the present Government of the Shawnee Nation." Wawahchepaekar asked the president of the United States to dissolve the National Council and restore "their old form of Government," with its hereditary, kin-based leadership. In particular, he insisted that federal officials must divide tribal annuities and other treaty monies "equally amongst all the people." No money should be given "to the chiefs & councellors for national purposes." The resistance of the Black Bobs was rooted deep in history. Descendants of the Chalaakaathas who had emigrated from the Ohio Country to the Trans-Mississippi West in the late eighteenth century, they had long viewed themselves as distinct from the Ohio Shawnees. Wide cultural differences separated Wawahchepaekar's followers from the prosperous Ohioan and Missourian elites. When the Parkses, Bluejackets, Rogerses, and many other prominent—and even ordinary—families converted to Christianity and sent their children to the Methodist, Baptist, and Quaker mission schools, "not one" of the Black Bobs "could read and but a very few . . . could speak the English language." According to Wawahchepaekar's ardent enemy Charles Bluejacket, the Chalaakaathas "were opposed to the Education of their children or of receiving any religious instruction and also opposed the adoptions of the habits of the white man." Wawahchepaekar himself claimed that he had "the blood of the chiefs in his veins." As "a direct decenant of the Old Shawnee Cheifs," he denied the legitimacy of the National Council and its elected leaders.[51]

The criticism against the National Council was not simply an outburst of disgruntled traditionalists. In the late 1850s some prosperous Christian Shawnees such as Paschal Fish and George Bluejacket (the brother of Charles) joined forces with Wawahchepaekar and protested vocally against the council's authoritarian actions and alleged greed. Despite their wide cultural differences, many traditionalists and wealthy Christian families shared the concern that the National Council did not use national resources for common good. Together, Wawahchepaekar, Fish, George Bluejacket, and others flooded the federal officials with complaints against the council and demanded that the U.S. authorities withdraw their support from it. But federal officials did not heed their requests. As a republican institution, the council enjoyed the trust of the Americans. Its opponents were easily dismissed as uncivilized savages, like Wawahchepaekar, or as self-interested malcontents, like Fish.[52]

Amidst such disunity, the struggle over the Shawnee land continued. The federal government finally finished the survey of the Shawnee reservation in 1856—two years after the Manypenny Treaty—and the Shawnees proceeded to select their allotments. Technically, this should have given their land rights stronger legal protection, but instead, bureaucratic fumbling continued. It took four more years for government officials to compile patents for the Shawnee landowners for their allotments. Squatters used this lack of proper documentation as an excuse to steal Native lands and resources. "They tell us to show somthing to prove that it is our land and timber. . . . Some of them laugh [at] the idea of an Indian suing him and making him pay for trespassing," complained Samuel Cornatzer, the clerk of the National Council, in 1858. As Cornatzer pointed out, timber was often at the heart of the conflicts between Shawnees and squatters. The Shawnee lands along the Kansas River were rich with timber, a valuable resource on the sparsely wooded prairie where hundreds of American newcomers needed wood for building and fuel. Many Missourians intruded on Shawnee lands precisely to steal timber; some even opened a commercial sawmill just outside the reservation and supplied it with timber robbed from the Indians. As tensions rose, violence followed. In June 1858 squatters murdered a Shawnee man named Tooly after he had accused them of stealing his timber. In revenge, a group of angry young Shawnee men attacked one of the squatter settlements and burned it to the ground.[53]

The Shawnees finally got their patents in 1860, but this simply led to further trouble. When Kansas was organized into a state a year later, its northeastern corner became Johnson County, which covered most of the Shawnee allotments. The county promptly proceeded to tax the allotments. Legally, tribal land had always been outside state jurisdiction, but now the Johnson County authorities reasoned that the allotments, owned by individual Shawnees, were no longer tribal property and therefore could be taxed like any other private landholdings. The National Council took the matter to court. The Kansas Supreme Court sided with the county and argued that "the Shawnees who hold their lands in severalty under patents from the government, have the abstract title thereto." No longer a sovereign tribal domain, their "lands are subject to taxation." The court's ruling had an even more profound implication. The judges argued that since the "Shawnees do not hold their land in common, nor are they contiguously located," it was "difficult to conceive a national existence" of the tribe.[54]

The decision of the Kansas Supreme Court was a powerful assault on Shawnee nationhood. It continued the aggressive efforts of the states, begun by Georgia in the 1820s, to enforce their sovereignty by detribalizing Indian nations and extending state jurisdiction over tribal lands. The court ruling posed an immense political and economic threat to the Shawnee nation. Politically, the decision amounted to a forced assimilation of the severalty Shawnees to the U.S. body politic as second-class citizens. Economically, the Johnson County taxes were a heavy burden to many Shawnees, whose farms, land, cattle, hogs, and timber the squatters had been stealing for years. In 1861 Agent James Abbot reported that a poor harvest had forced many Shawnees to sell their allotments to survive. The forced taxation led to the development of an impoverished, landless class of Shawnees that grew at an intimidating pace.[55]

The outbreak of the Civil War multiplied Shawnee problems. It first hit the Shawnees settled not in Kansas, but in Oklahoma. When slavery split the United States into two warring factions, both the "Seneca-Shawnees" on the Neosho River and the "Absentee Shawnees" on the Canadian River found themselves on a dangerous frontier between the belligerents. The Absentees and Seneca-Shawnees wished to remain neutral in the war. "It is between the whites—no good comes to us from the war—let them fight their own fight," the Absentees reasoned. Unfortunately, the Oklahoma Shawnees found neutrality in a war zone to be "almost impossible." In the east and south they were flanked by the rebellious Confederate states that courted the allegiance of the Native nations in the Indian Territory. Many of these nations, especially the Cherokees and the Absentees' Creek allies, divided into Northern and Southern factions and began to slide toward civil wars of their own. As a small child, Thomas Alford experienced the growing tension and confusion in the Indian Territory. He later reminisced how both pro-Union and pro-Confederacy factions among the Creeks demanded that the Absentees must "take sides, that we express ourselves, show upon which side our sympathies lay." Pressured by both sides, the Absentees fled to Kansas in 1862–1863. Similarly harassed, the Seneca-Shawnees likewise sought refuge among their relatives in the north.[56]

Kin networks facilitated such migrations. The Absentees quickly found relatives and generous help among the Black Bobs, for both groups descended from the Shawnees who had ventured across the Mississippi in the late eighteenth century. "They took up their life together with no jar or discord and again they were an undivided people," Alford wrote later. But the gathering of several hundred refugees on the diminished lands of the Kansas Shawnees also presented dire problems, as it put increased strain on the already limited resources of the locals. Neither was Kansas a safe haven in a world at war. Vicious guerilla warfare between Northern and Southern sympathizers had raged on the Kansas-Missouri borderlands since the mid-1850s. In September 1862 the Southern guerilla chief William Quantrill attacked the Black Bob settlement to revenge the pro-Union leanings of the Chalaakaathas. Quantrill's troops killed one Shawnee man serving in the Union Army and raped several women. The survivors fled to the western part of the old Shawnee reservation. Six hundred to seven hundred refugees lived there through the rest of the war, subsisting largely on buffalo hunting. Despite their Union sympathies, the federal government overlooked them. "The U.S. Indian Agent for the Kansas Shawnees seemed only to be the agent for those who had taken their lands in severalty" and "the refugees were entirely neglected," a group of Black Bob and Absentee headmen complained.[57]

In the spiral of violence and impoverishment, increasing numbers of Shawnees wanted to leave Kansas. Many turned their eyes to the Indian Territory. Despite the ravages of the Civil War, Oklahoma was still Indian country and outside the jurisdiction of U.S. territories and states. Even if many Cherokees and Creeks held strong Southern sympathies, far older ties of kinship and alliance connected them to the Shawnees. As early as 1859 many severalty

Shawnees harassed by squatters had planned to sell their allotments and "go south among the Cherokees, who want them to come."[58] There was nothing new in their plans; thirty years earlier hundreds of western Shawnees driven from Missouri had sought refuge among the Arkansas River Cherokees. A populous and powerful nation, the Cherokees seemed an ideal protector to the harassed Shawnees.

In 1862 the National Council opened negotiations with the federal government about one final removal to Oklahoma. But while many severalty Shawnees supported the negotiations, the Black Bobs and Absentees vehemently opposed a new removal. They insisted that the National Council had "no rights in our land" and "no right to interfere in our affairs." According to Wawahchepaekar and his allies, the council represented only the Shawnees living on allotments. The National Council tried to assert its authority by all means fair and foul. When the councilmen concluded a removal treaty with Agent James Abbott, someone forged the signatures of Wawahchepaekar and two other Black Bob headmen in the treaty in order to create an impression that the Shawnee delegation truly represented the entire nation. Wawahchepaekar protested to the commissioner of Indian affairs that the National Council and Abbott had plotted "a formal conspiracy" to disturb "the relation which subsists between [Wawahchepaekar] and those who have settled with him and are holding their property in common." Drawing from their long history of independence, the Black Bobs insisted that they lived under a distinct government, separate from the National Council and the severalty Shawnees. According to Wawahchepaekar and Paschal Fish, the National Council chiefs were mere "usurper[s] recognized by Agent Abbott." Even the death of Wawahchepaekar in the spring of 1864 did not break the resistance of his people. "We the Black Bobb Band still claim that we have a Chief and council and will have nothing to do with elections that are called by the other council," they declared.[59]

The National Council struck back. Led by Chief Charles Bluejacket, the councilmen dismissed the Black Bobs as uneducated pagans manipulated by scheming American swindlers. Only the council, they insisted, represented a legitimate and democratic government among the Shawnees. While most federal authorities were inclined to agree, the Black Bob resistance did reap some success. Between 1862 and 1867 the National Council concluded no fewer than five removal treaties with the federal government. Yet Congress did not ratify a single one of these, partially because of the constant flow of complaints and protests flooding in from the Black Bobs.[60]

The National Council was more successful in defending the sovereignty of the Shawnee nation. Charles Bluejacket took the Johnson County taxation dispute to the U.S. Supreme Court. He and his lawyers constructed their arguments carefully to demonstrate that the Shawnees formed an independent nation whether they lived on common land or on privately owned allotments amidst U.S. citizens. The Shawnees, Bluejacket argued, "have and still do keep up their tribal organization in said [Johnson] county, being an independent nation, having their own laws, usages, and customs; are governed by their own council, regulate their domestic affairs in their own way, and have, ever since the organization of the federal government, been recognized and treated by the United States as an independent nation." The mode of landownership was irrelevant. Sovereignty, according to Charles Bluejacket, was based on the fact that the Shawnees had their own government and laws that predated the birth of the United States. They "never had surrendered to the United States nor to the State of Kansas their national existence and the right to regulate their own affairs in their own way."[61] It was a logical argument from a people known as "the greatest Travellers in America"; a people who had for two centuries been driven across the continent by warfare, disease, and trade; a people who had repeatedly taken refuge among more powerful nations—and a people who had through all this retained their distinctive identity and political structures.

The Supreme Court agreed with Bluejacket. In a landmark case, it ruled in 1867 that the Shawnees remained an independent nation. The state of Kansas held no jurisdiction over them nor possessed any right to tax their land. Unfortunately, the victory came too late. Many Shawnee allotments had already been sold to cover unpaid taxes and other debts. Other Shawnees had lost their farms to con men of various sorts. For many severalty Shawnees there was little future left in Kansas. In June 1869 the National Council chiefs Graham Rogers and Charles Tucker concluded a three-party treaty with the United States and the Cherokees, agreeing to cede the remaining Shawnee lands in Kansas to the United States. The federal government, in turn, pressured the Cherokees to receive the Shawnees in their country and incorporate the migrants into the Cherokee Nation "on equal terms in every respect." In exchange for land and political rights in the Cherokee Nation, the Shawnees agreed to "abandon their tribal organization" and allow their annuities to be funneled through the Cherokee leadership.[62]

It was a hard bargain. The Shawnees had to leave their homes once more, fewer than forty years after their previous removal. The planned incorporation in the Cherokee Nation threatened their political sovereignty and independent control of national resources. But migration and alliances with larger peoples were nothing new to the Shawnees. With two hundred years of experience, they knew they would remain Shawnees even when living among the Cherokees. They would also remain divided. Most of the severalty Shawnees removed to the Cherokee Nation, but the Seneca-Shawnees returned to their own reservation on the Neosho, and the Absentees moved back to the Canadian River. The Black Bob Chalaakaathas initially planned to settle among the Absentees, but some of them also joined the severalty Shawnees in the Cherokee country.[63] This suggests that despite the bitter political conflicts between the leaders of the two groups, the relations among the common people had remained more amiable. This is not surprising. After all, Shawnees were used to divisions and disagreements. Although they had worked to construct national cooperation and unity for centuries, most of them had always recognized that such goals could be achieved only by respecting the fundamental independence of each community. For most, Shawnee peoplehood lay not in eradicating autonomous clans and towns, but in building consensus, alliances, and social networks among them. When Haudenosaunee warfare had scattered Shawnees from the Ohio Valley in the seventeenth century, these alliances and networks had remained. They had remained also when American expansion had shattered the Shawnee communities in the 1780s and 1790s. And they had remained after squatters, guerillas, and tax collectors drove the Shawnees from Kansas.

These ties still remain. So do the Shawnees.

CONCLUSION

A Living Nation

Around the time when American politicians and settlers expelled the Shawnees from Kansas, American scholars welcomed them into history books. Benjamin Drake led the way, publishing *Life of Tecumseh, and of His Brother the Prophet* in 1841. A decade later Francis Parkman gave Shawnees an important role in *The Conspiracy of Pontiac*. Henry Harvey, the Quaker missionary who had worked among the Shawnees in Ohio and Kansas, followed with *History of the Shawnee Indians* in 1855. As both fiction and nonfiction literature on the American past and frontier life proliferated over the next several decades, many authors incorporated Shawnees into the nation's history and mythology as one of the most fearsome opponents of the westward march of the Anglo-American civilization. "Of all the western Indians," George Bancroft wrote in his multivolume *History of the United States of America*, they "were the fiercest."[1] In the late nineteenth century it appeared as if books about the past were the only place where Americans might find room for the Shawnees and other Indian peoples.

When weaving the story of the Shawnees into the broader narrative of U.S. history, the nineteenth-century scholars emphasized some aspects of the past and ignored others. Most of them were fascinated by the wide-ranging diaspora and travels of the Shawnees. "The Shawanoes," asserted Drake, were "a restless, wandering people, averse to the pursuits of agriculture, prone to war and the chase." According to Bancroft, the Shawnees were a "restless nation of wanderers" who "roved to and fro in the wildernesses." There are several reasons why the seemingly endless migrations of the Shawnees interested early U.S. historians. Americans were themselves, of course, a nation of migrants, and in the late nineteenth century both emigration from Europe and the ongoing westward expansion made mobility a ubiquitous part of American society. But while this may have made many scholars interested in the Shawnee migrations, it did not encourage them to consider the similarities between the Shawnee and American experiences. On the contrary, they focused on the differences between the two groups. For them, the Shawnees pursued "eccentric wanderings" that ultimately stemmed from their "roving, and adventurous spirit." Americans, in turn, fulfilled a divine Manifest Destiny by spreading over the continent and winning it for a Christian, agrarian civilization.[2]

In the nineteenth century American writers portrayed Shawnees, and Indians in general, as transient vagabonds to stress the differences between the "savage" Natives and the "civilized" Euroamericans. They divorced Indian mobility from colonial expansion, warfare, and land theft and presented it as an inherent characteristic of Native culture, even personality. The discursive stereotype of wandering savages became important in justifying the Indian removal. Many writers evoked Indian mobility as evidence that the Natives could not possess legal title to any lands where they happened to camp at any given moment. Moreover, if Indians were transient rovers by nature, their migration beyond the Mississippi River would be inevitable at some point and therefore did not really disrupt their normal life.[3]

The image of the wandering Indian also influenced how nineteenth-century historians portrayed Shawnee society. The powerful trope of the Shawnees as "the greatest Travellers in America," constantly scattering and moving west in the face of the advancing Anglo-American frontier, made the Shawnee people appear fragmented, unstable, and landless. In short, they became almost the antithesis to what most contemporary Euroamericans regarded as a nation. When early scholars focused almost exclusively on the migrations of the Shawnees, they erased from history the recurrent Shawnee attempts to gather their people together, the Wapakonetan efforts to gain federal recognition for their territorial boundaries, and the spiritual vision of kindred communities uniting by sharing sacred power. Essentially, American historians downplayed or ignored the political and cultural expressions of Shawnee nationhood precisely at a time when U.S. authorities from the Johnson County officials to the designers of the 1869 removal treaty sought to dismantle the real Shawnees as a distinct, sovereign nation.

This was not a coincidence. The nineteenth century witnessed a dramatic transformation in the ways in which Americans conceptualized the Indian peoples living across the continent that was rapidly being incorporated into the United States. In the seventeenth and eighteenth centuries the British, French, and Spaniards had called the Natives they encountered, negotiated, traded, and fought with in America "nations." At the time, the word's meaning in most European languages was ambiguous and shifting. In both English and French, "nation" could refer to "a formal political entity" with a shared territory and a collective leadership, as well as to "a vaguely defined body of people linked only by a common language and culture." Nevertheless, the fact that European colonists chose to call Indian peoples nations suggests that they understood the Native societies to be at some level comparable to and equal with their own.[4]

This changed in the United States during the nineteenth century. Already in the late 1700s European Enlightenment philosophers and politicians had begun to define nationhood in increasingly narrow terms. Especially after the French Revolution many of them associated nationhood with a centralized political order and exclusive territorial boundaries. Nation, in other words, became synonymous with state. When the rapid westward expansion brought the United States into constant conflict with Indian peoples over land and jurisdiction, the Americans too reconsidered who should be counted as a nation and what such an appellation meant in terms of landownership and sovereignty. In 1831 and 1832 Supreme Court Chief Justice John Marshall defined Native Americans as "domestic dependent nations." As the cumbersome phrase suggests, Marshall no longer viewed the Indian nations as entirely equal with the American nation. Even though they retained the right to self-government, their relationship to the United States resembled that of "a ward to his guardian."[5]

Other U.S. officials, too, changed their rhetoric in ways that eroded the nationhood of Indians. Instead of nations, they increasingly labeled the Natives "tribes." While both words had diffuse meanings, their usage had long been markedly different. "Nation," with all its fussiness, denoted an extensive political or cultural community; "tribe," in contrast, singled out a smaller group—for instance, a local community, division, or kin group—within a nation. Categorizing Indian peoples as tribes therefore carried a powerful message: the Natives were, at best, semiautonomous dependents living within the United States, not sovereign political and territorial bodies comparable to, say, Mexico or France. Words can be potent "instruments of conquest," and in the early nineteenth century Indian realities were often shaped by American words. When federal and state officials, for example, sought to expulse the Cherokees from their homelands in Tennessee, Georgia, and Alabama, they reconstituted the Cherokees "from a 'nation' with a country to a 'tribe' with territory, or, worse, to 'tenants' with mere claims." Language made it possible to reimagine the place of the Indians in the rapidly changing continent and justify their subjugation and dispossession.[6]

Scholars participated in this linguistic shift undermining Indian nationhood, sovereignty, and land rights. Both anthropologists and historians adopted "tribe" as the term to designate Indian peoples. This had enduring ramifications for conceptualizing both Native American past and present. The emerging discipline of anthropology inherited from Enlightenment philosophers the idea of cultural evolution. According to the early anthropologists, the various societies of the world represented different stages in the universal cultural development of the human race. When they defined Indians as tribes, they assigned the Native peoples on the lower levels of evolution, far removed from the contemporary European and Euroamerican nation-states touted as the pinnacle of human progress. Tribes were, essentially, unchanging relics from the savage past of humankind. Because they had not evolved into higher forms of society, their history was unimportant; indeed, they had no real history. Instead, tribes could serve anthropology by illustrating the barbarian level of cultural evolution the Euroamericans had long since left behind. Historians did not confine Indians outside history, but they too saw little intrinsic value in Native history. For Bancroft, Parkman, and their colleagues, mere tribal history could not be meaningful; it became worth researching and writing about only when combined with the grander story of the growth of the United States from English colonies to an independent nation-state. Just as U.S. officials sought to assimilate Indian tribes into the American nation, historians subsumed Indian history into the national epic of the United States.[7]

Although history and anthropology have long since shed their nineteenth-century Eurocentrism and racism, Indian nationhood and the place of Indian peoples in American history remain problematic in both fields. Many scholars, for example, question whether seventeenth- or eighteenth-century Native societies can be called nations. This time their doubts rise from cultural sensitivity rather than from evolutionary fantasies or ethnocentrism. They point out that political terms are so culturally specific that using the terminology of one culture to describe the political life of another may inevitably distort our interpretations of the past people whose lives we seek to understand. This is a major problem in all historical research. Because scholars seek to make the past understandable to contemporary people, they have to work in a language that is meaningful to that audience. Often, this is not the language spoken by the people in the past. Even when studying the more distant past of his or her own community, the scholar typically encounters a linguistic universe not readily understandable to the contemporary speakers of the same language. The challenge is to find words that express how people in the past envisioned their world but at the same time make sense to modern audiences.[8]

Shawnee history has proved that this is not always easy. Shawnee dispersals and diasporas continue to "perplex" modern students as much as they did Parkman. Faced with the recurrent migrations and fragmentations, many scholars continue to think that the Shawnees in the 1760s, for example, were "even less" a "political entity" than other eastern Indians and that fifty years later their descendants possessed only "a weakened sense of tribal loyalty." Both statements contain a lot of truth. The Shawnees certainly did not create a unified statelike polity in the mid-eighteenth century, and their grandchildren in the 1810s underwent traumatic intracommunity strife during which the very Shawnee identity of some tribespeople was questioned. Nevertheless, the above statements miss the consistent and sophisticated Shawnee efforts to foster collaboration and unity through these difficult times. Clearly, scholars have trouble conceptualizing a people who were often both scattered and united at the same time. What seems to be missing is the vocabulary to describe a people who go through repeated diasporas yet maintain a distinct sense of themselves as a people. Likewise, historians struggle to understand a people who envisioned themselves as a nation but whose cultural ideas of nationhood differed radically from the modern Euroamerican ones that prioritize political centralization, sendentariness, and territorial boundaries.[9]

How should we grasp the history and politics of Shawnees and other Native peoples who were both dispersed and unified and whose understandings of peoplehood and society do not always correspond to the contemporary Western or academic ones? The innovative theorizing on "imagining" nations offers one solution. Since the 1980s many anthropologists, historians, Indigenous scholars, and sociologists have emphasized that all nations are, fundamentally, "imagined communities." What makes a group of people a nation is not a specific form of political organization or territoriality, but their belief that they share a common origin and future and belong together. Crucially, such imagining is inherently a dynamic and transformative process. Seeing nations as imagined is to focus on nations-in-the-making. It also draws attention to the fact that at different times and places people have imagined and constructed nationhood in dramatically different cultural ways. The question then becomes how the Shawnees (and other Native peoples) have imagined, debated, constructed, and deconstructed their society and their ideas about belonging, boundaries, and authority.[10]

Throughout this book I have argued that dispersal and consolidation—diaspora and nation-building—constituted two alternative Shawnee strategies for coping with the transformation of North America from Indian homelands to Euroamerican nation-states. Moreover, I have asserted that these strategies were based on two competing and continually evolving visions of society, peoplehood, and space. It is important to understand that neither vision was more or less "authentic" or "traditional" than the other. Both stemmed from ideas and philosophies that were unquestionably old; yet Shawnees always reworked these ideas creatively in conversations with each other, other Indian peoples, and Euroamerican newcomers, often to respond to the massive changes that colonialism brought to their world. Based on traditional roots, both dispersal and national consolidation made cultural sense to the Shawnees. Because both visions drew on many of the very same social and cultural materials, they probably appeared less contradictory to the eighteenth-century Shawnees, for instance, than to modern historians. In fact, national consolidation and dispersal were intimately connected and fed one another. The dangers that many Shawnees encountered during their great diaspora in the late seventeenth century motivated their descendants to seek unity, cooperation, and bordered homelands. On the other hand, the conflicts of authority among leaders, towns, and clans that the consolidation sparked, especially after the mid-eighteenth century, contributed greatly to the new dispersals of the Shawnees.

Both diaspora and national consolidation were fundamentally based on kinship. At least until the decline of the clan system in the mid-nineteenth century, one's m'shoma was probably the single most important source of identity, belonging, and security for most Shawnees. Each m'shoma possessed its own sacred power and spiritual guardian; each also had its leadership that organized collective action, from war parties to agricultural work. Clans were not isolated and self-contained entities, however. Since Fort Ancient times Shawnees had forged multiple ties that connected m'shomas to one another. In many rituals the m'shomas performed reciprocal tasks; even more intimately, marriages bound these exogamous kin groups together. The interlocking clans, then, constituted a vast weblike network in which multiple and overlapping social, ritual, and emotional ties connected each m'shoma to all the others and gave every individual complex responsibilities, rights, and loyalties in relation to various people inside and outside her or his own clan. A person was a Shawnee first and foremost because she or he belonged to a Shawnee clan and was, through the m'shoma network, related to diverse other Shawnees.

From the seventeenth through the nineteenth century Shawnees drew on this shared background of kinship networks to imagine two divergent political strategies and visions of peoplehood. When warfare and slaving disrupted the Ohio Valley in the late seventeenth century, most Shawnees stuck with those nearest to them both emotionally and physically—fellow clan members, other close relatives, and townspeople—and migrated to new homes in search of security. Often, their decisions about where to move were shaped by existing kin ties and alliances with non-Shawnee communities. During the next half century many Shawnees settled with their old allies and trading partners among the Lenapes, Creeks, Susquehannocks, and other surrounding peoples; shared land with them; married them; and engaged in complex diplomatic, military, and ritual collaboration with them. Multiethnic networks and communities offered Shawnees safety in their diaspora. Such networks and communities became an integral part of the everyday experience of all Shawnees.

Through the eighteenth and nineteenth centuries many Shawnees preferred to live in this kin-centric yet multiethnic world and sought to re-create it everywhere they went. Their sense of space and belonging can be best visualized as a kinscape, a terrain of social and geographic space in which several overlapping networks of kinship radiated out from each community and connected it to dozens of others, both near and far, Shawnee and non-Shawnee. Mobility was a normal part of this world and did not unsettle its order. Individuals, families, and entire communities could follow the lines of kinship that connected them to other people in order to escape enemies; look for better trading, hunting, or farming opportunities; participate in shared rituals; or simply visit relatives and friends. Two important social institutions made it easy for Shawnees to fragment and regroup flexibly. First, the widespread webs of kin meant that any family or individual would very likely find some relatives, and thus hospitality and a home, in multiple places. Second, the inclusive and collective decision-making institutions of the Shawnee and neighboring Indian communities, especially the town councils, facilitated the smooth incorporation of new groups into any local community.[11]

For many Shawnees flexible kin-based migrations and dispersals across an extensive kinscape represented the best strategy for coping with the often rapid and traumatic transformations that shook their world during the eighteenth and nineteenth centuries. Migrations and widespread contacts offered a successful way to avoid military subjugation and to take advantage of shifting economic circumstances. Because this strategy hinged on local and clan autonomy, many Shawnees were deeply suspicious of any attempts to curtail these. These Shawnees never denied their Shawnee identity or the fundamental unity of the Shawnees, however. They envisioned the Shawnee people as a widespread network of autonomous yet related communities, connected by kinship, common origins, and shared rituals.

Other Shawnees used kinship as a starting point for a far more unified vision of nationhood. The violence, land loss, and political oppression that many Shawnees experienced during the diaspora of the late seventeenth century convinced some that only unity and cooperation would preserve them from similar trials in the future. In the 1720s and 1730s they began to gather their scattered people together in the Ohio Valley and foster diplomatic collaboration among the diverse divisions and towns. These advocates of national consolidation relied heavily on the kinship webs that their ancestors had been building for centuries. Kinship provided a mechanism to link disparate groups together on several levels. Men and women of leading families married one another, thus binding clans and communities and encouraging cooperation in regional politics. Leaders also evoked kin ties when calling dispersed Shawnees to collect to the Ohio. Most fundamentally, kinship provided Shawnees with the vocabulary and a model for imagining nationhood. By the early nineteenth century at the latest (and probably much earlier) they envisioned their five interlinked divisions as "the different families of our nation."[12]

Two other elements besides kinship were integral to the construction of nationhood by the Shawnee advocates of consolidation. The first was collective and consensual decision-making in public councils. As early as in the fifteenth century the Fort Ancient peoples had created town councils to foster social harmony in communities that were growing fast when deteriorating ecological and political conditions along the Ohio forced previously separate villagers to congregate on smaller pieces of land. In the 1730s Shawnee leaders on the Allegheny and upper Ohio extended this old local institution to a new regional level, when prominent men and women from several neighboring towns began gathering at joint meetings to discuss issues important to all. The ravages of the Seven Years' and Pontiac's wars gave rise to even larger meetings, as more and more communities and divisions threatened by the British empire sought security in unity. The councils became a successful mechanism for uniting Shawnees, because they both facilitated wide cooperation and protected the long-standing autonomy of clans and towns. Until the foundation of the National Council in 1852 most Shawnees did not associate nationhood with centralized and hierarchical leadership. Rather, the nation was based on sharing power and incorporating as many kin and local groups as possible in collective decision-making structures.

Second, the Shawnee advocates of national consolidation saw a common homeland as a fundamental element of nationhood. The importance of land stemmed from their diasporic experiences and repeated dislocations since the late seventeenth century. Driven from their homes repeatedly by the Haudenosaunees, Catawbas, and British during the decades of diaspora, many Shawnees learned to attach great emotional and practical value to land rights. They also surmised that the best strategy to defend their land rights in the dangerous colonial world was collective action. By the 1730s Shawnee groups migrating to the Allegheny and Ohio valleys were negotiating collectively with the western Indians to gain wide international recognition of their rights in the local lands. Twenty years later they took up arms against the British empire in defense of this same ground. In the early 1800s the Wapakonetan leaders could describe with precision the borders of the Shawnee country and requested that the United States recognize these boundaries. These Shawnees, then, envisioned themselves as a landed nation.

Undoubtedly, this vision developed partly as a response to the unrelenting Anglo-American expansion to Native lands. But the image of the Shawnees as a territorial nation also had important Native roots. It had distinctly Indigenous features that set it apart from Euroamerican notions of territoriality. Like most eastern Indians, the Shawnees were always willing to share their lands with allies and kin. They saw nothing confusing about different communities possessing differing rights to the same piece of land. Land rights were also deeply spiritual. Time and again Shawnee leaders asserted that their country was a gift from the Creator. Many Shawnees believed that the Creator had put them at the center of the Earth to become its heart. The Mekoches in turn said that they had been created underground and had emerged to their Ohio home-lands through a hole in the ground. Land was not just something that the Shawnees owned or controlled—it was a part of the nation.[13]

Focusing on Native constructions and debates over peoplehood has the potential to transform the fields of both Indian and American history. While much of Indian history has concentrated on the interaction between Natives and newcomers, whether political, cultural, or economic, an investigation of Indigenous nation-building will draw attention also to the intranational side of Indian history. An approach foregrounding Indian-Indian interaction is impor-tant because it stresses Native agency, motivations, and cultures. It likewise draws attention to the time depth of Indian history, to the fact that Natives had engaged in complex negotiations with one another and with their environment, constructing and deconstructing communities and nations, for thousands of years before Europeans invaded the Americas. This Indian-centric approach questions the persistent tendency of scholars to see the European invasion as the *sole* engine of change in postcontact America. Colonialism has certainly been a massive force since 1492, yet Indian peoples have engaged colonists "from within the networks of indigenous power" and resisted, avoided, and subverted colo-nialism. At the same time, they have continued to negotiate with one another who has the right to construct "the networks of indigenous power," on which cultural traditions such networks should be based, and how these traditions ought to be understood in a changing world.[14]

A focus on Indian nation-building will also encourage us to rethink the center of American history. Traditionally, American history has been a story of Euroamerican nation-building. Even when concentrating on Indians, Africans, or other ethnic or cultural "others," many historians have asked how these groups "fit" in the grand narrative of the development of the United States and how their particular contributions may have shaped this narrative. But if we recognize that Native peoples have long and complex histories of their own and that they have engaged in nation-building projects just as creative as the Euroamerican ones, we need to reconsider our questions. Like Colin Calloway has recently noted, it would now be far more appropriate to ask how we can "place U.S. history in the context of longer and larger North American conti-nental history that is, by definition, predominantly Native American." This calls attention to the contingency of Euroamerican nationhoods and pushes scholars to investigate how Indian and Euroamerican nation-building have shaped, and continue to shape, one another.[15]

These are not just academic questions. The traditional narrative that equates the past of North America with the rise of the Euroamerican nation-states (mainly the United States) not only confines Indigenous peoples to the margins of history. Even more importantly, it also denies them a meaningful, independent future as nations. And yet Shawnees, like other Indian peoples, remain living nations today. Unlike what many Americans hoped, the removal from Kansas to Oklahoma in the late 1860s did not put the Shawnees on a road to a quiet assimilation or extinction. Neither did the allotment of the Shawnee lands in Oklahoma some decades later, the spread of American education and missionary work, the federal termination policy seeking to extinguish tribal governments in the 1950s, or the shift from communal subsistence economies to individualized wage labor. The Shawnees have adapted to these changes, resisted destructive federal policies, and explored new ways to maintain their communities. Today, three federally recognized Shawnee tribes continue to live in Oklahoma: the Shawnee Tribe, the Absentee Shawnee Tribe, and the Eastern Shawnee Tribe. According to some estimates, about six thousand Shawnees live in the state.[16]

Colonialism, diaspora, and nationhood have continued to shape Shawnee lives after the removal to Oklahoma. The Shawnees who settled in the Cherokee Nation in accordance with the treaty of 1869 found themselves in a difficult position, dependent politically and economically on the Cherokee leadership and the federal government. They enjoyed voting rights in the Cherokee Nation, but their annuities were funneled to them through the Cherokee administration. Nevertheless, Shawnees established their own communities in the Cherokee reservation and, despite generations of cooperation and inter-marriage with their hosts, maintained a separate identity. In the 1980s many of these "Cherokee Shawnees" began advocating the restoration of their independent tribal status. A long process of lobbying and negotiation culminated in 2000, when Congress passed legislation that recognized them as the sovereign Shawnee Tribe.[17]

Other Shawnees refused to move to the Cherokee Nation despite federal pressure. Long independent travelers, the Absentee Shawnees migrated from Kansas to their old homelands at the forks of the Canadian River. But U.S. officials remained determined to consolidate Indian tribes on reservations under centralized governments and refused to admit that the recalcitrant Absentees could have any rights to the lands on the Canadian. Instead, in the 1870s the federal government assigned the area to the Citizen Band Potawatomis who were likewise forced to remove from Kansas to Oklahoma. As so often in the past, the Absentee Shawnees suddenly found themselves guests on lands they had long regarded as their own. Bitter arguments broke out between the Absentees and Potawatomis. Thomas Alford later reminisced that "there was a great deal of unpleasantness, hard feelings, and nearly a war between the two tribes." Although the Absentees were eventually able to stay on the Canadian River, land rights remain a pressing economic and political problem today. The federal government has recognized the sovereign tribal status of the Absentees, but its haphazard land policies curtail the ways the Absentees can use and develop tribally owned land for economic projects. Absentee leaders continue to negotiate over the issue with the Bureau of Indian Affairs.[18]

After the Civil War the "Seneca-Shawnees," too, avoided the Cherokee Nation and returned to their old reservation in northeastern Oklahoma. There they reestablished the communities that had been disrupted by the war. In 1940 they organized as the Eastern Shawnee Tribe. Although the United States forced the ancestors of the Eastern Shawnees to remove from their homes in Lewistown, Ohio, to Oklahoma almost two hundred years ago, they have not forgotten their ancestral lands. In the new millennium the tribe has pursued land claims, fishing and hunting rights, and economic projects in Ohio.[19]

For Shawnees, nationhood and diaspora are not things of the past; both are living processes that continue to shape communal life in the present. Federal law acknowledges the sovereignty of the federally recognized Indian tribes. Yet what Native sovereignty means in practical terms is often debated when Indian interests clash with those of the states, federal government, and non-Native business circles. As Shawnees defend their land rights, organize health care and housing, design tribal economic programs, and implement taxation, they continue to negotiate what it means to be a living nation within another nation. The ongoing vitality of the Shawnee people was eloquently summed up by one Shawnee woman when I discussed the past and present of her people with her in 2011. "We are not the descendants of the Shawnee," she remarked. "We are the Shawnee."[20]

ABBREVIATIONS

AA	*American Archives*, Peter Force, ed.
AOM	*Archives of Maryland*, William Hand Browne, Clayton Colman Hall, and Bernard Christian Steiner, eds.
ASPIA	*American State Papers, Class II: Indian Affairs*, Walter Lowrie, Matthew St. Clair Clarke, and Walter S. Franklin, eds.
BB	Simon Kenton Papers, Lyman C. Draper Manuscripts, OVGLEA
BL	British Library
BTHCA	Barker Texas History Center Archives and Manuscripts
CC	Kentucky Papers, Lyman C. Draper Manuscripts, OVGLEA
CO	Colonial Office Papers, TNA
CVSP	*Calendar of Virginia State Papers and Other Manuscripts*ß William P. Palmer, Sherwin McRae, Raleigh Edward Colston, and Henry W. Flournoy, eds.
DAR	*Documents of the American Revolution, 1770–1783*, Kenneth G. Davies, ed.
DEF	*Découvertes et établissements des Français dans l'ouest et dans le sud de l'Amérique septentrionale, 1614–1754*, Pierre Margry, ed.

DM	Lyman C. Draper Manuscripts, OVGLEA
DRCHNY	*Documents Relative to the Colonial History of the State of New York*, Edmund B. O'Callaghan and Berthold Fernow, eds.
EAID 1	*Early American Indian Documents: Treaties and Laws, 1607–1789*, Vol. 1: *Pennsylvania and Delaware Treaties, 1692–1737*, Donald H. Kent, ed.
EAID 2	*Early American Indian Documents: Treaties and Laws, 1607–1789*, Vol. 2: *Pennsylvania Treaties, 1737–1756*, Donald H. Kent, ed.
EAID 3	*Early American Indian Documents: Treaties and Laws, 1607–1789*, Vol. 3: *Pennsylvania Treaties, 1756–1775*, Alison Duncan Hirsch, ed.
EAID 5	*Early American Indian Documents: Treaties and Laws, 1607–1789*, Vol. 5: *Virginia Treaties, 1723–1775*, W. Stitt Robinson, ed.
EAID 6	*Early American Indian Documents: Treaties and Laws, 1607–1789*, Vol. 6: *Maryland Treaties, 1632–1775*, W. Stitt Robinson, ed.
EAID 8	*Early American Indian Documents: Treaties and Laws, 1607–1789*, Vol. 8: *New York and New Jersey Treaties, 1683–1713*, Barbara Graymont, ed.
EAID 18	*Early American Indian Documents: Treaties and Laws, 1607–1789*, Vol. 18: *Revolution and Confederation*, Colin Calloway, ed.
EWVP	Erminie Wheeler-Voegelin Papers, Newberry Library
Gage Papers	Thomas Gage Papers, OVGLEA
GMLB	George Morgan Letterbooks, OVGLEA
HSP	Historical Society of Pennsylvania
JLP	James Logan Papers, American Philosophical Society

JR	*Jesuit Relations and Allied Documents*, Reuben Gold Thwaites, ed.
LAC	Library and Archives Canada
MHS	Missouri Historical Society
MPA	*Mississippi Provincial Archives*, Dunbar Rowland, A. G. Sanders, and Patricia Kay Galloway, eds.
MPCP	*Minutes of the Provincial Council of Pennsylvania*, Samuel Hazard, ed.
MPHC	*Michigan Pioneer and Historical Collections*
NA	National Archives of the United States
NN	Pittsburgh and Northwest Virginia Papers, Lyman C. Draper Manuscripts, OVGLEA
NYSL	New York State Library
OHS	Ohio Historical Society
OVGLEA	Ohio Valley–Great Lakes Ethnohistory Archive
PA	*Pennsylvania Archives*, Samuel Hazard et al., eds.
Peters Letterbooks	Richard Peters Letterbooks, HSP
Peters Papers	Richard Peters Papers, HSP
PHB	*The Papers of Henry Bouquet*, Sylvester K. Stevens, Donald H. Kent, and Autumn L. Leonard, eds.
PSWJ	*The Papers of Sir William Johnson*, James Sullivan et al., eds.
Revolutionary Virginia	*Revolutionary Virginia: The Road to Independence*, Robert L. Scribner and Brent Tarter, eds.
Simcoe Papers	*The Correspondence of Lieutenant-Governor John Graves Simcoe*, Ernest A. Cruikshank, ed.

SMV	*Spain in the Mississippi Valley*, Lawrence Kinnaird, ed.
SRM	*The Spanish Regime in Missouri*, Louis Houck, ed.
TNA	The National Archives of the United Kingdom
TPUS	*The Territorial Papers of the United States*, Clarence E. Carter and John Porter Bloom, eds.
U	Frontier Wars Manuscripts, Lyman C. Draper Manuscripts, OVGLEA
UCCO	Ulster County Clerk's Office
Wilderness Chronicles	*Wilderness Chronicles of Northwestern Pennsylvania*, Sylvester K. Stevens and Donald H. Kent, eds.
YY	Tecumseh Papers, Lyman C. Draper Manuscripts, OVGLEA

NOTES

INTRODUCTION

1. Quaife, "Henry Hay's Journal," 255 ("now going . . ."), 257; Jacobs, *Indians of the Southern Colonial Frontier*, 65 ("the greatest . . ."); Treaty of Logstown, May 28–June 13, 1752, *EAID* 5:138 ("dispersed . . ."); Spero, "Stout, Bold, Cunning"; Gallay, *Indian Slave Trade*, 55–56.

2. Historians have used the concept of diaspora to describe the dispersals of Lenapes, Alabamas, and Coushattas; Marsh, "Creating Delaware Homelands," 27; Shuck-Hall, "Alabama and Coushatta Diaspora." See also Schutt, *Peoples of the River Valleys*. For Kickapoos, Cherokees, Haudenosaunees (Iroquois), and Tuscaroras, see Callender, Pope, and Pope, "Kickapoo," 656–657, 662–667; Everett, *Texas Cherokees*; McLoughlin, *Cherokee Renascence*; Frisch, "Iroquois in the West"; Parmenter, "Iroquois and the Native American Struggle"; Feeley, "Tuscarora Trails." For developments in Europe and Africa, see Sidbury and Cañizares-Esguerra, "Mapping Ethnogenesis"; Morgan, "Africa and the Atlantic"; Phillips, "Europe and the Atlantic"; Wolf, *Europe and the People without History*, 195–231. The modern world-system perspective was developed in Wallerstein, *Modern World-System I*. For an anthropological discussion, see Nash, "Ethnographic Aspects"; Roseberry, *Anthropologies and Histories*, 10–12, 52–53.

3. For criticism of nation-centric models of American history, see Richter, *Before the Revolution*; Taylor, *American Colonies*. The borderlands perspective is most powerfully stated in Adelman and Aron, "From Borderlands to Borders" ("peoples in between" from 814, "bordered lands" from 816); for a more recent approach that is more careful to center Indians, see Hämäläinen and Truett, "On Borderlands." See also Aron, *American Confluence*; Cayton, "Writing North American History"; Hämäläinen, *Comanche Empire*, 1 ("resist, retreat . . ."); Taylor, "Divided Ground" ("porous" from 56). For examples of scholars who believe that the borderlands approach may obscure Native American borders and nationhoods, see Barr, "Geographies of Power"; DuVal, *Native Ground*; Hämäläinen, *Comanche Empire*; Preston, *Texture of Contact*, 12–14; Wunder and Hämäläinen, "Of Lethal Places."

4. For the development of ethnohistory and "new Indian history," see Edmunds, "Native Americans, New Voices," 737–739; Shoemaker, "Introduction," viii–ix; Trigger,

"Ethnohistory"; Wunder, "Native American History." Pathbreaking studies that utilize and expand the programs of ethnohistory and new Indian history and focus on Indian-European encounters include White, *Middle Ground*; Axtell, *Invasion Within*; Cayton and Teute, eds., *Contact Points*; Jennings, *Ambiguous Iroquois Empire*; Merrell, *Indians' New World*; Merrell, *Into the American Woods*; Merritt, *At the Crossroads*; Miller and Hamell, "New Perspective"; Richter, *Facing East*; Usner, *Indians, Settlers*. Scholars who argue that Indian dominance impeded the development of cultural and political "middle grounds" in their study areas and build more Native-centric narratives based on this foundation include Barr, *Peace Came*; DuVal, *Native Ground*; Hämäläinen, *Comanche Empire*. For "ethnopolitical history," see Hahn, *Invention of the Creek Nation*, 4–5 (quotation). In addition to Hahn, important studies that center power, politics, and political ideologies in Indian societies include Ethridge, *From Chicaza to Chickasaw*; Hämäläinen, *Comanche Empire*; Kugel, *To Be the Main Leaders*; Piker, *Okfuskee*; Piker, " 'White & Clean' "; Richter, *Ordeal of the Longhouse*; Saunt, " 'Domestick' "; Saunt, *New Order of Things*; Saunt, "Taking Account of Property"; Warren, *Shawnees and Their Neighbors*; Witgen, *Infinity of Nations*.

5. For anthropological definitions of tribal societies and discussion on their place in human political evolution, see Haas, "Warfare," 172; Lewellen, *Political Anthropology*, 24–26; Sahlins, *Tribesmen*, 14–27. For the problems of the evolutionary typologies, see Feinman and Neitzel, "Too Many Types." The position that tribes are produced by colonial expansion was formulated in Fried, *Notion of Tribe*. For a more recent and more refined version of this argument, one that emphasizes the complex interplay between tribal formation and colonial state-building, see Ferguson and Whitehead, "Violent Edge of Empire"; Whitehead, "Tribes Make States."

6. Drake, *Life of Tecumseh*; Parkman, *Conspiracy of Pontiac*, 32 ("a tribe . . ."); Witthoft and Hunter, "Seventeenth-Century Origins," 43 ("the Shawnee . . .").

7. Spero, "Stout, Bold, Cunning"; Gallay, *Indian Slave Trade*, 55–56. See also Warren and Noe, "Greatest Travelers." The definition of diaspora is from Shuck-Hall, "Alabama and Coushatta Diaspora," 250.

8. Dowd, *Spirited Resistance*, 66 ("weak"); Aron, *How the West Was Lost*, 38 ("lacked . . ."); Indians at Allegheney to Gov., March 20, 1738, *PA*, 1st Ser., 1:551 ("Gether . . ."); Shawnees to Lewis Cass, February 7, 1835, RG 75, M234, roll 300, frame 0666, NA ("again . . ."); George Croghan to Thomas Gage, March 2, 1765, Gage Papers, reel 10 ("Council . . .").

9. Ethridge, "Introduction"; Ethridge, *From Chicaza to Chickasaw*; Beck, "Catawba Coalescence"; Galloway, *Choctaw Genesis*; Rodning, "Reconstructing"; Shuck-Hall, "Alabama and Coushatta Diaspora"; Marsh, "Creating Delaware Homelands"; Schutt, *Peoples of the River Valleys*.

10. Schutt, *Peoples of the River Valleys*; Hahn, *Invention of the Creek Nation*; McLoughlin, *Cherokee Renascence*; Spero, "Stout, Bold, Cunning"; Shuck-Hall, "Alabama and Coushatta Diaspora"; Parmenter, "Iroquois and the Native American Struggle," 108–109.

11. For important community-centric analyses of Indian history, see Calloway, *American Revolution in Indian Country*; Hatley, "Three Lives of Keowee"; Henderson, "Lower Shawnee Town"; McConnell, "Kuskusky Towns"; Merrell, "Shamokin"; Piker, " 'White & Clean' "; Piker, *Okfuskee*; Tanner, "Glaize in 1792"; White, *Middle*

Ground; Willig, "Prophetstown on the Wabash." Studies that take a critical view of a tribal model and emphasize instead multiethnicity and pan-Indian networks also include Dowd, *Spirited Resistance*; Warren, *Shawnees and Their Neighbors*. For the importance of supralocal political entities and identities and the language and other symbols used to express these, see Shoemaker, *Strange Likeness*, 6–7, 39, 44, 70; Steele, "Shawnee Origins," 677; Waselkov, "Indian Maps." For the Shawnee terms, see Voegelin, *Shawnee Stems*, 317–318, 351.

12. Shoemaker, *Strange Likeness*, 8 ("the existence . . ."); Womack, *Red on Red*, 14 ("a key . . ."). For scholars who see nations as a post-Enlightenment European phenomenon, possibly because they equate nations with nationalism, see Anderson, *Imagined Communities*; Calhoun, *Nationalism*; Hobsbawm, *Nations and Nationalism*. For critiques, see Lavezzo, "Introduction," xv–xix; Shrank, *Writing the Nation*, 2–7; Moore, *Cheyenne Nation*, 8–18. The idea of imagining a nation comes from Anderson, *Imagined Communities*. Some scholars and Native peoples fear that applying the concept of "imagined communities" to Indigenous nations can make them appear less than authentic and thus weaken them in their struggles to maintain or reassert their sovereignty and rights; yet Anderson makes clear that the term does not imply inauthenticity. For a discussion, see Braun, "Imagining Un-Imagined Communities." Scholars continue to disagree on whether "nation" is a suitable term for conceptualizing Native American societies of the past. Hudson, "Introduction," xx, doubts the utility of the term "nation" for describing early postcontact Indian societies in the East. Jortner, *Gods of Prophetstown*, 18, argues that it was only the "Enlightenment zeal for classification" that prompted eighteenth-century Europeans to record the diverse and complex Native American communities "as 'tribes.' " In contrast, Barr, *Peace Came*, 8; Hahn, *Invention of the Creek Nation*, 8; and Stark, "Marked by Fire," 122–124, find that "nation" best captures the sociopolitical reality and ideology of the Indian peoples they discuss. Witgen, *Infinity of Nations*, argues that seventeenth-century Native social formations in the Great Lakes region were not nations, because they did not consider fixed communal membership or exclusive territorial borders important in their social life. However, Witgen's approach stressing the importance of understanding how Indians imagined their communities is very close to the one I employ in this book. The problems of defining and conceptualizing Native American nationhoods and nationalisms receive a thoughtful and thorough treatment in Hosmer and Nesper, eds., *Tribal Worlds*. See also Sturtevant, "Tribe and State."

13. Moore, *Cheyenne Nation*, 13.

14. Piker, " 'White & Clean,' " 320.

15. For studies that seek to balance Indian and Euroamerican agendas in Native nation-building, see Hahn, *Invention of the Creek Nation*; Warren, *Shawnees and Their Neighbors*. In an innovative recent study, historian Michael Witgen argues that in the seventeenth century French explorers and colonial administrators used various discursive, rhetorical, and ritual strategies to impose nationhood on the fluid and mobile Algonquian communities in the Great Lakes region in order to attach these peoples to the French empire as subject nations; Witgen, *Infinity of Nations*, 69–107. Several scholars have argued for looking beyond 1492 to understand postcontact Indian history and have emphasized that Native nations cannot be seen simply as the products of colonialism; see Edmunds, "Native Americans, New Voices," 726–728;

Ethridge, *From Chicaza to Chickasaw*; Hämäläinen, "Lost in Transitions"; Richter, *Before the Revolution*; Salisbury, "Indians' Old World"; Saunt, "Indians' Old World." Anthropology today emphasizes the malleability of traditions. This is not to claim that traditions are cynically "invented" for strategic purposes or that their authenticity is somehow dubious. See Darnell, "Private Discourse," 72–73 ("the creation . . .").

16. Cayton, " 'Separate Interests' "; Hinderaker, *Elusive Empires*, 199–204; Taylor, *Civil War of 1812*, 126.

17. Colin Calloway, "2008 Presidential Address," 200–201, has likewise recently argued for placing Indian history within the context of continental North American, rather than U.S., history.

18. Sturtevant, "Tribe and State," 10–13; Duthu, *American Indians and the Law*; Harring, *Crow Dog's Case*. My thanks to Christina Snyder for directing my attention to the importance that historicizing Indian nationhoods has for contemporary debates over tribal sovereignty.

19. Literature on the ethical and methodological challenges of writing Native American history is wide. For a discussion of Indian history as a colonizing or decolonizing project, see Deloria, *Red Earth, White Lies*; Edmunds, "Native Americans, New Voices," 721, 737–739; Mihesuah, "Introduction"; Richter, "Whose Indian History?" For a broader view on research on Indigenous peoples, see Smith, *Decolonizing Methodologies*. Ethnohistorical methodology has been examined by many of the leading figures of the field, see especially Barber and Berdan, *Emperor's Mirror*; Galloway, *Practicing Ethnohistory*. For the importance and problems of Native voices in Euroamerican documents, consult Richter, *Facing East*, 110–150; Shoemaker, *Strange Likeness*, 9–11. The importance of archaeological data as an independent source of evidence is emphasized by Trigger, *Children of Aataentsic*, 20. For the prospects and problems of cultural and linguistic translation, see Miller, *Ogimaag*, 7–13.

20. Sugden, *Blue Jacket*, 27; Lepore, *Name of War*, ix–xx.

21. Hahn, *Invention of the Creek Nation*; Foster, *Being Comanche*.

CHAPTER ONE. "THE GREATEST TRAVELLERS IN AMERICA"

1. Jacobs, *Indians of the Southern Colonial Frontier*, 65.

2. Parkman, *Conspiracy of Pontiac*, 32 ("sudden . . ."); Callender, "Shawnee," 630 ("very obscure"); Spero, "Stout, Bold, Cunning," 7–21; Gallay, *Indian Slave Trade*, 55–56; Merrell, "Indians' New World." The term "shatter zone" was introduced in the study of the early postcontact East by anthropologist Robbie Ethridge. She initially used the term to describe the entire eastern part of North America during this era but has subsequently focused on the Mississippian shatter zone of the South. Ethridge, "Creating the Shatter Zone"; Ethridge, "Introduction"; Ethridge, *From Chicaza to Chickasaw*, 4–5.

3. This is a composite version of three Shawnee origin legends recorded in 1795, 1824, and 1825: Trowbridge, *Shawanese Traditions*, 1–7, 55–56, 60–63 (quotations from 3–5 and 55–56); and Speech of the Makujays to the King, Claus Papers, 7:124, reel C-1479, LAC. For the name of the Shawnee Creator, see Schutz, "Study of Shawnee Myth," 78.

4. For the five Shawnee divisions and theories of their coalescence, see Callender, "Shawnee," 623–624; Howard, *Shawnee!*, 25–30; Hudson, "Introduction," xxx; Pollack

and Henderson, "Toward a Model," 291–292. In rendering the names of the divisions, I follow Howard, *Shawnee!*. According to Warren and Noe ("Greatest Travelers," 182), "[c]ontemporary Shawnee spellings of the divisions are *kesepokofi, pekowefi, mekoga, galikifi,* and *hifiwakela.*" For a classic discussion of archaeology and ethnicity, see Hodder, *Symbols in Action.*

5. Archaeologists and ethnohistorians have long debated the precontact location of the Shawnees and the relationship between Shawnees and the Fort Ancient cultures. For a review of this literature, see Callender, "Shawnee," 623–624, 630; Drooker, *View from Madisonville,* 103–105, 227, 282, 327–329; Drooker, "Ohio Valley," 124–126; Drooker and Cowan, "Transformations," 83, 105–106; Griffin, *Fort Ancient Aspect,* 28–35; Henderson, Pollack, and Turnbow, "Chronology and Cultural Patterns," 277–279; Howard, *Shawnee!,* 1–6; Pollack and Henderson, "Mid-Eighteenth Century," 23–24; Pollack and Henderson, "Toward a Model," 291–292; Spero, "Stout, Bold, Cunning," 54–56; Witthoft and Hunter, "Seventeenth-Century Origins."

6. Drooker and Cowan, "Transformations," 90–91; Henderson, Pollack, and Turnbow, "Chronology and Cultural Patterns," 259–260, 273; Purtill, "Evidence"; Turnbow and Jobe, "Goolman Site." For the importance of the Medieval Warm Period for agriculturalists in eastern North America, see Milner, *Moundbuilders,* 124.

7. For the change in the Fort Ancient settlement patterns, see Drooker, *View from Madisonville,* 48, 69–71, 100–101, 203, 327; Drooker and Cowan, "Transformations," 90; Graybill, "Eastern Periphery of Fort Ancient," 57–58, 168–172; Griffin, "Fort Ancient Has No Class," 54–55; Henderson, Pollack, and Turnbow, "Chronology and Cultural Patterns," 261–262, 269, 273, 275; Pollack and Henderson, "Toward a Model," 282–290. For the general changes through the East, see also Milner, *Moundbuilders,* 177, 185–189; Snow, "American Indian Migrations," 79–80.

8. Keesing and Strathern, *Cultural Anthropology,* 182–198.

9. Linguistic evidence suggests that clans may have existed among proto-Algonquian speakers as early as 500 CE; Fiedel, "Some Inferences," 1, 9. For archaeological evidence of kin groups in one early Fort Ancient village, see Robertson, "Chipped Stone," 252. For the archaeology of Fort Ancient houses, households, and clans, see Cowan, *First Farmers,* 13, 15, 17, 20–21; Drooker, *View from Madisonville,* 48, 101, 119, 133, 280–281; Drooker and Cowan, "Transformations," 91–94; Griffin, "Fort Ancient Has No Class," 56; Hanson, "Hardin Village Site," 7–13; Henderson, Jobe, and Turnbow, *Indian Occupation and Use,* 209–210; Henderson, Pollack, and Turnbow, "Chronology and Cultural Patterns," 273–275; Holmes, "Hardin Village," 54, 177; Pollack and Henderson, "Toward a Model," 288. For the sociopolitical importance of household-centric storage systems, see Wesson, "Chiefly Power and Food Storage."

10. Most information on Shawnee clans comes from the nineteenth and early twentieth centuries, when the clan system was undergoing dramatic change. This information can be combined and compared with more scattered evidence in older colonial documents to make inferences on the clan system in the eighteenth century, a method known as "upstreaming" in ethnohistory. For the m'shomas and their spiritual dimension, see Callender, "Great Lakes–Riverine Sociopolitical Organization," 614–615; Callender, *Social Organization,* 40–41, 98, 102; Galloway, *Old Chillicothe,* 305; Howard, *Shawnee!,* 86–90; Trowbridge, *Shawanese Traditions,* 16–17, 26–27, 48; Schutz, "Study of Shawnee Myth," 475; Voegelin and Voegelin, "Shawnee Name Groups," 625, 628–631.

11. McDowell, *Colonial Records of South Carolina*, 427 (quotation). The political organization of Shawnee m'shomas is described in Trowbridge, *Shawanese Traditions*, 11–19, 53–54, on the basis of information supplied by Tenskwatawa, the Shawnee Prophet, in 1824. While seemingly straightforward, Trowbridge's account is occasionally contradictory and difficult to interpret. Most historians portray Trowbridge's peace and war officials as town or tribal leaders, but when Trowbridge specifies the constituency of the chiefs he discusses, he is almost always describing clan leaders. He also tends to speak of all "chiefs" in the plural, which reinforces the sense that he depicts a system in which several similar leaders existed side by side in any single town. This again suggests that the "chiefs" were in fact clan leaders. It is important to notice that for Trowbridge "tribe" meant not a nationlike political or ethnic community but what we would now call a clan. For Shawnee leadership terms, see Voegelin, *Shawnee Stems*, 386; Wheeler-Voegelin, "Mortuary Customs," 403. The correct plural form of hokima is *hokimaaki*; however, for the convenience of the readers, throughout this book I pluralize Shawnee words as if they were English ones. For pictographs in treaties, see Proceedings of Sir William Johnson with the Ohio Indians, July 4–14, 1765, *DRCHNY* 7:751. For clans, their political organization, and individual identity among other eastern Indians, see Bohaker, "*Nindoodemag*"; Bohaker, "Reading Anishinaabe Identities"; Fenton, "Northern Iroquoian Culture Patterns," 306–312; Miller, *Ogimaag*, 65–112; Perdue, *Cherokee Women*, 59.

12. Trowbridge, *Shawanese Traditions*, 24–25; Voegelin and Voegelin, "Shawnee Name Groups," 629–630; Kowalewski, "Coalescent Societies."

13. For archaeological evidence of council houses, see Drooker and Cowan, "Transformations," 91; Henderson, Pollack, and Turnbow, "Chronology and Cultural Patterns," 274. For postcontact Shawnee council houses, see Gist, "Christopher Gist's First and Second Journals," 16; Howard, *Shawnee!*, 79–81, 362–363. Shawnee town councils are depicted in Trowbridge, *Shawanese Traditions*, 12–13, 15 (quotation); Annual Report of Beauharnois and Hocquart, October 12, 1736, Thwaites, *French Regime in Wisconsin*, II, 243; Slover, "Narrative of John Slover," 63. Note that while Trowbridge portrays councils as all-male affairs, he also describes situations in which women with leadership positions appear to have been present. The Shawnee term for a council house is from Callender, *Social Organization*, 38. For town councils elsewhere in the East, see Bamann et al., "Iroquoian Archaeology," 439, 442; Hudson, *Southeastern Indians*, 223–229; Miller, *Ogimaag*, 75–77, 104–109; Trigger, "Prehistoric Social and Political Organization," 37.

14. Trowbridge, *Shawanese Traditions*, 11–12.

15. For Shawnee rituals and festivals, see Gist, "Journal," 121–122; Howard, *Shawnee!*, 307–327. For plazas, see Drooker, *View from Madisonville*, 100, 280; Hudson, *Southeastern Indians*, 78, 218–222; Wesson, *Households and Hegemony*, 51–53. Examples of early-eighteenth-century towns with divisional names include Pequa (Pekowi) and Chillisquaque (Chalaakaatha), Kent, Rice and Ota, "Map of 18th Century Indian Towns," 8, 10.

16. Drooker, *View from Madisonville*, 231–233, 246–247, 274, 279, 282, 292–293, 327–329; Drooker, "Ohio Valley," 121; Drooker and Cowan, "Transformations," 87, 94, 96; Pollack and Henderson, "Toward a Model," 289, 291–292. For the power of serpents, see Trowbridge, *Shawanese Traditions*, 42; Hudson, *Southeastern Indians*, 166.

17. The early Shawnee oral histories are in Speech of the Makujays to the King, Claus Papers, 7:124, reel C-1479, LAC (Catahecassa, Biaseka, and the Red-Faced Fellow); Trowbridge, *Shawanese Traditions*, 1–8 (Tenskwatawa), 60–64 (Catahecassa). Alford's versions can be found in Alford, *Civilization*, 44, 200; and Galloway, *Old Chillicothe*, 181, 307–308. For the identity of the narrators of the 1795 version, see Ironside to McKee, February 6, 1795, Indian Affairs, 9:8840, reel C-10 999, LAC. The political nature of oral histories and the problems this causes for historians are discussed in Knight, "Formation of the Creeks," 377; Hahn, "Cussita Migration Legend."

18. Speech of the Makujays to the King, Claus Papers, 7:124, reel C-1479, LAC; Trowbridge, *Shawanese Traditions*, 61–62.

19. For miišaami power and sacred bundles, see Trowbridge, *Shawanese Traditions*, 3–8, 44–45, 55–57 ("rolled . . ." from 57); Galloway, *Old Chillicothe*, 180, 304–305 ("potency . . ." from 304); Howard, *Shawnee!*, 212–221; Schutz, "Study of Shawnee Myth," 152, 187–194; Voegelin, *Shawnee Female Deity*, 18. For Tenskwatawa's description of the alliance-building, see Trowbridge, *Shawanese Traditions*, 5–8 ("appointed . . ." from 5, "counsellor . . ." from 8). Alford describes a system of divisional duties, apparently based on the miišaami of each division, in Alford, *Civilization*, 44–45; and Galloway, *Old Chillicothe*, 180–181, 303–309. Note that Tenskwatawa seems to describe a single tribal sacred bundle, while other traditions portray each division with its own bundle. Even in Tenskwatawa's account, however, it is clear that the various responsibilities of the divisions are based on their spiritual potency, whether based on a divisional bundle or not. Alford's statement on the specific duties of the divisions is problematic, because it contradicts earlier sources, such as the accounts of Charles Trowbridge and John Johnston. Such disagreements should come as no surprise, for according to oral histories, Shawnees have often disagreed over the respective strength of each division. See Johnston, "Account of the Present State," 275; Trowbridge, *Shawanese Traditions*, 5–8, 54; Sugden, *Blue Jacket*, 269; Schutz, "Study of Shawnee Myth," 477.

20. Hahn, *Invention of the Creek Nation*, 239–241; Hudson, *Southeastern Indians*, 235–236; O'Brien, *Choctaws in a Revolutionary Age*, 12–22; Tooker, "League of the Iroquois"; Richter, *Ordeal of the Longhouse*, 30 ("spiritual and . . ."). Stephen Warren and Randolph Noe have similarly suggested that "assigning differential values to kin groups" may have been a strategy of coalescence for the early proto-Shawnee divisions: Warren and Noe, "Greatest Travelers," 170.

21. Griffin, "Fort Ancient Has No Class," 54–56. This is exactly how scholars now conceptualize the early Iroquois League, Richter, *Ordeal of the Longhouse*, 40.

22. For the formation of some of these confederacies, see Galloway, "Confederacy as a Solution"; Galloway, *Choctaw Genesis*; Rodning, "Reconstructing," 155–160; Waselkov and Smith, "Upper Creek Archaeology," 242; Worth, "Lower Creeks," 266–274.

23. Pollack and Henderson, "Toward a Model," 291–292; Speech of the Makujays to the King, Claus Papers, 7:124, reel C-1479, LAC; Trowbridge, *Shawanese Traditions*, 5–8, 62 ("to be . . ."), 64.

24. Howard, *Shawnee!*, 1, 5–6; Hunter, "History of the Ohio Valley," 588–590; Spero, "Stout, Bold, Cunning," 30–44; Erminie Wheeler-Voegelin, "Shawnee: An American Indian Culture," EWVP, box 31, folder 276, 6–7.

25. Howard, *Shawnee!*, 5; *JR* 59:145 ("villages," "districts"); Clark, *Shawnee*, 3.

26. For a similar portrayal of the Lenapes, see Schutt, *Peoples of the River Valleys*, 30.

27. The literature on the Spanish entradas and the Mississippian collapse is vast; see for example Hudson, *Knights of Spain*; Ethridge, *From Chicaza to Chickasaw*, 11–88. Scholarly interpretations of the impact and dating of Old World diseases have undergone major shifts in recent years. Following the groundbreaking work of Alfred Crosby and Henry Dobyns, anthropologists and historians agree that epidemics caused a massive demographic catastrophe among the Indigenous peoples of eastern North America, as well as across the continent. However, most scholars now doubt that pandemics devastated the East in the sixteenth century. While some areas, especially in the South, did experience foreign diseases, larger panregional epidemics occurred only in the next century. See Crosby, "Virgin Soil Epidemics"; Dobyns, *Their Number Became Thinned*; Kelton, "Great Southeastern Smallpox Epidemic"; Kelton, *Epidemics and Enslavement*; Snow and Lanphear, "European Contact and Indian Depopulation."

28. Trigger and Swagerty, "Entertaining Strangers," 339–342, 349–355; Gallay, *Indian Slave Trade*, 298–299; Ethridge, "Creating the Shatter Zone," 209–216; Ethridge "Introduction," 24–34 ("militaristic slaving societies" from 24); White, *Middle Ground*, 1 ("world made . . .").

29. Drooker, *View from Madisonville*, 283–294; Drooker and Cowan, "Transformations," 100.

30. Richter "War and Culture," 537–544; Richter, *Ordeal of the Longhouse*, 53–74; Trigger, "Early Iroquoian Contacts with Europeans," 354–355; Hunter, "History of the Ohio Valley," 588–590; White, *Middle Ground*, 1–10; Warren and Noe, "Greatest Travelers," 165–166.

31. *MPCP* 2:403 (quotations); Drooker, "Ohio Valley," 123–133; Drooker and Cowan, "Transformations," 100–102, 105–106; Hunter, "History of the Ohio Valley," 588–590. For Ohioan groups migrating across the Mississippi, see Jeter, "From Prehistory through Protohistory"; and DuVal, *Native Ground*, 67–68.

32. Although several scholars have passingly referred to the Shawnee dispersal as a diaspora, this argument is most analytically advanced in Spero, "Stout, Bold, Cunning," 7–21. My discussion owes much to Spero's groundbreaking work. See also Gallay, *Indian Slave Trade*, 55 (quotation).

33. For the Savannah River migration, see Drooker and Cowan "Transformations," 105–106; Warren and Noe, "Greatest Travelers," 174. In the 1730s both Pennsylvanians and Haudenosaunees agreed that the "Asswikales" or "Shawaygiras" who had recently settled on the upper Ohio had come "lately from S. Carolina." See "Number of Indians, 1731," *PA*, 1st Ser., 1:302 (quotation); *MPCP* 3:608–609. The history of the Alabama group is traced in Knight, *Tukabatchee*, 23–27; Waselkov and Smith, "Upper Creek Archaeology." For Fort St. Louis, see *DEF* 1:570–571; *DEF* 2:149–150, 314; Minet, "Voyage Made from Canada," 63–64; Deliette, "Memoir of De Gannes," 307; White, *Middle Ground*, 1–49. No primary document indicates the division of the Shawnees who settled at Fort St. Louis. The Shawnees who migrated from there to the Susquehanna River in the 1690s established a town called Pequa, suggesting that they were Pekowis. The Mekoche identity of some of the Fort St. Louis Shawnees is more difficult to prove. In the 1690s some Shawnees from Fort St. Louis migrated to the Delaware River where they founded a community known as Pechoquealin. In 1728 the Pechoquealin Shawnees moved to the Wyoming Valley on the Susquehanna's North

Branch. Two prominent late-eighteenth-century Mekoche headmen, Kisinoutha (Hardman) and Colesquo (Cornstalk), seem to have been descendants of Wyoming leaders. *AOM* 8:345–346, 517–518; *AOM* 19:520; Kent, Rice, and Ota, "Map of 18th Century Indian Towns"; Wallace, *Indians in Pennsylvania*, 121–122. For Kisinoutha and Colesquo, see Chapter 3.

34. The demise of the Savannah communities and their role in the Yamasee War are detailed in Spero, "Stout, Bold, Cunning," 146–149, 173–200; *MPCP* 2:404, 406; Ramsay, *Yamasee War*, 101–126; Jacobs, *Indians of the Southern Colonial Frontier*, 65. For the Illinois River Shawnees, see *AOM* 8:345–346, 517–518, 524; *AOM* 19:319, 519–520, 525; Peter Schuyler to Governor Fletcher, February 14, 1694, *DRCHNY* 4:96; Journal of Captain Arent Schuyler's Visit to the Minisinck Country, ibid., 99; Jennings, *Ambiguous Iroquois Empire*, 196–198.

35. For the Hudson River group, see At a meeting of the Justices of the peace & the Chiefe Sachims of the Esopus Indians, June 2, 1712, and Meeting with Esopus Sachems, June 30, 1712, both in UCCO, 101 Box Collection, Minutes Common Pleas/Sessions Court/ Justices of the Peace Meetings, 1711/12–1720. I am indebted to Tom Arne Midtrød for sharing the Kingston material with me. Drooker, "Ohio Valley," 126–127, 130; Drooker and Cowan, "Transformations," 105–106. For documented examples of Shawnees contacting Indians and Europeans living in the regions where they wished to move, see Journal of Captain Arent Schuyler's Visit to the Minisinck Country, *DRCHNY* 4:99; A Conference had between Benjamin Fletcher and the Mahikanders and Showanna's, August 28, 1694, *EAID* 8:322–323.

36. *AOM* 8:346 (quotation).

37. James Logan to Governor Clarke, August 4, 1737, JLP 4:7–8 ("had two . . ."). For the Shawnee negotiation with the Iroquois, see Copy of the Mayor's Letter to the Council concerning Arent, September 6, 1692, Leider, *Livingston Indian Records*, 168–169; Propositions of the Schaghticoke and Five Nations of Indians, [July 4, 1693], *DRCHNY* 4:43; Jennings, *Ambiguous Iroquois Empire*, 200–201. For the alliances and ritual and kin ties between the Alabama Shawnees and the Creeks, see Jacobs, *Indians of the Southern Colonial Frontier*, 43, 64–65; Knight, *Tukabatchee*, 21–27; Witthoft and Hunter, "Seventeenth-Century Origins," 52.

38. *MPCP* 2:252 ("upon Susquehannagh"); *MPCP* 3:313 ("in the . . .").

39. *MPCP* 3:150 ("Cousin"); Merrell, *Into the American Woods*, 116. Later in the eighteenth century marriages between Shawnee women, many of them from chiefly families, and British Indian agents and traders were very common: McLean to Green, August 27, 1799, Military Papers, 252:234, reel C-2850, LAC. For the importance of elite marriages in extending alliances among other Algonquian peoples, see Miller, *Ogimaag*, 69–72.

40. For Shawnee vision quest and hopawaaka, see Galloway, *Old Chillicothe*, 304, 309–310; Alford, *Civilization*, 24–25; Callender, "Shawnee," 626; Howard, *Shawnee!*, 136–139; Schutz, "Study of Shawnee Myth," 101–108, 197; Sugden, *Shawnee in Tecumseh's Time*, 44–46; Trowbridge, *Shawanese Traditions*, 36; Voegelin, *Shawnee Female Deity*, 18–19; Voegelin, *Shawnee Stems*, 444. Ritualized Shawnee council behavior is detailed in Propos: by the Showenoes Indians to his Excel: Rt hunter, October 21, 1710, *EAID* 8:627; *MPCP* 2:403–404; Speeches at an Indian Council, 1732, *Wilderness Chronicles*, 9. The use of tobacco is not documented during this period,

but it was so prevalent later that it must have been an old practice; see At a Council held at Detroit, April 5, 1781, Haldimand Papers 21 783:18–20, BL; At a Council held at Detroit, April 26, 1781, Haldimand Papers 21 783:29–32, BL. My interpretation of Shawnee council rituals and alliances has been influenced by Druke, "Linking Arms," 29–33; Richter, *Facing East*, 149; White, *Middle Ground*, 129.

41. For a very similar interpretation of Lenape alliances and migrations, see Schutt, *Peoples of the River Valleys*, 4–5, 22–31.

42. Warren and Noe, "Greatest Travelers," 168–170, 178–179; Howe, *Historical Collections of Ohio*, 299 (quotation); Marsh, "Creating Delaware Homelands," 38–40.

43. AOM 8:345–346, 517–518, 524–525; Spero, " 'Stout, Bold, Cunning,' " 77; *MPCP* 2:404, 557 ("to Messasippi . . ."); *MPCP* 4:633 ("in their . . .").

44. In the 1790s Shawnees from northern Ohio visited their tribespeople in eastern Missouri: The Information of James Day, Claus Papers, 8:35–39, reel C-1479, LAC; Report of Joseph Jackson, May 5, 1799, Claus Papers, 8:89–91, reel C-1479, LAC. For similar travels among the Lenapes, see Schutt, *Peoples of the River Valleys*, 101–106.

45. Trowbridge, *Shawanese Traditions*, 16–17; Urban, "Social Organizations of the Southeast," 176–178; Fenton, "Northern Iroquoian Culture Patterns," 313.

46. My ideas of kinscape owe a great deal to recent ethnohistorical analyses of Native concepts of space: Brooks, "Two Paths to Peace," 99; Preston, *Texture of Contact*, 1–2; Waselkov, "Indian Maps," 445–447; Witgen, *Infinity of Nations*, 42. For Shawnees introducing themselves as Shawnees, see AOM 8:524; Spero, "Stout, Bold, Cunning," 41.

47. Jennings, *Ambiguous Iroquois Empire*, 215–240, 249–250; Jennings, " 'Pennsylvania Indians.' "

48. AOM 8:345–346, 517–518, 524–525; Propositions of the Schaghticoke and Five Nations of Indians, [July 4, 1693], *DRCHNY* 4:43; Governor Fletcher to the Sachims of the Five Nations, July 31, 1693, ibid., 51; *MPCP* 2:10 ("at all . . ."), 12 ("true . . ."); *MPCP* 3:24 ("belong[ed]"). On William Penn's ideas of Indian-colonial relations, see Jennings, *Ambiguous Iroquois Empire*, 244–245.

49. For the new Iroquois strategy, see Aquila, *Iroquois Restoration*, 60–81, 156–193; Jennings, *Ambiguous Iroquois Empire*, 205–211, 215–219. For the Iroquois interference in Shawnee affairs and English support for the Shawnees, see *MPCP* 2:9–12, 148, 256, 403–404; Conference with the Five Nations, May 4–5, 1694, *EAID* 8:306. While older studies of the peace of 1701 tend to emphasize Iroquois weakness, recent reanalyses have argued that the Haudenosaunees succeeded in attaining many of their long-term goals through peace-making: Brandão and Starna, "The Treaties of 1701"; Preston, *Texture of Contact*, 23–27.

50. *MPCP* 3:97 ("no Chief . . ."); Extract from a Talk from Melonthy, June 8, 1786, *EAID* 18:355 ("only . . .").

51. Confirmation of the Treaty of Friendship with Shawnees, Delawares, and Susquehannocks, August 28–29, 1700, *EAID* 8:249 ("his great Men"); *MPCP* 2:403 ("spoke . . ."), 557 ("and his . . ."; "to the Woods"). For more information about Opessa's career, see Lakomäki, "Singing the King's Song," 80–81.

52. *MPCP* 2:557 (all quotations); Trowbridge, *Shawanese Traditions*, 13–14.

53. *MPCP* 3:97 ("their King . . ."); *MPCP* 2:600; Jennings, " 'Pennsylvania Indians,' " 85 ("anarchy").

54. *MPCP* 2:600 ("new Elected . . ."). For Cakundawanna, see Jennings, *Ambiguous Iroquois Empire*, 265; Jennings, " 'Pennsylvania Indians,' " 85.

55. Jennings, *Ambiguous Iroquois Empire*, 259–260, and Jennings, " 'Pennsylvania Indians,' " 82–84, date the beginning of intensifying Iroquois-Pennsylvania cooperation to 1710.

56. Aquila, "Down the Warrior's Path"; Aquila, *Iroquois Restoration*, 205–206; Jennings, *Ambiguous Iroquois Empire*, 145–150, 168; Merrell, " 'Their Very Bones Shall Fight,' " 116–119. The expression "Southern Indians" was often used vaguely by the Haudenosaunees, Shawnees, and British alike to refer to the diverse Native peoples in the South; see, for example, *MPCP* 3:92.

57. *MPCP* 2:140, 404; *MPCP* 3:93, 95 ("Young . . ."). For the roots of the Shawnee-Catawba conflict, see Spero, "Stout, Bold, Cunning," 122, 190. Shawnee hunting on the Potomac is documented in *AOM* 19:520; *MPCP* 3:116.

58. *MPCP* 3:23–24 (all quotations), 96, 98–99. For British views on the warfare, see Jennings, *Ambiguous Iroquois Empire*, 285–286; Aquila, *Iroquois Restoration*, 212–214.

59. The negotiations are documented in *MPCP* 3:45–49, 78–81, 92–98, 121–133, 209–215 (quotations from 97); Treaty in Civility's Cabin at Conestoga, April 6–7, 1722, *EAID* 1:225–230.

60. For peace women, see Trowbridge, *Shawanese Traditions*, 12–13 ("not countenanced . . ." from 13). For evidence of Shawnee women encouraging their kinsmen to go to war, see Council at Detroit, February 7, 1779, Kellogg, *Frontier Advance*, 218–219.

61. Aquila, *Iroquois Restoration*, 163–166; Jennings, *Ambiguous Iroquois Empire*, 294–299 (quotation from 295).

62. *MPCP* 3:209–211, 215.

CHAPTER TWO. "THE SHEYNARS IN GENERAL"

1. Indian Resolution Respecting Rum, March 15, 1738, *PA*, 1st Ser., 1:549 ("the Sheynars . . ."); Indians at Allegheney to Gov, March 20, 1738, ibid., 551 ("Gether . . .").

2. I have borrowed the metaphor of unity and diversity from Schutt, *Peoples of River Valleys*, especially ch. 6.

3. *MPCP* 3:218.

4. Sugrue, "Peopling and Depeopling," 27; Preston, *Texture of Contact*, 116–146; *MPCP* 4:234–235 ("without . . ."). For the retreat of the Shawnee communities, see *MPCP* 2:556; *MPCP* 3:49, 216–218, 220, 329–331, 599.

5. *MPCP* 3:49 (quotation). For famines and lack of food, see Treaty in Civility's Cabin at Conestoga, April 6–7, 1722, *EAID* 1:230; *MPCP* 3:152, 164, 218, 361; Wright to Logan, May 2, 1728, *PA*, 1st Ser., 1:213. For hunting, see *MPCP* 3:221. For colonial free-grazing, see Sugrue, "Peopling and Depeopling," 23–24; Richter, *Facing East*, 58–59.

6. Increasingly authoritarian British attitudes toward their Indian allies can best be seen in colonial demands that the Shawnees and their neighbors deliver to the British slaves who had escaped to the Indian towns and capture Indians suspected of killing colonists. See *AOM* 25:394–395; Indian Council at Conestogoe, May 26–27, 1728, *EAID* 1:288; *MPCP* 3:205, 211, 215, 285–286, 330 ("to preside . . ."). For Shickellamy, see Merrell, "Shickellamy." Literature on the relations between the Haudenosaunees and

the "Pennsylvania" Indians is vast. See Aquila, *Iroquois Restoration*, 160–183; Jennings, *Ambiguous Iroquois Empire*, 322–346; Jennings, " 'Pennsylvania Indians' "; Schutt, *Peoples of the River Valleys*, 66–69.

7. *MPCP* 3:219 ("King . . ."); Logan to Gooch, May 11, 1738, JLP 4:15; De Beauharnois and D'Aigremont to the Minister, October 1, 1728, *Wilderness Chronicles*, 4 ("with . . ."); Number of Indians, 1731, *PA*, 1st Ser., 1:302. No colonial source mentions the divisional background of the Conemaugh settlers. Ocowellos lived on the Conemaugh, and since he had been known as the "King of the upper [Susquehanna] Shawnese," he may have come from Chillisquaque (Chalaakaatha), located on the West Branch of the Susquehanna; see Kent, Rice, and Ota, "Map of 18th Century Indian Towns," the map supplement. For another reference suggesting that Chalaakaathas were among the earliest settlers on the Conemaugh, see Message of Shawnee Chiefs to Gov. Gordon, June 7, 1732, *PA*, 1st Ser., 1:329. One of the Conemaugh Shawnee leaders, Nucheconner, was often associated with Opessa's son Laypareawah. This hints that he and at least some of his followers may have been Pekowis like Opessa. Furthermore, in 1732 Nucheconner and other Conemaugh leaders spoke of "our friends ye Conestogoes," which links them to the lower Susquehanna where Conestogas and Pekowis had long shared land; Message of Shawnee Chiefs to Gov. Gordon, June 7, 1732, *PA*, 1st Ser., 1:330.

8. *MPCP* 8:126 ("his . . ."); *MPCP* 3:116 ("a hunting . . ."); Logan to Clark, August 4, 1737, JLP 4:8; McConnell, *Country Between*, 15.

9. McConnell, "Peoples 'in Between,' " 96–97; McConnell, *Country Between*, 14–15, 20; *MPCP* 3:403–404, 442–443, 445–446, 608–609 ("pressed . . .," "so closely . . .," "seized . . ."); Logan to Gooch, May 11, 1738, JLP 4:15 ("how little . . ."); Jennings, *Ambiguous Iroquois Empire*, 314–316. Francis Jennings has argued that the Haudenosaunees ordered the Shawnees to move west to further Iroquois interests. His evidence — a badly garbled Shawnee talk written down in 1732 — is ambiguous at best. The Shawnees who gave the speech were trying to justify their Ohio migration to Pennsylvanian authorities and may well have done so by explaining that they had only followed the orders of Pennsylvania's Iroquois allies. Throughout the talk they portrayed the Iroquois in an unflattering light. Jennings, " 'Pennsylvania Indians,' " 87–88; Message of Shawnee Chiefs to Gov. Gordon, June 7, 1732, *PA*, 1st Ser., 1:329.

10. Memorial on Trade with Indians, 1730, *PA*, 1st Ser., 1:261 ("Gott . . ."); Hinderaker, *Elusive Empires*, 24, 30–33; Simcoe to the Privy Council for Trade and Plantations, December 20, 1794, *Simcoe Papers*, 3:228 ("the Warriors . . ." and "worth . . ."). For examples of the kinds of clothing sold to Shawnees in the mid-eighteenth century, see Bailey, *Ohio Company Papers*, 37–40, 44–45, 73, 123, 167–171. For McKee's background, see Nelson, *Man of Distinction*, 24–28.

11. The best general treatments of these movements are in McConnell, *Country Between*, 9–20; and Tanner, *Atlas*, 40–44. For details about specific tribes, see Dowd, *War under Heaven*, 30–31; Schutt, *Peoples of the River Valleys*, 109–111; Callender, "Miami," 681, 686. The population estimate is from McConnell, "Peoples 'in Between,' " 95.

12. The lack of violence in the Ohio Country has been noted by Hinderaker, *Elusive Empires*, 52. McConnell, *Country Between*, 20–21, argues that the interaction and alliance-building among the various emigrant Indians was so intense that they came to

identify themselves collectively as "Ohio Indians." For land sharing in the Native East, see Schutt, *Peoples of the River Valleys*, 31–40, 69–70, 158, 175; Shoemaker, *Strange Likeness*, 85–99.

13. Beauharnois to the French Minister, October 15, 1732, *Wilderness Chronicles*, 5–6 ("would . . ."); Beauharnois & Hocquart to the French Minister, October 14, 1733, Thwaites, *French Regime in Wisconsin, II*, 185–186. Several colonial observers reported the ongoing negotiations between the Shawnees and Wyandots, although they rarely knew much about the content of the talks. See *MPCP* 4:234; Annual Report of Beauharnois and Hocquart, October 12, 1736, Thwaites, *French Regime in Wisconsin, II*, 243; Yearly Report of Beauharnois, 1737, ibid., 264. For the Shawnee towns, see Tanner, *Atlas*, 40–41.

14. For Shawnees and Lenapes, see Logan to Clark, August 4, 1737, JLP 4:8; Logan to Gooch, May 11, 1738, ibid., 15; A True account of all the Men in the Three Towns in Allegania of the Shawnise Nation, September 27, 1737, ibid., 68; *MPCP* 7:382 ("a Relation . . ."); Schutt, *Peoples of the River Valleys*, 109. The presence of Iroquois in Shawnee towns is attested in Indians at Allegheney to Gov., March 20, 1738, *PA*, 1st Ser., 1:551. For Ojibwe and Miami visits, see Newchecomer to James Logan, April 9, 1738, JLP 4:69; Message of King of Shawnees to Governor Gooch, August 4, 1738, *EAID* 5:23; *MPCP* 4:562, 574.

15. State of Canada in 1730, *MPHC* 34:76; *MPCP* 4:234; Weiser to Logan, September 2, 1736, JLP 4:57; Indians at Allegheney to Gov., March 20, 1738, *PA*, 1st Ser., 1:551; Message of King of Shawnees to Governor Gooch, August 4, 1738, *EAID* 5:23; McConnell, *Country Between*, 48–50.

16. Anderson, *Crucible of War*, 16–18.

17. For the Shawnees' "play off" strategy, see Hinderaker, *Elusive Empires*, 30. For similar strategies among other Native peoples, see Adelman and Aron, "From Borderlands to Borders" ("in between" from 814); Hahn, *Invention of the Creek Nation*; Richter, *Facing East*, 164–171; Richter, *Ordeal of the Longhouse*.

18. The experiences and strategies of the Haudenosaunees and the Creeks are traced most fully in Hahn, *Invention of the Creek Nation*; Richter, *Ordeal of the Longhouse*. The differences between British and French trade in the Ohio Country are discussed in Eccles, "Fur Trade," 356; White, *Middle Ground*, 211.

19. *MPCP* 3:219 ("Father"), 461 ("had no . . ."); De Beauharnois and D'Aigremont to the Minister, October 1, 1728, *Wilderness Chronicles*, 3 ("they were . . ."); Speeches at an Indian Council, 1732, ibid., 9 ("we all . . ."). For Algonquian ideas about fathers, see White, *Middle Ground*, 84–85.

20. Scholarship on Indian factionalism and its connection to neutralist strategies is considerable. See Hahn, *Invention of the Creek Nation*, chs. 3 and 4; Kugel, *To Be the Main Leaders*, 7–10; Richter, *Ordeal of the Longhouse*; Richter, *Facing East*, 164–171; and White, *Roots of Dependency*, 64–65. For Ocowellos, see *MPCP* 3:219. For Paguasse, see Examination of Edmund Cartlidge, December 7, 1731, *PA*, 1st Ser., 1:306; and Message of Shawnee Chiefs to Gov. Gordon, June 7, 1732, ibid., 329–330. For Nucheconner, see Indians' Letter to Gov. Gordon, April 24, 1733, *PA*, 1st Ser., 1:395; Message of King of Shawnees to Governor Gooch, August 4, 1738, *EAID* 5:22–24; and A True account of all the Men in the Three Towns in Allegania of the Shawnise Nation, September 27, 1737, JLP 4:68.

21. For the 1729 visit to Montreal, see Beauharnois to the French Minister, July 21, 1729, Thwaites, *French Regime in Wisconsin*, II, 64. The minutes of the 1732 Philadelphia council are in *MPCP* 3:459–463. Given the emphasis the Shawnee spokesman Opakethwa put on the Thawikilas' flight from the Potomac, it appears likely that at least one of the four Shawnees at the council represented them. At least one of the other leaders, Opakeita, represented the Allegheny-Conemaugh communities: he was involved in their diplomacy throughout the 1730s; see Message of Shawnee Chiefs to Gov. Gordon, June 7, 1732, *PA*, 1st Ser., 1:330; Indians' Letter to Gov. Gordon, April 24, 1733, ibid., 395; and Indian Letter Respecting Indian Traders, May 1, 1734, ibid., 425. Quassenung was the son of the Wyoming chief Kakewatchiky, *MPCP* 3:463. The minutes of the 1739 council are in *MPCP* 4:336–347 (quotation from 342). Nucheconner, Missemediqueety, and Tamany Buck can be connected to the Allegheny and Ohio communities; see, for example, Message of Shawnee Chiefs to Gov. Gordon, June 7, 1732, *PA*, 1st Ser., 1:330; Indian Letter to President and Council, May 1, 1747, ibid., 1:737; Gist, "Christopher Gist's First and Second Journals," 17; *MPCP* 5:289–290, 315–318, 352, 570. Kishacoquillas (Kaashawkaghquillas) is linked to the Juniata in Number of Indians, 1731, *PA*, 1st Ser., 1:302. Kakewatchiky was from the Wyoming Valley: *MPCP* 4:643, 648. For a similar identification of the Shawnee participants, see *EAID* 2:472.

22. The letters are in Message of Shawnee Chiefs to Gov. Gordon, June 7, 1732, *PA*, 1st Ser., 1:329–330; Indians' Letter to Gov. Gordon, April 24, 1733, ibid., 394–395; Indian Letter Respecting Indian Traders, May 1, 1734, ibid., 425 ("att Our . . ."); Indian Resolution Respecting Rum, March 15, 1738, ibid., 549–550; Indians at Allegheney to Gov., March 20, 1738, ibid., 550–552; Newchecomer to Logan, April 9, 1738, JLP 4:69; Message of King of Shawnees to Governor Gooch, August 4, 1738, *EAID* 5:22–24. For councils, see Annual Report of Beauharnois and Hocquart, October 12, 1736, Thwaites, *French Regime in Wisconsin*, II, 243 ("have frequent . . .").

23. For Coyacolinne, see Indians at Allegheney to Gov., March 20, 1738, *PA*, 1st Ser., 1:551–552 ("Chefe Counciler" from 552). Nucheconner is dubbed a king in Message of King of Shawnees to Governor Gooch, August 4, 1738, *EAID* 5:24 ("King of . . ."); Proceedings of William Fairfax with Iroquois Chiefs and Their Allies at Winchester, ibid., 183; A True account of all the Men in the Three Towns in Allegania of the Shawnise Nation, September 27, 1737, JLP 4:68; Newchecomer to James Logan, April 9, 1738, ibid., 69; *MPCP* 5:685. For Shawnee orators, see Trowbridge, *Meeārmeer Traditions*, 13–15; Trowbridge, *Shawnese Traditions*, 61. In the 1970s Shawnees told anthropologist James Howard that Pekowis were traditionally tribal speakers: Howard, *Shawnee!*, 28–29. For evidence of Nucheconner's Pekowi identity, see note 7 of this chapter.

24. For the connections between Nucheconner, Laypareawah, and Opessa, see Indian Resolution Respecting Rum, March 15, 1738, *PA*, 1st Ser., 1:549; and Indians at Allegheney to Gov, March 20, 1738, ibid., 552. For Opessa and the Potomac, see Hanna, *Wilderness Trail*, 1:153. The individual whom the British usually called "the young King" is sometimes named as Loapeckaway, Lapechkewe, or Capechque. Although it is not certain that this man is the same as Laypareawah, the names are similar. Moreover, both Laypareawah and Lapechkewe are consistently associated with "kingship" and Nucheconner, suggesting that we are dealing with only one man. For the "young King" and Lawachkamicky, see *MPCP* 6:153 ("a noted . . ."). For

Obocketoy and Obokater, see A True account of all the Men in the Three Towns in Allegania of the Shawnise Nation, September 27, 1737, JLP 4:68.

25. Indians at Allegheney to Gov., March 20, 1738, *PA*, 1st Ser., 1:551 ("Gether . . ."). The exact time of Lower Shawneetown's founding is not known, but it was in existence by 1739. For the history of the town, see Hanna, *Wilderness Trail*, 2:130, 140–143; Henderson, Jobe, and Turnbow, *Indian Occupation and Use*, 22–26, 30, 48–49, 50; Henderson, "Lower Shawneetown," 28, 30, 34, 38–42; Gist, "Christopher Gist's First and Second Journals," 16; Callender, "Shawnee," 625.

26. Gist, "Christopher Gist's First and Second Journals," 16; *MPCP* 5:708 ("the Place . . ."); Indians at Allegheney to Gov., March 20, 1738, *PA*, 1st Ser., 1:551 ("Oppointed . . ."); Sergeant to Williams, May 14, 1739, John Sergeant Letters, Box Ayer Ms 800, Newberry Library.

27. *MPCP* 4:234; Howard, *Shawnee!*, 6 (quotation); *MPCP* 3:608–609; Number of Indians, 1731, *PA*, 1st Ser., 1:302.

28. Hahn, *Invention of the Creek Nation*, 102–110, 139–145; Oatis, *Colonial Complex*, 269–287; D'Artaguette to Maurepas, October 17, 1729, *MPA* 4:20. D'Artaguette does not specify whether the English warehouse was in a Shawnee town on the Chattahoochee or on the Tallapoosa. The fact that it was destroyed by Cowetas from the Chattahoochee suggests that it was in the same region.

29. D'Artaguette to Maurepas, October 17, 1729, *MPA* 4:28; for identifying the Shawnee migrants, see the editors' note 16 on p. 30. Later French documents from the 1740s consistently associate the Shawnees with the Alabamas, rather than the Koasatis; see, for example, Beauchamp's Journal, *MPA* 4:276; Extract from an Anonymous Letter, ibid., 309.

30. Oatis, *Colonial Complex*, 214–215; Hahn, *Invention of the Creek Nation*, 101–102; D'Artaguette to Maurepas, October 17, 1729, *MPA* 4:28–29 ("completely . . ."); Extract from an Anonymous Letter, ibid., 308 ("the red . . ."); Vaudreuil to Maurepas, November 5, 1748, ibid., 337 ("they . . .").

31. Jacobs, *Indians of the Southern Colonial Frontier*, 43 ("intirely . . ."); Vaudreuil to Rouillé, September 22, 1749, *MPA* 5:36 ("in the . . ."); Vaudreuil to Maurepas, November 5, 1748, *MPA* 4:337. In 1754 South Carolinian trader Edmond Atkin estimated that 185 Shawnee men lived among the Upper Creeks. Depending on whether Atkin meant men in general or only warriors, his estimate brings the total Tallapoosa Shawnee population to somewhere between six hundred and one thousand. Jacobs, *Indians of the Southern Colonial Frontier*, 43.

32. Jacobs, *Indians of the Southern Colonial Frontier*, 65–66; Memoir of the King, February 2, 1732, *MPA* 3:552; Kerlérec to De Machault d'Arnouville, September 15, 1754, *MPA* 5:144; Bienville and Salmon to Maurepas, June 2, 1736, *MPA* 1:315.

33. D'Artaguette to Maurepas, October 24, 1737, *MPA* 4:147; Vaudreuil to Maurepas, April 1, 1746, ibid., 266 ("the project . . ."); Beauchamp's Journal, ibid., 276, 289; Vaudreuil to Maurepas, March 15, 1747, ibid., 305; Jacobs, *Indians of the Southern Colonial Frontier*, 50–52, 66.

34. For imperial fears, see White, *Middle Ground*, 196–197. For Shawnee hopes of making the paths safe for travelers, see Jacobs, *Indians of the Southern Colonial Frontier*, 66.

35. *MPCP* 3:608–609 ("to the . . ."); Vaudreuil to Maurepas, December 12, 1744, *MPA* 4:222 ("Canada"); Beauchamp's Journal, ibid., 276 ("the people . . ."); Jacobs, *Indians of the Southern Colonial Frontier*, 66 ("they only . . .").

36. Wunder and Hämäläinen, "Of Lethal Places," 1229 ("lethal places"). The idea of the Ohio Valley and the South as "zones of international friction" comes from Gipson, *British Empire*, especially chs. 6–9.

37. *MPCP* 4:587–589, 630–634 ("are known . . ." from 634), 739 ("the Six Nations . . ."); Logan to Thomas, July 19, 1742, JLP 4:39–40.

38. For Chartier robbing the traders, see Deposition of Peter Tostee, James Dinnen and George Croghan, May 14, 1745, JLP, 4:112–114; Richard Peters to [?], June 6, 1745, Peters Papers, 2:36; *MPCP* 4:757–758. Chartier's debts and problems with the Pennsylvanian leadership are discussed in Peters to Penn, May 5, 1745, Peters Letterbooks, 276; Peters to the Proprietors, November 19, 1747, ibid., 279; and Jennings, *Ambiguous Iroquois Empire*, 269–270. The movements of Chartier's community can be traced in Anonymous Diary of a Trip from Detroit to the Ohio River, pp. 3–7, Shawnee File, OVGLEA; Beauharnois to the French Minister, October 28, 1745, *Wilderness Chronicles*, 23; *MPCP* 5:311 ("great things . . ."); Vaudreuil to Rouillé, June 24, 1750, MPA 5:48. The French had promised to build a fort on the Wabash to serve Shawnee needs: Kerlérec to Rouillé, July 18, 1753, MPA 5:140–141. For opposition to Chartier and the British-Iroquois reactions, see *MPCP* 5:314 ("Chastize"), 352 ("protested . . ."). For the hostilities between Chartier's Shawnees and the Wabash and Illinois tribes, see Vaudreuil to Maurepas, June 15, 1748, MPA 4:323 ("offended"); Vaudreuil to Rouillé, May 8, 1749, MPA 5:27; Vaudreuil to Rouillé, May 10, 1751, ibid., 75; LaJonquière to the French Minister, September 25, 1751, Thwaites, *French Regime in Wisconsin*, 90–92.

39. French Minister to La Jonquière, May 4, 1749, Thwaites, *French Regime in Wisconsin*, 20–21; Vaudreuil to Maurepas, June 15, 1748, MPA 4:323; Vaudreuil to Maurepas, November 5, 1748, ibid., 336–337; Jacobs, *Indians of the Southern Colonial Frontier*, 66 ("Shartie's . . ."); Vaudreuil to Rouillé, June 24, 1750, MPA 5:48 ("entirely . . ."); Vaudreuil to Rouillé, May 10, 1751, ibid., 75; Vaudreuil to Rouillé, September 22, 1749, ibid., 36 ("The Shawnees . . .").

40. *MPCP* 4:747. Kakewatchiky is linked to Logstown in *MPCP* 5:351–352, 531. For Ossoghqua, see *MPCP* 4:585; *MPCP* 5:317–318.

41. Anderson, *Crucible of War*, 24–25; Hinderaker, *Elusive Empires*, 39–44; McConnell, *Country Between*, 61–67; White, *Middle Ground*, 198–202.

42. McConnell, "Peoples 'in Between,'" 97–102; McConnell, *Country Between*, 67–77; *MPCP* 5:119, 147–150 ("had concluded . . ." from 148), 166–167, 349–358.

43. La Jonquière to the French Minister, September 25, 1751, Thwaites, *French Regime in Wisconsin*, 90–91 ("we . . ." from 91); French Minister to La Galissonière, February 23, 1748, Thwaites, *French Regime in Wisconsin*, 12 ("been . . ."); *MPCP* 5:310 ("the strongest . . .").

44. McConnell, *Country Between*, 82–88, 99–100; White, *Middle Ground*, 202–215, 227–230; Indian Letter to President and Council, May 1, 1747, PA, 1st Ser., 1:737–738; *MPCP* 5:308–310; Lambing, "Celeron's Journal," 363–370.

45. LaJonquière to the French Minister, September 25, 1751, Thwaites, *French Regime in Wisconsin*, 90–92 ("it would be . . ." from 91); *MPCP* 5:497, 569 ("not suffer . . ."; "a Place . . ."), 732; McConnell, *Country Between*, 98–99; William Trent's Account of Proceedings with Iroquois and Their Allies at Logstown, *EAID* 5:172.

46. Jennings, *Empire of Fortune*, 8–13; McConnell, *Country Between*, 91; Preston, *Texture*

of Contact, 123–127, 131–144; Gist, "Christopher Gist's First and Second Journals," 39 (quotation).

47. Treaty of Logstown, May 28–June 13, 1752, *EAID* 5:133–146; Proceedings of William Fairfax with Iroquois Chiefs and Their Allies at Winchester, ibid., 191; Jennings, *Empire of Fortune*, 38–44; McConnell, *Country Between*, 95–99; Goodwin, *Journal of Captain William Trent*, 93 ("a suit . . .").

48. McDowell, *Colonial Records of South Carolina*, 421–429, 456–457; *MPCP* 5:682–683, 696–700; *MPCP* 6:153; Proceedings of William Fairfax with Iroquois Chiefs and Their Allies at Winchester, *EAID* 5:190–191 (quotations). For a thorough account of the incident, see Steele, "Shawnee Origins." Although Steele identifies Lawachkamicky as an "upper" Shawnee, the headman himself said that he came from a "River called Laiota." This probably refers to the Scioto River and suggests that the war party was from Lower Shawneetown; McDowell, *Colonial Records of South Carolina*, 423.

49. Anderson, *Crucible of War*, 30–32; Jennings, *Empire of Fortune*, 50–52; Ward, *Breaking the Backcountry*, 30; White, *Middle Ground*, 232–237.

50. McConnell, *Country Between*, 100–105; *MPCP* 5:676–677; *MPCP* 6:36–37; Kent, *French Invasion*, 43–52 ("we . . ." from 51); William Trent to Governor Dinwiddie, August 11, 1753, Bailey, *Ohio Company Papers*, 24 ("while the . . .").

51. Steele, "Shawnee Origins," 671–672, 677; *MPCP* 6:153 ("Death . . ."); Spero, "Stout, Bold, Cunning," 333, 337 ("to live . . .").

52. *MPCP* 6:153 ("we are . . ."), 159–160 ("large . . ."; "made . . ."; "see . . ."); Speech of the Makujays to the King, Claus Papers, 7:125, reel C-1479, LAC ("when . . ."; "thought . . ."; "not to . . .").

53. Bond, "Captivity of Charles Stuart," 63–64 ("that No . . ." and "the Greater . . ."); The Speech of Ackowanothio, 1758, *PA*, 1st Ser., 3:549 ("coming . . ."); Anderson, *Crucible of War*, 94–107; Ward, *Breaking the Backcountry*, 38–45.

54. *MPCP* 6:727, 766–768, 781–782; *MPCP* 7:299, 532; Ward, *Breaking the Backcountry*, 46–52; Speech of the Makujays to the King, Claus Papers, 7:126, reel C-1479, LAC (quotation).

55. Whereas older scholarship tended to treat Indians as mere pawns in the European imperial struggle, more recently historians have given Native peoples a much more important role in the Seven Years' War and reanalyzed the conflict from Native perspectives. This has meant questioning the standard chronology of the war, paying attention to the very different motives and strategies of different Native communities, and reassessing the outcome and consequences of the war. See Anderson, *Crucible of War*; Barr, " 'This Land Is Ours' "; Jennings, *Empire of Fortune*; Preston, *Texture of Contact*, 147–215; Richter, *Before the Revolution*, 369–414; Steele, "Shawnee Origins"; Steele, "Shawnees and the English"; Ward, *Breaking the Backcountry*; White, *Middle Ground*, 240–244. For Missiweakiwa, see Conference at Fort Pitt, April 7–12, 1760, *EAID* 3:544 ("The God Who . . .").

CHAPTER THREE. "THE CHIEF OF ALL THE TRIBES"

1. Anderson, *Crucible of War*, xv–xxiii (quotation from xv).

2. Speech of the Makujays to the King, Claus Papers, 7:124, reel C-1479, LAC (quotation). The Mekoche speakers are identified in Ironside to McKee, February 6, 1795,

Indian Affairs, 9:8840, reel C-10 999, LAC. Several classic and recent works discuss the transformative effects of the Seven Years' and Pontiac's wars in the Indian country. See especially Anderson, *Crucible of War*, 633–637; Calloway, *Scratch of a Pen*; Calloway, *Shawnees and the War for America*, 29–42; Dowd, *War under Heaven*; Jennings, *Empire of Fortune*; Steele, "Shawnees and the English"; White, *Middle Ground*, 223–314. Scholars who emphasize national consolidation among Indians or efforts by Indians to present at least a façade of national unity to the British include Galloway, " 'So Many Little Republics' "; Hahn, *Invention of the Creek Nation*, 229–270; Merritt, *At the Crossroads*, 169–308; Schutt, *Peoples of the River Valleys*, 126–149.

3. Barr, " 'This Land Is Ours,' " 29–40; Jennings, *Empire of Fortune*, 384–403; McConnell, *Country Between*, 120–132; Preston, *Texture of Contact*, 144, 153, 226; Steele, "Shawnees and the English," 11; Ward, *Breaking the Backcountry*, 44–73, 130–141, 145–156, 178–182; Ward, "Fighting the 'Old Women' "; Ward, "Redeeming the Captives," 162.

4. Barr, " 'This Land Is Ours,' " 37–39; Hunter, "Provincial Negotiations," 216–219; McConnell, *Country Between*, 126–139; Preston, *Texture of Contact*, 153, 226; Ward, *Breaking the Backcountry*, 157–188. For British promises to abandon Fort Pitt, *MPCP* 8:389.

5. The progress of the Anglo-French war in 1759–1763 is traced in Anderson, *Crucible of War*, 330–339, 344–368, 400–409. For the gradual deterioration of Indian-British relations in the Ohio Valley, see Dowd, *War under Heaven*, 54–113; Calloway, *Scratch of a Pen*, 66–69; McConnell, *Country Between*, 159–181.

6. For Pontiac's War, the Royal Proclamation, and somewhat differing interpretations of their legacies, see Dowd, *War under Heaven*, especially chs. 4–8; Ward, *Breaking the Backcountry*, 200–254, Calloway, *Scratch of a Pen*, 70–100; Sosin, *Whitehall and the Wilderness*, 39–78. For Shawnee negotiations, see *MPCP* 9:259 ("our Father . . ."); Proceedings of Sir William Johnson with the Ohio Indians, July 4–14, 1765, *DRCHNY* 7:750–758; Speech of the Makujays to the King, Claus Papers, 7:125, reel C-1479, LAC ("drawn . . ."). The 1758 Treaty of Easton stated that the permanent Indian-British boundary would be set by Crown officers and the Haudenosaunees. British officers later agreed that this would be the legitimate way of making revisions in the proclamation boundary as well. Some historians have therefore argued that the Royal Proclamation again strengthened Haudenosaunee power over such Ohio Indians as the Shawnees. This was certainly the British interpretation of the situation. Shawnees and their neighbors did not accept such a view, however. When the Six Nations and Crown officers moved the boundary without consulting the Ohio peoples in 1768, Shawnees vehemently disputed their right to do so. This suggests that even if the Shawnees had originally accepted the Haudenosaunees as their representatives in boundary negotiations, they expected that their leaders would also be heard in any decision. See Dowd, *War under Heaven*, 186–187; McConnell, *Country Between*, 205.

7. For Shawnee battlefield losses, see *MPCP* 7:381–382; *MPCP* 8:135–137; Minutes of Conference of Croghan with Indians, March 29–May 21, 1757, *PSWJ* 9:740. For famines among the Ohio Indians, see Conference at Fort Pitt, April 7–12, 1760, *EAID* 3:547 ("poor people" and "Starving . . ."); Mercer to Bouquet, August 15, 1759, *PHB* 3:565; Heckewelder, *History, Manners, and Customs*, 159. For the epidemics, see MacLeod, "Microbes and Muskets," 47–50; Hutchins's Journal, April 4–September

24, 1762, Bouquet Papers 21 655, f. 181–186, BL ("mostly Sick . . ."); Jordan, "Journal of James Kenny," 172, 178 ("sent from . . ."); Journal of Indian Affairs, March 1–3, 1765, *PSWJ* 11:618; William Grant to [?], April 14, 1764, Gage Papers, reel 11. For the British spreading smallpox, see Calloway, *Scratch of a Pen*, 73; Dowd, *War under Heaven*, 190.

8. Conference at Fort Pitt, April 7–12, 1760, *EAID* 3:544 ("[driven] us . . ."); Croghan to Johnson, December 10, 1762, *PSWJ* 3:964 ("begin . . ."); Wainwright, "George Croghan's Journal," 438 ("the English . . ."); Jordan, "Journal of James Kenny," 187 ("grown too . . ."). For Anglo-American spiritual interpretations of the British victory, see Anderson, *Crucible of War*, 373–376; Bloch, *Visionary Republic*, 36–50.

9. For upper Shawnees moving to Lower Shawneetown, see *MPCP* 7:172, 381, 466; Examination of a Delaware Prisoner, 1757, *PA*, 1st Ser., 3:148; Journal of Frederick Post from Pittsburgh, 1758, ibid., 560. For inviting the Alabama Shawnees, see Wainwright, "George Croghan's Journal," 356 ("sent . . ."). For the Trans-Mississippi Shawnees, see Jordan, "Journal of James Kenny," 177. For Paxinosa and Wyoming Shawnees, see *MPCP* 8:126–127; Post, "Two Journals of Western Tours," 193, 201; Diary of the Indian Congregation in Welhik Thuppeck, on the Muskingum, of the Month of Sept. to October 18, 1772, Moravian Records, reel 8, box 141, folder 13, item 1, p. 6, NYSL. For the situation in 1762, see Hutchins, "Description," 194–195. For Kittanning, see McConnell, *Country Between*, 126; Preston, *Texture of Contact*, 173–177. Wakatomika was the old Shawnee name for the South Branch of the Potomac River, suggesting that some Wakatomikans traced their roots there; Kercheval, *History of the Valley of Virginia*, 30, 34. A British estimate from 1762 places the number of the Ohio Shawnees at "about three hundred fighting men." Other estimates from the late 1750s and early 1760s generally hover around that figure, although it is sometimes unclear whether the estimate includes only the Scioto communities; see A List of Indian Nations, their places of abode & Chief Hunting, Bouquet Papers 21 655, f. 91–92, BL.

10. Steele, "Shawnees and the English," 12; McConnell, *Country Between*, 187, 193, 197; *MPCP* 9:223 ("Chief Captain"); Bouquet to Gage, November 15, 1764, Gage Papers, reel 5 ("the Chiefs . . ."); Croghan to Johnson, May 13, 1765, *PSWJ* 11:737 ("ye Warrers . . ."). For Shawnee councils during wartime, see Trowbridge, *Shawnese Traditions*, 12, 17. Anthropologist Erminie Wheeler-Voegelin likewise argued that the mid-eighteenth-century warfare drew Shawnee divisions to closer collaboration, Erminie W. Voegelin, "The Shawnee in Relation to Tecumseh's Proposed Uprising," 6–7, EWVP, box 35, folder 321.

11. Conference at Fort Pitt, April 7–12, 1760, *EAID* 3:545 (quotation). A careful analysis of British treaty minutes and other documents shows that the Shawnee delegations to Fort Pitt grew and became more broad-based during 1759 and 1760: *MPCP* 8:293–295, 383, 387; Wainwright, "George Croghan's Journal," 316–317, 331, 337, 342, 354, 368–369. No document explicitly identifies Missiweakiwa as a Mekoche; however, in 1760 he described how the Shawnees emerged into this world from a hole in the ground. In the early twentieth century this was a Mekoche belief, suggesting Missiweakiwa's association with this division: Conference at Fort Pitt, April 7–12, 1760, *EAID* 3:544; Erminie Wheeler Voegelin, "Shawnee: An American Indian Culture," 21, 62–63, EWVP, box 31, folder 276.

12. Wainwright, "George Croghan's Journal," 402 ("taking . . ."), 443 ("a gineral . . ."). For other references to tribal councils during the war years, see Jordan, "Journal of James Kenny," 185; Croghan to Gage, March 2, 1765, Gage Papers, reel 10.

13. Most of the older headmen simply disappear from the documents, suggesting that they died. The death of Kishacoquillas is reported in *MPCP* 6:153–154, and that of Paxinosa in Fliegel, *Index to the Records of the Moravian Mission*, 324. For the relationship between Kakewatchiky and Kisinoutha, see Schaaf, *Wampum Belts and Peace Trees*, 136; for Paxinosa, Nimwha, and Colesquo, see Fliegel, *Index to the Records of the Moravian Mission*, 324; Sugden, *Blue Jacket*, 48, 236. For examples of hokimas and war leaders joining forces in negotiations, see Wainwright, "George Croghan's Journal," 337; Conference at Fort Pitt, April 7–12, 1760, *EAID* 3:544; *MPCP* 9:229, 256. For the importance of linking old men, young men, and women to create legitimate communal decisions among other eastern Indians, see Fur, *Nation of Women*, 31; Kugel, *To Be the Main Leaders*, 71–72; Miller, *Ogimaag*, 1–2.

14. Proceedings of Sir William Johnson with the Ohio Indians, July 4–14, 1765, *DRCHNY* 7:755 (clan eponyms). For examples of Anglo-Americans calling Kisinoutha a king: Wainwright, "George Croghan's Journal," 400; Jones, *Journal of Two Visits*, 52. For Kisinoutha speaking collectively for Shawnees, see *MPCP* 9:220, 528–529, 538–539. Significantly, even when he did not speak in conferences, Crown officers listed him as the first of the Shawnee "Chiefs" present: Conference at Fort Pitt, April 7–12, 1760, *EAID* 3:544; *MPCP* 9:256, 515. For Kisinoutha calling a tribal council, see Col. Richard Butler's Journal, 1775, 34–35, HSP; Diary 1775, Thwaites and Kellogg, *Revolution on the Upper Ohio*, 57–62. Kisinoutha's identity as a Raccoon clan member is reported in Yeates, "Indian Treaty at Fort Pitt in 1776," 484. John Sugden has argued that Kisinoutha lived in Wakatomika and had only "a cabin" on the Scioto, but evidence for this is slim. In 1764 Kisinoutha claimed that the distance from the Muskingum River to his own town was "great." This indicates that he lived on the Scioto. Several documents from the early 1770s place him there. Sugden, *Blue Jacket*, 33; *MPCP* IX, 220 ("great"); Jones, *Journal of Two Visits*, 52.

15. A Speech Delivered by the Hard fellow, July 9, 1761, Bouquet Papers 21 655, f. 128, BL (quotation); Wainwright, "George Croghan's Journal," 443. For the divisional background of Nimwha and Oweeconnee, see The Delaware Chiefs to the Shawnee Chiefs, April 8, 1779, Kellogg, *Frontier Advance on the Upper Ohio*, 280. Miskapalathy's division is never identified in the documents. His constant association with Mekoche leaders like Kisinoutha and the fact that his son died on a diplomatic mission with the Mekoche headman Colesquo lead me to conjecture that he too was a Mekoche; Edward Hand to Patrick Henry, December 9, 1777, DM, 3NN69.

16. Proceedings of Sir William Johnson with the Ohio Indians, July 4–14, 1765, *DRCHNY* 7:755 ("for . . ."); *MPCP* 9:217 ("it is . . ."), 229–233; Orders and Regulations Published at Fort Pitt, Bouquet Papers 21 655, f. 195, BL. Stephen Hahn has emphasized the importance of "British colonial practices," including "trade, land acquisition, and the creation of British-sponsored 'chiefs' " in pushing the Creeks toward a "new concept of nationhood." Anthropologist Fred Gearing in turn argued that the fear of unlimited British retaliation against all Cherokees forced Cherokee leaders to centralize tribal leadership and coordinate Cherokee-British relations: Hahn, *Invention of the Creek Nation*, 8; Gearing, "Priests and Warriors," 85.

17. Steele, "Shawnees and the English," 12–13, 16; Croghan to Johnson, July 25, 1761, *PSWJ* 10:317 ("a property . . ."); *MPCP* 9:259–260; Trowbridge, *Shawnese Traditions*, 19–21, 53–54, 64. For the role of women in adopting captives in the East, see Dowd, *War under Heaven*, 86–87; Fur, *Nation of Women*, 23; Ward, "Redeeming the Captives," 168.

18. Smith, *Historical Account of Bouquet's Expedition*, 66–67; *MPCP* 9:259–260 ("our . . ." from 259); Croghan to Johnson, October 12, 1761, *PSWJ* 3:550; Croghan to Johnson, July 25, 1761, *PSWJ* 10:317–318 ("in the utmost . . ."); Jordan, "Journal of James Kenny," 185 ("pleaded . . ."); Wainwright, "George Croghan's Journal," 400 ("some Confusion . . .").

19. Dowd, *War under Heaven*, 153–158, 162–164; Journal of M. Dabbadie, 1763–1764, Alvord and Carter, *Critical Period*, 203–204; St. Ange to D'Abbadie, November 9, 1764, ibid., 356–358; Speeches by Indian Chiefs, February 24, 1765, ibid., 444–449; *MPCP* 9:207, 212–233 ("very Obstinate" from 207; "as soon . . ." from 232). For the returned captives, see also Bouquet to Murray, December 12, 1764, Bouquet Papers 21 655, f. 252–253, BL; Bouquet to Gage, November 15, 1764, Gage Papers, reel 5; Steele, "Shawnees and the English," 16. While older histories tended to portray Bouquet's Ohio expedition as an unqualified British success, more recently scholars have emphasized the ability of the Indian leaders to stop the invasion with promises of peace and the return of some captives. See especially Dowd, *War under Heaven*, 163–168.

20. Journal of Indian Affairs, March 1–3, 1765, *PSWJ* 11:617 ("unwilling . . ."); Croghan to Gage, March 2, 1765, Gage Papers, reel 10 ("called . . ." and "determined . . .").

21. *MPCP* 9:256, 259 ("came . . ."), 260 ("with a . . ."). In 1786 Richard Butler wrote a detailed description of the arrival of a Mekoche delegation to the Treaty of Fort Finney. The Mekoches marched to the fort in a ceremonial procession with the hokimas in the front, followed first by war leaders and warriors and then by a Peace Woman, women, and children; Craig, "Gen. Butler's Journal," 512–513.

22. Fraser to Gage, May 15, 1765, Gage Papers, reel 10 ("he will . . ."); Sterling to Gage, October 10, 1765, ibid.; Croghan's Official Journal, May 15–September 25, 1765, Alvord and Carter, *New Regime*, 41. Though the evidence is ambiguous, Charlot Kaské seems to have been the individual British often called "Corn Cobb"; see Calloway, *Shawnees and the War for America*, 41. In 1768 Corn Cobb/Kaské was described as having "lived long with the French": Indian Intelligence, September 30, 1768, *PSWJ* 12:602; see also Robert Fraser to Thomas Gage, December 16, 1765, and Robert Farmar to Thomas Gage, April 24, 1766, both in Gage Papers, reel 10; Government Order of Ensign Willm. Connolly, and Indian Department Order of Lieut. Fowler, both in Gage Papers, reel 12. For Kaské's activities in Illinois, see Dowd, *War under Heaven*, 217–232; White, *Middle Ground*, 300–305. For the captives, see Steele, "Shawnees and the English," 16; Johnson to Gage, July 5, 1765, *PSWJ* 4:786.

23. Anderson, *Imagined Communities*, 6; Kertzer, *Ritual, Politics, and Power*, 15–24.

24. Negotiations with the Shawnees, July 16, 1775, *Revolutionary Virginia* 7, pt. 2, 765 ("Principal Tribe"); Speech of the Makujays to the King, Claus Papers, 7:127, reel C-1479, LAC ("King Tribe" and "none . . .").

25. Galloway, *Old Chillicothe*, 54. Note that Alford uses the term "clan" or "sept" for the groups modern scholars call "divisions."

26. For the Mekoche miišaami, see Galloway, *Old Chillicothe*, 181; Alford, *Civilization*, 44; Johnston, "Account of the Present State," 275; Trowbridge, *Shawnese Traditions*, 6. For the connections of the color white, healing, purification, and peace among Shawnees and other eastern Indians, see Miller and Hamell, "New Perspective," 324; Hudson, *Southeastern Indians*, 223–224, 235–236; Fenton, "Structure, Continuity, and Change," 22–23; *MPCP* 8:736; O'Brien, *Choctaws in a Revolutionary Age*, 35; Trowbridge, *Shawnese Traditions*, 6, 60. A partly differing interpretation of the role of miišaami in the Shawnee consolidation is offered by Schutz, "Study of Shawnee Myth," 190–194.

27. Speech of the Makujays to the King, Claus Papers, 7:124–126, reel C-1479, LAC. Although we do not know who translated and wrote down the Mekoche speech, Indian agent George Ironside was present when the headmen delivered it. He spoke at least some Shawnee and may have both translated and recorded the talk. It is also possible that Red-Faced Fellow was a former American captive, James McPherson, who often served as an interpreter for the Indians. Ironside to McKee, February 6, 1795, Indian Affairs, 9:8840, reel C-10 999 LAC; Quaife, *Indian Captivity of O. M. Spencer*, 103; Sugden, *Blue Jacket*, 310.

28. Speech of the Makujays to the King, Claus Papers, 7:125, reel C-1479, LAC ("Our . . ."); Trowbridge, *Shawnese Traditions*, 8 ("very ancient"), 62 ("grandfathers"); Speech of Blackbeard, 1806, Shawnee File, OVGLEA ("first born"); Jones, *Journal of Two Visits*, 56 ("chief town").

29. Fenton, *Great Law and the Longhouse*, 224–234 ("noted for . . ." from 224; "public treasury" from 231); Foster, "Another Look"; Richter, *Facing East*, 137; Merrell, *Into the American Woods*, 187–197; Schutt, *Peoples of the River Valleys*, 11; *MPCP* 5:358 ("Council Bag"); Shoemaker, *Strange Likeness*, 68–69.

30. For customs of storing wampum belts among other Indians of the East, see Fenton, *Great Law and the Longhouse*, 231–233.

31. *MPCP* 9:230.

32. Three of the four documents in Miskapalathy's possession are easy to trace. Since there are no records of a Shawnee-English treaty made in April 1711, the first document is almost certainly the Philadelphia Treaty of April 1701; see *MPCP* 2:9–11. The dating of the second document, too, must be a clerical error. Patrick Gordon served as the lieutenant governor of Pennsylvania from 1726 to 1736 and could not have sent the letter in 1750. Most likely the document in question was the letter sent by Gordon to "Ollepoonoe, Achquaillemoe, &c., Chiefs of the Shawanese & Assekelaes, at or near Alleghening" in December 1731: From the Governr. to the Shawanese Indians, 1731, *PA*, 1st Ser., 1:301–302; see also *MPCP* 3:459. "Assakelaes" were Thawikilas. "Ollepoonoe" may have been the Chalaakaatha leader Ocowellos; see Number of Indians, *PA*, 1st Ser., 1:301. For the letter by Governor George Thomas, see *MPCP* 4:588–590, and Governor Thomas to Cacowachico & Nochiconna, August 16, 1742, JLP 4:79–81. I have not been able to track down Thomas Penn's letter. It is worth noting that at least Gordon's letter had originally been accompanied by a wampum belt, and the same may be true for the other documents. While Bouquet omitted mentioning belts in 1764, Miskapalathy may well have presented them with the papers. For the 1765 belt and the Mekoches, see Speech of Techkumthai, November 15, 1810, CO 42/143, f. 43–44. For the Shawnee term, see M. R. Harrington: "Shawnee Indian Notes," p. 83, EWVP, box 35, folder 319.

33. Journal of Alexander McKee, *PSWJ* 7:185; Croghan to Gage, January 1, 1770, *DAR* 2:22; Extract Taken from my Journal, October 7, 1773, to May 5, 1774, Indian Records, 2, 16:25, reel C-1224, LAC ("only . . ."). For the Thawikilas on the Ohio, see Alford, *Civilization*, 201.

34. Conference at Fort Pitt, April 7–12, 1760, *EAID* 3:544 ("God Who . . ."); *MPCP* 9:528 ("This Country . . ."); Speech of Cornstalk to Congress, November 7, 1776, *EAID* 18:147 ("esteem . . ."); Trowbridge, *Shawnese Traditions*, 55–56 ("the centre . . ."); Speech of the Makujays to the King, Claus Papers, 7:124, reel C-1479, LAC ("hold . . ."); Extract Taken from my Journal, October 7, 1773, to May 5, 1774, Indian Records, 2, 16:29, reel C-1224, LAC ("the Great . . .").

35. Speech of the Makujays to the King, Claus Papers, 7:125, reel C-1479, LAC ("Line"); Major Snake, Capt. Jonny, Thomas Snake, and Chiaxey to Alexander McKee, March 20, 1785, CO 42/48, f. 49 ("the whole . . ."); Wellenreuther and Wessel, *Moravian Mission Diaries*, 109, 113 ("reached . . ." and "many . . .").

36. Adelman and Aron, "From Borderlands to Borders," 816 ("bordered land").

37. Examination of a Delaware Prisoner, 1757, *PA*, 1st Ser., 3:148; Henderson, Jobe, and Turnbow, *Indian Occupation and Use*, 50–54, 60–61; Croghan's Journal, May 15 to October 8, 1765, Alvord and Carter, *New Regime*, 27; Hutchins, "A Description," 194–195 ("in . . ."); Jones, *Journal of Two Visits*, 50–57, 85–89; Extract of a Letter from a Gentleman at Redstone, August 18, 1774, *AA*, 4th Ser., 1:723; Diary of the Indian Congregation in Welhik Thuppeck, on the Muskingum, of the Month of Sept. to October 18, 1772, Moravian Records, reel 8, box 141, folder 13, item 1, pp. 6, 9, NYSL.

38. For the Grenadier Squaw, see A List of the Prisoners Supposed to be at the different Shanoes Towns on Sioto, November 15, 1764, Bouquet Papers 21 655, f. 251, BL; Col. Richard Butler's Journal, 1775, 48, HSP; Kellogg, "Non-hel-ma, Shawnee Princess," 291; Thwaites and Kellogg, *Frontier Defense on the Upper Ohio*, 26. For Anipassicowa, Sepettekenathé, and Wockachaalli, see Jones, *Journal of Two Visits*, 52, 57, 87 (all quotations). Jones does not name the woman chief, but his description fits the details Colesquo gave about Anipassicowa two years later: Treaty at Pittsburgh, 1775, Thwaites and Kellogg, *Revolution on the Upper Ohio*, 115–116. For "fair words," Extract from a Talk from Melonthy, June 8, 1786, *EAID* 18:355.

39. *MPCP* 9:220; Journal of Alexander McKee, October 10–November 27, 1762, *PSWJ* 10:576–577; Conference with Kayaghshota, January 5–15, 1774, *PSWJ* 12:1052 ("Wakatawicks"). The following leaders are directly or indirectly identified as living in the Scioto towns: Kisinoutha (Jones, *Journal of Two Visits*, 52); Miskapalathy (Smallman to Murray, May 16, 1767, Gage Papers, reel 11), Colesquo and Lawoughgua (both in Croghan to Gage, July 6, 1766, Gage Papers, reel 11); Benewessica (*MPCP* 9:232; Benewessica's Speech, January 8, 1765, Bouquet Papers 21 655, f. 261, BL); and Wapemashaway (White Horse) (Jordan, "Journal of James Kenny," 30–31). Just as importantly, *no* leader is identifiable as an Upper Shawnee. The only Muskingum Shawnee headman who is named in the colonial documents is Othawakeesquo, who appears only when he was murdered by Virginian squatters in 1774: Cornstalk to McKee, May 28, 1774, *EAID* 5:375.

40. Croghan to Gage, July 6, 1766, Gage Papers, reel 11 ("Tired . . ."); Aron, *How the West Was Lost*, 5, 13; Dowd, *War under Heaven*, 241–246; Preston, *Texture of Contact*, 217,

223–225, 229–231; Sosin, *Whitehall and the Wilderness*, 107–108; Ward, *Breaking the Backcountry*, 184–185, 201–202, 257–259.

41. Jones, *Journal of Two Visits*, 65, ("God . . ."), 67, 69 ("a very . . ."); Col. Richard Butler's Journal, 1775, 44–48, HSP ("head woman . . ."). For women speaking for peace, see also Turnbull to Gage, September 30, 1769, Gage Papers, reel 5.

42. Speech of Red Hawk, *PSWJ* 7:407–408 ("foolish," "rash," "unthinking"); Voegelin, *Shawnee Stems*, 372 (mayaanileni); Richard Cummins to Thomas H. Harvey, January 13, 1849, RG 75, M234, roll 303, frame 0128, NA ("a common Indian"); McKenney and Hall, *Indian Tribes of North America*, 243.

43. *MPCP* 9:222; Smallman to McKee, November 8, 1764, *PSWJ* 11:403–404; Croghan to Gage, July 7, 1766, Gage Papers, reel 11; Smallman to Murray, May 16, 1767, ibid.; Jehu Hay to William Johnson, *PSWJ* 5:649. For the French removal to the west side of the Mississippi, see Aron, *American Confluence*, 50–51, 54–55. Rumors of French return persisted in the Mississippi Valley and elsewhere for years, suggesting that some Indians hoped for such a development; Dowd, "French King Wakes Up in Detroit," 266–268.

44. Croghan to Gage, July 7, 1766, Gage Papers, reel 11; *MPCP* 9:528 (quotation); Dowd, *War under Heaven*, 217–233.

45. Johnson to Gage, December 16, 1768, *PSWJ* 6:536 ("Every . . ."). For the Treaty of Fort Stanwix and its complex background, see Campbell, *Speculators in Empire*; McConnell, *Country Between*, 239, 244–260; Sosin, *Whitehall and the Wilderness*, 105–110, 169–180. For the efforts of the British military and officials to evict squatters from Indian lands, see also Preston, *Texture of Contact*, 253–259.

46. Journal of Alexander McKee, *PSWJ* 7:184–185 ("in a . . ." and "complained . . ."); Speech of Red Hawk, ibid., 406–407 ("the Six Nations . . ."); Indian Speech, June 26, 1775, Haldimand Papers 21 845, f. 483, BL ("we cannot . . ."); Extract Taken from my Journal, October 7, 1773, to May 5, 1774, Indian Records, 2, 16:27, reel C-1224, LAC ("dissapointed . . ."); Aron, *How the West Was Lost*, 18–19; Callender to Penn, April 21, 1771, *PA*, 1st Ser., 4:412.

47. Preston, *Texture of Contact*, 231–243. To estimate the number of Shawnees involved in the murders I have followed the detailed table offered by David Preston (Table 3) but added six reported cases of violence (in 1762, 1765, 1769, two in 1773, and 1774) not included in his data. For these incidents, see Jordan, "Journal of James Kenny," 43; Wainwright, "George Croghan's Journal," 421–422; Croghan to Amherst, October 5, 1762, *PSWJ* 10:543–544; Extract of a Letter from Fort Loudoun, 1765, *PA*, 1st Ser., 4:218; McKee to Croghan, February 20, 1770, *PSWJ* 7:404; Speech of Red Hawk, *PSWJ* 7:407; Basset to Gage, April 29, 1773, Haldimand Papers 21 730, f. 44, BL; Diary of the Congregation in Welhik Thuppek and Gnadenhütten, March 27 to June 8, 1773, Moravian Records, reel 8, box 141, folder 13, p. 3, NYSL; Journal of Alexander McKee, February 26 to March 1, 1774, *PSWJ* 7:1080; McKee to Johnson, March 3, 1774, *PSWJ* 7:1082. For the cultural context of the violence, see Heckewelder, *Narrative of the Mission of the United Brethren*, 246–247; McConnell, *Country Between*, 238–245; White, *Middle Ground*, 339–351.

48. *MPCP* 9:517–520 ("foolish . . ." and "unhappy . . ." from 520). For other condolence ceremonies, see also Croghan to Gage, June 15, 1766, Gage Papers, reel 10; Edmonstone to Gage, February 12, 1768, McKee to Croghan, February 13, 1768, and Croghan to

Gage, April 14, 1768, all in Gage Papers, reel 11. For British fears of a new Indian war, see Preston, *Texture of Contact*, 224; Sosin, *Whitehall and the Wilderness*, 107–109.

49. Trowbridge, *Shawnese Traditions*, 13–14; Speech of Red Hawk, *PSWJ* 7:407–408 ("involves . . ."; "some of . . ."); Sugden, *Shawnee in Tecumseh's Time*, 39; Croghan to Gage, June 15, 1766, Gage Papers, reel 10 ("young men . . ."; "their young People"); McKee to Croghan, February 13, 1768, Gage Papers, reel 11.

50. Croghan to Johnson, *PSWJ* 7:182 (quotation); Dowd, *Spirited Resistance*, 25–27; Dowd, *War under Heaven*, 264–266. For the importance of the Shawnees' wide kinship networks and alliances for their pan-Indian activities, see Spero, "Stout, Bold, Cunning."

51. Journal of Alexander McKee, *PSWJ* 7:184–185 ("to Defend . . ." from 184); Gage to Hillsborough, August 18, 1770, and Gage to Hillsborough, November 12, 1770, both in *DAR* 2:169, 253; Johnson to Hillsborough, April 4, 1772, *DAR* 5:59–60; Johnson to Darthmouth, February 13, 1775, *DAR* 9:46–47; Journal of George Croghan, October 16–December 17, 1767, *PSWJ* 13:433; Croghan to Gage, January 1, 1770, *DAR* 2:22; Lord to Gage, September 11, 1772, Gage Papers, reel 12; Turnbull to Gage, September 30, 1769, Gage Papers, reel 5; Stuart to Lord Botetourt, January 13, 1770, and Stuart to Hillsborough, May 2, 1770, both in CO 5/71, p. 1, f. 61–62, 105–106; Stuart to Cameron, February 23, 1771, *DAR* 3:43 ("at the head . . ."). For the Scioto conferences, see also Dowd, *Spirited Resistance*, 44–46; Dowd, *War under Heaven*, 264–266; McConnell, *Country Between*, 264–269.

52. For accommodationists and militants, see Dowd, *Spirited Resistance*, xviii–xxi. There were several Ohio Iroquois settlements north of the lower Shawnee towns on the Scioto, and some Iroquoians had settled in Wakatomika: Tanner, *Atlas*, 80; Extract Taken from a Journal of Indian Transactions, *AA*, 4th Ser., 1:481. For headmen lamenting their difficulties in controlling the Iroquois, see Journal of Alexander McKee, October 7, 1773, *PSWJ* 12:1032–1033. The problems posed by multiethnic communities to tribal leaders have also been emphasized by Calloway, *American Revolution in the Indian Country*, 60.

53. Conference with Kayagshota, January 5–15, 1774, and Journal of Alexander McKee, February 26–March 1, 1774, both in *PSWJ* 12:1046–1049, 1056–1059, 1080–1081; Extract Taken from my Journal, October 7, 1773, to May 5, 1774, Indian Records, 2, 16:27, reel C-1224, LAC ("out of . . ."); Croghan to Gage, June 15, 1766, Gage Papers, reel 10 ("Ignorant . . ."); Speech of Red Hawk, *PSWJ* 7:408 ("the English . . ."); Extract from a Talk from Melonthy to John Wyllys, June 8, 1786, *EAID* 18:355 ("only . . ."). For Native perceptions of colonial political and legal systems, especially the use of coercion, see White, *Middle Ground*, 344; Dowd, *War under Heaven*, 65–66; Saunt, *New Order of Things*, 27–31.

54. For British retrenchment in the West, see Dowd, *War under Heaven*, 233–246; Hinderaker, *Elusive Empires*, 170–175; White, *Middle Ground*, 353–356.

55. For the killings, see Stevens, "His Majesty's 'Savage' Allies," 166. For Wakatomikans among the victims, see Zeisberger's Letter, May 27, 1774, *AA*, 4th Ser., 1:285. For Lower Shawnees, see Account of the Rise of the Indian War, 1774, *PA*, 1st Ser., 4:569; Cornstalk to McKee, May 28, 1774, *EAID* 5:375. For Wakatomikan retaliation, Mr. McKee's 3rd Journal, May 30–June 13, 1774, Indian Records, 2, 16:5–6, 8, reel C-1224, LAC; Diary of Schönbrunn, from May 22 to September 12, 1774, Moravian Records, reel 8, box 141, folder 14, item 1, p. 2, NYSL. For the Treaty of Camp Charlotte,

see William Fleming's Journal, and Christian to Preston, November 8, 1774, both in Thwaites and Kellogg, *Documentary History of Dunmore's War*, 290–291, 304; Stevens, "His Majesty's 'Savage' Allies," 244–245.

CHAPTER FOUR. "A STRUGGLE WITH DEATH"

1. Cashin, "'But Brothers,'" 241; Jennings, "Indians' Revolution," 322; Calloway, *American Revolution in the Indian Country*, 288; Calloway, "Continuing Revolution in Indian Country," 3.
2. Cruzat to Miró, August 23, 1784, SMV 2:117.
3. Stevens, "His Majesty's 'Savage' Allies," 354–357; Diary 1775, Thwaites and Kellogg, *Revolution on the Upper Ohio*, 36, 44, 47–48, 54, 58–63 ("Confirm . . ." from 59; "do every . . ." from 61).
4. Diary 1775, Thwaites and Kellogg, *Revolution on the Upper Ohio*, 58 ("the Shawanese . . ."), 63 ("the Indians . . ."). For the famine, see Diary of Schönbrunn, from September 13, 1774, to the end of February 1775, Moravian Records, reel 8, box 141, folder 15, item 1, p. 26, NYSL; Diary of Schönbrunn for March, April, and May 1775, ibid., p. 8. For Shawnee losses in Dunmore's War, see Stevens, "His Majesty's 'Savage' Allies," 243.
5. For the divisions in colonial communities, see Crow, "Liberty Men and Loyalists"; Sleeper-Smith, "'Ignorant Bigots and busy rebels'"; Sosin, *Revolutionary Frontier*, 93–102. For Native divisions, see Calloway, *American Revolution in the Indian Country*, 26–46 ("division and confusion" from 26; "family quarrel" from 28; "they never . . ." from 33); Graymont, *Iroquois in the American Revolution*, 48–85; O'Donnell, *Southern Indians in the American Revolution*, 12–33; Stevens, "His Majesty's 'Savage' Allies," 306–312, 404–406; White, *Middle Ground*, 366–367.
6. Historians agree that the Indian-colonial warfare in the Ohio Valley during the Revolutionary War continued the older struggle for Kentucky; see Calloway, *American Revolution in the Indian Country*, 163–164. For insightful analyses of state intervention and its results, see Harper, "State Intervention"; and Hinderaker, *Elusive Empires*, 199–204. For British and colonial views on using Indians as military allies and their policies in the Ohio Country, see Allen, *His Majesty's Indian Allies*, 44–48; Sosin, *Revolutionary Frontier*, 87–89; Stevens, "His Majesty's 'Savage' Allies," 314, 322, 354–356, 396–405, 410–416.
7. Stevens, "His Majesty's 'Savage' Allies," 314, 321–322; Diary 1775, Thwaites and Kellogg, *Revolution on the Upper Ohio*, 61 ("Virginians . . ."); Indian Speech, June 26, 1775, Haldimand Papers 21 845, f. 483, BL ("coming . . ." and "not come . . .").
8. Shawnee Message to Morgan, February 28, 1777, GMLB 1 ("sit still"); Arbuckle to Fleming, August 15, 1776, Thwaites and Kellogg, *Revolution on the Upper Ohio*, 187 ("Constantly . . ."); Report of William Wilson, September 20, 1776, GMLB 2 ("heart . . ."; "it was . . ."); Speech of Cornstalk to Congress, November 7, 1776, EAID 18:147. For Mekoche diplomacy at Pittsburgh, see also Treaty at Pittsburgh, 1775, Thwaites and Kellogg, *Revolution on the Upper Ohio*, 74–127; and Meeting with the Chiefs and Warriors of the Several Tribes of the Shawanese at Fort Dunmore, July 16–19, 1775, *Revolutionary Virginia*, 7, pt. 2, 764–774. The Mekoche presence in British councils in Detroit (Colesquo and Kisinoutha) and Niagara (Oweeconnee) in 1776 is documented in Report of William Wilson, September 20, 1776, GMLB 2. For demands that

neither Americans nor British send armies through Indian lands, see Speech of the Shawnees to Morgan, April 24, 1776, *EAID* 18:116; Conference with Indians at Fort Pitt, July 6, 1776, *AA* 5, pt. 1, 36–37.

9. For the raids in 1775, see Treaty at Pittsburgh, 1775, Thwaites and Kellogg, *Revolution on the Upper Ohio*, 92–93, 101–102, 117–118; Council at Pittsburgh, October 29 to November 6, 1776, *EAID* 18:139. For the 1776 raids, see Commissioners to the Committee of Congress, August 2, 1776, and Report of William Wilson, September 20, 1776, both in GMLB 2; Arbuckle to Fleming, August 15, 1776, Thwaites and Kellogg, *Revolution on the Upper Ohio*, 186–187; Wellenreuther and Wessel, *Moravian Mission Diaries*, 331, 336. For Shawnee neutrality in 1776, see Lockhart to the Chairman of the Committee of Botetourt, May 14, 1775, *Revolutionary Virginia*, 7, pt. 1, 135 ("the Shanese . . ."). For the connections between Pluggy's Iroquois and the Shawnees, see Morgan to the Commissioner or Agent of Indian Affairs, March 9, 1777, GMLB 1; Morgan to Hancock, November 8, 1776, ibid.; Minutes of Intelligence received from the White Mingo, October 18, 1776, GMLB 2. The role of the Ohio Iroquois is discussed in Calloway, *American Revolution in the Indian Country*, 32–33; Parmenter, "Iroquois and the Native American Struggle," 114. For a detailed analysis of the early hostilities, see Stevens, "His Majesty's 'Savage' Allies," 473, 483, 540–541.

10. Col. Richard Butler's Journal, 1775, 34–47, HSP (quotations from 35 and 45).

11. Hand to Yeates, July 12, 1777, Thwaites and Kellogg, *Frontier Defense on the Upper Ohio*, 20 (quotation). For Aquitsica's and Sepettekenathé's cooperation with the Mekoches, see Meeting with the Chiefs and Warriors of the Several Tribes of the Shawanese at Fort Dunmore, July 16, 1775, *Revolutionary Virginia*, 7, pt. 2, 765; Council at Pittsburgh, October 29 to November 6, 1776, *EAID* 18:139; Shawnee Message to Morgan, February 28, 1777, GMLB 1. Kisinoutha's house is described in Jones, *Journal of Two Visits*, 52–54. For Sepettekenathé's trading activities and possible kin connections to the Mekoches, see Sugden, *Blue Jacket*, 26–27, 33, 275.

12. For intensifying Shawnee attacks, see Clark's "Diary," December 25, 1776, to March 30, 1777, James, *George Rogers Clark Papers*, 1:22–23; Delaware Council to Morgan, February 26, 1777, and Shawnee Message to Morgan, February 28, 1777, both in GMLB 1; Council held at Detroit, June 17–24, 1777, CO 42/37, f. 70–77. The attacks and changing British policies are analyzed in Stevens, "His Majesty's 'Savage' Allies," 884–885, 915–916, 960, 963–968, 973–975, 1029–1039. For Shawnee perspectives on the Shawnee-British alliance, see Calloway, *American Revolution in the Indian Country*, 163–167; Sugden, *Blue Jacket*, 50–54. For Black Fish, see Galloway, *Old Chillicothe*, 55–56; Stevens, "His Majesty's 'Savage' Allies," 2190.

13. A Message from the Delaware Council to Morgan, February 26, 1777, GMLB 1 ("foolish . . .," "Virginians"); Morgan to Hancock, November 8, 1776, ibid.; Arbuckle to Hand, July 26, 1777, DM, 3NN71–73; Diary of Gnadenhütten, from January to May 25, 1777, Moravian Records, reel 9, box 144, folder 13, item 1, NYSL ("his people . . ."); Speech of the Shawnees to Morgan, April 24, 1776, *EAID* 18:116.

14. Shawnee Message to Morgan, February 28, 1777, GMLB 1; Arbuckle to Hand, July 26, 1777, DM, 3NN71–72; Wilson, "An Acc't of the Indian Towns," 345; Zeisberger to Hand, November 16, 1777, Thwaites and Kellogg, *Frontier Defense on the Upper Ohio*, 166; White Eyes and Killbuck to Morgan, March 14, 1778, GMLB 3; White Eyes, Teytapaukasheh, William Chillaways, and Isaac Leykhickon to Morgan, April 25,

1778, ibid.; Wellenreuther and Wessel, *Moravian Mission Diaries*, 383, 421, 424, 430–431, 433, 443; Tanner, *Atlas*, 80–81; Wheeler-Voegelin, "Ethnohistory of Indian Use and Occupancy," 554–583. For Colesquo's murder, Arbuckle to Hand, October 6, 1777, Arbuckle to Hand, November 7, 1777, and Portion of the Narrative of Capt. John Stuart, all in Thwaites and Kellogg, *Frontier Defense on the Upper Ohio*, 126–127, 149–150, 157–163; White Eyes and Killbuck to Morgan, March 14, 1778, GMLB 3; Stevens, "His Majesty's 'Savage' Allies," 1508–1512. For Coshocton, see Dowd, *Spirited Resistance*, 68–83.

15. Shawnee Message to Morgan, February 28, 1777, GMLB 1 ("not see . . ."); Sugden, *Blue Jacket*, 52–54. Although Sugden asserts that Aquitsica followed the Mekoches east, he was in Detroit demanding British military assistance as early as September 1779, when the Mekoches still remained at peace on the Muskingum: Indian Speech to Capt. R. B. Lernoult, September 26, 1779, *MPHC* 19:468–470.

16. Hamilton to Carleton, April 25, 1778, CO 42/38, f. 98–100; Council held at Detroit, June 14–20, 1778, Haldimand Papers 21 782, f. 45–51, BL; Hamilton to Haldimand, September 15–16, 1778, ibid., f. 105–106; Bowman to Clark, October 14, 1778, James, *George Rogers Clark Papers*, 1:69–70. For the marriages, see Sugden, *Blue Jacket*, 31–32; Nelson, *Man of Distinction*, 63; Last Will of Louis Lorimier, March 12, 1808, Rodney Family Papers, MHS.

17. Brodhead to Washington, April 24, 1780, *PA*, 1st Ser., 12:223; Wheeler-Voegelin, "Ethnohistory of Indian Use and Occupancy," 571–573; Stuart to Stuart, August 25, 1776, *DAR* 7:201–206 (quotation from 203); Cameron to Lord George Germain, July 18, 1780, *DAR* 18:121; Dowd, *Spirited Resistance*, 55, 58–59, 109–110; Bird to De Peyster, Haldimand Papers 21 760, f. 316, BL; McKee to De Peyster, ibid., f. 316–317.

18. Brodhead to Washington, April 24, 1780, *PA*, 1st Ser., 12:223 ("renegadoes . . ."); Montgomery, "Journal of Samuel Montgomery," 272 ("banditti . . ."); Knox to St. Clair, Smith, *Life and Public Services of Arthur St. Clair*, 2:148 ("regular tribes").

19. Zeisberger to Morgan, August 19, 1778, GMLB 3; Wellenreuther and Wessel, *Moravian Mission Diaries*, 455, 457–458, 501.

20. Kelleleman to Maghingive Keeshuch, September 21, 1779, *EAID* 18:194–195; Heckewelder, *Narrative of the Mission of the United Brethren*, 329–330; Wellenreuther and Wessel, *Moravian Mission Diaries*, 493; A Council held at Detroit, April 5, 1781, Haldimand Papers 21 783, f. 18–20, BL ("our Chief"). Nimwha's death is reported in Delawares and Mequochoke-Shawnee to Brodhead, February 17, 1780, Kellogg, *Frontier Retreat on the Upper Ohio*, 139. Kisinoutha's death is not mentioned in any contemporary document, but I have seen no reference to him after February 1780, and even that document refers to him in the past tense. For the perils of neutrality in the upper Ohio Valley, see Dowd, *Spirited Resistance*, 65–89.

21. Dowd, *Spirited Resistance*, 59; De Peyster to Bolton, March 10, 1780, Haldimand Papers 21 760, f. 273–274, BL ("surrounded"); Speech of the Delawares & Shawanese to De Peyster, August 22, 1780, Haldimand Papers 21 782, f. 383, BL; De Peyster to Haldimand, November 3, 1781, Haldimand Papers 21 783, f. 113–114, BL.

22. Bolton to Haldimand, June 27, 1779, Haldimand Papers 21 760, f. 147–148, BL; McKee to De Peyster, August 22, 1780, and Speech of the Delawares & Shawanese to De Peyster, August 22, 1780, both in Haldimand Papers 21 782, f. 381–383, BL; Clark to

Jefferson, August 22, 1780, James, *George Rogers Clark Papers*, 1:452 ("destroyed . . ."); McKee to De Peyster, November 15, 1782, Haldimand Papers 21 783, f. 270, BL; Clark to Irvine, November 13, 1782, James, *George Rogers Clark Papers*, 2:153.

23. Speech of the Delawares & Shawanese to De Peyster, August 22, 1780, Haldimand Papers 21 782, f. 383, BL ("Our Women . . ."); De Peyster to Haldimand, August 31, 1780, ibid., f. 387–388 ("wretched . . ."); Bolton to Haldimand, August 10, 1779, Haldimand Papers 21 760, f. 187, BL ("very . . ."). For British presents, see To the Chiefs and Warriors of the Mingoes, Hurons, Delawares, and Shawanese, December 4, 1779, Haldimand Papers 21 782, f. 301, BL; McKee to De Peyster, October 10, 1781, *MPHC* 10:525–526. For the development of Indian dependence on British supplies during the Revolutionary War, see Calloway, *American Revolution in the Indian Country*, 57, 129; Mancall, "Revolutionary War and the Indians."

24. At a Council held at Detroit, April 5, 1781, Haldimand Papers 21 783, f. 18–20, BL ("They are . . ."); Turney to De Peyster, June 7, 1782, ibid., f. 169–170; A Letter from Captain Caldwell, August 26, 1782, ibid., f. 231–232; De Peyster to Haldimand, January 7, 1783, ibid., f. 282–283; De Peyster to Maclean, January 7, 1783, Haldimand Papers 21 763, f. 1, BL ("to fear . . .").

25. Haldimand to Townshend, October 23, 1783, *DAR* 21:126 ("thunderstruck"); Maclean to Haldimand, May 18, 1783, Haldimand Papers 21 763, f. 118–119, BL ("Conduct . . .," "King could . . ."); Craig, "Gen. Butler's Journal," 522 ("You seem . . ."). For general treatments of the Treaty of Paris and Native reactions, see Allen, *His Majesty's Indian Allies*, 55–56; Calloway, *Crown and Calumet*, 5–13; Calloway, *American Revolution in the Indian Country*, 272–277; Graymont, *Iroquois in the American Revolution*, 258–260; Horsman, "American Indian Policy," 35–40; Horsman, *Expansion and American Indian Policy*, 3–5; Horsman, "Indian Policy of an 'Empire of Liberty,'" 37. For an excellent discussion on how the Revolution changed American policies toward Indian lands, see Banner, *How the Indians Lost Their Land*, 112–129.

26. Major Wall's Speech to the Shawanese, July 7, 1783, CO 42/45, f. 7 ("neglected . . ."); In Council at Detroit, July 30, 1783, Haldimand Papers 21 763, f. 207–209, BL; Minutes of Transactions with Indians at Sandusky, CO 42/45, f. 9–14. For British policies, see also Allen, *His Majesty's Indian Allies*, 55–68; Calloway, *Crown and Calumet*, 3, 6–16; Graymont, *Iroquois in the American Revolution*, 277–278; Willig, *Restoring the Chain of Friendship*, 12–30. For the role of the British Indian agents, see Horsman, "British Indian Department"; Nelson, *Man of Distinction*, 149–152, 175.

27. Daniel to Harrison, May 21, 1784, *CVSP* 3:586 ("he hoped . . ."); Speeches from the Shawanees and Wyandots, March 2, 1784, ibid., 565; Major Snake, Capt. Jonny, Thomas Snake, and Chiaxey to Alexander McKee, March 20, 1785, CO 42/48, f. 49.

28. Tanner, *Atlas*, 81; McKee to De Peyster, June 4, 1780, Haldimand Papers 21 760, f. 326, BL ("Wakitumikée . . ."); McKee to De Peyster, May 24, 1783, Haldimand Papers 21 763, f. 125, BL ("some . . ."); Major Snake, Capt. Jonny, Thomas Snake, and Chiaxey to McKee, March 20, 1785, CO 42/48, f. 49 ("that they . . ."). For the identity of Peteusha and Shemonetoo, see Heckewelder, *Narrative of the Mission of the United Brethren*, 352; Sugden, *Blue Jacket*, 285–286.

29. Cruzat to Miró, March 19, 1782, *SRM* 1:209–210; Cruzat to Miró, August 23, 1784, *SMV* 2:117–119. For more information on the Shawnee migrants and Spanish motives,

see Chapter 6. Warren, *Shawnees and Their Neighbors*, 69, has described the Shawnee migration to the west as "a third way."

30. Minutes of Transactions with Indians at Sandusky, CO 42/45, f. 9–14 (quotations). For the Sandusky council and its context, see Calloway, *Crown and Calumet*, 14–16; Downes, *Council Fires on the Upper Ohio*, 282–284; Sugden, *Blue Jacket*, 66–67; White, *Middle Ground*, 413–416. For the novel idea of collective Indian landownership, see Sugden, *Tecumseh*, 44–45; Wallace, "Political Organization and Land Tenure," 311–312.

31. Speeches from the Shawanees and Wyandots, March 2, 1784, CVSP 3:565 ("Great . . ."); Major Snake, Capt. Jonny, Thomas Snake, and Chiaxey to Alexander McKee, March 20, 1785, CO 42/48, f. 49 ("the whole . . ."); A Council held at Wakitumikee, May 18, 1785, CO 42/47, f. 370–371 ("you will . . ."). For the treaties of Fort Stanwix and Fort McIntosh, see Graymont, *Iroquois in the American Revolution*, 273–284; Downes, *Council Fires on the Upper Ohio*, 292–295; Horsman, *Expansion and American Indian Policy*, 17–21.

32. Montgomery, "Journal of Samuel Montgomery," 272; Indian Speech to Alexander McKee, September 20, 1785, CO 42/48, f. 211 ("determined . . ."); Peteusha's Speech, November 8, 1785, CO 42/49, f. 41 ("nothing . . ."); Craig, "Gen. Butler's Journal," 512. For Aquitsica's death, see Speeches from the Shawanees and Wyandots, March 2, 1784, CVSP 3:565.

33. Craig, "Gen. Butler's Journal," 513 ("go . . ."), 522 ("on the . . ."); McKee to Johnson, February 25, 1786, CO 42/49, f. 258–259 ("to enter . . ."); Stephen Ruddell's Narrative, DM, 2YY120 ("a king . . ."). For Ruddell's background, see Sugden, *Tecumseh*, 4–5. For Nehinissica, see Craig, "Gen. Butler's Journal," 529–530 ("young chief," "value[d] highly"); Logan to the Shawnees, August 20, 1787, DM, 18CC7 ("the Young Prince"). Richard White has presented a similar interpretation of the motives of the Lenape and Wyandot leaders to participate in the Treaty of Fort McIntosh; White, *Middle Ground*, 436–437.

34. Craig, "Gen. Butler's Journal," 513–531; Reply of the Indians to the Commissioners of the United States, August 13, 1793, MPHC 24:588 ("Through fear . . ."); Articles of a Treaty Concluded at the Mouth of the Great Miami, January 21, 1786, Peters, *Public Statutes at Large*, 7:27; Denny, *Military Journal of Major Ebenezer Denny*, 72–76, 86–87, 93 ("their king . . ." from 87); McKee to Johnson, February 25, 1786, CO 42/49, f. 258–259; McDowell to Henry, April 18, 1786, CVSP 4:118; May to Henry, April 19, 1786, CVSP 4:119; Report of Mr. Philip Liebert, July 20, 1786, Smith, *Life and Public Services of Arthur St. Clair*, 2:17; Wheeler-Voegelin, "Ethnohistory of Indian Use and Occupancy," 565; Message from the Shawanese, April 29, 1786, CO 42/49, f. 349; Extract of a Talk from Melonthy to John Wyllys, June 8, 1786, EAID 18:355 ("very . . .," "young men," "under . . .").

35. Horsman, *Expansion and American Indian Policy*, 32–37; Denny, *Military Journal of Major Ebenezer Denny*, 93–94; Girty to McKee, October 11, 1786, MPHC 24:34; Ancrum to [?], October 20, 1786, MPHC 24:37–38; Sword, *President Washington's Indian War*, 31–41.

36. The Speech of Captain Johnny, August 20, 1787, DM, 18CC7 ("all my . . ."). I base my estimate of the number of the Maumee migrants on British censuses from the early 1790s, for example, List of Nations who receive Presents at Swan Creek, December 4,

1794, Claus Papers, 6:289, reel C-1479, LAC. For the western migrants, see Hamtramck to Harmar, October 13, 1788, Thornbrough, *Outpost on the Wabash*, 123–124; Hamtramck to Harmar, April 11, 1789, ibid., 167; Sugden, *Tecumseh*, 420; Du Lac, *Travels through the Two Louisianas*, 45 ("two tribes"). For an overall picture of these migrations, see Tanner, *Atlas*, 86–89, 93, 95.

37. Gamelin's Journal, April 5 to May 5, 1790, *ASPIA* 1:93–94; Denny, *Military Journal of Major Ebenezer Denny*, 145–147; Quaife, "Henry Hay's Journal," 223, 248, 255; Proceedings of the General Council held at the Glaize, September 30 to October 9, 1792, Indian Affairs, 8:8251, reel C-10 999, LAC; Quaife, *Indian Captivity of O. M. Spencer*, 77–86, 89–90, 95–97; Sugden, *Blue Jacket*, 79–80; Tanner, "Glaize in 1792"; Tanner, *Atlas*, 87–91.

38. White, *Middle Ground*, 448–456; Nelson, *Man of Distinction*, 149, 157–158; Tanner, "Glaize in 1792," 25–30.

39. For confederacy councils held between the Sandusky and Brownstown meetings, see At a Council held at Wakitumikee, May 18, 1785, CO 42/47, f. 370–371; Report of the Council at Loyal Village, August 2, 1785, CO 42/48, f. 121–125; A Council held at Niagara, July 25, 1786, CO 42/49, f. 375–378. For the Brownstown conference, see Speech of the United Indian Nations to Congress, December 18, 1786, *EAID* 18:356–358 (quotations from 357).

40. Putnam to Knox, July 8, 1792, Smith, *Life and Public Services of Arthur St. Clair*, 2:303 (quotation); Indian Speech to Alexander McKee, September 20, 1785, CO 42/48, f. 211; Sugden, *Blue Jacket*, 88–97.

41. At a Council held at Wakitumikee, May 18, 1785, CO 42/47, f. 370–371 ("the people . . ."); Indian Speech to Alexander McKee, September 20, 1785, CO 42/48, f. 211 ("Brown Skins"); Proceedings of the General Council held at the Glaize, September 30 to October 9, 1792, Indian Affairs, 8:8242–8281 ("all nations . . ."; "with . . ."), reel C-10 999, LAC. For the eastern prophetic tradition and its influence on the Indian Confederacy, see Dowd, *Spirited Resistance*, 23–46, 90–115.

42. The rise of the racial ideology among the Indians of eastern North America is discussed by Richter, *Facing East*, 180–182, 189–208; Shoemaker, "How Indians Got to Be Red"; Shoemaker, *Strange Likeness*, 125–140.

43. Waweyapiersenwaw's career is traced in Sugden, *Blue Jacket*. For his commission, see Wayne to Knox, February 6, 1795, Knopf, *Anthony Wayne*, 390 ("War Chief"). For Peteusha, Speech of Captain Snake, June 8, 1782, Butterfield, *Washington–Irvine Correspondence*, 369–370; Hamtramck to Harmar, May 21, 1788, Thornbrough, *Outpost of the Wabash*, 80–81; Kekewepelethy is identified as a Wakatomikan and a war leader in Craig, "Gen. Butler's Journal," 513; Denny, *Military Journal of Major Ebenezer Denny*, 73. For Kekewepelethy's reputation after the Treaty of Fort Finney, see Sugden, *Blue Jacket*, 71–72.

44. Anglo-Americans usually called Biaseka "Wolf." In an important message that the Indian Confederacy sent to the U.S. peace commissioners in 1793 the Shawnees were represented by a picture of a wolf, making it quite possible that the Shawnee signatory was Biaseka: Speech of the Chiefs of the Western Nations in behalf of the Indian American Confederacy, August 13, 1793, *MPHC* 24:598. For Musquaconocah as an advocate of the confederacy, see Proceedings of the General Council held at the Glaize, September 30 to October 9, 1792, Indian Affairs, 8:8251–8281, reel C-10 999,

LAC. For Biaseka and Peteusha, see Quaife, "Henry Hay's Journal," 255 ("to gather . . ."). The relationship between Waweyapiersenwaw and Musquaconocah is traced in Sugden, *Blue Jacket*, 26. For Kekewepelethy as an "aid" of the Mekoche leaders, see Denny, *Military Journal of Major Ebenezer Denny*, 68–69.

45. Diary of an Officer in the Indian Country, *Simcoe Papers*, 5:91 ("for his . . ."); Journal, *MPHC* 24:221 ("Maycoché," "Pickeardé"); Quaife, "Henry Hay's Journal," 248 ("Chilicothe"); List of Nations who Received Presents at Swan Creek, December 4, 1794, Claus Papers, 6:291, LAC ("Kiskapoo").

46. The Secretary of Congress to Governor St. Clair, October 26, 1787, *TPUS* 2:79 ("every . . ."); St. Clair to the President, May 2, 1789, *ASPIA* 1:10 ("general . . ."). For the Treaty of Fort Harmar and its context, see Horsman, *Expansion and American Indian Policy*, 38–49; Downes, *Council Fires on the Upper Ohio*, 303–309; Kelsay, *Joseph Brant*, 418–426.

47. Downes, *Council Fires on the Upper Ohio*, 310–314; Kelsay, *Joseph Brant*, 434–436; Cayton, " 'Separate Interests.' " For the battles, see Denny, *Military Journal of Major Ebenezer Denny*, 143–149, 164–171; Meek, "General Harmar's Expedition," 74–108; St. Clair to the Secretary of War, November 9, 1791, Smith, *Life and Public Services of Arthur St. Clair*, 2:262–267; Sugden, *Blue Jacket*, 99–106, 113–127; Sword, *President Washington's Indian War*, 89–120, 155–191.

48. For Indian hunger and need for British goods, see Aupaumut, "Narrative of an Embassy to the Western Indians," 86; Blue Jacket's Speech and Answer, CO 42/73, f. 39–41; McKee to Johnson, November 1, 1791, *MPHC* 24:330; A Speech of the Shawanoes & other Western Nations, May 16, 1792, Indian Affairs, 8:8242–8243, reel C-10 999, LAC. For the fields along the Maumee, see Quaife, *Indian Captivity of O. M. Spencer*, 85–86, 96–97; Wayne to Knox, August 28, 1794, Knopf, *Anthony Wayne*, 354–355. The dependence is discussed in White, *Middle Ground*, 454–456.

49. Aupaumut, "Narrative of an Embassy to the Western Indians," 86–125; Proceedings of the General Council held at the Glaize, September 30 to October 9, 1792, Indian Affairs, 8:8251–8281, reel C-10 999, LAC; Brant to Simcoe, September 2, 1793, CO 42/317, f. 298; McKee to Simcoe, August 22, 1793, CO 42/317, f. 309–310; Brant's Journal, *Simcoe Correspondence*, 2:5–17; Expedition to Detroit, 1793, *MPHC* 17:605 ("the young . . ."); Lincoln, Randolph, and Pickering to Knox, August 21, 1793, *ASPIA* 1:359 ("near . . ."); Sugden, *Blue Jacket*, 144.

50. Sugden, *Blue Jacket*, 156–168; White, *Middle Ground*, 464–467.

51. Sugden, *Blue Jacket*, 168–180; Sword, *President Washington's Indian War*, 287–311. Shawnees long remembered the English betrayal at Fort Miamis: T. Worthington and Duncan McArthur to Governor Kirker, September 22, 1807, DM, 7BB49.

52. Wayne to Knox, December 24, 1794, Knopf, *Anthony Wayne*, 370–371 ("succeeded . . ."); Instructions to Capt. Elliot, May 14, 1795, Claus Papers, 7:47, reel C-1479, LAC; Articles of Peace Between Gen. Anthony Wayne and the Indians, *MPHC* 20:393–394; Ironside to McKee, February 6, 1795, Indian Affairs, 9:8840, reel C-10 999, LAC ("more . . ."); Speech of the Makujays to the King, Claus Papers, 7:127, reel C-1479, LAC ("none . . ." and "Younger . . .").

53. Report of the Committee on Northern Indians, August 8, 1787, *EAID* 18:457–458 ("select . . ."; "in the . . ."); The Secretary of Congress to Governor St. Clair, October 26, 1787, *TPUS* 2:79 ("attach . . ."); White, "Fictions of Patriarchy," 73–74.

54. Minutes of a Treaty at Greenville, June 16 to August 10, 1795, *ASPIA* 1:564–583; Treaty of Greenville, August 3, *TPUS* 2:525–534; Sugden, *Blue Jacket*, 184, 202–207. The presence of Chalaakaathas at Greenville is not explicitly stated in the documents. One of the Shawnee signatories of the treaty was "Hah-goo-see-kaw," or "Captain Reed." He may have been the same person as the Chalaakaatha headman Paytakootha, also known as Captain Reed. This identification is not conclusive, however, for in the early nineteenth century several Shawnee leaders were known among English-speakers as Captain Reed. For Paytakootha, see McKenney and Hall, *Indian Tribes of North America*, 172–173.

55. Minutes of a Treaty at Greenville, June 16 to August 10, 1795, *ASPIA* 1:569–578; Treaty of Greenville, August 3, 1795, *TPUS* 2:528–529 ("useful goods").

56. The Secretary of War to the President, September 28, 1795, *TPUS* 2:537 ("the chiefs . . ."); Minutes of a Treaty at Greenville, June 16 to August 10, 1795, *ASPIA* 1:580–581; Wayne to Pickering, March 8, 1795, Knopf, *Anthony Wayne*, 389–390; Pickering to Wayne, May 7, 1795, ibid., 414; Sugden, *Blue Jacket*, 212–216.

57. Many Shawnees and other Maumee Indians planned to move across the Mississippi immediately after the Battle of Fallen Timbers; McKee to Chew, August 27, 1794, *MPHC* 20:372. For the Shawnee migration to Canada, see Ironside to Shelby, July 7, 1796, Claus Papers, 7:247, reel C-1479, LAC; Ironside to Shelby, July 18, 1796, *MPHC* 20:458. The Kishpoko movements are traced in Sugden, *Tecumseh*, 97. For the witchcraft killings, see Elliot to McKee, September 30, 1797, Indian Affairs, 26:15133, reel C-11 006, LAC.

58. Speech of Blackbeard, 1806, Shawnee File, OVGLEA. Note that this document is erroneously dated at 1806. That Nenessica made this speech in 1807 is established in Thomas Jefferson to the Chiefs of the Shawnee Nation, February 19, 1807, Washington, *Writings of Thomas Jefferson*, 206.

CHAPTER FIVE. "BECOME AN INDEPENDENT PEOPLE"

1. The Shawanoes in Answer to Kirk, April 14, 1809, RG 107, M221, roll 25, NA. Although the documents do not identify Catahecassa as the speaker who gave this talk, this is likely, for he had just made two other speeches at Kirk's farm on behalf of the Wapakonetans. See The Shawnee Chiefs to the Quakers of Baltimore, April 10, 1809, Thornbrough, *Letter Book*, 45–46; The Shawnee Chiefs to the President and Secretary of War, April 10, 1809, ibid., 46–47.

2. Address of Black Hoof, February 5, 1802, Oberg, *Papers of Thomas Jefferson*, 36:517–518 (quotations). For Shawnee fears, see McKee to Chew, October 24, 1795, Indian Affairs, 8:9038, reel C-10 999, LAC. For Shawnee dependence on American and British supplies, see Sargent to Pickering, August 9, 1796, *TPUS* 2:563; Hamtramck to Wayne, April 25, 1795, *MPHC* 34:737; Talk Between Capt. Mayne and Indian Chiefs, June 30, 1797, *MPHC* 20:520–521. For insightful analyses on the connections between land loss, American and Native overhunting, and Indian dependence, see Aron, "Pigs and Hunters," 196; White, *Middle Ground*, 489–493.

3. Speech of Blackbeard, 1806, Shawnee File, OVGLEA (quotation); Sugden, *Tecumseh*, 97; Sugden, *Blue Jacket*, 212.

4. Literature on the civilization program is wide. For general treatments, see Horsman, "American Indian Policy," 47–53; Horsman, *Expansion and American Indian Policy*,

53–65; Sheehan, *Seeds of Extinction*; Wallace, *Death and Rebirth of the Seneca*, 217–220. For American understandings of Indian economies, see Richter, "'Believing That Many of the Red People'"; Usner, "Iroquois Livelihoods and Jeffersonian Agrarianism." The gender aspects of the civilization mission are analyzed by Perdue, *Cherokee Women*, 109–184.

5. Jefferson to Harrison, February 27, 1803, Esarey, *Messages and Letters of William Henry Harrison*, 1:71.

6. Treaty of Greenville, August 3, 1795, *TPUS* 2:529 ("in domestic . . ."); Address of Black Hoof, February 5, 1802, Oberg, *Papers of Thomas Jefferson*, 36:518–519 ("some Farming . . ."; "all necessary . . ."; "some domestick . . ."); Speech of Blackbeard, 1806, Shawnee File, OVGLEA ("to act . . ."); Blackhoof & others to the President and Secretary of War, December 12, 1807, RG 107, M221, roll 4, NA ("We make . . ."). For similar Indian strategies of manipulating the civilization program for Native goals, see Bernstein, "'We Are Not Now as We Once Were'"; Kugel, *To Be the Main Leaders*; Saunt, *New Order of Things*.

7. Report of George Ellicott and Gerard T. Hopkins to Baltimore Yearly Meeting, October 15, 1804, Shawnee File, OVGLEA ("40 head . . ."; "making . . ."); Kirk to Dearborn, May 25, 1807, RG 107, M221, roll 9, NA; Kirk to Dearborn, July 20, 1807, ibid.; Kirk to Dearborn, April 12, 1808, RG 107, M221, roll 25, NA; The Shawnees to the President and Secretary of War, December 1, 1808, ibid.; Duchouquet's Statement, December 4, 1808, ibid. ("built . . .," "at least . . .," "a plentiful . . ."). For Kirk's activities in Wapakoneta, see Edmunds, "'Evil Men Who Add to Our Difficulties.'" For Quakers in other Indians communities, see Rothenberg, "Mothers of the Nation," 72–80; Richter, "'Believing That Many of the Red People,'" 603–604; Wallace, *Death and Rebirth of the Seneca*, 220–228.

8. Duchouquet's Statement, December 4, 1808, RG 107, M221, roll 25, NA ("the advances . . ."); Kirk to Dearborn, April 12, 1808, ibid.; Klinck and Talman, *Journal of Major John Norton*, 189 ("the Men . . ."); Green, "Journal of Ensign William Schillinger," 82.

9. For Kirk, see Edmunds, "'Evil Men Who Add to Our Difficulties,'" 8–11. For Wapakoneta's growth, see Kirk to Dearborn, April 12, 1808, RG 107, M221, roll 25, NA; Johnston to Thomas, April 15, 1809, Thornbrough, *Letter Book*, 41; Diary of an Exploratory Journey of the Brethren Luckenbach and Haven, in Company of the Indian Brother Andreas, August 26–September 13, 1808, Shawnee File, OVGLEA. For Chalaakaathas and Kishpokos at or near Wapakoneta, see Minutes of a Council held at Wapaghkonetta, May 1825, RG 75, M1, roll 28, p. 362, NA; Johnston to Draper, August 21, 1847, Knopf, Papers of John Johnston, 90, OHS.

10. Lewistown seems to have been in existence by 1802; see Johnston to Eustis, January 7, 1812, Knopf, *Document Transcriptions of the War of 1812*, 6, pt. 1, 7. It is less clear when Hog Creek was established. Early population estimates for these communities are not available, but for an 1819 estimate, see Johnston, "Account of the Present State," 270. That at least some of the Hog Creek Shawnees were Chalaakaathas is testified by an 1825 report: Minutes of a Council held at Wapaghkonetta, May 1825, RG 75, M1, roll 28, p. 362, NA. Note that the Captain Johnny of Captain Johnny's Town was not the Wakatomikan leader Kekewepelethy, also known as Captain Johnny. For this community, see Sugden, *Tecumseh*, 128, 431.

11. Wells to Dearborn, December 31, 1807, RG 107, M221, roll 15, NA ("each . . ."); Wells to Dearborn, October 20, 1807, ibid.; Wells to the Secretary of War, September 30, 1807, ibid.; Kirk to Drake, September 16, 1807, DM, 3YY; Address to the Chiefs of the Wyandot, Delaware and Munsee Nation, & the Shawnees, by William Hull, November 11, 1806, Shawnee File, OVGLEA; Blackhoof & others to the President and Secretary of War, December 12, 1807, RG 107, M221, roll 4, NA; An Abstract of Disbursements, Johnston Papers, reel 1, OHS. For American efforts to centralize the tribes of the Old Northwest, see Warren, *Shawnees and Their Neighbors*, 18–23.

12. Blackhoof & others to the President and Secretary of War, December 12, 1807, RG 107, M221, roll 4, NA ("none . . ."); Speech of the Makujays to the King, Claus Papers, 7:124, reel C-1479, LAC ("in the . . ."; "to hold . . ."); Johnston, "Account of the Present State," 275 ("the priesthood . . ."); Trowbridge, *Shawanese Traditions*, 6. The claim that Catahecassa and his Wapakonetan allies were "Americanizing Indians" who "made common cause with the government in Washington" and even "agreed to its aggressive settlement plans" has most recently been advanced in Jortner, *Gods of Prophetstown*, 4, 144. Other historians have disputed such interpretations and demonstrated the commitment of the Wapakonetan leadership to maintaining Shawnee traditions and land rights; see Sugden, *Tecumseh*, 129. Portraying Catahecassa and his associates as politically corrupt cultural apostates may reflect a persistent Euroamerican ideology that deems only unchanging Indigenous cultures as "authentic." It is probably also linked to the fact that, until recently, most scholars have been more interested in the militant Native Americans who took up arms to challenge the U.S. hegemony in the Great Lakes region than in those who chose less violent strategies for defending their autonomy.

13. Minutes of a Council held at Wapaghkonetta, May 1825, RG 75, M1, roll 28, p. 378, NA ("the different . . ."). For Catahecassa, see McKenney and Hall, *Indian Tribes of North America*, 238–246; Sugden, *Blue Jacket*, 128–129; Kirk to Dearborn, May 28, 1807, RG 107, M221, roll 9, NA ("the Principal . . ."). Several documents identify Catahecassa as the speaker for larger delegations of Shawnees; see The Shawanoes to the President and Secretary of War, December 1, 1808, RG 107, M221, roll 25, NA; The Chiefs and Head men of the Shawanoes to their friends the Quakers of Baltimore, April 10, 1809, Thornbrough, *Letter Book*, 45; Minutes of a Council held at Wapaghkonetta, May 1825, RG 75, M1, roll 28, pp. 358–382, NA. For Catahecassa's background as a war chief, see Johnston to Drake, December 14, 1831, DM, 11YY18.

14. Shemanetoo's background is difficult to identify, because several Shawnees around the time were known to Anglo-Americans as "Snake." Shemanetoo was apparently the brother of the Wakatomikan headman Peteusha; Sugden, *Blue Jacket*, 285–286. For his possible Kishpoko connection, see Johnston to Draper, August 21, 1847, Knopf, Papers of John Johnston, 90, OHS. Kayketchheka (William Perry) acted as the spokesman of Pekowis in 1825, and since he seems to have been Pemthala's brother, I surmise that Pemthala was a Pekowi; see Minutes of a Council held at Wapaghkonetta, May 1825, RG 75, M1, roll 28, pp. 380–381, NA.

15. Johnston to Cass, June 14, 1816, RG 75, M1, roll 2, p. 237, NA ("When . . ."); McLoughlin, *Cherokee Renascence*, 59 ("traditionally . . ."); Johnston to Eustis, January 7, 1812, Knopf, *Document Transcriptions of the War of 1812*, 6, pt. 1, 7; McKenney and Hall, *Indian Tribes of North America*, 168–170.

16. The Treaty of Greenville, August 3, 1795, *TPUS* 2:529 (quotation); Owens, "Jeffersonian Benevolence on the Ground"; Sugden, *Tecumseh*, 105–108. For examples of Harrison selecting the "rightful" Indian owners of land, and of his superiors' justification of this, see for example Harrison to Secretary of War, March 25, 1803, Esarey, *Messages and Letters of William Henry Harrison*, 1:47; Jefferson to Harrison, December 22, 1808, ibid., 323; Dearborn to Hull, July 22, 1806, Shawnee File, OVGLEA.

17. Address of Black Hoof, February 5, 1802, Oberg, *Papers of Thomas Jefferson*, 36:517 ("give . . ." and "We . . ."); Dearborn's Reply, February 10, 1802, ibid., 523–524 ("the President . . ."); Blackhoof & others to the President and Secretary of War, December 12, 1807, RG 107, M221, roll 4, NA ("the proportial . . ."); Shawnee Chiefs' Speech to the Secretary of War, December 29, 1815, Shawnee File, OVGLEA. For Lenapes, see Weslager, *Delaware Indians*, 329–333. For a similar development of territorial nationhood among the Creeks, see Hahn, *Invention of the Creek Nation*, 258–270.

18. A Treaty Between the United States and . . . the Wyandot, Ottawa, Chipawa, Munsee, and Delaware, Shawanee, and Pottawatima nations, July 4, 1805, Peters, *Public Statutes at Large*, 7:87–89; Blackhoof & others to the President and Secretary of War, December 12, 1807, RG 107, M221, roll 4, NA ("have received . . ."); For the Shawanoese Annuity 1812, Thornbrough, *Letter Book*, 99–100; John Johnston to William Crawford, September 13, 1815, Shawnee File, OVGLEA; Wyandotts' Talk to William H. Crawford, June 22, 1816, Shawnee File, OVGLEA ("the Shawnees . . .").

19. Sugden, *Blue Jacket*, 239–240; Blackhoof & others to the President and Secretary of War, December 12, 1807, RG 107, M221, roll 4, NA (quotation).

20. For the history of these Kishpokos, see Edmunds, *Shawnee Prophet*, 31–32; Sugden, *Tecumseh*, 52–110.

21. For differing interpretations on when and where Lalawéthika received his first vision, see Edmunds, *Shawnee Prophet*, 28–35; and Sugden, *Tecumseh*, 116. The first written descriptions of Lalawéthika's visions were penned in 1807; see MacLean, "Shaker Mission to the Shawnee Indians," 223–224 ("where . . .," "people . . .," and "sins" from 223); Substance of a Talk by Le Maygaus, May 4, 1807, RG 107, M221, roll 8, NA ("different manners . . .," "with different . . .," "such as . . ."); Worthington & McArthur to Kirker, September 22, 1807, DM, 7BB49 (8) ("would . . .").

22. Sugden, *Tecumseh*, 118 ("nativist gospel"). For Lalawéthika's new name, see Sugden, *Tecumseh*, 168; Cave, *Prophets of the Great Spirit*, 69. Libby, "Thomas Forsyth to William Clark," 192–194 ("all kind . . ."); Substance of a Talk by Le Maygaus, May 4, 1807, RG 107, M221, roll 8, NA ("Skins . . .," "for their . . ."); MacLean, "Shaker Mission to the Shawnee Indians," 223–226. For thorough analyses of Tenskwatawa's teachings, see Cave, *Prophets of the Great Spirit*, 63–79; Edmunds, *Shawnee Prophet*, 34–40; Sugden, *Tecumseh*, 117–120. The nativist prophets' views on the fur trade are discussed by Dowd, *Spirited Resistance*, 130–131. Anthropological literature on revitalization movements is wide; see Wallace, "Revitalization Movements," 264–281; Harkin, "Introduction," xv–xxxvi.

23. Substance of a Talk by Le Maygaus, May 4, 1807, RG 107, M221, roll 8, NA ("cultivate . . ."). For Tenskwatawa's pan-Indianism, see also Dowd, *Spirited Resistance*, 139–147; Cave, *Prophets of the Great Spirit*, 69–70.

24. Shawanoes in Answer to Kirk, April 14, RG 107, M221, roll 25, NA ("to make . . ."); Kirk to Dearborn, May 28, 1807, RG 107, M221, roll 9, NA ("Poisonous Medicine," "if they . . ."); Sugden, *Tecumseh*, 121, 128.

25. Several scholars have detailed the rise of distrust of traditional leaders, witchcraft accusations, and intracommunity conflicts related to the increasingly racialized climate among the Natives from the mid-eighteenth century: Cave, "Failure of the Shawnee Prophet's Witch-Hunt," 447–451; Dowd, *Spirited Resistance*, 29–31. For Colesquo, see A Message from the Delaware Council to Morgan, February 26, 1777, GMLB 1 ("esteemed . . ."); Diary of Gnadenhütten, from January to May 25, 1777, Moravian Records, reel 9, box 144, folder 13, item 1, NYSL.

26. Proceedings of a Council held with the Indians at Springfield, June 24–25, 1807, DM, 5U183; Blackhoof & others to the President and Secretary of War, December 12, 1807, RG 107, M221, roll 4, NA ("that part . . ."); Sugden, *Tecumseh*, 151–154. For the 1806 Lenape witch hunt, see Cave, "Failure of the Shawnee Prophet's Witch-Hunt"; Edmunds, *Shawnee Prophet*, 42–48; Miller, "1806 Purge"; Sugden, *Tecumseh*, 121–126.

27. Sugden, *Tecumseh*, 131–132, 151–154, 169; Libby, "Thomas Forsyth to William Clark," 193; Hull to Dearborn, September 9, 1807, RG 107, M221, roll 8, NA ("considered . . ."). For the Pekowi background of Tenskwatawa's mother, Methoataaskee, see Sugden, *Tecumseh*, 13–14. According to another interpretation, she may have been a Creek; Edmunds, *Shawnee Prophet*, 29.

28. Edmunds, *Shawnee Prophet*, 42–54; Sugden, *Tecumseh*, 143–148, 155; Wells to Harrison, August 20, 1807, Esarey, *Messages and Letters of William Henry Harrison*, 1:239 (quotations).

29. Substance of a Talk by Le Maygaus, RG 107, M221, roll 8, NA ("Scum . . ."); Harrison to Dearborn, July 11, 1807, ibid. ("an Engine . . ."); Wells to Dearborn, June 4, 1806, RG 107, M221, roll 15, NA ("absolutely . . ."); Johnston to Dearborn, December 31, 1807, RG 107, M221, roll 9, NA ("assemblage . . ."); Sugden, *Tecumseh*, 148–150, 156–158. Edmunds (*Shawnee Prophet*, 92) and Sugden (*Tecumseh*, 113–134, 157) agree that Tenskwatawa initially prescribed spiritual, not military, solutions to the problems of the Indians. For the U.S.-British tensions in 1807, see Hickey, *War of 1812*, 16–17.

30. Hull to Johnston, September 27, 1810, Thornbrough, *Letter Book*, 86–87 (quotations).

31. Sugden, *Tecumseh*, 133–134, 155–156, 163–168; Edmunds, *Shawnee Prophet*, 63–69; Wells to Dearborn, March 6, 1808, RG 107, M221, roll 15, NA.

32. Wells to the Secretary of War, April 20–23, 1808, TPUS 7:558 ("the Indians . . ."); Edmunds, *Shawnee Prophet*, 69–71 ("collect . . ." from 71); Sugden, "Early Pan-Indianism."

33. Harrison to the Secretary of War, August 22, 1810, Esarey, *Messages and Letters of William Henry Harrison*, 1:465, 469 ("jealousies," "distinctions," "distractions"); Wells to the Secretary of War, April 20, 1808, TPUS 7:558 ("sanctioned . . .").

34. Journal of the Proceedings of the commissioners plenipotentiary, July 1–23, 1814, ASPIA 1:829 ("so absurd . . ."); Cass to McArthur, May 24, 1818, RG 75, M1, roll 3, p. 419, NA ("Once . . ."); Annual Message, November 12, 1810, Esarey, *Messages and Letters of William Henry Harrison*, 1:489 ("the Prophet . . ."); Edmunds, *Shawnee Prophet*, 80–81; Owens, "Jeffersonian Benevolence on the Ground," 427–434; Sugden, *Tecumseh*, 183–185.

35. Brouillet to Harrison, June 30, 1810, Esarey, *Messages and Letters of William Henry Harrison*, 1:436; Harrison to the Secretary of War, July 4, 1810, ibid., 439; Harrison to the Secretary of War, August 22, 1810, ibid., 465 ("destroy . . ."); Speech of Techkumthai, November 15, 1810, CO 42/43, f. 43–44 ("our great . . ."). For the Treaty of Fort Wayne and its repercussions, see also Edmunds, *Shawnee Prophet*, 80–82, 92; Owens, "Jeffersonian Benevolence on the Ground," 427–434; Sugden, *Tecumseh*, 182–189.

36. The most comprehensive accounts of Prophetstown's destruction and the War of 1812 from the point of view of Tecumseh, Tenskwatawa, and their followers are Cave, "Shawnee Prophet"; Edmunds, *Shawnee Prophet*, 98–116, 125–152; Edmunds, *Tecumseh and the Quest for Indian Leadership*, 163–214; Sugden, *Tecumseh*, 226–236, 279–386. The story of the Shawnees of Wapakoneta and Lewistown is told in Edmunds, "A Watchful Safeguard."

37. Edmunds, *Shawnee Prophet*, 140–152; Harrison to Secretary of War, December 14, 1812, Esarey, *Messages and Letters of William Henry Harrison*, 2:247; Johnston to Secretary of War, May 4, 1815, RG 107, M221, roll 63, NA ("agricultural . . ."); Johnston to Monroe, March 20, 1815, ibid. ("more . . ."); Tupper to Meigs, January 26, 1813, Knopf, *Document Transcriptions of the War of 1812*, 2:116; Johnston to Meigs, August 22, 1813, ibid., 174.

38. Benn, *Iroquois in the War of 1812*, 175–178; Hickey, *War of 1812*, 289–296; Taylor, *Civil War of 1812*, 411–439; Godfroy to Caldwell, July 5, 1816, Indian Affairs, 12:10810–10811, reel C-11001, LAC ("lawfull Chiefs"); Stickney to Crawford, November 12, 1815, RG 75, M1, roll 2, p. 154, NA ("to exercise . . ."); Cass to Crawford, April 24, 1816, ibid., p. 185, ("that if . . .").

39. Shawnee Talk to John Johnston, April 27, 1815, RG 107, M221, roll 63, NA ("come back . . ."); Cass to Johnston, October 17, 1817, RG 75, M1, roll 3, p. 193, NA; Edmunds, *Shawnee Prophet*, 154–161; Taylor, *Civil War of 1812*, 126 ("treated . . .").

40. Hurt, *Ohio Frontier*, 375; Cayton, *Frontier Indiana*, 264, 267. The advocates of states' rights were especially vocal against Indian nations in the South, but similar arguments were important in the northern states too. Dennis, *Seneca Possessed*, 10–11; Green, *Politics of Indian Removal*, 69–173; Perdue and Green, *Cherokee Nation and the Trail of Tears*, 57–61.

41. The standard work on the rise of the racial ideology is Horsman, *Race and Manifest Destiny*. See also McLoughlin, *Cherokee Renascence*, xv–xvii; Perdue and Green, *Cherokee Nation and the Trail of Tears*, 42–46.

42. Shawnee Chiefs to the Secretary of War, December 29, 1815, Shawnee File, OVGLEA.

43. Graham to Cass, March 23, 1817, ASPIA 2:136; Johnston to Cass, May 21, 1817, RG 75, M1, roll 3, p. 47, NA; Johnston to Cass, June 13, 1817, ibid., pp. 81–82; Johnston to Cass, June 26, 1817, ibid., pp. 112–113; Cass to McArthur, June 16, 1817, ibid., pp. 85–86; Diary of Joseph and Martha Rhodes' Mission to the Shawnee Indians 1817, 5–7, OHS; Hill, *John Johnston and the Indians*, 175; Johnston, "Account of the Present State," 270.

44. Treaty with the Wyandots, Senecas, Delawares, Shawanees, Pattawatamies, Ottawas, and Chippewas, ASPIA 2:131–135.

45. Shawnee Chiefs to the Secretary of War, December 29, 1815, Shawnee File, OVGLEA ("the war . . ."); Col. Lewis, Civil John and Wackanachy: Memorial to the President, January 1816, Shawnee File, OVGLEA ("we . . .").

46. A plow cost from sixteen to eighteen dollars in Ohio in the late 1810s, and only a black-smith could repair broken ones; Hurt, *Ohio Frontier*, 235. See also McLoughlin, *Cherokee Renascence*, 65.

47. Harvey, *History of the Shawnee Indians*, 138; Johnston to Crohan, March 31, 1817, Hill, *John Johnston and the Indians*, 97; Johnston to Cass, June 14, 1816, RG 75, M1, roll 2, p. 236, NA; Diary of Joseph and Martha Rhodes' Mission to the Shawnee Indians 1817, 4–6, OHS; James Ellicott and Philip E. Thomas: Report on the feasibility of introducing farming and other civilizing activities among the Indians at Wapaghkonnetta and Lewis Town, August 1, 1816, Shawnee File, OVGLEA ("busily . . ."); Johnston, "Account of the Present State," 273, 276 ("their attention . . .," "cows . . .").

48. James Ellicott and Philip E. Thomas: Report on the feasibility of introducing farming and other civilizing activities among the Indians at Wapaghkonnetta and Lewis Town, August 1, 1816, Shawnee File, OVGLEA ("fully . . ."). For cattle and hogs among the Shawnees, see Jones, *Journal of Two Visits*, 57; Johnston, "Account of the Present State," 298–299. For the importance of pork trade to the American farmers of Ohio, see Hurt, *Ohio Frontier*, 213–217; for Shawnees, see Warren, *Shawnees and Their Neighbors*, 61. Other early-nineteenth-century Indians also began to raise cattle and hogs for commercial purposes, partly in order to replace the declining fur trade: Ethridge, *Creek Country*, 158–161; Taylor, "Native Americans, the Market Revolution, and Culture Change," 183–199; White, *Roots of Dependency*, 103–104. For "hybrid economies of survival," see Dennis, *Seneca Possessed*, 8.

49. Memorial of the Society of Friends in Regard to the Indians, 1, OHS (quotation); Johnston, "Account of the Present State," 276; Diary of an Exploratory Journey of the Brethren Luckenbach and Haven, in Company of the Indian Brother Andreas, August 26–September 13, 1808, Shawnee File, OVGLEA; James Ellicott and Philip E. Thomas: Report on the feasibility of introducing farming and other civilizing activities among the Indians at Wapaghkonnetta and Lewis Town, August 1, 1816, Shawnee File, OVGLEA.

50. James Ellicott and Philip E. Thomas: Report on the feasibility of introducing farming and other civilizing activities among the Indians at Wapaghkonnetta and Lewis Town, August 1, 1816, Shawnee File, OVGLEA ("the chiefs . . ."); Diary of Joseph and Martha Rhodes' Mission to the Shawnee Indians 1817, 6, OHS. For chiefs leading farm work and collecting war parties, see Trowbridge, *Shawanese Traditions*, 12–13, 17–19; Quaife, "Henry Hay's Journal," 255. For the free use of the mills, see Harvey, *History of the Shawnee Indians*, 138. Anthropological literature on labor mobilization in noncapital-ist societies is wide; see for example Dietler and Hayden, "Digesting the Feast"; Donham, *History, Power, Ideology*.

51. Johnston to Cass, August 19, 1816, RG 75, M1, roll 2, p. 292, NA ("becoming . . ."); Johnston to Crohan, March 31, 1817, Hill, *John Johnston and the Indians*, 97 ("many . . ."; "ploughs . . ."); Johnston to Calhoun, January 20, 1819, Shawnee File, OVGLEA ("every . . .").

52. Clark to Porter, January 15, 1829, RG 75, M234, roll 300, frames 0051–0064, NA ("good . . ."); Klinck and Talman, *Journal of Major John Norton*, 173 ("the houses . . ."). For eighteenth-century Shawnee settlement structure, see Henderson, "Lower Shawnee Town," 34.

53. Clark to Porter, January 15, 1829, RG 75, M234, roll 300, frames 0051–0064, NA; An Enumeration of all the Shawanees remaining in the State of Ohio, April 9, 1830, ibid., frame 0136; An Enumeration of the Shawanees who have Emigrated West of the Mississippi, April 8, 1830, ibid., frames 0138–0139; An Enumeration of all the mixed blood Shawnees & Senecas of Lewistown, April 15, 1830, ibid., frame 0141. For the flexibility and persistence of Native social organization amidst economic changes, see Ethridge, *Creek Country*, 172–173; Hatley, "Cherokee Women Farmers," 325.

54. Trowbridge, *Shawnese Traditions*, 13; Harvey, *History of the Shawnee Indians*, 174–178; Treaty with the Wyandots, Senecas, Delawares, Shawanees, Pattawatamies, Ottawas, and Chippewas, September 29, 1817, *ASPIA* 2:132.

55. Hopkins, *Mission to the Indians*, 77 ("women . . ."); Harvey, *History of the Shawnee Indians*, 140 ("the intolerable . . .," "furnishing . . ."); Minutes of a Council held at Wapaghkonetta, May 1825, RG 75, M1, roll 28, p. 364, NA ("enjoy . . ."); Trowbridge, *Shawanese Traditions*, 65 ("Shawnee men . . ."). For detailed analyses of the gender ideology of the Quaker missionaries and the civilization program, see Richter, "'Believing That Many of the Red People,'" 612–613; Rothenberg, "Mothers of the Nation," 73–74; Saunt, *New Order of Things*, 139–163. Warren, *Shawnees and Their Neighbors*, 43–55, offers an insightful analysis of these debates among the preremoval Ohio Shawnees. Bowes, *Exiles and Pioneers*, 104–106, offers evidence that Shawnee women continued to farm through the nineteenth century, while Trowbridge, *Shawanese Traditions*, 34, describes men taking a more active role in such work in the 1820s. Note that two Wapakonetan leaders, Pemthala and Lalloway, were known to Americans as John Perry and are sometimes confused in the literature.

56. The survey was undertaken to determine how much compensation the federal government would have to pay to individual Shawnees when the nation was removed to the reservation in Kansas. The main source for the estimates are Payments for the Improvements at Lewistown, April 1833, and Payments for the Improvements at Wapaghkonetta, April 1833, both in *Document 512*, 5:90–94. One of the government appraisers, the Quaker missionary Henry Harvey, later published an account in which he gave significantly higher evaluations to the wealthiest farms. Harvey explained that the appraisers had been compelled to underestimate the value of the richest farms, sometimes by 40 percent, because the federal government had decided the total amount of the compensations it was prepared to make before any evaluations were made. Harvey, *History of the Shawnee Indians*, 224–227; Articles of Agreement and Convention Made at Lewistown, July 20, 1831, Peters, *Public Statutes at Large*, 7:352; Articles of Agreement and Convention Made at Wapaghkonnetta, August 8, 1831, ibid., 356.

57. Clark to Porter, January 15, 1829, RG 75, M234, roll 300, frames 0063–0064, NA.

58. Saunt, "Taking Account of Property," 746; Saunt, *New Order of Things*, 164–185, 272; McLoughlin, *Cherokee Renascence*, 326–328; White, *Roots of Dependency*, 109–146; Harvey, *History of the Shawnee Indians*, 148 (quotation).

59. Harvey, *History of the Shawnee Indians*, 226, 282 ("noble . . ."); McElvain to Herring, May 3, 1833, *Document 512*, 4:200 ("worth . . ."); Cummins to Harvey, January 13, 1849, RG 75, M234, roll 303, frame 0128, NA ("a common . . ."); Articles of Agreement and Convention Made at Wapaghkonnetta, August 8, 1831, Peters, *Public Statutes at Large*, 7:358 ("a quarter . . ."). For Joseph Parks's background, see Parks to Cass, September

19, 1831, *Document 512*, 2:594; Relinquishment by Shawnees from river Huron of land, RG 75, M234, roll 301, frame 0419, NA; Spencer, "Shawnee Indians," 399; Lutz, "Methodist Missions," 186; Bowes, *Exiles and Pioneers*, 155–158. For Joseph Parks's Shawnee name, see LC Draper's 1868 Shawnee & Delaware Field Notes, EWVP, box 320, folder 320, p. 9.

60. Harvey, *History of the Shawnee Indians*, 282 ("always . . ."); Payments for the Improvements at Wapaghkonetta, April 1833, *Document 512*, 5:94; Speech of Black Hoof, RG 75, M234, roll 300, frame 0507, NA; Shawnee Message to Cass, April 7, 1834, ibid., frame 0628.

61. Cornstalk, John Perry, Nolaseesay & Shemanetoo to Vashon, April 10, 1830, RG 75, M234, roll 300, frames 0144–0145, NA; Johnston to Draper, September 13, 1847, DM, 11YY31 ("go . . .").

62. For American violence and other problems facing Shawnees in Ohio, see Warren, *Shawnees and Their Neighbors*, 60–64. For Quitewepea's migration, see Clark to Calhoun, September 5, 1823, Shawnee File, OVGLEA; Menard to Clark, September 30, 1825, RG 75, M234, roll 747, NA; Proceedings in Council with General Clark, November 10, 1825, ibid.; An Enumeration of the Shawanees & Senecas of Lewistown, who have Emigrated to the West of the Mississippi, April 15, 1830, RG 75, M234, roll 300, frame 0142, NA; Warren, *Shawnees and Their Neighbors*, 92–94. Tenskwatawa's removal is discussed in Edmunds, *Shawnee Prophet*, 166–183.

63. Clark to Eaton, April 9, 1829, RG 75, M234, roll 300, frame 0067, NA; Copy of Speech from Emigrating Shawnees from Wapaghconnetta & Lewis Town, April 3, 1827, ibid., frame 0083; Cornstalk, John Perry, Nolaseesay & Shemanetoo to Vashon, April 10, 1830, ibid., frame 0145 (quotations); Graham to Clark, April 7, 1829, ibid., frames 0087–0089.

64. For the Ohio Shawnees' struggle against removal, see Warren, *Shawnees and Their Neighbors*, 60–68. The removal negotiations of 1831 are described in Harvey, *History of the Shawnee Indians*, 190–207. For the Cherokee and Creek situation, see McLoughlin, *Cherokee Renascence*, 408–451; Green, *Politics of Indian Removal*, 69–186; Perdue and Green, *Cherokee Nation and the Trail of Tears*, 57–61.

65. Harvey, *History of the Shawnee Indians*, 190; Articles of Agreement and Convention Made in Lewistown, July 20, 1831, Peters, *Public Statutes at Large*, 7:351–354; Articles of Agreement and Convention Made at Wapaghkonnetta, August 8, 1831, ibid., 355–358.

CHAPTER SIX. "DISPERSED LIKE TURKEYS"

1. Speech of a Shawnie Chief formerly of Cape Girardeau, January 7, 1825, RG 75, M234, roll 747, NA ("disperced . . ."); Shawnee Chiefs to the President, June 29, 1829, RG 75, M234, roll 300, frame 0109, NA ("Land . . ."). For the Indian emigration across the Mississippi, see Warren, *Shawnees and Their Neighbors*, 71–75; Aron, *American Confluence*, 80–82; Usner, "American Indian Gateway."

2. Talk of the Shawnanoes to the President, November 20, 1831, RG 75, M234, roll 300, frame 0249, NA (quotation). The emergence of the Shawnee communities in the West is best analyzed in Warren, *Shawnees and Their Neighbors*, 69–96.

3. Drooker, *View from Madisonville*, 89–95, 332; Drooker and Cowan, "Transformations," 96, 102–103; DuVal, *Native Ground*, 67–68; 104; Jeter, "From Prehistory through

Protohistory"; Spero, "Stout, Bold, Cunning," 58–59, 138–142; Jordan, "Journal of James Kenny," 177 (quotation).

4. Aron, *American Confluence*, 50–51, 54–55; St. Ange to D'Abbadie, November 9, 1764, Alvord and Carter, *Critical Period*, 356–357; Smallman to McKee, November 8, 1764, *PSWJ* 11:403–404; Indian Intelligence, September 30, *PSWJ* 12:602; The Government Order of Ensign Willm. Connolly; The Indian Department Order of Lieut. Fowler; Lord to Gage, September 11, 1772; Gage to Lord, February 20, 1773, all in Gage Papers, reel 12.

5. Cruzat to Miró, March 19, 1782, *SRM* 1:209–210; Cruzat to Miró, August 23, 1784, *SMV* 2:117 (quotation); Cruzat to Lorimier, July 9, 1787, ibid., 42; Hamtramck to Harmar, October 13, 1788, Thornbrough, *Outpost on the Wabash*, 123–124; Hamtramck to Harmar, April 11, 1789, ibid., 167. For the divisional identity of the migrants, see Alford, *Civilization*, 200–201; Sugden, *Tecumseh*, 420.

6. Usner, "American Indian Gateway," 44–47; Din and Nasatir, *Imperial Osages*, 51–176; Rollings, *Osage*, 131–153; Military Report on Louisiana and West Florida by Baron de Carondelet, November 24, 1794, Robertson, *Louisiana under the Rule of Spain*, 297–302; Aron, *American Confluence*, 60–61, 72–84; Weber, *Spanish Frontier in North America*, 265–285.

7. Cruzat to Miró, March 19, 1782, *SRM* 1:209–210; Cruzat to Miró, August 23, 1784, *SMV* 2:117–119; Report of Joseph Jackson, May 5, 1799, Claus Papers, 8:90, reel C-1479, LAC ("for the . . ."). For the Cape Girardeau land grant, see Articles of Convention between William Clark and the Chiefs and Head Men of the Shawonee Nation, November 7, 1825, Peters, *Public Statutes at Large*, 7:284.

8. In the early 1790s some Shawnees demanded that the Spanish mediate a peace between them and the Osages. Even this indirect diplomatic initiative came after Shawnees had been moving across the Mississippi and fighting against the Osages for several years. The negotiations never materialized. Some Shawnees negotiated occasionally with the Quapaws of the lower Arkansas River Valley in order to receive permission to settle and hunt close to the Quapaw lands. The Quapaws in general fostered peaceful relations with the eastern Indian emigrants and allied with them against the Osages. The Shawnees' willingness to establish good relations with them underlines the absence of Shawnee-Osage diplomacy. Northern Indians to Trudeau, *SMV* 3:111; Browne to the Secretary of War, January 6, 1807, *TPUS* 14:72; DuVal, *Native Ground*, 128–163.

9. Rollings, *Osage*, 6–9, 136–138, 181–188; Din and Nasatir, *Imperial Osages*, 43, 50; DuVal, *Native Ground*, 103–127.

10. Rollings, *Osage*, 186–187 ("scarcely . . ."); Northern Indians to Trudeau, *SMV* 3:111 ("we . . ."); Ekberg, *Colonial Ste. Genevieve*, 98; Warren, *Shawnees and Their Neighbors*, 75 ("chose . . ."; "the ongoing . . .").

11. Delino to Miró, March 4, 1791, *SMV* 2:406; Portell to Lorimier, August 16, 1793, *SRM* 2:53; Trudeau to Lorimier, September 10, 1793, ibid., 55–56; Northern Indians to Trudeau, *SMV* 3:111; Carondelet to Trudeau, December 22, 1792, ibid., 107; Lorimier to Carondelet, September 17, 1793, ibid., 204–205 ("a sincere . . ."); Trudeau to Carondelet, September 28, 1793, ibid., 206–207; Journal of Lorimier, 1793–1795, *SRM* 2:73. For more detailed analyses of the failed Spanish campaign, see Din and Nasatir, *Imperial Osages*, 217–254; DuVal, *Native Ground*, 165–169; Aron, *American Confluence*, 92–93.

12. Cruzat to Lorimier, July 9, 1787, *SRM* 2:42; Journal of Lorimier, 1793–1795, ibid., 59–60, 72, 82; Ekberg and Foley, *Account of Upper Louisiana*, 34–35; Du Lac, *Travels through the Two Louisianas*, 45; Stoddard, *Sketches*, 215; Houck, *History of Missouri*, 209, 214; Menard to Calhoun, September 29, 1820, Shawnee File, OVGLEA ("big shawneetown"). In 1807 twenty "fighting men" reportedly lived in Rogerstown. This would put the total population somewhere between eighty and one hundred people. See Bates to Lewis, April 28, 1807, Shawnee File, OVGLEA. For the importance of the St. Francis Basin as a hunting ground for the eastern Indian settlers, see Stoddard, *Sketches*, 210, 215; DuVal, *Native Ground*, 200; Usner, "American Indian Gateway," 45. For the western Shawnee population estimates, see A List of the nearest Indian tribes in Missouri Territory and west of Lake Michigan, September 20, 1815, Shawnee File, OVGLEA.

13. Stoddard, *Sketches*, 215 ("the most . . .," "well furnished . . .," "barns . . ."); Ekberg and Foley, *Account of Upper Louisiana*, 34 ("more . . ."; "soon . . ."); De Lac, *Travels through the Two Louisianas*, 45 ("maize . . ."); A List of Horses, Cattle, Hogs, and other property Stolen from the Shawnee and Delaware Indians, RG 75, M865, roll 2, frames 0034–0035, NA.

14. Ekberg and Foley, *Account of Upper Louisiana*, 34–35; Blanc to Miró, May 4, 1790, *SMV* 2:335; An Account of Indian Tribes in Louisiana, *TPUS* 9:64; The Nicholas Biddle Notes, Jackson, *Letters of the Lewis and Clark Expedition*, 522; Journal of Lorimier, 1793–1795, *SRM* 2:84; Delino to Miró, March 4, 1791, *SMV* 2:406.

15. For Shawnee divisions and Creek contacts, see Alford, *Civilization*, 200–201. Log of His Majesty's Galiot, La Fleche, January 5 to March 25, 1793, SMV 3:129 (quotations). In May 1793 Governor Baron de Carondelet sent "a medal" and other marks of respect to "the principal chief of the Chaouesnons." Less than a year later Louis Lorimier mentioned that Metipouiosa had received a medal from the governor. This makes it likely that Metipouiosa was Carondelet's "principal chief" and possibly "the great chief" of the Shawnees; Carondelet to Lorimier, May 8, 1973, *SRM* 2:52; Journal of Lorimier, 1893–1795, ibid., 60. Metipouiosa's ties to Lorimier suggest that he was well connected to the Ohio Shawnees. His plans to lead the western Shawnees to the Creek country indicate a close relationship with the Shawnee communities in Alabama.

16. For examples of Shawnees traveling back and forth between the Mississippi Valley and the Maumee, see The Information of James Day, Claus Papers, 8:39, reel C-1479, LAC; Report of Joseph Jackson, May 5, 1799, Claus Papers, 8:89, reel C-1479, LAC; Houck, *History of Missouri*, 208–209. For Pemanpich and her relationship to Nenessica and Lorimier, see Last Will of Louis Lorimier, March 12, 1808, Rodney Family Papers, MHS; McKee to Shelby, January 10, 1803, Claus Papers, 8:244, reel C-1480, LAC; Sugden, *Blue Jacket*, 275. Nenessica's movements are reported in Ironside to Shelby, July 7, 1796, Claus Papers 7:247, reel C-1479, LAC; Elliott to Claus, June 28, 1809, Indian Affairs, 11:10040, reel C-11 000, LAC; Klinck and Talman, *Journal of Major John Norton*, 189. For Kishkalwa, see McKenney and Hall, *Indian Tribes of North America*, 32, 39, 42; Alford, *Civilization*, 201. For an excellent discussion on the Native connections and networks that crossed the Mississippi, see Bowes, *Exiles and Pioneers*, 19–52.

17. Robertson to Portell, February 13, 1792, *SMV* 2:3; Carondelet to Las Casas, April 20, 1794, *SMV* 3:276–277; St. Clair to the Secretary of State, 1796, Smith, *Life and Public Services of Arthur St. Clair*, 2:402.

18. Journal of Lorimier, 1793–1795, *SRM* 2:72–73; Du Lac, *Travels through the Two Louisianas*, 45 (quotation).

19. Most historians follow Alford's identification of the early western emigrants as predominantly Thawikilas, Kishpokos, and Pekowis. The small size of these divisions in British lists documenting the Shawnee population on the Maumee supports Alford's oral sources. Alford, *Civilization*, 200–201; List of Indians who Received Presents at Swan Creek, December 4, 1794, Claus Papers, 6:291, reel C-1479, LAC; Sugden, *Tecumseh*, 420. The fact that one of the Apple Creek towns was sometimes called Chillicothe or Chilliticaux indicates that a number of Chalaakaathas joined the migration; Houck, *History of Missouri*, 214. For the Thawikilas, see Trowbridge, *Shawanese Traditions*, 8, 62.

20. The Information of James Day, Claus Papers, 8:36, reel C-1479, LAC.

21. Weber, *Spanish Frontier in North America*, 290–291.

22. Aron, *American Confluence*, 82–84, 95–104, 115–116; Din, "Immigration Policy of Governor Esteban Miró"; Ekberg and Foley, *Account of Upper Louisiana*, 35; Faragher, " 'More Motley than Mackinaw,' " 304–314 ("frontier . . .").

23. Usner, "American Indian Gateway," 49; Lorimier to Browne, February 19, 1807, *TPUS* 14:112; Proclamation by Governor Lewis, April 6, 1809, ibid., 261; Clark to the President, April 10, 1811, ibid., 445–446 ("provent . . ."; "a permanent . . .").

24. Sugden, *Tecumseh*, 209–211; Clark to the Secretary of War, August 20, 1814, *TPUS* 14:786; Aron, *American Confluence*, 155–158; Faragher, " 'More Motley than Mackinaw,' " 316–323.

25. Faragher, "'More Motley than Mackinaw,'" 304, 316; Clark, Edwards, and Chouteau to Crawford, October 18, 1815, *ASPIA* 2:11 ("early . . ."); Shawnee and Delaware Indians to the President, September 16, 1820, Shawnee File, OVGLEA ("Since . . ."; "the Whites . . ."); Menard to Bowlbury or Fullbright, March 10, 1822, Deposition of Pitatawa (or Shot Pouch), and Graham to Brown, December 18, 1822, all in Richard Graham Papers, box 2-12, MHS; Graham to Thompson, April 27, 1823, Graham to Easton, September 18, 1823, Thompson to Graham, December 17, 1823, and Complaint of Petatwa, September 1826, all in Richard Graham Papers, box 3-12, MHS.

26. Faragher, "'More Motley than Mackinaw,'" 317–324 ("the club . . ." from 321); Anderson, *Conquest of Texas*, 7 ("forced . . ."); A Proclamation, December 4, 1815, *TPUS* 15:191–192; Clark to the President, January 22, 1816, ibid., 105; Resolutions of the Territorial Assembly, ibid., 105–107 ("permission . . ."; "a Considerable . . ."); Resolutions of the Territorial Assembly, January 24, 1817, ibid., 234–235 ("greatly"; "the prosperity . . ."); Warren, *Shawnees and Their Neighbors*, 82–84.

27. Clark to Calhoun, June 5, 1823, Shawnee File, OVGLEA ("for fear . . ."); Clark, Edwards, and Choteau to Crawford, October 18, 1815, *ASPIA* 2:11; Menard to Calhoun, September 29, 1820, Clark to Calhoun, August 9, 1822, ("scattered . . ."), Talk of the Shawnee, September 23, 1822, Graham to Calhoun, December 23, 1823, all from Shawnee File, OVGLEA; Crittenden to the Secretary of War, September 28, 1823, *TPUS* 19:549. For the persistence of some St. Francis communities to the mid-1820s, see Hopkins to Graham, August 6, 1825, Richard Graham Papers, box 3-12, MHS. For evidence of Rogerstown, see Lewis Rogers et al. to Cummins, March 6, 1838, RG 75,

M234, roll 301, frames 0176–0177, NA; Report of places designated for carrying on Trade with Different Indian Tribes, December 21, 1824, RG 75, M234, roll 747, NA.

28. Shawnee and Delaware Indians to the President, September 16, 1820, ("worth . . ."), Calhoun to Menard, October 25, 1820, Talk of the Shawnee, September 23, 1822, all from Shawnee File, OVGLEA; Shawnee chiefs to the President, June 29, 1829, RG 75, M234, roll 300, frame 0109, NA ("Land . . .").

29. Clark to Calhoun, June 5, 1823, Shawnee and Delaware Indians to the President, September 16, 1820, ("hilly . . ."), Statement of Wm. Marshall & others, April 16, 1823, ("the most crying . . ."), all from Shawnee File, OVGLEA; Stoddard, *Sketches*, 215 ("the most wealthy"); Kiseallawa, Mayesweskaka & Petecaussa to Calhoun, February 28, 1825, RG 75, M234, roll 300, frame 0008, NA ("rich . . ."). For Shawnee losses of property, see also Talk of the Shawnee chiefs to the President, June 29, 1829, RG 75, M234, roll 300, frame 0109, NA; Speech of Shawnie Chief formerly of Cape Girardeau, January 7, 1825, RG 75, M234, roll 747, NA; A List of Horses, Cattle, Hogs, and other property Stolen from the Shawnee and Delaware Indians, RG 75, M865, roll 2, frames 0034–0035, NA.

30. Onothe and Noma to the President, March 29, 1811, RG 75, M271, roll 1, frame 0551, NA.

31. DuVal, *Native Ground*, 196–210; McLoughlin, *Cherokee Renascence*, 128–167; Thornton, *Cherokees*, 59–60; Rollings, *Osage*, 233–241.

32. Secretary of War to Clark, May 8, 1818, *TPUS* 15:390–391; DuVal, *Native Ground*, 199, 210–226; Rollings, *Osage*, 236–244; Long to Smith, January 30, 1818, *TPUS* 19:7 ("several").

33. Crittenden to Secretary of War, September 28, 1823, *TPUS* 19:549 ("hoards . . ."; "extort . . ."); Speech of a Shawnie Chief formerly of Cape Girardeau, January 7, 1825, RG 75, M234, roll 747, NA; Kisceallawa, Mayesweskaka & Petecaussa to Calhoun, February 28, 1825, RG 75, M234, roll 300, frames 0008–0009, NA; Calhoun to Kiscallawa, Mayesweskaka, and Petecaussa, March 2, 1825, RG 75, M1, roll 28, pp. 401–402, NA; Clark to Barbour, April 19, 1825, RG 75, M234, roll 747, NA; Articles of Convention between William Clark and the Chiefs and Head Men of the Shawonee Nation, November 7, 1825, Peters, *Public Statutes at Large*, 7:284–285. For analyses of the Cherokee-led Indian coalition, see Warren, *Shawnees and Their Neighbors*, 85–96; Foreman, *Indians and Pioneers*, 184–198.

34. Calhoun to Kiscallawa, Mayesweskaka, and Petecaussa, March 2, 1825, RG 75, M1, roll 28, pages 401–402, NA; Articles of Convention between William Clark and the Chiefs and Head Men of the Shawonee Nation, November 7, 1825, Peters, *Public Statutes at Large*, 7:284–285; McKenney and Hall, *Indian Tribes of North America*, 33; Barry, *Beginning of the West*, 376; The United States Indian Department to Robert Rollins, May 23, 1828, Richard Graham Papers, box 4-12, MHS.

35. Talk of the Shawnee chiefs to the President, June 29, 1829, RG 75, M234, roll 300, frames 0109–0110, NA; Talk of Shawnanoes from the White River to the President, November 20, 1831, ibid., frame 0250 (quotations); Talk of a deputation of Shawanoes from White River to the President, July 20, 1832, ibid., frames 0349–0350.

36. Pope to the Secretary of War, November 24, 1831, *Document 512*, 2:691 ("good . . ."); Trimble & Caldwell to the President, November 3, 1831, ibid., 640–641 ("bickerings . . ."); Pope to Eaton, September 9, 1830, ibid., 112; Talk of the Shawnee chiefs to the

President, June 29, 1829, RG 75, M234, roll 300, frames 0109–0110, NA; Articles of a Treaty Made at Castor Hill, October 26, 1832, Peters, *Public Statutes at Large*, 7:397–398. For the American settlement of Arkansas and the removal of the Arkansas Cherokees, see DuVal, *Native Ground*, 228–229, 237–242.

37. Clark to Herring, December 4, 1833, *Document 512*, 4:745; Shawnees to Cass, February 7, 1835, RG 75, M234, roll 300, frame 0666, NA ("all . . ."; "refuse . . ."); Talk of the Shawnee chiefs to the President, June 29, 1829, ibid., frame 0109 ("When . . ."); Armstrong to Herring, January 23, 1835, ibid., frames 0652–0653; Talk from Shawnees from Cape Girardeau, August 1, 1835, ibid., frames 0822–0823. For the long-standing contacts between the Lewistown and White River Shawnees, see An Enumeration of the Shawanees & Senecas of Lewistown, who have Emigrated West of the Mississippi, RG 75, M234, roll 300, frame 0142, NA; Clark to Calhoun, September 5, 1823, Shawnee File, OVGLEA; Speech of Col. Lewis, January 7, 1825, RG 75, M234, roll 747, NA.

38. Herring to Clark, March 30, 1833, *Document 512*, 3:635 ("It . . ."); Armstrong to Herring, January 23, 1835, RG 75, M234, roll 300, frames 0652–0653, NA ("if . . .").

39. Everett, *Texas Cherokees*, 11–23; May, "Alabama and Koasati," 407–408; Smith, *From Dominance to Disappearance*, 101–103; La Vere, *Contrary Neighbors*, 44–45; White, *Roots of Dependency*, 92–94; Weber, *Spanish Frontier in North America*, 295–296. For the estimate of ten thousand emigrant Indians, see Anderson, *Conquest of Texas*, 4.

40. Miller to the Secretary of War, June 20, 1820, *TPUS* 19:194; Gray to the Secretary of War, February 28, 1824, ibid., 612; Cumming to the Adjutant General, January 18, 1826, ibid., 185; Gray to the Secretary of War, April 1824, ibid., 665; Colquhoun to Cummings, August 1, 1827, RG 94, M567, roll 26, frames 0652–0653, NA (all quotations); McKenney and Hall, *Indian Tribes of North America*, 33.

41. Weber, *Spanish Frontier in North America*, 295–300 ("in ruins"); Hämäläinen, *Comanche Empire*, 358; Smith, *From Dominance to Disappearance*, 96–102; Everett, *Texas Cherokees*, 17–18.

42. Smith, *From Dominance to Disappearance*, 101–102.

43. Smith, *From Dominance to Disappearance*, 133–134, 139; Petition to Governor Izard by Citizens of Miller County, March 20, 1828, *TPUS* 20:629; Izard to Rector, April 7, 1828, ibid., 641; Rector to Izard, May 8, 1828, ibid., 677; Hyde to the Adjutant General, November 17, 1828, ibid., 784; Birch to Galt, April 9, 1829, RG 94, M567, roll 41, frame 0974, NA; Almonte, "Statistical Report on Texas," 215, 222.

44. An Account of Indian Tribes in Louisiana, *TPUS* 9:64 ("Vagabonds"); Herring to Clark, March 30, 1833, *Document 512*, 3:635 ("without chiefs"); Cummings to the Adjutant General, January 18, 1826, *TPUS* 20:185 ("generally . . ."); Miller to the Secretary of War, *TPUS* 19:194–195 ("a Banditti . . ."); Gray to the Secretary of War, June 13, 1827, *TPUS* 20:480 ("the whirlpool"; "in a little . . ."); Gray to the Secretary of War, April 1824, *TPUS* 19:665.

45. For Cherokee factionalism, see Everett, *Texas Cherokees*, 14–19. The migration of many of Kishkalwa's Shawnees to Texas after the 1825 treaty, when the headman himself moved to the Kansas reservation, suggests that factional disagreements lay behind Shawnee movements, too; see McKenney and Hall, *Indian Tribes of North America*, 33. For the role of the Cherokees among the emigrant Indians, see Everett, *Texas Cherokees*, 33, 71–73; for Caddos, see Smith, *From Dominance to Disappearance*, 112

(quotation). Miller to the Secretary of War, June 20, 1820, *TPUS* 19:194; Gray to the Secretary of War, April 30, 1826, *TPUS* 20:298.

46. For the divisional background of the Texas Shawnees, see Alford, *Civilization*, 200–202. For Paukesaa, see Sugden, *Tecumseh*, 386–387; Talk of a deputation of Shawanoes from White River to the President, July 20, 1832, RG 75, M234, roll 300, frames 0349–0350, NA. For the White River leaders' signs, see also Talk of the Shawnanoes from White River to the President, November 20, 1831, ibid., frame 0250.

47. Sánchez, "Trip to Texas," 283 ("intermingled . . ."); Almonte, "Statistical Report on Texas," 215; Berlandier, *Indians of Texas in 1830*, 49 ("use . . ."), 52 ("look . . ."); An Account of the Indian Tribes in Louisiana, *TPUS* 9:64.

48. Smith, *From Dominance to Disappearance*, 120–139; Anderson, *Conquest of Texas*, 96; Burnet to Bustamante, July 2, 1827, Barker, *Austin Papers*, 1668–1669 (quotations).

49. Everett, *Texas Cherokees*, 69–118; Smith, *From Dominance to Disappearance*, 154–160, 169–173; Anderson, *Conquest of Texas*, 103–105, 172–179; Commissioners' Journal, July 11–15, 1839, Rusk Papers, Box 2G34, BTHCA; Treaty between Texas and the Shawnee Indians, August 2, 1839, Winfrey and Day, *Texas Indian Papers*, 1:80–81; A Valuation of the Property belonging to the Shawnee tribe of Indians, August 5, 1839, Rusk Papers, Oversize 2.116/OD 1223A, item 4, BTHCA. Despite the violence, small groups of Shawnees remained in Texas until 1859; Anderson, "The Delaware and Shawnee Indians," 246–260.

50. Foreman, *Traveler in Indian Territory*, 30, 111–116, 121, 145–146, 159 (quotation from 154); Alford, *Civilization*, 202; Foreman, *Last Trek of the Indians*, 162–164; La Vere, *Contrary Neighbors*, 81–87, 94. For the Indian Country, see Unrau, *Rise and Fall of Indian Country*, 2–3.

51. Foreman, *Last Trek of the Indians*, 162; Foreman, *Traveler in Indian Territory*, 30 (quotation); La Vere, *Contrary Neighbors*, 113–118, 123–126.

52. Foreman, *Marcy and the Gold Seekers*, 137–138 ("gardens . . ."), 159 ("They . . .").

53. Alford, *Civilization*, 200 (quotations).

CHAPTER SEVEN. "REUNION"

1. Herring, *Enduring Indians of Kansas*, 1, 17–22; King et al. to Cooley, March 12, 1866, RG 75, M234, roll 814, frames 0762, 0766, NA (quotations). The development of the National Council and the controversies surrounding it are analyzed in detail in Warren, *Shawnees and Their Neighbors*, 127–173. The most powerful expression of the emerging view of Indians as the wards of the federal government was Chief Justice John Marshall's "domestic dependent nations" formulation that compared the tribal-federal relationship to that between a ward and a guardian; Harring, *Crow Dog's Case*, 31.

2. Articles of Convention between William Clark and the Chiefs and Head Men of the Shawonee Nation, November 7, 1825, Peters, *Public Statutes at Large*, 7:284–285; Treaty with the Shawnees, May 10, 1854, Minot, *Statutes at Large*, 1053. For population estimates from the late 1830s and early 1840s, see McCoy, *History of the Baptist Indian Missions*, 566; Cummins to Harris, September 25, 1838, RG 75, M234, roll 301, frame 0318, NA; Census of the Shawnee Tribe for the Year 1842, ibid., frames 1154–1161.

3. The Rogerstown removal can be dated on the basis of Barry, *Beginning of the West*, 376; The United States Indian Department to Jacob Barton, April 22, 1822, Richard

Graham Papers, box 4-12, MHS. For the background of the Rogers and Fish families, see Babcock, *Forty Years of Pioneer Life*, 112–113; LC Draper's 1868 Shawnee and Delaware Field Notes, EWVP, box 35, folder 320, pp. 3, 16–18; Faragher, " 'More Motley than Mackinaw,' " 310–313. For the other removals, see Edmunds, *Shawnee Prophet*, 173–183; McKenney and Hall, *Indian Tribes of North America*, 33; Cummins to Cass, December 1832, RG 75, M234, roll 300, frame 0459, NA; Articles of Agreement and Convention Made at Wapaghkonnetta, August 8, 1831, Peters, *Public Statutes at Large*, 7:356; Harvey, *History of the Shawnee Indians*, 233–234.

4. Cornstalk, John Perry, Nolaseesay, and Shemanetoo to Vashon, April 10, 1830, RG 75, M234, roll 300, frame 0146, NA ("we felt . . ."); Copy of a Speech from Emigrating Shawnees from Wapaghconnetta & Lewis Town to the Secretary of War, April 3, 1827, ibid., frame 0082 ("to subsist . . ."); Graham to Clark, April 4, 1827, ibid., frame 0070 ("in a . . ."); Gardiner to Gibson, October 8, 1832, *Document* 512, 1:704–706.

5. Cobb to Cass, November 27, 1833, RG 75, M234, roll 300, frames 0451–0453, NA; Harvey, *History of the Shawnee Indians*, 233–235; Johnston to Drake, December 14, 1831, DM, 11YY18-1 ("removing . . ."; "to collect . . ."). For Lalloway, see Morgan, *Indian Journals*, 86; Harvey, *History of the Shawnee Indians*, 188 ("the head chief"); Clark to Clark, November 12, 1834, RG 75, M234, roll 300, frame 0594, NA. For Biaseka's death, see Johnston to Draper, April 27, 1849, Knopf, Papers of John Johnston, 120, OHS.

6. Shawnees to Cass, February 7, 1835, RG 75, M234, roll 300, frame 0666, NA. George Williams is identified as Pamothaway in Harvey, *History of the Shawnee Indians*, 245.

7. Clark to Harris, August 14, 1838, RG 75, M234, roll 301, frame 0238, NA; Muster rolls of Shawnees under Tecumseh's Son, July 31, 1838, ibid., frame 0240; Lalahsekah et al. to Pilcher, August 1, 1839, ibid., frames 0451–0452; Muster Roll of a Company of Shawnee Indians from Neosho, ibid., frame 0467; Van Horne to Gibson, December 7, 1832, *Document* 512, 1:923–930; Articles of Agreement made and concluded at the Seneca Agency, Peters, *Public Statutes at Large*, 7:411–413.

8. Wheeler-Voegelin, "Mortuary Customs," 422 ("claimed . . ."); "Shawnee in Old Mexico," EWVP, box 31, folder 281 ("mekoče went . . ."). For Mr. Clark's divisional background, see Voegelin and Voegelin, "Shawnee Name Groups," 617. For other Missourian complaints against the Ohio Shawnees, see Rogers et al. to Cummins, March 6, 1838, RG 75, M234, roll 301, frames 0176–0178, NA. Spito is a sixth division of the Shawnees, sometimes mentioned in oral histories; see Erminie Wheeler Voegelin, "Shawnee: An American Indian Culture: Its Bearers and Its Background," 17–18, EWVP, box 31, folder 276.

9. Articles of a Convention, Peters, *Public Statutes at Large*, 7:284 ("to . . ."). In 1838 a Rogerstown leader admitted that they had asked the government for a territory "large enough for myself & my friends in Ohio," but in 1866 the Missourians claimed that they had thought the Ohioans would remain on the reservation only "temporarily." Rogers et al. to Cummins, March 6, 1838, RG 75, M234, roll 301, frame 0177, NA; Guthrie in behalf of the Fish Party, Spring 1866, RG 75, M234, roll 814, frame 0753, NA. For the Wapakoneta Treaty and the locals' expectation of their own reservation, see Articles of Agreement and Convention, August 8, 1831, Peters, *Public Statutes at Large*, 7:356; Perry et al. to Crawford, March 30, 1844, RG 75, M234, roll 302, frames 0353–0354, NA.

10. Rogers et al. to Cummins, March 6, 1838, RG 75, M234, roll 301, frames 0176–0178, NA (all quotations). The Wapakoneta trust fund is described in Articles of Agreement and Convention, August 8, 1831, Peters, *Public Statutes at Large*, 7:357. For the additional compensation, see Harvey, *History of the Shawnee Indians*, 213, 237–238; Shawnees to Cass, February 7, 1835, RG 75, M234, roll 300, frame 0665, NA. Some Missourians later claimed that the Ohioans had always given them a share of their annuities in recognition of the Missourians' stronger claim to the reservation land; Guthrie in behalf of the Fish Party, Spring 1866, RG 75, M234, roll 814, frame 0753, NA.

11. Act on the part of the Delawares, Shawnees, Kaskaskias, & Peorias, Piankashaws & Weas, October 21, 1836, RG 75, M234, roll 300, frames 0966–0967, NA; Harvey, *History of the Shawnee Indians*, 242–249 ("stormy" from 243, "the United States . . ." from 244, "very much . . ." from 247, and "they would . . ." from 245). Identifying Chawwe is confusing. He is variously called John or George Francis, Kos-qua-the, and Tep-a-ta-go-the. Parks, Chawwe, and Barnett to the President, December 22, 1849, RG 75, M234, roll 303, frame 0476, NA; Parks, Wahwee, and Barnett to Brown, December 27, 1849, ibid., frame 480; Morgan, *Indian Journals*, 86; Spencer, "Shawnee Indians," 392.

12. Shawnee Message to Cass, March 21, 1834, RG 75, M234, roll 300, frame 0626, NA (quotations); Clark to Porter, January 15, 1829, ibid., frames 0051–0064; Cobb to Cass, November 27, 1833, ibid., frames 451–0453; Harvey to Vance, April 15, 1834, ibid., frame 0632; Harvey, *History of the Shawnee Indians*, 234–235. For a broader treatment of the ecological challenges faced by the Shawnees and other removed Indians in Kansas, and their subsequent adaptation strategies, see Bowes, *Exiles and Pioneers*, 91–96.

13. Articles of a Convention, Peters, *Public Statutes at Large*, 7:285 ("for . . ."); Articles of Agreement and Convention, August 8, 1831, ibid., 356; Clark to Herring, January 18, 1834, RG 75, M234, roll 300, frames 0510–0511, NA; Mayahwathhucker et al. to Crawford, March 30, 1844, RG 75, M234, roll 302, frame 0348, NA.

14. Harring, *Crow Dog's Case*, 30–34. The development of U.S. Indian policy during the first half of the nineteenth century is traced in Prucha, *Great Father*, 135–177, 283–338. Shawnees to Cass, February 7, 1835, RG 75, M234, roll 300, frame 0665, NA; Crawford to Bancroft, June 20, 1845, RG 75, M234, roll 302, frames 0406–0407, NA.

15. The coming of the missionaries to the reservation is narrated in detail in Abing, "Fall from Grace," 61–71; Abing, "Holy Battleground"; Warren, "Baptists, Methodists, and the Shawnees"; Warren, *Shawnees and Their Neighbors*, 97–126.

16. The alliances between the various Shawnee communities and missionaries can be traced through the following sources: Caldwell, *Annals*, 8, 10; Harvey, *History of the Shawnee Indians*, 234–239, 250–257; Lutz, "Methodist Missions," 166–167; McCoy, *History of Baptist Indian Missions*, 404–405; Johnson to Ruland, July 19, 1833, RG 75, M234, roll 300, frame 0425, NA. For the Johnson-Campbell feud, see also Campbell to Clark, May 20, 1833, RG 75, M234, roll 300, frames 0409–0412, NA; Shawnee Speech, June 3, 1833, ibid., frame 0414 (quotations). For the turf wars between the missionaries, see Abing, "Holy Battleground." How the Shawnees' alliances with the missionaries reflected older political divisions is analyzed in Warren, "Baptists, Methodists, and the Shawnees"; and Warren, *Shawnees and Their Neighbors*, 99–126.

17. Shawnee Speech, June 3, 1833, RG 75, M234, roll 300, frame 0414, NA ("this man . . .," "meddles . . ."); Marston Clark to William Clark, October 7, 1834, ibid., frame 0499 ("In . . .," "Missionareys . . ."); McCoy, *History of Baptist Indian Missions*, 482.

18. For the number of Christians, see Census and Statistics of the Shawanee Tribe of Indians for the year 1846, RG 75, M234, roll 302, frame 0556, NA ("national . . ."). The most detailed discussion of Shawnee conversions is in Warren, *Shawnees and Their Neighbors*, 97–126. For references to friction between Christians and traditionalists, see Caldwell, *Annals*, 19. For examples of Christian converts participating in traditional rituals, see Spencer, "Shawnee Indians," 391. For discarding traditional rituals, see Morgan, *Indian Journals*, 53. The tensions between converts and non-Christians are also discussed in Abing, "Fall from Grace," 178–182; Abing, "Holy Battleground," 135–136; Warren, "Baptists, Methodists, and the Shawnees," 161.

19. The spiritual roots of traditional Shawnee leadership are explored in more detail in Lakomäki, "Singing the King's Song," 46–53. For the views of the Christian Shawnees in the 1860s, see LC Draper's 1868 Shawnee & Delaware Field Notes, EWVP, box 35, folder 320, p. 3 ("the best . . ."). For interpreters and Christian Shawnees, see A List of persons employed within the Northern Agency of Western Territory, September 30, 1835, RG 75, M234, roll 300, frame 0795, NA; Cummins to Clark, December 12, 1836, RG 75, M234, roll 301, frame 0019, NA ("in the . . ."; "information . . ."); A list of all persons connected with the Indian Department within the Fort Leavenworth Agency, September 30, 1838, ibid., frame 0307.

20. Herring to McElvain, April 5, 1833, *Document 512*, 3:649 (quotation); Shawnee Message to Cass, April 7, 1834, RG 75, M234, roll 300, frame 0628, NA; Shawnees to Cass, February 7, 1835, RG 75, M234, roll 300, frame 0666, NA. Parks's career is analyzed in detail in Bowes, *Exiles and Pioneers*, 152–178.

21. Cummins to Harris, January 29, 1838, RG 75, M234, roll 301, frame 0166, NA; Cummins to Clark, December 12, 1836, ibid., frames 0019–0020; Cummins to Mitchell, February 2, 1843, RG 75, M234, roll 302, frame 0077, NA; Petition of Charles Findlay, January 10, 1848, RG 75, M234, roll 303, frame 0034, NA; Jesup to Bell, March 29, 1848, ibid., frame 0040; Findlay to Bell, ibid., frames 0055–0060. For the business connections of Parks, see Barry, *Beginning of the West*, 343, 350; Caldwell, *Annals*, 58.

22. Cummins to Crawford, February 19, 1839, RG 75, M234, roll 301, frame 0417, NA ("much . . .").

23. Cummins to Mitchell, September 16, 1842, RG 75, M234, roll 301, frame 1115, NA ("Their . . .," "Comfortable . . .," "Out houses . . .," "enclosed . . ."); Cummins to Harris, September 25, 1838, ibid., frame 0320 ("the Shawnees . . ."); Census and Statistics of the Shawanee Tribe of Indians for the Year 1846, RG 75, M234, roll 302, frame 0555, NA.

24. Cummins to Harris, September 25, 1838, RG 75, M234, roll 301, frame 0320, NA ("The Shawnees . . ."); Census of the Shawanee Tribe of Indians for the Year 1842, ibid., frames 1154–1161.

25. Trowbridge, *Shawnese Traditions*, 16–17, 26–28, 31, 33; Morgan, *Indian Journals*, 49–53, 86; Voegelin and Voegelin, "Shawnee Name Groups."

26. Callender, *Social Organization*, 98, 100–103, 107–109; Howard, *Shawnee!*, 87–90.

27. Cummins to Mitchell, September 16, 1842, RG 75, M234, roll 301, frame 1115, NA; Cummins to Harvey, September 26, 1848, RG 75, M234, roll 302, frame 1104, NA (quotations); Abing, "Before Bleeding Kansas." In 1847 a visitor to the reservation reported

that "one Shawnee Indian chief" owned slaves and "some" other Indians had taken up runaway slaves. The "chief" was undoubtedly Parks; Caldwell, *Annals*, 58, 61. See also Barry, *Beginning of the West*, 723.

28. Harvey, *History of the Shawnee Indians*, 286–288 (the Blackhoofs and Bluejackets); Babcock, *Forty Years of Pioneer Life*, 112–113 (the Rogerses and Fishes). Quaskey quoted in Abing, "Holy Battleground," 134.

29. For the death of the headmen, see Barry, *Beginning of the West*, 498, 566, 573.

30. Harvey, *History of the Shawnee Indians*, 281, 286 (quotations). Warren, *Shawnees and Their Neighbors*, 97–126, emphasizes the aggressive rise of formerly marginal mixed-blood men from the Hog Creek and Rogerstown communities to national prominence in the 1840s and argues that they owed their influence largely to federal and missionary support, while "[f]ew Shawnees trusted them." While I agree with the thrust of Warren's argument, he downplays the support the new leaders had among the Shawnees. True, they had many critics; yet men like Parks and the Rogerses had long been influential in their local communities and had wide kinship networks that guaranteed them a strong base of support.

31. Letho et al. to Harris, January 8, 1838, RG 75, M234, roll 301, frames 0351–0353, NA; Cummins to Clark, May 24, 1838, ibid., frames 0205–0209; Perry et al. to Crawford, March 30, 1844, RG 75, M234, roll 302, frames 0356–0359, NA; Heaton to Medill, April 10, 1848, ibid., frame 0954.

32. For Parks's travels and authorization, see Cummins to Crawford, February 2, 1842, RG 75, M234, roll 301, frame 0833, NA; Perry et al. to Crawford, March 30, 1844, RG 75, M234, roll 302, frame 0358, NA; Lea to Mitchell, November 23, 1849, RG 75, M234, roll 303, frame 0409, NA; Shawnee Chiefs, March 2, 1852, RG 75, M234, roll 364, frames 0396–0397, NA; Power of Attorney to Joseph Parks, December 10, 1852, ibid., frames 0628–0630.

33. Parks, Chawwe, and Barnett to Brown, RG 75, M234, roll 303, frame 0854, NA. Warren, *Shawnees and Their Neighbors*, 130, likewise notes how Shawnee delegates in Washington built their arguments on the notion of national sovereignty. For lawyers, see for example Thompson to Lea, April 12, 1852, RG 75, M234, roll 364, frames 0432–0433, NA.

34. Parks, Chawwe, and Barnett to Brown, RG 75, M234, roll 303, frames 0850–0855, NA; Thompson to Manypenny, April 4, 1853, RG 75, M234, roll 364, frame 616, NA ("national purposes"); Cummins to Harvey, November 3, 1847, RG 75, M234, roll 302, frame 0750, NA; Cummins to Harvey, January 13, 1849, RG 75, M234, roll 303, frame 0126, NA ("for their . . ."). The involvement of Parks and his business partners for various debt-collecting schemes was extremely complex and is documented in a myriad of papers in RG 75, M234, rolls 302–303, NA. For the plans of the reservation leaders to use treaty money for mills and a council house, see Moseley to Mitchell, March 4, 1852, RG 75, M234, roll 364, frame 0390, NA.

35. Prucha, *Great Father*, 173, 299, 309–310; Cummins to Harvey, January 13, 1849, RG 75, M234, roll 303, frames 0126–0128, NA; Bowes, *Exiles and Pioneers*, 176.

36. Cumming to Manypenny, July 11, 1853, RG 75, M234, roll 364, frame 0479, NA; Thompson to Manypenny, April 4, 1853, ibid., frame 616 ("national purposes"); Parks et al. to the commissioner of Indian affairs, July 22, 1853, ibid., frame 0637 ("induce . . ."); Robinson to Cumming, July 27, 1853, ibid., frame 0482–0483;

Cumming to Manypenny, August 2, 1853, ibid., frames 0484–0485; Thompson to Manypenny, August 10, 1853, ibid., frames 0661–0696 ("war chiefs").

37. Lea to Mitchell, January 22, 1850, RG 75, M234, roll 303, frame 0709, NA ("within . . ."); Thompson to Longhery, October 3, 1850, ibid., frames 0920–0923. For American wishes and plans of expansion, see Herring, *Enduring Indians of Kansas*, 6; Unrau, *Rise and Fall of Indian Country*, 52–53, 109–110, 115–128. For the emigrants and other intruders in the Kansas reservations, see also Warren, *Shawnees and Their Neighbors*, 128.

38. Thompson to Longhery, October 3, 1850, RG 75, M234, roll 303, frame 0923, NA (quotation); Moseley to Lea, July 20, 1852, RG 75, M234, roll 364, frames 0305–0306, NA.

39. No contemporary document details the founding of the National Council, but indirect evidence and later oral histories date the event to 1852. December is suggested by the fact that it was then that the Shawnee agent, Thomas Moseley Jr., reported the "recent union of the Shawnee parties" and a group of fourteen Ohioan and Missourian headmen signed a power of attorney for Parks, authorizing him to negotiate for tribal lands and money in Washington. I surmise that the leaders authorizing Parks were the same who negotiated the "union" of the two "parties" and that this union meant the establishment of the National Council. Moseley to Mitchell, December 10, 1852, RG 75, M234, roll 364, frame 0559, NA; Power of Attorney to Joseph Parks, December 10, 1852, ibid., frames 0628–0630.

40. Guthrie in behalf of the Fish party in the spring of 1866, RG 75, M234, roll 814, frames 0753–0754, NA (quotations). Ohioan chiefs gave a far more positive account of the birth of the National Council in 1866: King et al. to Cooley, March 12, 1866, ibid., frames 0759–0772.

41. For the establishment and organization of the National Council, see Moseley to Mitchell, December 10, 1852, RG 75, M234, roll 364, frame 0559, NA ("union . . ."); Newsom to Robinson, September 5, 1860, RG 75, M234, roll 811, frame 0402, NA ("1st . . ."); LC Draper's 1868 Shawnee & Delaware Field Notes, EWVP, box 35, folder 320, pp. 2–3; Deposition of Moses Silverheels, November 30, 1865, RG 75, M234, roll 814, frame 0634, NA. For the meeting places, see "Charles Blue-Jacket v. The Commissioners of Johnson County," 301–302. My analysis of the transformation from communal consensus to a representative government follows Kidwell, *Choctaws in Oklahoma*, 42.

42. King et al. to Cooley, March 12, 1866, RG 75, M234, roll 814, frames 0766–0767, NA (quotation). For appreciative American opinions, see for example Morgan, *Indian Journals*, 54. For the early chiefs and other National Council members, see "Charles Blue-Jacket v. The Commissioners of Johnson County," 300; Answer to the Objections, 1855, RG 75, M234, roll 810, frame 0096, NA; Newsom to Robinson, October 25, 1860, RG 75, M234, roll 811, frame 0438, NA.

43. "Charles Blue-Jacket v. The Commissioners of Johnson County," 301–305; Miller to Cumming, July 24, 1855, RG 75, M234, roll 809, frame 0034, NA; Pay Roll of Orphan Shawnees, February 18, 1858, RG 75, M234, roll 810, frame 0113, NA; Harvey, *History of the Shawnee Indians*, 281–288 (quotation from 285).

44. Articles of Agreement and Convention, Peters, *Statutes at Large*, 357 ("shall never . . ."); Herring, *Enduring Indians of Kansas*, 6–7; Miner and Unrau, *End of Indian Kansas*, 3–12; Unrau, *Rise and Fall of Indian Country*, 125–136; Harvey, *History of the Shawnee Indians*, 292 ("This . . .").

45. Harvey, *History of the Shawnee Indians*, 274, 308–310; Gates, *Fifty Million Acres*, 15–17; Unrau, *Rise and Fall of Indian Country*, 134; Treaty with the Shawnees, May 10, 1854, Minot, *Statutes at Large*, 1058. Wawahchepaekar identified himself as a Chalaakaatha and a hereditary leader, Black Bob and Paschal Fish to Usher, March 12, 1864, RG 75, M234, roll 813, frame 0520, NA; Abbott to Dole, April 6, 1863, ibid., frame 0019. Long Tail's background is more difficult to ascertain. Henry Harvey reported that two of the eight leaders in the Shawnee delegation were Missourians. Since Wawahchepaekar and Graham Rogers were from Missouri, Long Tail must have been an Ohio Shawnee. In 1860 a man named Black Wolf who lived at Long Tail's community hosted a traditional ritual, probably a Bread Dance, which suggests that Long Tail may have leaned toward traditional Shawnee spirituality. Harvey, *History of the Shawnee Indians*, 310; Kimbro, " 'Genuine Western Man Never Drinks Tea,' " 174–175; King and Fish to Denver, September 1, 1857, RG 75, M234, roll 809, frame 0577, NA.

46. Treaty with the Shawnees, May 10, 1854, Minot, *Statutes at Large*, 1053–1058; Abing, "Fall from Grace," 334–335. For the ideology of allotment, see Banner, *How the Indians Lost Their Land*, 258–262.

47. Treaty with the Shawnees, May 10, 1854, Minot, *Statutes at Large*, 1054–1057. The treaty gave Long Tail's people, too, the right to hold their lands in common, but they later chose to take allotments; Ragsdale, "Dispossession of the Kansas Shawnees," 236–240.

48. Gates, *Fifty Million Acres*, 19–21, 48 ("not an . . ." from 19); Miner and Unrau, *End of Indian Kansas*, 7–15; Treaty with the Shawnees, May 10, 1854, Minot, *Statutes at Large*, 1056.

49. Gates, *Fifty Million Acres*, 58–60; Herring, *Enduring Indians of Kansas*, 7–8; Robinson to Cumming, December 22, 1854, RG 75, M234, roll 364, frame 1168, NA; Miller to Cumming, May 21, 1855, RG 75, M234, roll 809, frame 0011–0012, NA ("object . . .").

50. Meeker quoted in Warren, *Shawnees and Their Neighbors*, 99 ("The Shawanoes . . ."); Taylor to [?], July 17, 1857, RG 75, M234, roll 809, frame 0769, NA ("a number . . ."; "buying out"; "that will sell"); Miller to Cumming, July 24, 1855, ibid., frame 0033 ("strictly . . ." and "long continued . . ."); Morgan, *Indian Journals*, 53.

51. Robinson to Cumming, March 31, 1855, RG 75, M234, roll 364, frames 1236–1237, NA ("a majority"; "opposed . . ."; "their old . . ."; "equally . . ."; "to the chiefs . . ."); Bluejacket to Cooley, November 30, 1865, RG 75, M234, roll 814, frame 0639 ("not one . . .," "were opposed . . ."), 0641 ("the blood . . ."), NA; Abbot to Dole, April 6, 1863, RG 75, M234, roll 813, frame 0019, NA ("a direct . . ."), Alford, *Civilization*, 201–202.

52. Robinson to Cumming, March 31, 1855, RG 75, M234, roll 364, frames 1236–1237, NA; Young to Denver, August 22, 1857, RG 75, M234, roll 809, frame 0489, NA; King and Fish to Denver, September 1, 1857, ibid., frames 0576–0578; Charles Fish et al. to the President, February 6, 1861, RG 75, M234, roll 812, frames 0067–0068, NA. For accusations of corruption against Paschal Fish, see Bluejacket to Cooley, November 30, 1865, RG 75, M234, roll 814, frames 0640–0644, NA; Bowes, *Exiles and Pioneers*, 225–226.

53. Arnold to Manypenny, November 22, 1856, RG 75, M234, roll 809, frame 0290, NA; Receipt for Shawnee Patents, January 9, 1860, RG 75, M234, roll 811, frame 0039, NA; Cornatzer to Thompson, July 8, 1858, RG 75, M234, roll 810, frame 0014,

NA (quotation); Street to Cumming, February 17, 1857, RG 75, M234, roll 809, frame 0518, NA; Newsom to Robinson, September 2, 1858, RG 75, M234, roll 810, frames 0128–0129, NA.

54. "Charles Blue-Jacket v. The Commissioners of Johnson County," 297–300, 352 ("Shawnees do not . . ."; "difficult to . . ."), 358 ("the Shawnees who . . ."; "lands are . . ."); Gates, *Fifty Million Acres*, 38, 46; Rosen, *American Indians and State Law*, 47–48.

55. For the struggles between Indians and states, see Harring, *Crow Dog's Case*, 25–56; Rosen, *American Indians and State Law*. For the economic problems and taxation, see Abbott to Branch, July 8, 1861, RG 75, M234, roll 812, frame 0016, NA; "Charles Blue-Jacket v. The Commissioners of Johnson County," 296–297; Bowes, *Exiles and Pioneers*, 228–236; Gates, *Fifty Million Acres*, 46.

56. Alford, *Civilization*, 6–13 ("It is . . ." from 6; "almost . . ." and "take . . ." from 7); Abbott to Branch, May 26, 1862, RG 75, M234, roll 812, frame 0220, NA.

57. Alford, *Civilization*, 13 ("They took . . ."); Abbott to Branch, September 25, 1862, RG 75, M234, roll 812, frames 0223–0225, NA; Abbott to Branch, June 8, 1863, RG 75, M234, roll 813, frames 0130–0132, NA; Guthrie to Dole, September 29, 1864, ibid., frame 0568; Fish et al. to Cooley, December 5, 1865, RG 75, M234, roll 814, frame 0418, NA ("The U.S. . . .").

58. Morgan, *Indian Journals*, 53.

59. Treaty with the Shawnee, April 4, 1862, Deloria and De Mallie, *Documents of American Indian Diplomacy*, 2:1344–1346; Black Bob Statement, RG 75, M234, roll 814, frame 0646, NA ("no rights . . ."); Wawahchepaekar et al. to the Commissioner of Indian Affairs, RG 75, M234, roll 812, frame 516, NA ("a formal . . ."); Black Bob & Fish to Usher, March 12, 1864, RG 75, M234, roll 813, frame 0591, NA ("usurper[s] . . ."); Fish et al. to Dole, September 15, 1864, ibid., frames 0563–0564 ("We . . ."). For the death of Wawahchepaekar, see Alford, *Civilization*, 12; and Bluejacket to Cooley, November 30, 1865, RG 75, M234, roll 814, frames 0643–0644, NA. Bluejacket gives the time of death as 1854, but this is clearly a clerical error.

60. Bluejacket to Cooley, November 30, 1865, RG 75, M234, roll 814, frames 0638–0645, NA. For the treaties, see Deloria and De Mallie, *Documents of American Indian Diplomacy*, 2:871–874, 886–891, 912–918, 1344–1346, 1348–1350.

61. "Charles Blue-Jacket v. The Commissioners of Johnson County," 297.

62. Bowes, *Exiles and Pioneers*, 236–237; Warren, *Shawnees and Their Neighbors*, 158–159; Agreement between the Shawnee and Cherokee, June 7, 1869, Deloria and De Mallie, *Documents of American Indian Diplomacy*, 1:717–718. For the loss of the Kansas lands, see Ragsdale, "Dispossession of the Kansas Shawnees," 242–247.

63. For the Shawnee removal to Oklahoma, see Warren, *Shawnees and Their Neighbors*, 170–171. For the Black Bobs, see "Black Bob's Band of Kansas Shawnee Join the Cherokee Nation (Jim Clark, 1935)," EWVP, box 31, folder 281.

CONCLUSION

1. Bancroft, *History of the United States of America*, 4:87.

2. Drake, *Life of Tecumseh*, 20 ("The Shawanoes . . ."); Bancroft, *History of the United States of America*, 2:397 ("restless nation . . ."), 407 ("roved . . ."); Parkman, *Conspiracy of Pontiac*, 32 ("eccentric wanderings" and "roving . . .").

3. Buss, *Winning the West with Words*, 206–207.

4. Shoemaker, *Strange Likeness*, 6 ("a formal . . ." and "a vaguely . . ."); Godechot, "New Concept," 13–14. For Spanish and French practices, see Barr, *Peace Came*, 8; Witgen, *Infinity of Nations*, 69–107.

5. For the transformation of European concepts of nation during the era of the French Revolution, see Godechot, "New Concept," 13–19. For Marshall, see Shoemaker, *Strange Likeness*, 101–102 (all quotations).

6. For examples of a nineteenth-century writer using "tribe" as a subdivision of a "nation," see for example Trowbridge, *Shawanese Traditions*, 11, 16. For "instruments of conquest," see Buss, *Winning the West with Words*, 7. The changing rhetorical status of the Cherokees is traced in Cumfer, "Local Origins of National Indian Policy," 44 ("from . . ."). For a broader discussion on changing American discourses on Indian nationhood and land rights in the nineteenth century, see Banner, *How the Indians Lost Their Land*, 247–251.

7. Early anthropology and its primitivization of Native Americans are analyzed by Vincent, *Anthropology and Politics*, 38, 130–131, 172. For a broader treatment of how nineteenth-century anthropologists invented a "primitive" society, see Kuper, *Invention of Primitive Society*.

8. For ethnohistorians who draw attention to the difficulty of finding culturally meaningful words for depicting Indian social formations of the past, see Saunt, *New Order of Things*, 36–37; Shoemaker, *Strange Likeness*, 36, 39; Witgen, *Infinity of Nations*, 26–27.

9. Parkman, *Conspiracy of Pontiac*, 32 ("perplex"); Dowd, *War under Heaven*, 217 ("even less" and "political entity"); Warren, *Shawnees and Their Neighbors*, 18 ("a weakened . . .").

10. Anderson, *Imagined Communities*; Womack, *Red on Red*, 14; Moore, *Cheyenne Nation*, 10. Witgen, *Infinity of Nations*, 33, likewise emphasizes the importance of exploring how Indians imagined social formations as well as collective identities, even though he argues that "nationhood" is not an appropriate concept to capture these formations and identities among the seventeenth-century Anishinaabeg he studies.

11. That the ability of Indian peoples to combine diversity and unity successfully hinged largely on kinship and collective decision-making is emphasized in two excellent studies of the Lenapes: Schutt, "Forging Identities," and Schutt, *Peoples of the River Valleys*. My analysis owes a great deal to Schutt's insightful studies.

12. Minutes of a Council held at Wapaghkonetta, May 1825, RG 75, M1, roll 28, p. 378, NA ("the different . . .").

13. For the Mekoche belief, see Erminie Wheeler Voegelin, "Shawnee: An American Indian Culture," 21, 62–63, EWVP, box 31, folder 276.

14. Hämäläinen and Truett, "On Borderlands," 347 ("from within . . ."). For the importance of the time depth of Indian history, see for example Salisbury, "Indians' Old World"; Saunt, "Indians' Old World." Indian-Indian interaction is emphasized by Foster, *Being Comanche*, 13–19.

15. Calloway, "2008 Presidential Address," 200 ("place . . ."). For recentering American history, see also Hämäläinen and Truett, "On Borderlands," 345–354.

16. Sugden, "Shawnee," 583–584.

17. Warren, *Shawnees and Their Neighbors*, 170–171.

18. Alford, *Civilization*, 70 (quotation); Warren, *Shawnees and Their Neighbors*, 171–172; "Blanchard–Little Axe Meet with Assistant Secretary, Larry Echo Hawk"; author field notes, November 17, 2011.

19. Sugden, "Shawnee," 583; Provance, "Eastern Shawnee Tribe to Seek Federal Approval."

20. Author field notes, November 17, 2011.

BIBLIOGRAPHY

ARCHIVAL MATERIAL

American Philosophical Society, Philadelphia

James Logan Papers

Barker Texas History Center Archives and Manuscripts,
University of Texas at Austin

Thomas Jefferson Rusk Papers, 1824–1859

British Library, London

Bouquet Papers, Additional Manuscripts 21631–21660 (cited by volume and folio)
Haldimand Papers, Additional Manuscripts 21661–21892 (cited by volume and folio)

Historical Society of Pennsylvania, Philadelphia

Col. Richard Butler's Journal, 1775
Richard Peters Letterbooks
Richard Peters Papers

Library and Archives Canada, Ottawa, Ontario

William Claus Papers, MG 19
Indian Affairs Papers, RG 10
Indian Records, series II, RG 10
Military Papers, RG 8

Missouri Historical Society, St. Louis

Richard Graham Papers
Rodney Family Papers

The National Archives of the United Kingdom, Kew

CO 5: Colonial Office Papers: Board of Trade and Secretaries of State Original Correspondence on America and West Indies (cited by volume, part, and folio)
CO 42: Colonial Office Papers: Canada, original correspondence (cited by volume and folio)

National Archives of the United States, Washington, DC

RG 75: Records of the Bureau of Indian Affairs (cited by microcopy number [M])
RG 94: Letters Received by the Office of the Adjutant General (cited by microcopy number [M])
RG 107: Records of the Office of the Secretary of War (cited by microcopy number [M])

Newberry Library, Chicago

Erminie Wheeler-Voegelin Papers
John Sergeant Letters

New York State Library, Albany

Records of the Moravian Mission among the Indians of North America. A microfilm publication of Research Publications, Inc., of New Haven, Connecticut; photographed from original material at the Archives of the Moravian Church, Bethlehem, Pa.

Ohio Historical Society, Columbus

The Diary of Joseph and Martha Rhodes' Mission to the Shawnee Indians, 1817 [Part of the Story]
John Johnston Papers
Knopf, Richard C. (transcriber), The Papers of John Johnston, Indian Agent, from the Draper Collection Vol. 11YY
Memorial of the Society of Friends in Regard to the Indians

Ohio Valley–Great Lakes Ethnohistory Archive, Glenn A. Black Archaeology Laboratory, Indiana University, Bloomington

Lyman C. Draper Manuscripts (microfilm copy):
  Kentucky Papers (CC)
  Frontier Wars Manuscripts (U)
  Pittsburgh and Northwest Virginia Papers (NN)

Simon Kenton Papers (BB)
Tecumseh Papers (YY)
Thomas Gage Papers (microfilm copy)
George Morgan Letterbooks I–III (microfilm copy)
Shawnee File

Ulster County Clerk's Office, Kingston, N.Y.

101 Box Collection, Minutes of Common Pleas/Sessions Court/Justice of the Peace
Meetings, 1711/2–1720

PUBLISHED PRIMARY SOURCES

Alford, Thomas Wildcat. *Civilization: As Told to Florence Drake*. Norman: University of
Oklahoma Press, 1936.

Almonte, Juan M. "Statistical Report on Texas." *Southwestern Historical Quarterly* 28
(January 1925): 177–222.

Alvord, Clarence Walworth, and Clarence Edwin Carter, eds. *The Critical Period, 1763–
1765*. Collections of the Illinois State Historical Library, Vol. 10. Springfield: Trustees of
the Illinois State Historical Library, 1915.

———. *The New Regime, 1765–1767*. Collections of the Illinois State Historical Library,
Vol. 11. Springfield: Trustees of the Illinois State Historical Library, 1916.

Aupaumut, Hendrick. "A Narrative of an Embassy to the Western Indians, from the
Original Manuscript of Hendrick Aupaumut." In *Memoirs of the Historical Society of
Pennsylvania*, Vol. 2, 61–132. Philadelphia: Carey, Lea & Carey, 1827.

Babcock, Rufus, ed. *Forty Years of Pioneer Life: Memoir of John Mason Peck, D.D.*
Carbondale: Southern Illinois University Press, 1965.

Bailey, Kenneth P., ed. *The Ohio Company Papers, 1753–1817: Being Primarily Papers of
the "Suffering Traders" of Pennsylvania*. Arcata, CA, 1947.

Barker, Eugene C., ed. *The Austin Papers, Part 2*. Annual Report of the American Historical
Association for the Year 1919, Vol. 2. Washington, DC: Government Printing Office, 1924.

Berlandier, Jean Louis. *The Indians of Texas in 1830*. Edited by John C. Ewers. Washington,
DC: Smithsonian Institution Press, 1969.

Bond, Beverly W., Jr., ed. "The Captivity of Charles Stuart, 1755–57." *Mississippi Valley
Historical Review* 13 (1/1926): 58–81.

———. *The Correspondence of John Cleves Symmes, the Founder of the Miami Purchase*.
New York: Macmillan, 1926.

Browne, William Hand, Clayton Colman Hall, and Bernard Christian Steiner, eds.
Archives of Maryland. 72 vols. Baltimore: Maryland Historical Society, 1883–.

Butterfield, C. W., ed. *Washington–Irvine Correspondence: The Official Letters which
Passed between Washington and Brig.-Gen. William Irvine and between Irvine and
Others Concerning Military Affairs in the West from 1781 to 1783*. Madison, WI: David
Atwood, 1882.

Calloway, Colin G., ed. *Revolution and Confederation. Early American Indian Documents:
Treaties and Laws, 1607–1789*, Vol. 18. General editor Alden T. Vaughan. Bethesda,
MD: University Publications of America, 1994.

Carter, Clarence E., and John Porter Bloom, eds. *The Territorial Papers of the United States.* 28 vols. Washington DC: Government Printing Office, 1934–1975.

"Charles Blue-Jacket v. The Commissioners of Johnson County et al." *3 Kansas Reports 294* (1865): 294–358.

Craig, Neville, ed. "Gen. Butler's Journal." In *The Olden Time*, Vol. 2, 433–468, 481–525, 529–531. Pittsburgh: Dumars, 1846–1848.

Cruikshank, Ernest A., ed. *The Correspondence of Lieutenant-Governor John Graves Simcoe.* 5 vols. Toronto: Ontario Historical Society, 1923–1931.

Davies, Kenneth G., ed. *Documents of the American Revolution, 1770–1783.* 19 vols. Shannon: Irish University Press, 1972–1978.

Deliette, Louis. "Memoir of De Gannes Concerning the Illinois Country." In *The French Foundations, 1680–1693.* Collections of the Illinois State Historical Library, Vol. 23: French Series, Vol. 1. Edited by Theodore Calvin Pease and Raymond C. Werner. Springfield: Illinois State Historical Library, 1934.

Deloria, Vine, Jr., and Raymond J. DeMallie, eds. *Documents of American Indian Diplomacy: Treaties, Agreements, and Conventions, 1775–1979.* 2 vols. Norman: University of Oklahoma Press, 1999.

Denny, Ebenezer. *Military Journal of Major Ebenezer Denny, an Officer in the Revolutionary and Indian Wars.* 1859. Reprint, New York: Arno, 1971.

Document 512: Correspondence on the Subject of the Emigration of Indians, between the 30th November, 1831, and 27th December, 1833, with Abstracts of Expenditures by Disbursing Agents, in the Removal and Subsistence of Indians, &c., &c. Furnished in Answer to a Resolution of the Senate, of 27th December, 1833, by the Commissary General of Subsistence. 5 vols. Washington, DC: Duff Green, 1834–1835.

Du Lac, Perrin. *Travels through the Two Louisianas, And Among the Savage Nations of the Missouri; Also, in the United States, along the Ohio, and the Adjacent Provinces, in 1801, 1802, & 1803 with a Sketch of the Manners, Customs, Character, and Civil and Religious Ceremonies of the People of those Countries.* London: Richard Phillips, 1807.

Ekberg, Carl J., and William E. Foley, eds. *An Account of Upper Louisiana.* Columbia: University of Missouri Press, 1989.

Esarey, Logan, ed. *Messages and Letters of William Henry Harrison.* 2 vols. Indianapolis: Indiana Historical Commission, 1922.

Force, Peter, ed. *American Archives.* 4th and 5th series, 9 vols. Washington, DC: M. St. Clair Clarke and Peter Force, 1837–1853.

Foreman, Grant, ed. *Marcy and the Gold Seekers: The Journal of Captain R. B. Marcy, with an Account of the Gold Rush over the Southern Route.* Norman: University of Oklahoma Press, 1939.

———. *A Traveler in Indian Territory: The Journal of Ethan Allen Hitchcock, late Major-General in the United States Army.* Norman: University of Oklahoma Press, 1996.

Gist, Christopher. "Christopher Gist's First and Second Journals September 11, 1750–March 29, 1752 For the Honble Robert Dinwiddie Esquire Governor & Commander of Virginia." In *George Mercer Papers: Relating to the Ohio Company of Virginia*, edited by Lois Mulkearn, 7–40. Pittsburgh: University of Pittsburgh Press, 1954.

———. "A Journal." In *George Mercer Papers: Relating to the Ohio Company of Virginia*, edited by Lois Mulkearn, 97–122. Pittsburgh: University of Pittsburgh Press, 1954.

Goodman, Alfred T., ed. *The Journal of Captain William Trent from Logstown to Pickawillany, A.D. 1752.* Cincinnati, OH: Robert Clarke, 1871.

Graymont, Barbara, ed. *New York and New Jersey Treaties, 1683–1713. Early American Indian Documents: Treaties and Laws, 1607–1789,* Vol. 8. General editor Alden T. Vaughan. Bethesda, MD: University Publications of America, 1985.

Green, James A., ed. "Journal of Ensign William Schillinger, a Soldier of the War of 1812." *Ohio Archaeological and Historical Quarterly* 41 (1/1932): 51–85.

Harvey, Henry. *History of the Shawnee Indians, from the Year 1681 to 1854, Inclusive.* Millwood, NY: Kraus Reprint, 1977.

Hazard, Samuel, ed. *Minutes of the Provincial Council of Pennsylvania.* 16 vols. Harrisburg, PA: 1838–1853.

Hazard, Samuel, John Blair Linn, William Henry Egle, George Edward Reed, Thomas Lynch Montgomery, Gertrude MacKinney, and Charles Francis Hoban, eds. *Pennsylvania Archives.* 9 series, 138 vols. Philadelphia, 1852–1949.

Heckewelder, John. *History, Manners, and Customs of the Indian Nations who Once Inhabited Pennsylvania and the Neighbouring States.* Philadelphia: Historical Society of Pennsylvania, 1876.

———. *A Narrative of the Mission of the United Brethren among the Delaware and Mohegan Indians: From Its Commencement in the Year 1740 to the Close of the Year 1808.* Edited by William Elsey Connelley. Cleveland, OH: Burrows Bros., 1907.

Hirsch, Alison Duncan, ed. *Pennsylvania Treaties, 1756–1775. Early American Indian Documents: Treaties and Laws, 1607–1789,* Vol. 3. General editor Alden T. Vaughan. University Publications of America, 2004.

Hopkins, Gerard T. *A Mission to the Indians from the Indian Committee of Baltimore Yearly Meeting, to Fort Wayne, in 1804.* Philadelphia: T. Ellwood Zell, 1862.

Houck, Louis, ed. *The Spanish Regime in Missouri.* 2 vols. Chicago: R. R. Donnelley & Sons, 1909.

Hutchins, Thomas. "A Description of the Country Westward of the River Ohio, with the Distances Computed from Fort Pitt to the several Indian Towns by Land & Water." In *The Wilderness Trail Or the Ventures and Adventures of the Pennsylvania Traders on the Allagheny Path with Some New Annals of the Old West, and the Records of Some Strong Men and Some Bad Ones,* by Charles A. Hanna, Vol. 2, 192–202. New York: G. P. Putnam's Sons, 1911.

Jackson, Donald, ed. *Letters of the Lewis and Clark Expedition, with Related Documents, 1783–1854, Vol. 2.* Urbana: University of Illinois Press, 1978.

Jacobs, Wilbur R., ed. *Indians of the Southern Colonial Frontier: The Edmond Atkin Report and Plan of 1755.* Columbia: University of South Carolina Press, 1954.

James, James Alton, ed. *George Rogers Clark Papers,* Vol. 1, 1771–1781. Collections of the Illinois State Historical Library, Vol. 7: Virginia Series, Vol. 3. Springfield: Trustees of the Illinois State Historical Library, 1912.

———. *George Rogers Clark Papers,* Vol. 2, 1781–1784. Collections of the Illinois State Historical Library, Vol. 19: Virginia Series, Vol. 4. Springfield: Trustees of the Illinois State Historical Library, 1926.

Johnston, John. "Account of the Present State of the Indian Tribes Inhabiting Ohio." *Archaeologia Americana: Transactions and Collections of the American Antiquarian Society* 1 (1820): 269–299.

Jones, David. *A Journal of Two Visits made to Some Indians on the West Side of the River Ohio In the Years 1772 and 1773.* New York: Reprinted for Joseph Sabin, 1865.

Jordan, John W., ed. "Journal of James Kenny, 1761–1763." *Pennsylvania Magazine of History and Biography* 37 (1–2/1913): 1–47, 152–201.

Kellogg, Louise Phelps, ed. *Frontier Advance on the Upper Ohio, 1778–1779.* State Historical Society of Wisconsin Collections, Vol. 22. Madison: State Historical Society of Wisconsin, 1916.

——. *Frontier Retreat on the Upper Ohio, 1779–1781.* State Historical Society of Wisconsin Collections, Vol. 24. Madison: State Historical Society of Wisconsin, 1917.

Kent, Donald H., ed. *Pennsylvania and Delaware Treaties, 1692–1737. Early American Indian Documents: Treaties and Laws, 1607–1789,* Vol. 1. General editor Alden T. Vaughan. Washington, DC: University Publications of America, 1979.

——. *Pennsylvania Treaties, 1737–1756. Early American Indian Documents: Treaties and Laws, 1607–1789,* Vol. 2. General editor Alden T. Vaughan. Frederick, MD: University Publications of America, 1984.

Kimbro, Harriet, ed. " 'A Genuine Western Man Never Drinks Tea': Gustavus French Merriam's Letters from Kansas in 1860." *Kansas History* 8 (Autumn 1985): 162–175.

Kinnaird, Lawrence, ed. *Spain in the Mississippi Valley, 1765–1794.* 3 vols. Washington, DC: Government Printing Office, 1946–1949.

Klinck, Carl F., and James J. Talman, eds. *The Journal of Major John Norton, 1816.* Toronto: Champlain Society, 1970.

Knopf, Richard C., ed. *Anthony Wayne: A Name in Arms. Soldier, Diplomat, Defender of Expansion Westward of a Nation. The Wayne-Knox-Pickering-McHenry Correspondence.* Pittsburgh: University of Pittsburgh Press, 1960.

——. *Document Transcriptions of the War of 1812 in the Northwest,* Vol. 2, *Return Jonathan Meigs Jr. and the War of 1812.* Columbus: Ohio Historical Society, 1957.

——. *Document Transcriptions of the War of 1812 in the Northwest,* Vol. 6, Part 1, *Letters to the Secretary of War Relating to the War of 1812 in the Northwest.* Columbus: Ohio Historical Society, 1959.

Lambing, A. A., ed. "Celeron's Journal." *Ohio Archaeological and Historical Society Publications* 29 (1920): 335–395, 481–483.

Leider, Lawrence H., ed. *The Livingston Indian Records, 1666–1723.* Gettysburg: Pennsylvania Historical Association, 1956.

Libby, Dorothy, ed. "Thomas Forsyth to William Clark, St. Louis, December 23, 1812." *Ethnohistory* 8 (Spring 1961): 179–195.

Lowrie, Walter, Matthew St. Clair Clarke, and Walter S. Franklin, eds. *American State Papers, Class II: Indian Affairs.* 2 vols. Washington, DC: Gales and Seaton, 1832–1834.

Lutz, J. J. "The Methodist Missions among the Indian Tribes in Kansas." *Transactions of the Kansas State Historical Society* 9 (1905–1906): 160–230.

McCoy, Isaac. *History of Baptist Indian Missions: Embracing Remarks on the Former and Present Condition of the Aboriginal Tribes; Their Settlement within the Indian Territory, and their Future Prospects.* Washington, DC: William M. Morrison, 1840.

McDowell, William L., Jr., ed. *Colonial Records of South Carolina: Documents relating to Indian Affairs, May 21, 1750–August 7, 1754.* Columbia: South Carolina Archives Department, 1958.

McKenney, Thomas L., and James Hall. *The Indian Tribes of North America with Biographical Sketches and Anecdotes of the Principal Chiefs*, Vol. 1. Edited by Frederick Webb Hodge. Edinburgh: John Grant, 1933.

MacLean, J. P., ed. "Shaker Mission to the Shawnee Indians." *Ohio Archaeological and Historical Publications* 11 (1903): 215–229.

Margry, Pierre, ed. *Découvertes et établissements des Français dans l'ouest et dans le sud de l'Amérique septentrionale, 1614–1754. Mémoires et documents originaux*. 6 vols. Paris: D. Jouaust, 1876–1886.

Meek, Basil, ed. "General Harmar's Expedition." *Ohio Archaeological and Historical Society Publications* 20 (1911): 74–108.

Michigan Pioneer and Historical Collections. 40 vols. Lansing: Pioneer and Historical Society of the State of Michigan, 1877–1929.

Minet. "Voyage Made from Canada Inland Going Southward during the Year 1682." In *LaSalle, the Mississippi, and the Gulf: Three Primary Documents*, edited by Robert S. Weddle, 29–68. College Station: Texas A&M University Press, 1987.

Minot, George, ed. *Statutes at Large and Treaties of the United States of America*, Vol. 10, *From December 1, 1851, to March 3, 1855*. Boston: Little, Brown, 1855.

Montgomery, Samuel. "Journal of Samuel Montgomery." *Mississippi Valley Historical Review* 2 (September 1915): 262–273.

Morgan, Lewis Henry. *The Indian Journals, 1859–1862*. Edited by Leslie A. White. New York: Dover, 1993.

Nasatir, A. P., ed. *Before Lewis and Clark: Documents Illustrating the History of Missouri, 1785–1804*, Vol. 1. St. Louis, MO: St. Louis Historical Documents Foundation, 1952.

Oberg, Barbara B., ed. *The Papers of Thomas Jefferson*, Vol. 36. Princeton, NJ: Princeton University Press, 2009.

O'Callaghan, Edmund B., and Berthold Fernow, eds. *Documents Relative to the Colonial History of the State of New York*. 15 vols. Albany, NY: Weed, Parsons, 1856–1887.

Palmer, William P., Sherwin McRae, Raleigh Edward Colston, and Henry W. Flournoy, eds. *Calendar of Virginia State Papers and Other Manuscripts*. 11 vols. Richmond: Virginia State Library, 1875–1893.

Peters, Richard, ed. *The Public Statutes at Large of the United States of America*, Vol. 7. Boston: Charles C. Little and James Brown, 1846.

Post, Charles [Christian] Frederick, "Two Journals of Western Tours, by Charles Frederick Post: One, to the Neighborhood of Fort Duquesne (July–September 1758); the Other, to the Ohio (October, 1758–January, 1759)." In *Early Western Travels, 1748–1846*, Vol. 1, edited by Reuben Gold Thwaites, 175–291. Cleveland, OH: Arthur H. Clark, 1904.

Quaife, M. M., ed. "Henry Hay's Journal from Detroit to the Miami River." In *Proceedings of the State Historical Society of Wisconsin*, 208–261. Madison: State Historical Society of Wisconsin, 1914.

Quaife, Milo Milton, ed. *The Indian Captivity of O. M. Spencer*. New York: Citadel, 1968.

Ridout, Thomas. "Narrative of the Captivity among the Shawanese Indians, in 1788, of Thomas Ridout, Afterwards Surveyor-General of Upper Canada, from the Original

Manuscript in Possession of the Family." In *Ten Years of Upper Canada in Peace and War, 1805–1815; Being the Ridout Letters with Annotations by Matilda Edgar. Also an Appendix of The Narrative of the Captivity among the Shawanese Indians, in 1788, of Thomas Ridout, Afterwards Surveyor-General of Upper Canada; and a Vocabulary, Compiled by Him, of the Shawanese Language*, edited by Matilda Edgar, 339–381. Toronto: William Briggs, 1890.

Robertson, James Alexander, ed. *Louisiana under the Rule of Spain, France, and the United States, 1785–1807, Vol. 1.* Cleveland, OH: Arthur H. Clark, 1911.

Robinson, W. Stitt, ed. *Maryland Treaties, 1632–1775. Early American Indian Documents: Treaties and Laws, 1607–1789*, Vol. 6. General editor Alden T. Vaughan. Frederick, MD: University Publications of America, 1987.

———. *Virginia Treaties, 1723–1775. Early American Indian Documents: Treaties and Laws, 1607–1789*, Vol. 5. General editor Alden T. Vaughan. Frederick, MD: University Publications of America, 1983.

Rowland, Dunbar, and A. G. Sanders, eds. *Mississippi Provincial Archives: French Dominion*, Vols. 1–3. Jackson: Press of the Mississippi Department of Archives and History, 1927–1932.

Rowland, Dunbar, A. G. Sanders, and Patricia Kay Galloway, eds. *Mississippi Provincial Archives: French Dominion*, Vols. 4–5. Baton Rouge: Louisiana State University Press, 1984.

Sánchez, José María. "A Trip to Texas in 1828." *Southwestern Historical Quarterly* 29 (April 1926): 249–288.

Scribner, Robert L., and Brent Tarter, eds. *Revolutionary Virginia: The Road to Independence.* 7 vols. Charlottesville: University Press of Virginia, 1973–1983.

Slover, John. "The Narrative of John Slover." In *A Collection of Some of the Most Interesting Narratives of Indian Warfare in the West, containing an account of the Adventures of Colonel Daniel Boone, one of the first settlers in Kentucky, Comprehending the most important occurrences relative to its early history—Also, an account of the Manners and Customs of the Indians, their Traditions and Religious Sentiments, their Police or Civil Government, their Discipline and method of War; To which is added an account of the Expeditions of Genl's Harmer, Scott, Wilkinson, St. Clair & Wayne*, compiled by Samuel Metcalf, 53–71. Lexington, KY: William G. Hunt, 1821.

Smith, William Henry, ed. *The Life and Public Services of Arthur St. Clair, a Soldier of the Revolutionary War; President of the Continental Congress; and Governor of the North-Western Territory, with his Correspondence and Other Papers.* 2 vols. Cincinnati, OH: Robert Clarke, 1882.

Smith, William Provost. *Historical Account of Bouquet's Expedition against the Ohio Indians in 1764.* Cincinnati, OH: Robert Clarke, 1907.

Spencer, Joab. "The Shawnee Indians: Their Customs, Traditions and Folk-Lore." *Transactions of the Kansas State Historical Society* 10 (1907–1908): 382–402.

Stevens, Sylvester K., and Donald H. Kent, eds. *Wilderness Chronicles of Northwestern Pennsylvania.* Harrisburg: Pennsylvania Historical Commission, 1941.

Stevens, Sylvester K., Donald H. Kent, Autumn L. Leonard, Louis M. Waddell, and John L. Tottenham, eds. *The Papers of Henry Bouquet.* 6 vols. Harrisburg: Pennsylvania Historical and Museum Commission, 1951–1994.

Stoddard, Amos. *Sketches, Historical and Descriptive of Louisiana.* Philadelphia: Matthew Carey, 1812.

Sullivan, James, Alexander C. Flick, Almon W. Lauber, Albert B. Corey, and Milton W. Hamilton, eds., *The Papers of Sir William Johnson*. 14 vols. Albany: State University of New York, 1921–1965.

Thornbrough, Gayle, ed. *Letter Book of the Indian Agency at Fort Wayne, 1809–1815*. Indianapolis: Indiana Historical Society, 1961.

———. *Outpost on the Wabash, 1787–1791: Letters of Brigadier General Josiah Harmar and Major John Francis Hamtramck and Other Letters and Documents Selected from the Harmar Papers in the William L. Clements Library*. Indianapolis: Indiana Historical Society, 1957.

Thwaites, Reuben Gold, ed. *The French Regime in Wisconsin, 1743–1760*. Collections of the State Historic Society of Wisconsin, Vol. 18. Madison: State Historical Society of Wisconsin, 1908.

———. *The French Regime in Wisconsin, II: 1727–1748*. Collections of the State Historic Society of Wisconsin, Vol. 17. Madison: State Historical Society of Wisconsin, 1906.

———. *Jesuit Relations and Allied Documents: Travel and Explorations of the Jesuit Missionaries in New France, 1610–1791; the Original French, Latin, and Italian Texts, with English Translations and Notes*. 73 vols. Cleveland, OH: Burrows Brothers, 1896–1901.

Thwaites, Reuben Gold, and Louise Phelps Kellogg, eds. *Documentary History of Dunmore's War, 1774*. Madison: State Historical Society of Wisconsin, 1905.

———. *Frontier Defense on the Upper Ohio, 1777–1778*. Madison: State Historical Society of Wisconsin, 1912.

———. *Revolution on the Upper Ohio, 1775–1777*. Madison: State Historical Society of Wisconsin, 1908.

Trowbridge, C. C. *Meeārmeer Traditions*. Edited by Vernon Kinietz. Occasional Contributions from the Museum of Anthropology of the University of Michigan, No. 7. Ann Arbor: University of Michigan Press, 1938.

———. *Shawanese Traditions: C. C. Trowbridge's Account*. Edited by Vernon Kinietz and Erminie W. Voegelin. Occasional Contributions from the Museum of Anthropology of the University of Michigan, No. 9. Ann Arbor: University of Michigan Press, 1939.

Wainwright, Nicholas B., ed. "George Croghan's Journal, 1759–1763." *Pennsylvania Magazine of History and Biography* 71 (October 1947): 311–444.

Washington, H. A., ed. *The Writings of Thomas Jefferson: Being His Autobiography, Correspondence, Reports, Messages, Addresses, and Other Writings, Official and Private*, Vol. 8. Washington, DC: Taylor & Maury, 1954.

Wellenreuther, Hermann, and Carola Wessel, eds. *The Moravian Mission Diaries of David Zeisberger, 1772–1781*. University Park: Pennsylvania State University Press, 2005.

Wilson, William. "An Acc't of the Indian Towns & Nations in the Western Department— Their Numbers & present Dispositions." *Virginia Magazine of History and Biography* 23 (October 1915): 345–346.

Winfrey, Dorman H., James M. Day et al., eds. *Texas Indian Papers*. 4 vols. Austin: Texas State Library, 1959–1961.

Yeates, Jasper. "Indian Treaty at Fort Pitt in 1776." *Pennsylvania Magazine of History and Biography* 5 (4/1881): 484–485.

SECONDARY SOURCES

Abing, Kevin. "Before Bleeding Kansas: Christian Missionaries, Slavery, and the Shawnee Indians in Pre-Territorial Kansas, 1844–1854." *Kansas History* 24 (Spring 2001): 54–70.

———. "A Fall from Grace: Thomas Johnson and the Shawnee Indian Manual Labor School, 1839–1862." Ph.D. diss., Marquette University, 1995.

———. "A Holy Battleground: Methodist, Baptist, and Quaker Missionaries among Shawnee Indians, 1830–1844." *Kansas History* 21 (Summer 1998): 118–137.

Adelman, Jeremy, and Stephen Aron. "From Borderlands to Borders: Empires, Nation-States and the Peoples in between in North American History." *American Historical Review* 104 (June 1999): 814–841.

Allen, Robert S. *His Majesty's Indian Allies: British Indian Policy in the Defence of Canada, 1774–1815.* Toronto: Dundurn, 1992.

Anderson, Benedict. *Imagined Communities: Reflections on the Origins and Spread of Nationalism.* Rev. ed. London: Verso, 1991.

Anderson, Fred. *Crucible of War: The Seven Years' War and the Fate of Empire in British North America, 1754–1766.* New York: Vintage, 2000.

Anderson, Gary Clayton. *The Conquest of Texas: Ethnic Cleansing in the Promised Land, 1820–1875.* Norman: University of Oklahoma Press, 2005.

Anderson, H. Allen. "The Delaware and Shawnee Indians and the Republic of Texas, 1820–1845." *Southwestern Historical Quarterly* 94 (October 1990): 231–260.

Andrist, Ralph K. *The Long Death: The Last Days of the Plains Indians.* New York: Collier, 1964.

Aquila, Richard. "Down the Warrior's Path: The Causes of the Southern Wars of the Iroquois." *American Indian Quarterly* 4 (August 1978): 211–221.

———. *The Iroquois Restoration: Iroquois Diplomacy on the Colonial Frontier, 1701–1754.* Detroit, MI: Wayne State University Press, 1983.

Aron, Stephen. *American Confluence: The Missouri Frontier from Borderland to Border State.* Bloomington: Indiana University Press, 2006.

———. *How the West Was Lost: The Transformation of Kentucky from Daniel Boone to Henry Clay.* Baltimore: Johns Hopkins University Press, 1996.

———. "Pigs and Hunters: 'Rights in the Woods' on the Trans-Appalachian Frontier." In *Contact Points: American Frontiers from the Mohawk Valley to the Mississippi, 1750–1830,* edited by Andrew R. L. Cayton and Frederika J. Teute, 175–204. Chapel Hill: University of North Carolina Press, 1998.

Axtell, James. *The Invasion Within: The Contest of Cultures in Colonial North America.* New York: Oxford University Press, 1985.

Bamann, Susan, Robert Kuhn, James Molnar, and Dean Snow. "Iroquoian Archaeology." *Annual Review of Anthropology* 21 (1992): 435–460.

Bancroft, George. *History of the United States of America from the Discovery of the Continent,* Vol. 2. Boston: Little, Brown, 1879.

———. *History of the United States of America from the Discovery of the Continent,* Vol. 4. New York: D. Appleton, 1884.

Banner, Stuart. *How the Indians Lost Their Land: Law and Power on the Frontier.* Cambridge, MA: Belknap, 2005.

Barber, Russell J., and Frances F. Berdan. *The Emperor's Mirror: Understanding Cultures through Primary Sources.* Tucson: University of Arizona Press, 1998.

Barr, Daniel P. " 'This Land Is Ours and Not Yours': The Western Delawares and the Seven Years' War in the Upper Ohio Valley." In *The Boundaries between Us: Natives and Newcomers along the Frontiers of the Old Northwest Territory, 1750–1850,* edited by Daniel P. Barr, 25–43. Kent, OH: Kent State University Press, 2006.

Barr, Juliana. "Geographies of Power: Mapping Indian Borders in the 'Borderlands' of the Early Southwest." *William and Mary Quarterly* 68 (January 2011): 5–46.

———. *Peace Came in the Form of a Woman: Indians and Spaniards in the Texas Borderlands.* Chapel Hill: University of North Carolina Press, 2007.

Barry, Louise. *The Beginning of the West: Annals of the Kansas Gateway to the American West, 1540–1854.* Topeka: Kansas State Historical Society, 1972.

Beck, Robin A., Jr. "Catawba Coalescence and the Shattering of the Carolina Piedmont." In *Mapping the Mississippian Shatter Zone: The Colonial Indian Slave Trade and Regional Instability in the American South,* edited by Robbie Ethridge and Sheri M. Shuck-Hall, 115–141. Lincoln: University of Nebraska Press, 2009.

Benn, Carl. *The Iroquois in the War of 1812.* Toronto: University of Toronto Press, 1998.

Bernstein, David. " 'We Are Not Now as We Once Were': Iowa Indians' Political and Economic Adaptations during U.S. Incorporation." *Ethnohistory* 54 (Fall 2007): 605–637.

"Blanchard–Little Axe Meet with Assistant Secretary, Larry Echo Hawk." http://www.absenteeshawneetribe-nsn.gov/BLANCHARD.pdf (accessed 5/3/2012).

Bloch, Ruth. *Visionary Republic: Millennial Themes in American Thought, 1756–1800.* Cambridge: Cambridge University Press, 1985.

Bohaker, Heidi. "*Nindoodemag*: The Significance of Algonquian Kinship Networks in the Eastern Great Lakes Region, 1600–1701." *William and Mary Quarterly* 63 (January 2006): 23–52.

———. "Reading Anishinaabe Identities: Meaning and Metaphor in *Nindoodem* Pictographs." *Ethnohistory* 57 (Winter 2010): 11–33.

Bowes, John P. *Exiles and Pioneers: Eastern Indians in the Trans-Mississippi West.* Cambridge: Cambridge University Press, 2007.

Brandão, José António, and William Starna. "The Treaties of 1701: A Triumph of Iroquois Diplomacy." *Ethnohistory* 43 (Spring 1996): 209–244.

Braun, Sebastian F. "Imagining Un-Imagined Communities: The Politics of Indigenous Nationalism." In *Tribal Worlds: Critical Studies in American Indian Nation Building,* edited by Brian Hosmer and Larry Nesper, 141–160. Albany, NY: SUNY Press, 2013.

Brooks, Lisa. "Two Paths to Peace: Competing Visions of Native Space in the Old Northwest." In *The Boundaries between Us: Natives and Newcomers along the Frontiers of the Old Northwest Territory, 1750–1850,* edited by Daniel P. Barr, 87–117. Kent, OH: Kent State University Press, 2006.

Buss, James Joseph. *Winning the West with Words: Language and Conquest in the Lower Great Lakes.* Norman: University of Oklahoma Press, 2011.

Caldwell, Martha B., comp. *Annals of the Shawnee Methodist Mission and Indian Manual Labor School.* Topeka: Kansas State Historical Society, 1939.

Calhoun, Craig. *Nationalism.* Buckingham: Open University Press, 1997.

Callender, Charles. "Great Lakes–Riverine Sociopolitical Organization." In *Handbook of North American Indians*, Vol. 15, *Northeast*, edited by Bruce G. Trigger, 610–621. Washington, DC: Smithsonian Institution, 1978.

——. "Miami." In *Handbook of North American Indians*, Vol. 15, *Northeast*, edited by Bruce G. Trigger, 681–689. Washington, DC: Smithsonian Institution, 1978.

——. "Shawnee." In *Handbook of North American Indians*, Vol. 15, *Northeast*, edited by Bruce G. Trigger, 622–635. Washington, DC: Smithsonian Institution, 1978.

——. *Social Organization of the Central Algonkian Indians*. Milwaukee Public Museum Publications in Anthropology, No. 7. Milwaukee: Milwaukee Public Museum, 1962.

Callender, Charles, Richard K. Pope, and Susan M. Pope. "Kickapoo." In *Handbook of North American Indians*, Vol. 15, *Northeast*, edited by Bruce G. Trigger, 656–667. Washington, DC: Smithsonian Institution, 1978.

Calloway, Colin G. *The American Revolution in the Indian Country: Crisis and Diversity in Native American Communities*. Cambridge: Cambridge University Press, 1995.

——. "The Continuing Revolution in Indian Country." In *Native Americans and the Early Republic*, edited by Frederick E. Hoxie, Ronald Hoffman, and Peter J. Albert, 3–33. Charlottesville: University Press of Virginia, 1999.

——. *Crown and Calumet: British-Indian Relations, 1783–1815*. Norman: University of Oklahoma Press, 1987.

——. *The Scratch of a Pen: 1763 and the Transformation of North America*. Oxford: Oxford University Press, 2006.

——. *The Shawnees and the War for America*. New York: Viking, 2007.

——. "2008 Presidential Address: Indian History from the End of the Alphabet; And What Now?" *Ethnohistory* 58 (Spring 2011): 197–211.

Campbell, William J. *Speculators in Empire: Iroquoia and the 1768 Treaty of Fort Stanwix*. Norman: University of Oklahoma Press, 2012.

Cashin, Edward J. " 'But Brothers, It Is Our Land We Are Talking About': Winners and Losers in the Georgia Backcountry." In *An Uncivil War: The Southern Backcountry during the American Revolution*, edited by Ronald Hoffman, Thad W. Tate, and Peter J. Albert, 240–275. Charlottesville: University of Virginia Press, 1985.

Cave, Alfred A. "The Failure of the Shawnee Prophet's Witch-Hunt." *Ethnohistory* 42 (Summer 1995): 445–475.

——. *Prophets of the Great Spirit: Native American Revitalization Movements in Eastern North America*. Lincoln: University of Nebraska Press, 2006.

——. "Shawnee Prophet, Tecumseh and Tippecanoe: A Case Study of Historical Myth-Making." *Journal of the Early Republic* 22 (Winter 2002): 637–673.

Cayton, Andrew R. L. *Frontier Indiana*. Bloomington: Indiana University Press, 1996.

——. " 'Separate Interests' and the Nation-State: The Washington Administration and the Origins of Regionalism in the Trans-Appalachian West." *Journal of American History* 79 (June 1992): 39–67.

——. "Writing North American History." *Journal of the Early Republic* 22 (Spring 2002): 105–111.

Cayton, Andrew R. L., and Frederika J. Teute, eds. *Contact Points: American Frontiers from the Mohawk Valley to the Mississippi, 1750–1830*. Chapel Hill: University of North Carolina Press, 1998.

Clark, Jerry E. *The Shawnee*. Lexington: University Press of Kentucky, 1977.

Cowan, C. Wesley. *First Farmers in the Middle Ohio Valley: Fort Ancient Societies, A.D. 1000–1670.* Cincinnati, OH: Cincinnati Museum of Natural History, 1987.

Crosby, Alfred. "Virgin Soil Epidemics as a Factor in the Aboriginal Depopulation in America." *William and Mary Quarterly* 33 (April 1976): 289–299.

Crow, Jeffrey J. "Liberty Men and Loyalists: Disorder and Disaffection in the North Carolina Backcountry." In *An Uncivil War: The Southern Backcountry during the American Revolution*, edited by Ronald Hoffman, Thad W. Tate, and Peter J. Albert, 125–178. Charlottesville: University of Virginia Press, 1985.

Cumfer, Cynthia. "Local Origins of National Indian Policy: Cherokee and Tennessean Ideas about Sovereignty and Nationhood, 1790–1811." *Journal of the Early Republic* 23 (Spring 2003): 21–46.

Darnell, Regna. "Private Discourse, Public Discourse and Algonquian Oral Tradition." In *Actes du vingt-cinquième congrès des algonquinistes*, edited by William Cowan, 72–82. Ottawa: Carleton University, 1994.

Deloria, Vine, Jr. *Red Earth, White Lies: Native Americans and the Myth of Scientific Fact.* Golden, CO: Fulcrum, 1995.

Dennis, Matthew. *Seneca Possessed: Indians, Witchcraft, and Power in the Early American Republic.* Philadelphia: University of Pennsylvania Press, 2010.

Dietler, Michael, and Brian Hayden. "Digesting the Feast—Good to Eat, Good to Drink, Good to Think: An Introduction." In *Feasts: Archaeological and Ethnographic Perspectives on Food, Politics, and Power*, edited by Michael Dietler and Brian Hayden, 1–20. Washington, DC: Smithsonian Institution Press, 2001.

Din, Gilbert C. "The Immigration Policy of Governor Esteban Miró in Spanish Louisiana." *Southwestern Historical Quarterly* 73 (October 1969): 155–175.

Din, Gilbert C., and A. P. Nasatir. *The Imperial Osages: Spanish-Indian Diplomacy in the Mississippi Valley.* Norman: University of Oklahoma Press, 1983.

Dobyns, Henry. *Their Number Became Thinned: Native American Population Dynamics in Eastern North America.* Knoxville: University of Tennessee Press, 1983.

Donham, Donald L. *History, Power, Ideology: Central Issues in Marxism and Anthropology.* Cambridge: Cambridge University Press, 1990.

Dowd, Gregory Evans. "The French King Wakes Up in Detroit: 'Pontiac's War' in Rumor and History." *Ethnohistory* 37 (Summer 1990): 254–278.

———. *A Spirited Resistance: The North American Indian Struggle for Unity, 1745–1812.* Baltimore: Johns Hopkins University Press, 1992.

———. *War under Heaven: Pontiac, the Indian Nations, and the British Empire.* Baltimore: Johns Hopkins University Press, 2002.

Downes, Randolph C. *Council Fires on the Upper Ohio: A Narrative of Indian Affairs in the Upper Ohio Valley until 1795.* Pittsburgh: University of Pittsburgh Press, 1940.

Drake, Benjamin. *Life of Tecumseh, and of His Brother the Prophet; with a Historical Sketch of the Shawnee Indians.* Cincinnati: E. Morgan, 1841.

Drooker, Penelope B. "The Ohio Valley, 1550–1750: Patterns of Sociopolitical Coalescence and Dispersal." In *The Transformations of the Southeastern Indians, 1540–1760*, edited by Robbie Ethridge and Charles Hudson, 115–133. Jackson: University Press of Mississippi, 2002.

———. *The View from Madisonville: Protohistoric Western Fort Ancient Interaction Patters.* Ann Arbor: University of Michigan Press, 1997.

Drooker, Penelope B., and C. Wesley Cowan. "Transformations of the Fort Ancient Cultures of the Central Ohio Valley." In *Societies in Eclipse: Archaeology of the Eastern Woodlands Indians, A.D. 1400–1700*, edited by David S. Brose, Robert C. Mainforth Jr., and C. Wesley Cowan, 83–106. Washington, DC: Smithsonian Institution Press, 2001.

Druke, Mary A. "Linking Arms: The Structure of Iroquois Intertribal Diplomacy." In *Beyond the Covenant Chain: The Iroquois and Their Neighbours in Indian North America, 1600–1800*, edited by Daniel K. Richter and James H. Merrell, 29–39. Syracuse, NY: Syracuse University Press, 1987.

Duthu, N. Bruce. *American Indians and the Law.* New York: Viking, 2008.

DuVal, Kathleen. *The Native Ground: Indians and Colonists in the Heart of the Continent.* Philadelphia: University of Pennsylvania Press, 2006.

Eccles, W. J. "The Fur Trade and Eighteenth-Century Imperialism." *William and Mary Quarterly 40* (July 1983): 341–362.

Edmunds, R. David. " 'Evil Men Who Add to Our Difficulties': Shawnees, Quakers, and William Wells, 1807–1808." *American Indian Culture and Research Journal 14* (4/1990): 1–14.

———. "Native Americans, New Voices: American Indian History, 1985–1995." *American Historical Review 100* (June 1995): 717–740.

———. *The Shawnee Prophet.* Lincoln: University of Nebraska Press, 1983.

———. *Tecumseh and the Quest for Indian Leadership.* Boston: Little, Brown, 1984.

———. " 'A Watchful Safeguard to Our Habitations': Black Hoof and the Loyal Shawnees." In *Native Americans and the Early Republic*, edited by Frederick E. Hoxie, Ronald Hoffman, and Peter J. Albert, 162–199. Charlottesville: University Press of Virginia, 1999.

Ekberg, Carl J. *Colonial Ste. Genevieve: An Adventure on the Mississippi Frontier.* Gerald, MO: Patrice, 1985.

Ethridge, Robbie. *Creek Country: The Creek Indians and Their World.* Chapel Hill: University of North Carolina Press, 2003.

———. "Creating the Shatter Zone: Indian Slave Traders and the Collapse of the Southeastern Chiefdoms." In *Light on the Path: The Anthropology and History of the Southeastern Indians*, edited by Thomas J. Pluckhahn and Robbie Ethridge, 207–218. Tuscaloosa: University of Alabama Press, 2006.

———. *From Chicaza to Chickasaw: The European Invasion and the Transformation of the Mississippian World, 1540–1715.* Chapel Hill: University of North Carolina Press, 2010.

———. "Introduction: Mapping the Mississippian Shatter Zone." In *Mapping the Mississippian Shatter Zone: The Colonial Indian Slave Trade and Regional Instability in the American South*, edited by Robbie Ethridge and Sheri M. Shuck-Hall, 1–62. Lincoln: University of Nebraska Press, 2009.

Everett, Dianna. *Texas Cherokees: A People between Two Fires, 1819–1840.* Norman: University of Oklahoma Press, 1990.

Faragher, John Mack. " 'More Motley than Mackinaw': From Ethnic Mixing to Ethnic Cleansing on the Frontier of the Lower Missouri, 1783–1833." In *Contact Points: American Frontiers from the Mohawk Valley to the Mississippi, 1750–1830*, edited by Andrew R. L. Cayton and Frederika J. Teute, 304–326. Chapel Hill: University of North Carolina Press, 1998.

Feeley, Stephen Delbert. "Tuscarora Trails: Indian Migrations, War, and Constructions of Colonial Frontiers." Ph.D. diss., College of William and Mary, 2007.

Feinman, Gary, and Jill Neitzel. "Too Many Types: An Overview of Sedentary Prestate Societies in the Americas." In *Advances of Archaeological Method and Theory*, Vol. 7, edited by Michael B. Schiffer, 39–102. Orlando, FL: Academic Press, 1984.

Fenton, William N. *The Great Law and the Longhouse: A Political History of the Iroquois Confederacy*. Norman: University of Oklahoma Press, 1998.

———. "Northern Iroquoian Culture Patterns." In *Handbook of North American Indians*, Vol. 15, *Northeast*, edited by Bruce G. Trigger, 296–321. Washington, DC: Smithsonian Institution, 1978.

———. "Structure, Continuity, and Change in the Process of Iroquois Treaty Making." In *The History and Culture of Iroquois Diplomacy: An Interdisciplinary Guide to the Treaties of the Six Nations and Their League*, edited by Francis Jennings, William N. Fenton, Mary A. Druke, and David R. Miller, 3–36. Syracuse, NY: Syracuse University Press, 1985.

Ferguson, R. Brian, and Neil L. Whitehead. "The Violent Edge of Empire." In *War in the Tribal Zone: Expanding States and Indigenous Warfare*, edited by R. Brian Ferguson and Neil L. Whitehead, 1–30. Santa Fe, NM: School of America Research Press, 1992.

Fiedel, Stuart J. "Some Inferences Concerning Proto-Algonquian Economy and Society." *Northeast Anthropology* 48 (Fall 1994): 1–11.

Fliegel, Carl John. *Index to the Records of the Moravian Mission among the Indians of North America*. New Haven, CT: Research Publications, 1970.

Foreman, Grant. *Indians and Pioneers: The Story of the American Southwest before 1830*. Norman: University of Oklahoma Press, 1936.

———. *The Last Trek of the Indians*. Chicago: University of Chicago Press, 1946.

Foster, Michael K. "Another Look at the Function of Wampum in Iroquois-White Councils." In *The History and Culture of Iroquois Diplomacy: An Interdisciplinary Guide to the Treaties of the Six Nations and Their League*, edited by Francis Jennings, William N. Fenton, Mary A. Druke, and David R. Miller, 99–114. Syracuse, NY: Syracuse University Press, 1985.

Foster, Morris W. *Being Comanche: A Social History of an American Indian Community*. Tucson: University of Arizona Press, 1991.

Fried, Morton H. *The Notion of Tribe*. Menlo Park, CA: Cummins, 1975.

Frisch, Jack A. "Iroquois in the West." In *Handbook of North American Indians*, Vol. 15, *Northeast*, edited by Bruce G. Trigger, 544–546. Washington, DC: Smithsonian Institution, 1978.

Fur, Gunlög. *A Nation of Women: Gender and Colonial Encounters among the Delaware Indians*. Philadelphia: University of Pennsylvania Press, 2009.

Gallay, Alan. *The Indian Slave Trade: The Rise of the English Empire in the American South, 1670–1717*. New Haven, CT: Yale University Press, 2002.

Galloway, Patricia. *The Choctaw Genesis, 1500–1700*. Lincoln: University of Nebraska Press, 1995.

———. "Confederacy as a Solution to Chiefdom Dissolution: Historical Evidence in the Choctaw Case." In *The Forgotten Centuries: Indians and Europeans in the American South, 1521–1704*, edited by Charles Hudson and Carmen Tesser, 393–420. Athens: University of Georgia Press, 1994.

——. *Practicing Ethnohistory: Mining Archives, Hearing Testimony, Constructing Narrative*. Lincoln: University of Nebraska Press, 2006.

——. " 'So Many Little Republics': British Negotiations with the Choctaw Confederacy, 1765." *Ethnohistory* 41 (Fall 1994): 513–537.

Galloway, William Albert. *Old Chillicothe: Shawnee and Pioneer History—Conflicts and Romances in the Old Northwest*. Xenia, OH: Buckeye Press, 1934.

Gates, Paul Wallace. *Fifty Million Acres: Conflicts over Kansas Land Policy, 1854–1890*. Norman: University of Oklahoma Press, 1997.

Gearing, Fred. "Priests and Warriors: Social Structures for Cherokee Politics in the 18th Century." *American Anthropological Association Memoir* 93 (1962).

Gipson, Lawrence Henry. *British Empire before the American Revolution*, Vol. 4, *Zones of International Friction: North America, South of the Great Lakes Region, 1748–1754*. New York: Alfred A. Knopf, 1961.

Godechot, Jacques. "The New Concept of the Nation and Its Diffusion in Europe." In *Nationalism in the Age of the French Revolution*, edited by Otto Dann and John Dinwiddy, 13–26. London: Hambledon, 1988.

Graybill, Jeffrey Robert. "The Eastern Periphery of Fort Ancient (A.D. 1050–1650): A Diachronic Approach to Settlement Variability." Ph.D. diss., University of Washington, 1981.

Graymont, Barbara. *The Iroquois in the American Revolution*. Syracuse, NY: Syracuse University Press, 1972.

Green, Michael D. *The Politics of Indian Removal: Creek Government and Society in Crisis*. Lincoln: University of Nebraska Press, 1982.

Griffin, James B. "Fort Ancient Has No Class: The Absence of an Elite Group in Mississippian Societies in the Central Ohio Valley." In *Lords of the Southeast: Social Inequality and the Native Elites of Southeastern North America*, edited by Alex W. Barker and Timothy R. Pauketat, 53–59. Washington, DC: American Anthropological Association, 1992.

Griffin, James Bennett. *The Fort Ancient Aspect: Its Cultural and Chronological Position in Mississippi Valley Archaeology*. Ann Arbor: University of Michigan Press, 1943.

Haas, Jonathan. "Warfare and the Evolution of Tribal Polities in the Prehistoric Southeast." In *The Anthropology of War*, edited by Jonathan Haas, 171–189. Cambridge: Cambridge University Press, 1992.

Hahn, Steven C. "The Cussita Migration Legend: History, Ideology, and the Politics of Mythmaking." In *Light on the Path: The Anthropology and History of the Southeastern Indians*, edited by Thomas J. Pluckhahn and Robbie Ethridge, 57–93. Tuscaloosa: University of Alabama Press, 2006.

——. *The Invention of the Creek Nation, 1670–1763*. Lincoln: University of Nebraska Press, 2004.

Hämäläinen, Pekka. *The Comanche Empire*. New Haven, CT: Yale University Press, 2008.

——. "Lost in Transitions: Suffering, Survival, and Belonging in the Early Modern Atlantic World." *William and Mary Quarterly* 68 (April 2011): 219–223.

Hämäläinen, Pekka, and Samuel Truett. "On Borderlands." *Journal of American History* 98 (September 2011): 338–361.

Hanna, Charles A. *The Wilderness Trail Or the Ventures and Adventures of the Pennsylvania Traders on the Allagheny Path with Some New Annals of the Old West, and the Records of Some Strong Men and Some Bad Ones*. 2 vols. New York: G. P. Putnam's Sons, 1911.

Hanson, Lee H., Jr. *The Hardin Village Site*. Lexington: University Press of Kentucky, 1966.

Harkin, Michael E. "Introduction: Revitalization as History and Theory." In *Reassessing Revitalization Movements: Perspectives from North America and the Pacific Islands*, edited by Michael E. Harkin, xv–xxxvi. Lincoln: University of Nebraska Press, 2004.

Harper, Rob. "State Intervention and Extreme Violence in the Revolutionary Ohio Valley." *Journal of Genocide Research* 10 (June 2008): 233–248.

Harring, Sidney L. *Crow Dog's Case: American Indian Sovereignty, Tribal Law, and United States Law in the Nineteenth Century*. Cambridge: Cambridge University Press, 1994.

Hatley, M. Thomas. "The Three Lives of Keowee: Loss and Recovery in the Eighteenth-Century Cherokee Villages." In *Powhatan's Mantle: Indians in the Colonial Southeast*, edited by Peter H. Wood, Gregory A. Waselkov, and M. Thomas Hatley, 223–248. Lincoln: University of Nebraska Press, 1989.

Hatley, Tom. "Cherokee Women Farmers Hold Their Ground." In *Powhatan's Mantle: Indians in the Colonial Southeast*, edited by Gregory A. Waselkov, Peter H. Wood, and Tom Hatley, 305–335. Lincoln: University of Nebraska Press, 2006.

Henderson, A. Gwynn. "The Lower Shawnee Town on the Ohio: Sustaining Native Autonomy in an Indian 'Republic.'" In *The Buzzel about Kentuck: Settling the Promised Land*, edited by Craig Thompson Friend, 24–55. Lexington: University Press of Kentucky, 1999.

Henderson, A. Gwynn, Cynthia E. Jobe, and Christopher A. Turnbow. *Indian Occupation and Use in Northern and Eastern Kentucky during the Contact Period (1540–1795): An Initial Investigation*. Lexington: University Press of Kentucky, 1986.

Henderson, A. Gwynn, David Pollack, and Christopher A. Turnbow. "Chronology and Cultural Patterns." In *Fort Ancient Cultural Dynamics in the Middle Ohio Valley*, edited by A. Gwynn Henderson, 253–279. Madison, WI: Prehistory Press, 1992.

Herring, Joseph B. *The Enduring Indians of Kansas: A Century and a Half of Acculturation*. Lawrence: University Press of Kansas, 1990.

Hickey, Donald R. *The War of 1812: A Forgotten Conflict*. Urbana: University of Illinois Press, 1989.

Hill, Leonard U. *John Johnston and the Indians in the Land of the Three Miamis*. Columbus, OH: Stoneman, 1957.

Hinderaker, Eric. *Elusive Empires: Constructing Colonialism in the Ohio Valley, 1673–1800*. Cambridge: Cambridge University Press, 1997.

Hobsbawm, E. J. *Nations and Nationalism since 1780*. Cambridge: Cambridge University Press, 1990.

Hodder, Ian. *Symbols in Action*. Cambridge: Cambridge University Press, 1982.

Holmes, William. "Hardin Village: A Northern Kentucky Late Fort Ancient Site's Mortuary Patterns and Social Organization." Master's thesis, University of Kentucky, Lexington, 1994.

Horsman, Reginald. "American Indian Policy in the Old Northwest, 1783–1812." *William and Mary Quarterly* 18 (January 1961): 35–53.

———. "The British Indian Department and the Resistance to General Anthony Wayne, 1793–1795." *Mississippi Valley Historical Review* 49 (September 1961): 269–290.

———. *Expansion and American Indian Policy, 1783–1812.* East Lansing: Michigan State University Press, 1967.

———. "The Indian Policy of an 'Empire of Liberty.' " In *Native Americans and the Early Republic*, edited by Frederick E. Hoxie, Ronald Hoffman, and Peter J. Albert, 37–61. Charlottesville: University Press of Virginia, 1999.

———. *Race and Manifest Destiny: The Origins of American Racial Anglo-Saxonism.* Cambridge, MA: Harvard University Press, 1981.

Hosmer, Brian, and Larry Nesper, eds. *Tribal Worlds: Critical Studies in American Indian Nation Building.* Albany, NY: SUNY Press, 2013.

Houck, Louis. *A History of Missouri, from the Earliest Explorations and Settlements until the Admission of the State into the Union, Vol. 1.* Chicago: R. R. Donnelley & Sons, 1908.

Howard, James H. *Shawnee! The Ceremonialism of a Native American Indian Tribe and Its Cultural Background.* Athens: Ohio University Press, 1981.

Howe, Henry. *Historical Collections of Ohio, Vol. 1.* Cincinnati, OH: C. J. Krehbiel, 1904.

Hudson, Charles. "Introduction." In *The Transformations of the Southeastern Indians, 1540–1760*, edited by Robbie Ethridge and Charles Hudson, xi–xxxix. Jackson: University Press of Mississippi, 2002.

———. *Knights of Spain, Warriors of the Sun: Hernando de Soto and the South's Ancient Chiefdoms.* Athens: University of Georgia Press, 1997.

———. *The Southeastern Indians.* Knoxville: University of Tennessee Press, 1976.

Hunter, William A. "History of the Ohio Valley." In *Handbook of North American Indians*, Vol. 15, *Northeast*, edited by Bruce G. Trigger, 588–593. Washington, DC: Smithsonian Institution, 1978.

———. "Provincial Negotiations with the Western Indians, 1754–1758." *Pennsylvania History* 18 (July 1951): 213–219.

Hurt, R. Douglas. *The Ohio Frontier: Crucible of the Old Northwest, 1720–1830.* Bloomington: Indiana University Press, 1996.

Jennings, Francis. *The Ambiguous Iroquois Empire: The Covenant Chain Confederation of Indian Tribes with English Colonies from Its Beginnings to the Lancaster Treaty of 1744.* New York: W. W. Norton, 1984.

———. *Empire of Fortune: Crowns, Colonies, and Tribes in the Seven Years' War in America.* New York: W. W. Norton, 1988.

———. "The Indians' Revolution." In *The American Revolution: Explorations in the History of American Radicalism*, edited by Alfred F. Young, 319–348. DeKalb: Northern Illinois University Press, 1976.

———. " 'Pennsylvania Indians' and the Iroquois." In *Beyond the Covenant Chain: The Iroquois and Their Neighbours in Indian North America, 1600–1800*, edited by Daniel K. Richter and James H. Merrell, 75–91. Syracuse, NY: Syracuse University Press, 1987.

Jeter, Marvin D. "From Prehistory through Protohistory to Ethnohistory in and Near the Northern Lower Mississippi Valley." In *The Transformations of the Southeastern Indians, 1540–1760*, edited by Robbie Ethridge and Charles Hudson, 177–223. Jackson: University Press of Mississippi, 2002.

Jortner, Adam. *The Gods of Prophetstown: The Battle of Tippecanoe and the Holy War for the American Frontier.* Oxford: Oxford University Press, 2012.

Keesing, Roger M., and Andrew J. Strathern. *Cultural Anthropology: A Contemporary Perspective.* Ft. Worth, TX: Harcourt Brace, 1998.

Kellogg, Louise Phelps. "Non-hel-ma, Shawnee Princess." In *Old Chillicothe: Shawnee and Pioneer History—Conflicts and Romances in the Old Northwest*, edited by William Albert Galloway. Xenia, OH: Buckeye Press, 1934.

Kelsay, Isabel Thompson. *Joseph Brant, 1743–1807: Man of Two Worlds.* Syracuse, NY: Syracuse University Press, 1984.

Kelton, Paul. *Epidemics and Enslavement: Biological Catastrophe in the Native Southeast, 1492–1715.* Lincoln: University of Nebraska Press, 2007.

———. "The Great Southeastern Smallpox Epidemic, 1696–1700: The Region's First Major Epidemic?" In *The Transformations of the Southeastern Indians, 1540–1760*, edited by Robbie Ethridge and Charles Hudson, 21–37. Jackson: University Press of Mississippi, 2002.

Kent, Barry C., Janet Rice, and Kakuko Ota. "A Map of 18th Century Indian Towns in Pennsylvania." *Pennsylvania Archaeologist 4* (December 1981): 1–18.

Kent, Donald H. *The French Invasion of Western Pennsylvania, 1753.* Harrisburg: Commonwealth of Pennsylvania and Pennsylvania Historical and Museum Commission, 1953.

Kercheval, Samuel. *A History of the Valley of Virginia.* 2nd ed. Woodstock, VA: John Gatewood, 1850.

Kertzer, David I. *Ritual, Politics, and Power.* New Haven, CT: Yale University Press, 1988.

Kidwell, Clara Sue. *The Choctaws in Oklahoma: From Tribe to Nation, 1855–1970.* Norman: University of Oklahoma Press, 2007.

Knight, Vernon J. "The Formation of the Creeks." In *The Forgotten Centuries: Indians and Europeans in the American South, 1521–1704*, edited by Charles Hudson and Carmen Tesser, 373–392. Athens: University of Georgia Press, 1994.

———. *Tukabatchee: Archaeological Investigations at an Historic Creek Town, Elmore County, Alabama.* Tuscaloosa: University of Alabama Office of Archaeological Research, 1985.

Kowalewski, Stephen A. "Coalescent Societies." In *Light on the Path: The Anthropology and History of the Southeastern Indians*, edited by Thomas J. Pluckhahn and Robbie Ethridge, 94–122. Tuscaloosa: University of Alabama Press, 2006.

Kugel, Rebecca. *To Be the Main Leaders of Our People: A History of Minnesota Ojibwe Politics, 1825–1898.* East Lansing: Michigan State University Press, 1998.

Kuper, Adam. *The Invention of Primitive Society: Transformations of an Illusion.* New York: Routledge, 1988.

Lakomäki, Sami. "Singing the King's Song: Constructing and Resisting Power in Shawnee Communities, 1600–1860." Ph.D. diss., University of Oulu, 2009.

La Vere, David. *Contrary Neighbors: Southern Plains and Removed Indians in Indian Territory.* Norman: University of Oklahoma Press, 2000.

Lavezzo, Kathy. "Introduction." In *Imagining a Medieval English Nation*, edited by Kathy Lavezzo, xv–xix. Minneapolis: University of Minnesota Press, 2004.

Lepore, Jill. *The Name of the War: King Philip's War and the Origins of American Identity.* New York: Vintage, 1998.

Lewellen, Ted C. *Political Anthropology: An Introduction.* South Hadley, MA: Bergin & Garvey, 1983.

MacLeod, D. Peter. "Microbes and Muskets: Smallpox and the Participation of the Amerindian Allies of New France in the Seven Years' War." *Ethnohistory* 39 (Winter 1991): 42–64.

Mancall, Peter C. "The Revolutionary War and the Indians of the Upper Susquehanna Valley." *American Indian Culture and Research Journal* 12 (December 1988): 39–57.

Marsh, Dawn. "Creating Delaware Homelands in the Ohio Country." *Ohio History* 116 (2009): 26–40.

May, Stephanie A. "Alabama and Koasati." In *Handbook of the North American Indians*, Vol. 14, *Southeast*, edited by Raymond D. Fogelson, 407–414. Washington, DC: Smithsonian Institution, 2004.

McConnell, Michael N. *A Country Between: The Upper Ohio Valley and Its Peoples, 1724–1774.* Lincoln: University of Nebraska Press, 1992.

———. "Kuskusky Towns and Early Western Pennsylvania Indian History." *Pennsylvania Magazine of History and Biography* 116 (January 1992): 33–58.

———. "Peoples 'in Between': The Iroquois and the Ohio Indians, 1720–1768." In *Beyond the Covenant Chain: The Iroquois and Their Neighbours in Indian North America, 1600–1800*, edited by Daniel K. Richter and James H. Merrell, 93–112. Syracuse, NY: Syracuse University Press, 1987.

McLoughlin, William G. *Cherokee Renascence in the New Republic.* Princeton, NJ: Princeton University Press, 1986.

Merrell, James H. *The Indians' New World: Catawbas and Their Neighbors from European Contact through the Era of Removal.* Chapel Hill: University of North Carolina Press, 1989.

———. *Into the American Woods: Negotiators on the Pennsylvania Frontier.* New York: W. W. Norton, 1999.

———. "Shamokin, 'the very seat of the Prince of darkness': Unsettling the Early American Frontier." In *Contact Points: American Frontiers from the Mohawk Valley to the Mississippi, 1750–1830*, edited by Andrew R. L. Cayton and Frederika J. Teute, 16–59. Chapel Hill: University of North Carolina Press, 1998.

———. "Shickellamy, 'a Person of Consequence.' " In *Northeastern Indian Lives, 1632–1816*, edited by Robert S. Grumet, 227–257. Amherst: University of Massachusetts Press, 1996.

———. " 'Their Very Bones Shall Fight': The Catawba-Iroquois Wars." In *Beyond the Covenant Chain: The Iroquois and Their Neighbours in Indian North America, 1600–1800*, edited by Daniel K. Richter and James H. Merrell, 115–133. Syracuse, NY: Syracuse University Press, 1987.

Merrit, Jane T. *At the Crossroads: Indians and Europeans on a Mid-Atlantic Frontier, 1700–1763.* Chapel Hill: University of North Carolina Press, 2003.

Mihesuah, Devon A. "Introduction." In *Natives and Academics: Researching and Writing about American Indians*, edited by Devon A. Mihesuah, 1–22. Lincoln: University of Nebraska Press, 1998.

Miller, Cary. *Ogimaag: Anishinaabeg Leadership, 1760–1845.* Lincoln: University of Nebraska Press, 2010.

Miller, Christopher L., and George R. Hamell. "A New Perspective on Indian-White Contact: Cultural Symbols and Colonial Trade." *Journal of American History* 73 (September 1986): 311–328.

Miller, Jay. "The 1806 Purge among the Indiana Delaware: Sorcery, Gender, Boundaries, and Legitimacy." *Ethnohistory* 41 (Spring 1994): 244–266.

Milner, George R. *The Moundbuilders: Ancient Peoples of Eastern North America.* London: Thames and Hudson, 2004.

Miner, H. Craig, and William E. Unrau. *The End of Indian Kansas: A Study of Cultural Revolution, 1854–1871.* Lawrence: University Press of Kansas, 1990.

Moore, John H. *The Cheyenne Nation: A Social and Demographic History.* Lincoln: University of Nebraska Press, 1987.

Morgan, Philip D. "Africa and the Atlantic, c. 1450 to c. 1820." In *Atlantic History: A Critical Appraisal*, edited by Jack P. Greene and Philip D. Morgan, 223–248. Oxford: Oxford University Press, 2009.

Nash, June. "Ethnographic Aspects of the World Capitalist System." *Annual Review of Anthropology* 10 (1981): 393–423.

Nelson, Larry L. *A Man of Distinction among Them: Alexander McKee and the Ohio Country Frontier, 1754–1799.* Kent, OH: Kent State University Press, 1999.

Oatis, Steven J. *A Colonial Complex: South Carolina's Frontiers in the Era of the Yamasee War, 1680–1730.* Lincoln: University of Nebraska Press, 2004.

O'Brien, Greg. *Choctaws in a Revolutionary Age, 1750–1830.* Lincoln: University of Nebraska Press, 2002.

O'Donnell, James H., III. *Southern Indians in the American Revolution.* Knoxville: University of Tennessee Press, 1973.

Owens, Robert M. "Jeffersonian Benevolence on the Ground: The Indian Land Cession Treaties with William Henry Harrison." *Journal of the Early Republic* 22 (Autumn 2002): 405–435.

Parkman, Francis. *The Conspiracy of Pontiac and the Indian War after the Conquest of Canada*, Vol. 1, *To the Massacre at Michilimackinac.* Lincoln: University of Nebraska Press, 1994.

Parmenter, Jon. "The Iroquois and the Native American Struggle for the Ohio Valley, 1754–1794." In *The Sixty Years' War for the Great Lakes, 1754–1814*, edited by David Curtis Skaggs and Larry Nelson, 105–124. East Lansing: Michigan State University Press, 2001.

Perdue, Theda. *Cherokee Women: Gender and Culture Change, 1700–1835.* Lincoln: University of Nebraska Press, 1998.

Perdue, Theda, and Michael D. Green. *The Cherokee Nation and the Trail of Tears.* New York: Viking, 2007.

Phillips, Carla Rahn. "Europe and the Atlantic." In *Atlantic History: A Critical Appraisal*, edited by Jack P. Greene and Philip D. Morgan, 249–275. Oxford: Oxford University Press, 2009.

Piker, Joshua. *Okfuskee: A Creek Indian Town in Colonial America.* Cambridge, MA: Harvard University Press, 2004.

Piker, Joshua A. " 'White & Clean' & Contested: Creek Towns and Trading Paths in the Aftermath of the Seven Years' War." *Ethnohistory* 50 (Spring 2003): 315–347.

Pollack, David, and A. Gwynn Henderson. "A Mid-Eighteenth Century Historic Indian Occupation in Greenup County, Kentucky." In *Late Prehistoric Research in Kentucky*, edited by David Pollack, Charles D. Hockensmith, and Thomas N. Sanders, 1–24. Frankfort: Kentucky Heritage Council, 1984.

——. "Toward a Model of Fort Ancient Society." In *Fort Ancient Cultural Dynamics in the Middle Ohio Valley*, edited by A. Gwynn Henderson, 281–294. Madison, WI: Prehistory Press, 1992.

Preston, David L. *The Texture of Contact: European and Indian Settler Communities on the Frontiers of Iroquoia, 1667–1783*. Lincoln: University of Nebraska Press, 2009.

Provance, Jim. "Eastern Shawnee Tribe to Seek Federal Approval for Ohio Casinos." *The Blade*, July 26, 2007, available at http://www.toledoblade.com/State/2007/07/26/Eastern-Shawnee-tribe-to-seek-federal-approval-for-Ohio-casinos.html (accessed 5/21/2012).

Prucha, Francis Paul. *The Great Father: The United States Government and the American Indians*, Vol. 1. Lincoln: University of Nebraska Press, 1984.

Purtill, Matthew P. "Evidence for a Late Fort Ancient Fall/Winter Occupation in Southwestern Ohio." *North American Archaeologist* 20 (2/1999): 105–133.

Ragsdale, John W., Jr. "The Dispossession of the Kansas Shawnee." *University of Missouri–Kansas City Law Review* 58 (Winter 1990): 209–256.

Ramsay, William L. *The Yamasee War: A Study of Culture, Economy, and Conflict in the Colonial South*. Lincoln: University of Nebraska Press, 2008.

Richter, Daniel K. *Before the Revolution: America's Ancient Pasts*. Cambridge, MA: Belknap, 2011.

——. " 'Believing That Many of the Red People Suffer Much for the Want of Food': Hunting, Agriculture, and a Quaker Construction of Indianness in the Early Republic." *Journal of the Early Republic* 19 (Winter 1999): 601–628.

——. *Facing East from Indian Country: A Native History of Early America*. Cambridge, MA: Harvard University Press, 2001.

——. *The Ordeal of the Longhouse: The Peoples of the Iroquois League in the Era of European Colonization*. Chapel Hill: University of North Carolina Press, 1992.

——. "War and Culture: The Iroquois Experience." *William and Mary Quarterly* 40 (October 1983): 528–559.

——. "Whose Indian History?" *William and Mary Quarterly* 50 (April 1993): 379–393.

Robertson, James A. "Chipped Stone and Functional Interpretations: A Fort Ancient Example." *Midcontinental Journal of Archaeology* 9 (2/1984): 251–265.

Rodning, Christopher B. "Reconstructing the Coalescence of Cherokee Communities in Southern Appalachia." In *The Transformations of the Southeastern Indians, 1540–1760*, edited by Robbie Ethridge and Charles Hudson, 155–175. Jackson: University Press of Mississippi, 2002.

Rollings, Willard H. *The Osage: An Ethnohistorical Study of Hegemony on the Prairie-Plains*. Columbia: University of Missouri Press, 1992.

Roseberry, William. *Anthropologies and Histories: Essays in Culture, History, and Political Economy*. New Brunswick, NJ: Rutgers University Press, 1994.

Rosen, Deborah A. *American Indians and State Law: Sovereignty, Race, and Citizenship, 1790–1880*. Lincoln: University of Nebraska Press, 2007.

Rothenberg, Diane. "The Mothers of the Nation: Seneca Resistance to Quaker Intervention." In *Women and Colonization: Anthropological Perspectives*, edited by Mona Etienne and Eleanor Leacock, 63–87. New York: Praeger, 1980.

Sahlins, Marshall. *Tribesmen*. Englewood Cliffs, NJ: Prentice-Hall, 1968.

Salisbury, Neal. "The Indians' Old World: Native Americans and the Coming of Europeans." *William and Mary Quarterly* 53 (July 1996): 435–458.

Saunt, Claudio. " 'Domestick … Quiet Being Broke': Gender Conflict among Creek Indians in the Eighteenth Century." In *Contact Points: American Frontiers from the Mohawk Valley to the Mississippi, 1750–1830*, edited by Andrew R. L. Cayton and Frederika J. Teute, 151–174. Chapel Hill: University of North Carolina Press, 1998.

——. "The Indians' Old World." *William and Mary Quarterly* 68 (April 2011): 215–218.

——. *A New Order of Things: Property, Power, and the Transformation of the Creek Indians, 1733–1816*. Cambridge: Cambridge University Press, 1999.

——. "Taking Account of Property: Stratification among the Creek Indians in the Early Nineteenth Century." *William and Mary Quarterly* 57 (October 2000): 733–760.

Schaaf, Gregory. *Wampum Belts and Peace Trees*. Golden, CO: Fulcrum, 1990.

Schutt, Amy C. "Forging Identities: Native Americans and Moravian Missionaries in Pennsylvania and Ohio, 1765–1782." Ph.D. diss., Indiana University, 1995.

——. *Peoples of the River Valleys: The Odyssey of the Delaware Indians*. Philadelphia: University of Pennsylvania Press, 2007.

Schutz, Noel William, Jr. "The Study of Shawnee Myth in Ethnographic and Ethnohistorical Perspective." Ph.D. diss., Indiana University, 1975.

Sheehan, Bernard W. *Seeds of Extinction: Jeffersonian Philanthropy and the American Indian*. New York: W. W. Norton, 1973.

Shoemaker, Nancy. "How Indians Got to Be Red." *American Historical Review* 102 (June 1997): 625–644.

——. "Introduction." In *Clearing a Path: Theorizing the Past in Native American Studies*, edited by Nancy Shoemaker, vii–xiii. New York: Routledge, 2002.

——. *A Strange Likeness: Becoming Red and White in Eighteenth-Century North America*. Oxford: Oxford University Press, 2004.

Shrank, Cathy. *Writing the Nation in Reformation England, 1530–1580*. Oxford: Oxford University Press, 2004.

Shuck-Hall, Sheri M. "Alabama and Coushatta Diaspora and Coalescence in the Mississippian Shatter Zone." In *Mapping the Mississippian Shatter Zone: The Colonial Indian Slave Trade and Regional Instability in the American South*, edited by Robbie Ethridge and Sheri M. Shuck-Hall, 250–271. Lincoln: University of Nebraska Press, 2009.

Sidbury, James, and Jorge Cañizares-Esguerra. "Mapping Ethnogenesis in the Early Modern Atlantic." *William and Mary Quarterly* 68 (April 2011): 181–208.

Sleeper-Smith, Susan. " 'Ignorant Bigots and busy rebels': The American Revolution in the Western Great Lakes." In *The Sixty Years' War for the Great Lakes, 1754–1814*, edited by David Curtis Skaggs and Larry Nelson, 145–165. East Lansing: Michigan State University Press, 2001.

Smith, F. Todd. *From Dominance to Disappearance: The Indians of Texas and the Near Southwest, 1786–1859*. Lincoln: University of Nebraska Press, 2005.

Smith, Linda Tuhiwai. *Decolonizing Methodologies: Research and Indigenous Peoples.* London: Zed Books, 1999.

Snow, Dean R. "American Indian Migrations: A Neglected Dimension of Paleodemography." In *Anthropology, History, and American Indians: Essays in Honor of William Curtis Sturtevant*, edited by William L. Merrill and Ives Goddard, 75–83. Washington, DC: Smithsonian Institution Press, 2002.

Snow, Dean, and Kim M. Lanphear. "European Contact and Indian Depopulation in the Northeast: The Timing of the First Epidemics." *Ethnohistory* 35 (Winter 1988): 15–33.

Sosin, Jack M. *The Revolutionary Frontier, 1763–1783.* Albuquerque: University of New Mexico Press, 1967.

———. *Whitehall and the Wilderness: The Middle West in British Colonial Policy, 1760–1775.* Lincoln: University of Nebraska Press, 1961.

Spero, Laura Keenan. " 'Stout, Bold, Cunning and the Greatest Travellers in America': The Colonial Shawnee Diaspora." Ph.D. diss., University of Pennsylvania, 2010.

Stark, Heidi Kiiwetinepinesiik. "Marked by Fire: Anishinaabe Articulations of Nationhood in Treaty Making with the United States." *American Indian Quarterly* 36 (Spring 2012): 119–149.

Steele, Ian. "Shawnee Origins of Their Seven Years' War." *Ethnohistory* 53 (Fall 2006): 657–687.

Steele, Ian K. "The Shawnees and the English: Captives and War, 1753–1765." In *The Boundaries between Us: Natives and Newcomers along the Frontiers of the Old Northwest Territory, 1750–1850*, edited by Daniel P. Barr, 1–24. Kent, OH: Kent State University Press, 2006.

Stevens, Paul Lawrence. "His Majesty's 'Savage' Allies: British Policy and the Northern Indians during the Revolutionary War. The Carleton Years, 1774–1778." Ph.D. diss., State University of New York at Buffalo, 1984.

Sturtevant, William C. "Tribe and State in the Sixteenth and Twentieth Century." In *The Development of Political Organization in Native North America*, edited by Elisabeth Tooker, 3–16. Washington, DC: American Ethnological Society, 1983.

Sugden, John. *Blue Jacket: Warrior of the Shawnees.* Lincoln: University of Nebraska Press, 2000.

———. "Early Pan-Indianism: Tecumseh's Tour of the Indian Country, 1811–1812." *American Indian Quarterly* 10 (Fall 1986): 273–304.

———. "Shawnee." In *Encyclopedia of North American Indians: Native American History, Culture, and Life from Paleo-Indians to the Present*, edited by Frederick E. Hoxie, 582–584. New York: Houghton and Mifflin, 1996.

———. *The Shawnee in Tecumseh's Time.* Abhandlungen der Völkerkundlichen Arbeitsgemeinschaft, Heft 66. Nortorf: Volkerkundliche Arbeitsgemeinschaft, 1990.

———. *Tecumseh: A Life.* New York: Henry Holt, 1997.

Sugrue, Thomas J. "The Peopling and Depeopling of Early Pennsylvania: Indians and Colonists, 1680–1720." *Pennsylvania Magazine of History and Biography* 116 (January 1992): 3–31.

Sword, Wiley. *President Washington's Indian War: The Struggle for the Old Northwest, 1790–1795.* Norman: University of Oklahoma Press, 1985.

Tanner, Helen Hornbeck. "The Glaize in 1792: A Composite Indian Community." *Ethnohistory* 25 (Winter 1978): 15–39.

Tanner, Helen Hornbeck, ed. *Atlas of Great Lakes Indian History*. Norman: University of Oklahoma Press, 1987.

Taylor, Alan. *American Colonies: The Settling of North America*. New York: Penguin, 2001.

———. *The Civil War of 1812: American Citizens, British Subjects, Irish Rebels, and Indian Allies*. New York: Alfred A. Knopf, 2010.

———. "The Divided Ground: Upper Canada, New York, and the Iroquois Six Nations, 1783–1815." *Journal of the Early Republic* 22 (Spring 2002): 55–75.

Taylor, James Carson. "Native Americans, the Market Revolution, and Culture Change: The Choctaw Cattle Economy, 1690–1830." In *Pre-Removal Choctaw History: Exploring New Paths*, edited by Greg O'Brien, 183–199. Norman: University of Oklahoma Press, 2008.

Thornton, Russell. *The Cherokees: A Population History*. Lincoln: University of Nebraska Press, 1990.

Tooker, Elisabeth. "The League of the Iroquois: Its History, Politics, and Ritual." In *Handbook of North American Indians*, Vol. 15, *Northeast*, edited by Bruce G. Trigger, 418–441. Washington, DC: Smithsonian Institution, 1978.

Trigger, Bruce G. *The Children of Aataentsic: A History of the Huron People to 1660*, Vol. 1. Montreal: McGill–Queen's University Press, 1976.

———. "Early Iroquoian Contacts with Europeans." In *Handbook of North American Indians*, Vol. 15, *Northeast*, edited by Bruce G. Trigger, 344–356. Washington, DC: Smithsonian Institution, 1978.

———. "Ethnohistory: Problems and Prospects." *Ethnohistory* 29 (Winter 1982): 1–19.

———. "Prehistoric Social and Political Organization: An Iroquoian Case Study." In *Foundations of Northeast Archaeology*, edited by Dean R. Snow, 1–50. New York: Academic Press, 1981.

Trigger, Bruce G., and William R. Swagerty. "Entertaining Strangers: North America in the Sixteenth Century." In *The Cambridge History of the Native Peoples of the Americas*, Vol. 1, *North America*, Part 1, edited by Bruce G. Trigger and Wilcomb E. Washburn, 325–398. Cambridge: Cambridge University Press, 1996.

Turnbow, Christopher A., and Cynthia E. Jobe. "The Goolman Site: A Late Fort Ancient Winter Encampment in Clark County, Kentucky." In *Late Prehistoric Research in Kentucky*, edited by David Pollack, Charles D. Hockensmith, and Thomas N. Sanders, 25–48. Frankfort: Kentucky Heritage Council, 1984.

Unrau, William E. *The Rise and Fall of Indian Country, 1825–1855*. Lawrence: University Press of Kansas, 2007.

Urban, Greg. "The Social Organizations of the Southeast." In *North American Indian Anthropology: Essays on Society and Culture*, edited by Raymond J. DeMallie and Alfonso Ortiz, 172–193. Norman: University of Oklahoma Press, 1994.

Usner, Daniel H., Jr. "An American Indian Gateway: Some Thoughts on the Migration and Settlement of Eastern Indians around Early St. Louis." *Gateway Heritage* 11 (Winter 1990–1991): 42–51.

———. *Indians, Settlers, and Slaves in a Frontier Exchange Economy: The Lower Mississippi Valley before 1783*. Chapel Hill: University of North Carolina Press, 1992.

———. "Iroquois Livelihood and Jeffersonian Agrarianism: Reaching behind the Models and Metaphors." In *Native Americans and the Early Republic*, edited by Frederick E.

Hoxie, Ronald Hoffman, and Peter J. Albert, 200–225. Charlottesville: University Press of Virginia, 1999.

Vincent, Joan. *Anthropology and Politics: Visions, Traditions, and Trends*. Tucson: University of Arizona Press, 1990.

Voegelin, C. F. *The Shawnee Female Deity*. Yale University Publications in Anthropology 10. New Haven, CT: Yale University Press, 1936.

———. *Shawnee Stems and the Jacob P. Dunn Miami Dictionary*. Prehistory Research Series 1, No. 3 (January 1938): 63–108; No. 5 (June 1938): 135–167; No. 8 (October 1939): 289–341; No. 9 (April 1940): 345–406; No. 10 (August 1940): 409–476. Indianapolis: Indiana Historical Society, 1938–1940.

Voegelin, C. F., and E. W. Voegelin. "Shawnee Name Groups." *American Anthropologist* 37 (October–December 1935): 617–635.

Wallace, Anthony F. C. *The Death and Rebirth of the Seneca*. New York: Vintage, 1969.

———. "Political Organization and Land Tenure among the Northeastern Indians, 1600–1830." *Southwestern Journal of Anthropology* 13 (4/1957): 301–321.

———. "Revitalization Movements." *American Anthropologist* 58 (2/1956): 264–281.

Wallace, Paul A. W. *Indians in Pennsylvania*. Harrisburg: Pennsylvania Historical and Museum Commission, 1964.

Wallerstein, Immanuel. *The Modern World-System I: Capitalist Agriculture and the Origins of the European World-Economy in the Sixteenth Century*. New York: Academic Press, 1974.

Ward, Matthew C. *Breaking the Backcountry: The Seven Years' War in Virginia and Pennsylvania, 1754–1765*. Pittsburgh: University of Pittsburgh Press, 2003.

———. "Fighting the 'Old Women': Indian Strategy on the Virginia and Pennsylvania Frontier, 1754–1758." *Virginia Magazine of History and Biography* 103 (July 1995): 297–320.

———. "Redeeming the Captives: Pennsylvania Captives among the Ohio Indians, 1755–1765." *Pennsylvania Magazine of History and Biography* 125 (July 2001): 161–189.

Warren, Stephen. *The Shawnees and Their Neighbors, 1795–1870*. Urbana: University of Illinois Press, 2005.

Warren, Stephen A. "The Baptists, Methodists, and the Shawnees: Conflicting Cultures in Indian Territory, 1833–1834." *Kansas History* 17 (Autumn 1994): 149–161.

Warren, Stephen, and Randolph Noe. " 'The Greatest Travelers in America': Shawnee Survival in the Shatter Zone." In *Mapping the Mississippian Shatter Zone: The Colonial Indian Slave Trade and Regional Instability in the American South*, edited by Robbie Ethridge and Sheri M. Shuck-Hall, 163–187. Lincoln: University of Nebraska Press, 2009.

Waselkov, Gregory A. "Indian Maps of the Colonial Southeast." In *Powhatan's Mantle: Indians in the Colonial Southeast*, edited by Gregory A. Waselkov, Peter H. Wood, and Tom Hatley, 435–502. Lincoln: University of Nebraska Press, 2006.

Waselkov, Gregory A., and Marvin T. Smith. "Upper Creek Archaeology." In *Indians of the Greater Southeast: Historical Archaeology and Ethnohistory*, edited by Bonnie G. McEwan, 242–264. Gainesville: University Press of Florida, 2000.

Weber, David J. *The Spanish Frontier in North America*. New Haven, CT: Yale University Press, 1992.

Weslager, C. A. *The Delaware Indians: A History*. New Brunswick, NJ: Rutgers University Press, 1972.

Wesson, Cameron B. "Chiefly Power and Food Storage in Southeastern North America." *World Archaeology* 31 (1/1999): 145–164.

———. *Households and Hegemony: Early Creek Prestige Goods, Symbolic Capital, and Social Power*. Lincoln: University of Nebraska Press, 2008.

Wheeler-Voegelin, Erminie. "Ethnohistory of Indian Use and Occupancy in Ohio and Indiana Prior to 1795." In *Indians of Ohio and Indiana Prior to 1795*, Vol. 2, edited by Erminie Wheeler-Voegelin and Helen Horbeck Tanner. New York: Garland, 1974.

———. "Mortuary Customs of the Shawnee and Other Eastern Tribes." *Indiana Historical Society, Prehistory Research Series 11*, No. 4 (March 1944): 227–444.

White, Richard. "The Fictions of Patriarchy: Indians and Whites in the Early Republic." In *Native Americans and the Early Republic*, edited by Frederick E. Hoxie, Ronald Hoffman, and Peter J. Albert, 62–84. Charlottesville: University Press of Virginia, 1999.

———. *The Middle Ground: Indians, Empires, and Republics in the Great Lakes Region, 1650–1815*. Cambridge: Cambridge University Press, 1991.

———. *The Roots of Dependency: Subsistence, Environment, and Social Change among the Choctaws, Pawnees, and Navajos*. Lincoln: University of Nebraska Press, 1983.

Whitehead, Neil L. "Tribes Make States and States Make Tribes: Warfare and the Creation of Colonial Tribes and States in Northeastern South America." In *War in the Tribal Zone: Expanding States and Indigenous Warfare*, edited by R. Brian Ferguson and Neil L. Whitehead, 127–150. Santa Fe, NM: School of America Research Press, 1992.

Willig, Timothy D. "Prophetstown on the Wabash: The Native Spiritual Defense of the Old Northwest." *Michigan Historical Review* 23 (Fall 1997): 115–158.

———. *Restoring the Chain of Friendship: British Policy and the Indians of the Great Lakes, 1783–1815*. Lincoln and London: University of Nebraska Press, 2008.

Witgen, Michael. *An Infinity of Nations: How the Native New World Shaped Early North America*. Philadelphia: University of Pennsylvania Press, 2012.

Witthoft, John, and William A. Hunter. "The Seventeenth-Century Origins of the Shawnee." *Ethnohistory* 2 (Winter 1955): 42–57.

Wolf, Eric. *Europe and the People without History*. Berkeley: University of California Press, 1982.

Womack, Craig S. *Red on Red: Native American Literary Separatism*. Minneapolis: University of Minnesota Press, 1999.

Worth, John E. "The Lower Creeks: Origins and Early History." In *Indians of the Greater Southeast: Historical Archaeology and Ethnohistory*, edited by Bonnie G. McEwan, 265–298. Gainesville: University Press of Florida, 2000.

Wunder, John R. "Native American History, Ethnohistory, and Context." *Ethnohistory* 54 (Fall 2007): 591–604.

Wunder, John R., and Pekka Hämäläinen. "Of Lethal Places and Lethal Essays." *American Historical Review* 104 (October 1999): 1229–1234.

INDEX

Note: Italicized page numbers refer to maps or figures.